NORTH AMERICAN MAMMALS

Books by Roger A. Caras

ANTARCTICA: LAND OF FROZEN TIME

DANGEROUS TO MAN

WINGS OF GOLD

THE CUSTER WOLF

LAST CHANCE ON EARTH

NORTH AMERICAN MAMMALS: FUR-BEARING ANIMALS
OF THE UNITED STATES AND CANADA

Charles Frace

NORTH AMERICAN
MAMMALS

Fur-bearing Animals
of the United States and Canada

by ROGER A. CARAS

GALAHAD BOOKS · NEW YORK

*This book is for my mother and father, who
gave me every opportunity to know and love animals.
They loved and tolerated dogs,
cats, rabbits, birds, turtles, snakes,
rats, mice, guinea pigs, hamsters, fish,
salamanders, and a host of other short-
and long-term visitors. Their patience and
understanding eventually led to this book.*

Library of Congress Catalog Card No. 73-85503
ISBN: 0-88365-072X

Published by Galahad Books, a division of A&W Promotional Book Corporation, 95 Madison Avenue, New York, N.Y. 10016 by arrangement with Hawthorn Books, 260 Madison Avenue, New York, N.Y. 10016.

Manufactured in the United States of America.

Introduction

FOR THE PAST 185,000,000 years there has existed on this planet an extremely interesting group of animals known as mammals. During the 57,000,000-year span known to science as the Jurassic Period of the Mesozoic Era, the first mammals appeared; they evolved at the same time as the birds from the much more ancient reptiles. This same Jurassic Period saw the great dinosaurs reach the peak of their incredible development and start down the long road to extinction. The previous period in geologic time, the 40,000,000-year Triassic Period, had seen the rise of the dinosaur and the diversification of the early mammal-like reptiles that had begun to appear in the preceding Permian Period.

Subsequent to the Jurassic Period was the Cretaceous, 66,000,000 eventful years during which the dinosaurs inexplicably disappeared forever as the mammals and flowering plants began their conquest of the world. Our own early roots are traceable to this period

In this great span of time since the first mammals evolved from primitive reptiles, much has happened to our own planet. Mountains have appeared, the results of great heavings in the surface crust, only to be eroded down to level plains by water and wind. Oceans have risen to flow across the bodies of land we erroneously think of as permanent continents, where they deposited untold billions of tons of fossil-bearing sediment. Later, when convulsive forces beneath the surface of these land masses again created new mountains, ocean bottoms became alpine meadows.

Time and again, great ice sheets covered much of the exposed land surface of the world, destroying the plants and animals that flourished there.

Land bridges rose out of the sea and formed links between continents, allowing animals to migrate over vast distances, and then sank beneath the sea again to isolate the travelers. What we today call North America has been as subject to these forces as any other part of our planet, and the result has been an endless parade of fascinating mammals that even today are in a state of transition.

As much as 53,000,000 years ago strange little horses, not much bigger than a house cat, roamed over North America. Although the ancestor of the modern horse, they hardly looked the part. They had four toes on each front foot and three on each hind. Strangely, none of their descendants are native to North America; the Western Hemisphere has no *native* wild horse left. Weird camels, giant sloths, huge short-faced bears, tremendously powerful saber-toothed cats, elephantlike mammoths and mastodons, hyenoid dogs, great animals that looked like rhinoceroses, and a host of other nightmarish creatures came and went, each in their turn.

The study of the mammal in North America, whether pursued by digging into hillsides for ancient forms or by observing living species still to be found in their natural environment, is endlessly fascinating. Fortunately, North America has long been endowed with a rich mammalian fauna. The most interesting of these can be observed by anyone curious enough about the world around him to go and look.

Mammals are readily distinguished from all other animals. A few characteristics will serve to make them immediately recognizable to anyone.

(1) Mammals, and mammals alone, have true fur. This is, of course, the most easily determined external characteristic. Some other animals appear to have hair (certain spiders make good examples), but true fur is a mammalian characteristic. Even mammals like whales, which appear to be furless, have bristles at some point in their life. No land mammal in North America is furless when mature. Some are born naked but remain that way only for a matter of days.

(2) All mammals are air breathers. No mammal, not even the great whale, is free of our atmosphere. This is of particular importance when observing animals which spend much of their time in the water; all must come up to breathe.

(3) All mammals, except a very few remote forms from Australia and nearby land areas, give birth to living young. All North American mammals except the opossums have a placenta, just as humans do. The young of all but the opossum are completely formed at birth—even if hairless, helpless, and somewhat difficult to recognize in the first few days.

(4) All mammals are warm-blooded, a characteristic they share on our planet only with the birds. They are able to tolerate temperature extremes that are impossible for most other animals to withstand. *There is no major surface environment on the North American continent to which mammals have not adapted*.

There are many other characteristics, of course, that distinguish mammals from other animal groups: brain structure, bone formation, and many more that are not of immediate concern to us here. With the exception of bats, which are atypical because they fly like birds, and the marine mammals, which differ from the norm because they have returned to an easy life in the sea, all North American mammals are easy to recognize for what they are—members of the most advanced group of animals yet evolved on this planet.

In this book we will treat the various mammal groups as specific projects. We will determine their habits, their habitats, the immediately recognizable differences between the more interesting members of the group, and outline the steps that must be taken to observe them.

There are few projects, for the family group or the individual, more satisfying than *successful* wildlife observation. The thrill of seeing a new species in its natural setting, or in watching a familiar species live out part of the drama of its wild existence—these are thrills available to all who are interested.

In this book, then, we will deal with two distinct problems, interwoven into one project outline: (1) what and where our mammals are, and (2) what we must do to find and identify them.

In each case we will establish a *preferred* common name for the animal under discussion. We will frequently give alternate common names as well, because as you travel from state to state or from region to region you will be endlessly confused, as the common name for the same animal changes. There are, however, preferred common names.

No common name, though, is acceptable for positive identification. For this purpose, only the established scientific name will do. These names, always in Latin and/or Greek, generally are more than the average reader or observer wishes to contend with. To satisfy the needs of the more scientific observer as well as those of the amateur, an appendix is provided that classifies all animals discussed in this book by scientific name and position.

From the outset we should acknowledge that this book does not provide a complete checklist of our mammals. It does provide a complete list of all the *groups* of mammals found on this continent, and it points out the more interesting species. It is a *practical guide* for the observation of nature. It is practical for the average observer in that it contains no project that can't be carried out and lists few, if any, distinctions that can't be observed by watching living animals in their natural environment.

For the nature watcher who wishes to delve deeper into mammalogy, who wishes to pursue the finer distinctions, a bibliography is provided listing many excellent guidebooks and scientific papers. These books, though often somewhat impractical as project books for the amateur observer, will provide the information necessary for the thrilling transformation from nature project to scientific study.

This book has been designed to help the reader locate our native mammals in their natural habitats, to help him identify them, and to enable him to watch them pursue their normal patterns of life. Attention to a few of the devices provided will not only help the reader to improve his wildlife "score," but will make the things he sees more meaningful.

The first chapter provides some general hints on the fine art of observation. These hints are well worth special attention. Subsequent chapters deal with specific animal groups and provide definite project outlines.

Few observers have the opportunity to travel endlessly and stay as long as they want in each region. For this reason a project involving the observation of all animals in any one group regardless of geography is generally impractical. The geographic approach is far more realistic for most of us. For this reason reference is made to the appendixes to this book. It will be noted that cross-references are given: geographic distribution and a number of other subject headings that will enable the average observer to make any trip in any state a potentially rewarding nature field trip. The most likely project for the average observer to adopt is the location and observation of the mammals in his own home state.

It is suggested, then, that the reader become familiar with the cross-referenced appendixes, that he pay particular attention to the suggestions for methods of observation, and that he then read the chapters on the individual mammal groups. It is hoped that the reader will then have the desire to put on some old clothes and head out to the country. When he gets there, he should keep in mind that what he is seeing is a legitimate part of a drama already 185,000,000 years old. The squirrel that scampers up a tree at his approach, the deer that gracefully arches over some roadside brush as his car turns the bend are playing out their roles just as their extremely primitive ancestors did when the quaking earth signaled to them the approach of a carnivorous dinosaur. It should be remembered that we, and not our wild animals, are aware of the time that has passed. To the squirrel and to the deer the problem is the same now as then. That is part of the charm, and a great part of the excitement, of nature observation. Life goes on in an endless parade, but a parade too little understood, too little appreciated in our day. If this book can help the reader in any small way regain his contact with this wonderful world of wild animals, it has served its purpose.

Contents

APPENDIX

COLOR PLATES

NORTH AMERICAN MAMMALS

1

The Role of the Observer

THIS BOOK presupposes that the interest of the reader is directed to the *observation* of wildlife. It does not provide hints or suggestions for killing, but rather for watching specimens, and, quite likely, photographing them. It is earnestly suggested that this be *your* role, that you enter an environment where wild animals live quietly and without despoiling. The observer who enriches his own life by watching the ancient wonder of wildlife and then leaves it as he found it is twice blessed. He has done something for himself and for the generations that follow him.

In most cases your success as an observer will depend in large measure on how unaware the animals are of your presence. If you can see them without their seeing you, if you can hear them without their hearing you, you are on the way to new adventures, to a new dimension in your own life.

Mammals, of course, are acutely aware of their surroundings. Those that hunt must be keenly observant or they will starve. Those that are hunted must be sharply alert or they will not survive to continue their species. The very fact that an animal exists is proof that it is successfully in balance with the forces in nature that support and protect it, and with the forces that would destroy it. If animals that are hunted as prey were so alert, so swift that no predatory animal could ever catch them, they would not only starve their enemies to death but issue their own death warrant as well. Predators would not thin their ranks of weak and inferior specimens who would then survive to breed and weaken the strain. The population would get out of hand and available food diminish to the point where poor nutrition would spell doom to the species as it weakened generation by generation.

[3]

If predatory animals, on the other hand, became so keen in their hunting prowess that no animal could escape them, they would soon reduce the breeding stock of their prey animals to the point where they themselves would eventually be overpopulated and starved out.

Nature is in dynamic balance. There are the hunters and the hunted, but both groups are in a finely drawn and highly successful relationship to each other. It is into this successful environment that you must enter if you will observe wildlife. If you do not give the impression that you are there to upset it, you will realize success. If you blunder in without regard for the sensitive relationship each animal has with its environment, you will fail in all but a few lucky instances. As you pass through the truly magic mirror from the world of man to the world of wildlife, tread lightly, go quietly, and go in peace.

Animals are, of course, aware of their surroundings by the same means we are, by their senses. To become a successful observer you must blend unobtrusively with natural surroundings. To accomplish this you must become aware of the sensory pattern with which you must contend.

SIGHT

With the exception of a few of the burrowing species, all North American mammals use their eyesight to good purpose. While many are nearsighted, all can see and all can be alarmed by what they see. In the chapters that follow we will discuss the sensory equipment of many animal types, but here is some general information:

(1) *Movement:* Most, if not all, mammals will not notice a stationary figure unless something else about it attracts their attention. That is to say, if the animal cannot smell or hear you, it probably will not notice you if you remain perfectly still. Indeed, you will be inspected by curious creatures only vaguely aware that you are new or different. Even animals as shy as foxes will approach closely to investigate a stationary figure. Not until they have the alarming man-scent will they run in such instances.

For the reasons outlined above, still-watching is a very good way of observing nature. As you read through the chapters that follow and learn of the life patterns of the animals that interest you, you will be able to determine a pattern for still-watching. Perhaps your own project will put you on a stump at the edge of a marsh or swamp an hour before sunrise, or at the edge of a blueberry patch an hour before sunset. However your project works out, still-watching is suggested. While involved do not smoke, do not speak, and move as little as possible. You will be richly rewarded.

(2) *Skylines:* There is no better way to scatter wild animals than by charging up over a high piece of ground and throwing yourself in silhouette against the sky. This is particularly true in seeking out animals that live on open ground (pronghorns, bison, some bears, wolves and coyotes, and many more).

If you are moving about in open country and you must pass over high ground, use great care. *Never* move along the crest of a hill, keep well below the skyline, and move parallel to the ridge. If you must cross the ridge to observe the lowland on the far side and you cannot find a pass or cut to use, go down on your stomach (or, at the very least, on all fours) and crawl. No animal, no matter how nearsighted, will miss you if you put yourself between it and the sky. *Do not become a silhouette.*

(3) *Clothing:* It is generally believed that all mammals except certain primates are color-blind. There is still some controversy over all this, but, generally speaking, any mammal you will be seeking out in North America will see in black, white, and gray only. One might suppose, then, that the clothing one chooses is of little account. Such is not the case.

Most mammals are aided in their battle to survive by their appearance. Even the gaudy striped and spotted species, when seen in their native environment, are generally made less obvious by their seemingly bizarre coats. We should take our lead from this fact.

Do not wear vibrant and brilliantly colored fabrics that have no correlation with natural surroundings. Some cloth reflects light, flashes in the sun. Some patterns are so bold that they will attract the attention of even nearsighted animals blind to color. There are, actually, no hard and fast rules and, indeed, this is a very good area for the observer to examine in original research. It is suggested, however, that subdued clothing that is neutral and blends with natural backgrounds will aid in your quest. Some Army surplus stores sell camouflage fabric, cloth with leaf patterns printed in shades of brown. Such material is excellent for your purpose. In general, shades of brown, gray, and green will tend to make you less obtrusive not because the animal can detect other colors as colors, but because the tones suggested will tend to absorb and reflect sunlight somewhat like natural materials in woods and fields. Sand-colored clothing is fine in desert areas, white in snowscapes.

(4) *Reflecting Surfaces:* Any surface that can catch and reflect sunlight is bad. Jewelry, shiny metal parts on cameras, any adornment or equipment of

this nature may alarm a sensitive creature and spoil your chances of observation. If your equipment is very shiny there are dulling sprays available that will cut down their reflecting power. These sprays, of course, cannot be used on camera and binocular lenses, and for this reason great care must be taken when in very bright sunlight. Move slowly, try not to catch the rays of the sun on your lens, and do not let such equipment flop around as you walk about.

(5) *Pace:* If you must move about in an area where you can anticipate wildlife, watch your pace. *Never run;* walk slowly. Not only will rapid movement create noise, it will be immediately noticeable and will alarm almost everything around. Fast movement is in itself attention-getting, and it causes bushes and other plant life to move abnormally. Trees, bushes, and reeds may move rapidly in the wind, but not a few at a time. One or two bushes or a few reeds moving suddenly will signal almost any mammal that trouble is at hand.

HEARING

Many mammals depend more on their hearing than on their eyesight, and no sense can cause more trouble in the field than this. The success you have as a nature watcher will be in large measure in direct proportion to the amount of noise you make.

It will be worth your while to try an experiment on yourself. The next time you walk down a city street make note of the sounds you hear. If you listen very, very carefully you will realize that you are subjected to a great many more sounds than you were aware of before. You will hear wind sounds, voices, mechanical sounds, unidentified sounds of all kinds, babies crying, dogs barking, an endless symphony of racket and static. If we were constantly aware of all the sounds around us, we would be driven mad in short order. We would be constantly exhausted, worn down by trying to sort out the sounds we need from those we don't. But nature is merciful, and our mind filters out that which we don't need.

All-knowing nature has been no less kind to our wild animals. They, too, have selective hearing. Whereas our hearing is alerted to a voice speaking our name or mentioning some fact of interest to us, or to a siren or car horn nearby, animals listen for a breaking twig, for fabric brushing against foliage, for a metallic click, or a human voice. Very often you will be thwarted because a squirrel or bird will note your presence and call a warning, but there is little you can do about that. What you can do, however, is make as little noise as possible. Try not to kick stones loose, try not to charge through heavy brush, keep your voice down, and don't let objects you are carrying rattle and clang. It is all very obvious: Try to keep your presence a secret for as long as possible and, once it is detected, try to keep it from appearing threatening.

THE SENSE OF SMELL

I am being neither facetious nor rude when I say that one of your greatest handicaps as an observer has to do with the way you smell, and there is just about nothing you can do about it. Obviously, if you put yourself in such a position that the wind is blowing from you toward the animal, you are diminishing your chances for success. It is not always possible, however, to avoid doing so. All that I can suggest is that you be so inconspicuous in every other way that even when an animal smells you he will take so long to become oriented to your position that you will have a chance to see him before he is gone.

There are perhaps a few things that can be done or at least tried, but so few people will take the trouble to do them that only a passing mention is warranted. You can take the clothing you will be wearing and "treat" it to reduce the scent. Instead of storing your clothing in a closet with a lot of other material loaded with the man-scent, pack it in a container where human apparel and equipment has not been packed before. Put natural materials in with it and let it all sit for a few days. Cedar shavings, moss, burlap sacks of loam, bark, particularly fragrant greenery like pine needles or various native herbs, all these will help. The effects are temporary, however, and not always worth the trouble. It is an interesting project to fool with when you are getting down toward the end of your lifetime checklist and are having trouble with a few tricky species.

IN GENERAL

In a word, literally one word, *blend*. It is truly amazing how quickly animals will accept that which is not endangering, not obtrusive. As you progress through the wonderland of our wildlife your skills will increase. One of them, one of the most important of them, will be your ability to melt into an environment. You will be able to measure that progress by the success you are having in observing new and different species of wild animals.

Several times in the chapters that follow I will suggest that traps be used. These are necessary if you are to examine some of our smaller and many of our nocturnal mammals. You just won't get to see them otherwise. I will point out again and again that I am referring to the type of trap that captures but does not harm specimens. But, then, if you were the kind of person who would destroy a life just so that you could make note that it had once existed, you probably wouldn't be reading this book.

There are several manufacturers of traps who advertise their humane devices in sporting magazines. These are box traps that have ends that snap shut once an animal is safely inside. Any trap that physically catches hold of an animal is not humane. Only those that do not make contact with the animal's body are harmless and only those should be used.*

On the subject of bait, here is a field for you to experiment with. A chunk of stewing beef or an open can of sardines left in the sun to ripen for a day or two will attract meat-eaters. C. B. Colby, the wonderful author of scores of books, has told me of his success with a combination of peanut butter, molasses, and salt in trapping rodents.† Salt licks from a farm-supply store and apples will attract many animals, if not into traps, at least into viewing range. If you are going to try to trap our wily predators, remember you will have to go to great pains. You will have to wear gloves, especially gloves that have been buried in manure, and you may also have to treat your shoes in a like manner. If you kneel on the ground you will have to do so on a drop cloth prepared and maintained for this purpose. Before you get a coyote or a fox, or a bobcat, into a box trap, you are going to have to develop a high order of skill and take great and elaborate pains.

In all trapping endeavors set your traps in natural animal runs. Put them where they and their enticing baits will be come upon naturally. Try not to disturb the surrounding landscape any more than necessary and try not to drench the area with your man-scent. One last word: Do not set traps that you cannot or will not visit at least once a day. Some of our smaller animals will starve to death if left alone for long, and it is cruel to trap them into so sad a fate without purpose or benefit to anyone.

There are many other aspects of wildlife observation that could go in this

---

* Also be sure you (1) put enough bait in your trap to sustain a captive animal for the period you will be away; (2) put some cotton or other nesting material in so that small animals can make themselves comfortable (metal can get *very* cold); and (3) if your trap has a closed end, face the opening downhill if on a slope in case of rain.

† Another good formula consists of rolled oats, raisins, and peanut butter.

chapter, but I think it better to intersperse the information with data about the animals themselves. They will be found where they best apply.

May I wish you luck. You are about to embark on *one of the great adventures left on this planet*. It is a trip away from yourself, away from the world of mankind. It is a trip into the past, into the future, and through one of the greatest looking glasses of the present. It is one way, truly, of enriching your life and giving it meaning in a grander context than our own societies can provide. *Remember always: The natural world in which you take pleasure is not the property of our generation*. It is not ours to do with as we will. It was given to us in trust by the generations that have preceded our tenure and carries with it awesome responsibility. We are honor-bound to pass it along in at least as good a condition as we inherited it and in a better one if our skill permits improvement.

2

North America's Most Primitive Mammal: The Opossum

BETWEEN seventy and a hundred million years ago, small primitive mammals known as marsupials cowered beneath exotic ferns and under piles of primeval plant debris to escape the depredations of carnivorous dinosaurs. Slowly, as mammals replaced reptiles as the dominant vertebrate forms on our planet, the marsupials died out, unable to compete with more alert and adaptable mammalian groups. In a few places, however, they survived. In Australia they were virtually the only mammals to reach the isolated area (with the ancestors of the platypus and echidna) and withstand the passage of eons. There they diversified into everything from kangaroos to koala bears in the absence of competitive placental mammals. In our own hemisphere, the region known as the New World, the marsupials remain only in the form of the opossums, from the aquatic species to the highly carnivorous forms.

The marsupials do not have a placenta and the young are born after a very abbreviated gestation period. Virtually embryos at birth, they are kept in a pouch on the outside of the female's stomach in most species and there suckle for many months before venturing forth into the world. Even when partially grown, the young regularly retreat to the warmth and safety of the pouch at the first sign of danger. Parental care is long and careful.

Central and South America have many opossums varying greatly in appearance. North America has only one, and it is our only marsupial. It is the most primitive mammal on our continent.

Today very widespread, the opossum is a common mammal in many

A sight many a hunter has seen, 'possum in a tree!

states and provides an instructive observation project. Neither alert, playful, nor particularly colorful in habit, it is a link with the earliest beginnings of the mammals. A few of its habits, unique in our hemisphere, are readily observable and interesting to note.

The old story of "playing 'possum" is true. Although equipped with many sharp teeth and often given to brief displays of bravado punctuated with loud hissing, the opossum generally will not fight. If the open-mouthed hissing fails to intimidate an intruder, the opossum "plays" dead. Whether the animal is consciously aware of putting on an act or goes into a kind of nervous shock has often been discussed, but the answer is not clear.* One way or another, a challenged opossum rolls over and looks very dead indeed. No amount of prodding will make it reveal itself. However, when the danger appears to have

* The weight of evidence seems to indicate a kind of catatonic shock.

passed, the animal soon makes off with its peculiar rolling gait. It is an excellent climber and swims well but is not particularly fast on the ground.

Names and Range

Possum or opossum is the *preferred common name* of the one North American species. It is also known as the common, Virginia, and eastern opossum.

Virginia opossum (diagonal lines).

The Virginia opossum started out in South America and has been steadily following the retreating glaciers of the last Ice Age (as its ancestors undoubtedly did several times before). Its range has increased until now it is found as far north as southern Canada. The "Virginia" in its name comes from its former scientific name *virginianus*.

In recent years the opossum has been introduced in the Far West and can be found in most of California and in pockets of northwest Washington and northeast Oregon. Where it is found, the Virginia opossum is often densely settled. The annual take in the United States for the fur trade alone is about three million animals.

Appearance and Distinguishing Characteristics

The opossum is not a large animal; about the size of a large house cat is average. Head and body length run from fifteen to twenty inches; tail length from nine to thirteen. Weights vary from four to twelve pounds.

The coarse fur has a grizzled appearance and is usually an off-white. The animal's name apparently comes from the Algonquian word *apasum,* meaning "white animal." It has a darker undercoat of shorter, somewhat softer, fur. The longer guard hairs tend to have darker tips in some areas, and black and cinnamon phases have been reported. Albino specimens are not too uncommon. The nose is pink and set well out at the end of a long, pointed snout. The eyes are black except in the case of albinos. The tips of the ears may be black, or at least darker than the animal's ground color, and the scaly, prehensile tail is black.

The overall appearance of the opossum can perhaps be best characterized as "untidy." It somehow looks as if it needs a haircut, a shave, or something it hasn't had for a long time (and it has been around for a very long time, indeed). Its charm lies not so much in its appearance but in its quiet insistence on surviving. Its maternal habits are particularly enchanting, and it very much looks as if it will have the last laugh in the race against its many competitors. Sleek and racy species become scarcer every year as civilization encroaches on their home ranges, but the patient, untidy little opossum continues to expand its range and maintain its numbers.

Habits

The opossum is essentially a nocturnal animal and will seldom be found abroad in daylight unless disturbed in its nest. It lies up during the day in a den in a rocky crevice, a hollow tree trunk, under logs, in the deserted burrow of a more energetic species, or in a brush pile. Although it often digs for food, it does not seem to excavate its own burrow.

Not a true hibernator, the opossum does become torpid during extremely cold weather and may lie up for several days at a time. Its ears and tail are subject to frostbite, and animals with cold injuries, even with part of the tail missing, are common.

Essentially a scavenger, the opossum eats just about everything. Its diet is known to include worms, millipedes, spiders, insects of all kinds, flesh living and dead, birds' eggs, mice, moles, lizards, snakes, nestling birds, fruits, and various vegetable matter. It is fond of all kinds of berries, particularly poke-berries, and appears to prefer persimmons above most other vegetable foods.

The opossum tends to establish a home range where it may spend all or most of its life if not driven out. This range, anywhere from fifteen to forty acres, generally includes a good water supply and may consist of woods, swamps, or wet bottomlands. Heavy forests are not generally inhabited, although some may be included in a range. Farm lands, particularly back pastures with clumps of trees near a stream or pond, are preferred habitats. Opossums regularly invade suburban and even urban areas, and in recent years specimens have been rescued from domestic dogs and cats by the SPCA in New York City!

In the course of a nighttime feeding, an animal may travel two or three miles in a circle, returning to the den or seeking suitable shelter before dawn.

The enemies of this inoffensive creature are many: bobcats, coyotes, wolves, dogs, foxes, ocelots, hawks, owls, and bears all take a toll in different parts of its vast range. Despite its rather repellent musky odor, the opossum feeds a great many wild creatures. In many places, particularly the South, the opossum is relished by man. Porklike in flavor, they are killed and eaten by the tens of thousands annually. The fur is used mainly as a trim for garments.

Reproduction

Part of the opossum's success story in North America is due to its fecundity. In the northern parts of its range it has reduced its reproductive cycle to one litter a year. In the South two litters are usual. Litters in the South appear in January or early February and again in May or June. In the North, the young appear in the early spring.

The female prepares its nest with various twigs and leaves, often carrying a load in the tightly curled end of the prehensile tail. (This same tail will support the animal on a limb if an effort is made to shake it from a tree.)

The opossum's pouch.

The gestation period is the shortest of any North American mammal, an incredibly brief twelve to thirteen days. The litter may contain anywhere from five to sixteen young. The female has only thirteen nipples, located inside her pouch in two rows of six, with the odd one in the middle.

As soon as the young are born, they instinctively crawl to the pouch and attach themselves to the nipples, which swell inside their mouths, providing a constant food supply and a firm attachment. Those born last, if there are more than thirteen, or those too weak to crawl the few inches to the pouch, soon perish. At the very outset nature begins weeding out the weaklings. The lot of the opossum is a tough one in this world, and weaklings that survived to reproduce would soon undermine the strength of the stock and bring an end to a lineage already older than many mountains. No more than thirteen in any litter can survive, at any rate.

At birth the young weigh approximately one seven-thousandth of a pound each. Sixteen to twenty can fit in the bowl of a tablespoon. Their front legs are developed to facilitate that first critical journey to the pouch, the opossum's first survival test, but the hind legs are still embryonic, mere stubs. The young, of course, are naked, blind, and deaf.

After about sixty days the eyes open. By this time the sucklings have increased their body weight five hundred fold. At the end of three months, the young are ready to leave the pouch and start foraging. They stay with the mother for some time, hanging onto her back and tail as the nightly rounds of the feeding range are made. At one year they reach maturity. Unless killed by accident or taken by a predator (which is more than likely to happen), the opossum has seven years of life. In the wild, few probably make it.

Observation

Seeing an opossum in the wild is night work. In farm country you may often encounter them along back roads and even on main highways. Many thousands are killed by cars each year when they come to the road to feed on other highway victims, scavengers that they are. Slow-witted and slow-paced, they are transfixed by approaching headlights and remain frozen until run over. A slow stroll with a strong flashlight down a country lane, particularly one that borders on a stream or marsh, will turn one up in most parts of their range. When berries or fruit are ripening, this type of growth is a likely place to look. In the fall, when fruit falls from the trees, they will often be found on the ground in orchards.

A word of caution about night-watching is in order. Care should be taken about announcing your intentions to the owner if private property is to be traversed. It is difficult for a farmer to tell a nature observer from a chicken thief in the dark. Even the excitement and charm of seeing a female opossum ambling along her ancient way with her half-grown young will not compensate for the discomfort engendered by a load of angry buckshot.

Refuges

The opossum can be found in the following refuges and sanctuaries, where they are protected and maintain a good population:

Aransas National Wildlife Refuge, Texas
Mattamuskeet National Wildlife Refuge, North Carolina
Okefenokee National Wildlife Refuge, Georgia
Ipswich River Wildlife Sanctuary, Massachusetts
Morton National Wildlife Refuge, Long Island, New York

Opossum tracks.

3

The Insectivores: The Moles and Shrews

THE INSECTIVORES, as the name implies, are insect-eaters. That is, however, misleading, for although the moles and shrews, the only two families of insectivores found in North America, do consume quantities of insects, their appetite is much more universal. The name refers more to their dental characteristics than to any limitation in their diet.

The moles and shrews have much in common besides the fact that science has placed them both among the insectivores. They are generally diminutive, long-snouted, and extremely active; their eyes are very small or, in the case of some moles, hidden; they have an elongated head and feet with five claw-bearing toes. The differences, however, are just as pronounced. The following chart will accent some that are immediately apparent when observing the living animal. Many others exist, but for recognition require dissection or skeletal examination.

Telling the Moles from the Shrews

	FAMILY TALPIDAE THE MOLES	FAMILY SORICIDAE THE SHREWS
Body	Stout and cylindrical.	More slender.
External Ears	Absent.	Present but hidden.
Eyes	Very small, sometimes not appearing through skin.	More prominent but still small.
Environment	Almost always found burrowing underground.	Usually found scampering about under surface debris; not as often underground.
Forefeet	Spadelike—soles turned outward; adapted for digging.	Not adapted for digging.

THE MOLES

Moles of one kind or another live over much of the United States and parts of eastern Canada. The Rocky Mountains and Great Basin areas are without them, and western Canada has them only in the extreme southwestern corner of British Columbia. Rarely seen aboveground, they do create certain external signs that make their detection possible. Their presence is announced by low ridges meandering across a lawn or other area where the vegetation is very short, or by characteristic earth mounds pushed up from below. These "mole hills" are created as the animal clears its burrow. The actual entrance to the burrow is hidden by the mound of earth. The ridges just under the surface are made as the animal seeks its food: earthworms, grubs, insects and insect larvae, millipedes, centipedes, spiders, snails, slugs, an occasional mouse or small snake, various seeds, and occasionally a potato. Animal food constitutes about 85 percent of the diet. They are insatiable eaters and eat at least one half of their own body weight daily. When projected to human proportions, this metabolic rate is startling: a large man eating a hundred pounds of food every twenty-four hours.

The mole's front feet and shoulders are greatly enlarged for digging. The forefeet may be twice the size of the hind, and the pink palms are turned outward. The mole is virtually blind, but it can distinguish between light and dark. Although the ears consist of no more than a minute hole in the skin, hearing is quite acute.

The rate at which a mole can move underground is startling. The eastern mole, at least, can tunnel along at the rate of a foot a minute, while its deeper excavations proceed at rates up to fifteen feet per hour. When the ground is frozen, they tunnel below the frost line.

Because life depends on their ability to burrow rapidly after the food they must have very frequently, moles are found in specific kinds of soil. Meadows, pastures, lawns, open woodlands, gardens, and stream banks are preferred because the soil is loose and contains a high percentage of humus which provides for a well-drained but moist environment. Dry, hard-packed or very rocky ground is avoided.

The velvetlike coat of the mole can be brushed either way without offering resistance. This is essential for the small creature moving about in its endless tunnels. The front and hind feet of the mole as well as the tail are fringed with sensory hairs to aid in its dark, close world. The senses of touch and smell are

A star-nosed mole photographed in Michigan. Those are its nostrils in the middle of the star, not its eyes!

highly developed, and the flexible snout helps keep the little burrower in close touch with its subterranean environment.

Names and Range

The eastern mole, the most widely distributed mole in North America, ranges from northern New England to the Florida Keys, west to South Dakota, and south to Mexico.

The western mole (actually a general name for several different species) has a much more limited range: British Columbia, Washington, Oregon, California, and extreme western Nevada.

The hairy-tailed mole is an animal of the Northeast. Also known as the Brewer mole, it ranges across much of eastern Canada and the United States.

The distinctive star-nosed mole is another creature of the Northeast, but with a vast range. It is found from southern Labrador across to the Great Lakes and south, in pockets at least, to Florida.

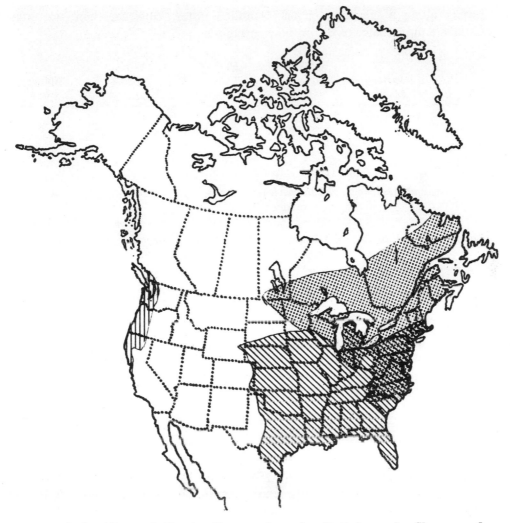

Eastern mole (diagonal lines). Star-nosed mole (dotted area). Shrew mole (vertical lines).

The shrew mole is a creature of the Far Northwest, found only in British Columbia, Washington, Oregon, and California.

Appearance and Distinguishing Characteristics

Ranges of the different moles often overlap. The only sure way of knowing what you have caught or seen is to make a trip to a local museum, taking along a specimen or very detailed notes. However, here are some details of appearance of the broader groupings:

	EASTERN MOLE	WESTERN MOLE	HAIRY-TAILED MOLE	STAR-NOSED MOLE	SHREW MOLE
Size (*Total length*)	6–7 in.	9 in.	6 in.	8 in.	4.5 in.
Tail	1 in.; sparsely furred	Slightly thicker than eastern mole: 1½–2 in.	Hairy 1–1½ in.	3 in.-plus	1½ in.
Color	Blackish-brown to silvery gray	Blackish-brown to black; purplish tinge	Blackish-brown tinge	Blackish-brown	Iridescent dark gray to black; purple or greenish tinge
Muzzle	Naked	Naked	Shorter than eastern mole	Rose-colored: *See* below	Long, naked
Feet	Slightly webbed	Not webbed	Not webbed	Not webbed	Not webbed and less well developed

The most bizarre member of the group is the star-nosed mole. Its snout ends in a rosy-pink star with twenty-two fleshy fingers, eleven to a side, on a wide, naked disk. This strange characteristic is apparently an aid to the animal's already delicate sense of touch.

Habits

As we have noted, moles spend much of their time underground, and for this reason their habits are little known. They apparently are not true hibernators but do retreat to deeper chambers to escape extremes of temperature. They are by no means silent and can issue a variety of sounds ranging from high-pitched squeals to harsh, guttural squeaks. They occasionally snort and grate their teeth.

Most of the mole's usually solitary life is spent tunneling after food in

Photo by Victor B. Scheffer, courtesy of U.S. Department of Interior, Fish & Wildlife Service

A coast mole photographed in Washington. Note the immense front digging feet.

soft, loose soil. When the soil proves too loose to support its tunnel, the little creature does a somersault and burrows off in another direction, bracing itself against the walls of the tunnel with its hind legs while working furiously with its greatly enlarged forefeet.

Reproduction

Moles mate in the spring, the single annual litter appearing from late March to early May. Gestation is from four to six weeks. A litter contains two to five blind and naked young. Growth is rapid, and the first fur appears in ten days. At one month the young are ready to go on their own.

Observation

Looking for moles is probably one of the least intriguing adventures in wildlife observation. Their most interesting activities are always out of sight and only the specialist involved in classification will find the pursuit particularly rewarding. They are, however, a part of our wildlife scene and therefore not to be passed over entirely. The judicious use of a spade may uncover an animal once a tunnel or mole hill is found and can offer the observer a close look at the little beast before returning it to its own world out of our sight and hearing. Most gardeners would probably suggest an alternate disposition of the specimen.

Mole hill.

THE SHREWS

The shrews are much more widely distributed than the moles. They spend a good part of their time aboveground but will, on occasion, take over the burrow or tunnel of another animal, or even make their own. They are belligerent little creatures with an insatiable appetite.

The shrew's metabolic rate is more than twice that of man and some species will starve to death in seven hours. A shrew breathes ten times in the

Courtesy U.S. Department of Interior, Fish & Wildlife Service

The short-tailed shrew, one of the very few venomous mammals in the world. Its bite is not a hazard to man.

length of time it takes a man to inhale and exhale once. These fussy, fastidious, nervous little balls of furry energy are found over most of the continent.

Names and Range

The common or masked shrew ranges through virtually all of Canada all the way north to the Arctic tundra. It is found throughout Alaska and down the backs of the Rocky and Appalachian Mountains.

Masked shrew (diagonal lines).

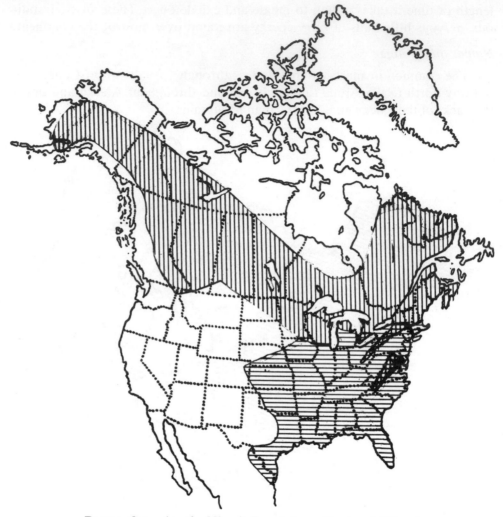

Pygmy shrew (vertical lines). Least shrew (horizontal lines).

The tiny two-and-a-half-inch pygmy shrew has an enormous range: from Alaska to Labrador, and south into the United States as far as North Carolina.

The desert shrew is limited to our Southwest and to Mexico.

The least shrew is another widespread species ranging from Florida to Texas, from southern New England to Nebraska.

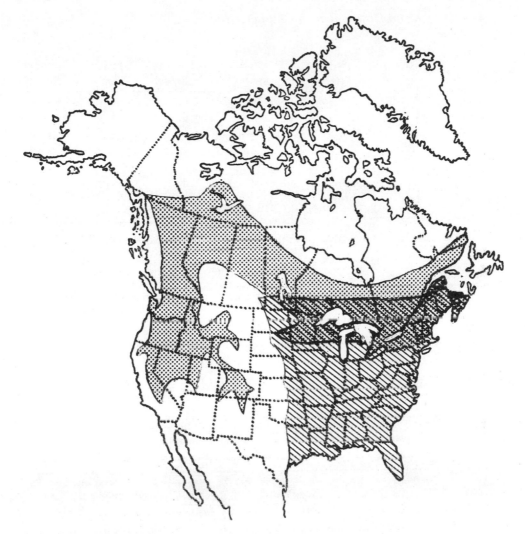

Short-tailed shrew (diagonal lines). Northern water shrew (dotted area).

The short-tailed shrew populates the entire eastern half of the United States. It is one of the commonest mammals of this great region.

In this survey we have barely touched upon the shrew family. Many of the ranges described are overlapping. With a few notable exceptions, most shrews are very hard to tell apart for anyone but the expert.

Appearance and Distinguishing Characteristics

	COMMON SHREW	PYGMY* SHREW	NORTHERN WATER SHREW†	DESERT SHREW	LEAST SHREW	SHORT-TAILED SHREW‡
Length	2–2½ in.	2–2½ in.	3½ in.	2 in.	2½ in.	3–4 in.
Tail	1½–2 in.	1–1½ in.	2½–3 in.	1 in.	½–¾ in.	¾ in.
Habitat	Moist	Dry clearings	Northern and mountain streams	Low desert	Open grassy	Varied
Color	Grayish-brown	Shades of brown	Blackish-gray (sharp two-tone effect)	Pale ashy	Cinnamon	Plumbeous (lead-colored)

* This is probably the world's smallest living mammal. Its weight is about that of a dime—2½ grams.

† The northern and Pacific water shrews are distinguishable from all others in that they alone have stiff hairs along the sides of their hind feet. They are almost certainly the only mammals that can walk on water, although only for a short distance.

‡ Distinguishable by having no visible external ears (they are hidden in the fur) and extremely small eyes.

Habits

The hyperactive little shrews live almost exclusively on animal food. Insects of all kinds predominate in their diet, supplemented by earthworms, snails, slugs, millipedes, centipedes, spiders, newts, salamanders, birds, snakes,

The pygmy shrew—one of the smallest mammals in the world.

lizards, mice, moles, and other shrews. In winter some roots, fruits, nuts, and berries are consumed.

Shrews in turn are hunted by snakes, hawks, owls, weasels, foxes, skunks, and a host of other carnivores.

Most shrews utter a variety of squeaks and shrill chatter; a low moan is sometimes issued while feeding. At least part of the shrew's sounds are at a pitch too high for the human ear. They are apparently seldom still.

The furious and brief life of the shrew is spent in hunting and, briefly, in reproducing. Active day and night, they can be found burrowing and nosing about almost any dark, damp wooded area or field, in weedy growth of all kinds, on open Arctic tundra, in alpine meadows, under snow, just about anywhere in North America. They are among our most common mammals, and only their extremely small size keeps them from being seen by us every time we go afield.

The short-tailed shrew is unique among shrews in that it is *venomous!* This three-to-four-inch bundle of fury actually has venom-producing glands. It does not inject its venom, as snakes do with their hypodermic fangs, but allows it to flow into the wounds it makes with its sharp but altogether solid teeth. The venom is harmless to man but deadly to the short-tailed shrew's prey.

Reproduction

Shrews have one or two litters annually, depending on species and range. One litter may appear in early spring and another in late fall. The gestation period is a brief 21 or 22 days for most species. Litter size varies from three to ten.

Newborn shrews are naked and are extremely small; they weigh about one hundredth of an ounce. It takes just one week for the young to double their size and start growing their velvet coat. After a month of care a shrew is on its own for a brief but hectic year of life. Some may survive into a second year, and some captives have lived three.

Observation

So utterly vast is the range of the shrew and so varied its habitat that their observation is possible just about everywhere from city park to Arctic wastes; virtually no North American habitat excludes them.

While not as exciting as spotting a mountain lion or watching a herd of bison, the observation of the shrew can be instructive in the ways of the wild.

Pick a likely locality, sit down quietly, focus on small things and forget the large, and sooner or later you will see your shrew. Their hearing is very acute, but it is doubtful that their vision can encompass anything as large as a human being. Avoid areas where dogs and cats roam because these are likely to have been hunted out. Quiet, good eyesight, and lots of patience are the prerequisites of shrew-watching.

Shrew tracks.

4

Mammals That Fly: The Bats

CONTRARY TO MANY LEGENDS, some quite ancient, not one bat is imbued with supernatural powers or given to attacking ladies' coiffures. As a matter of plain fact, bats consume so many hundreds of thousands of tons of insects each year they are extremely beneficial to our comfort and welfare.

Bats have many remarkable qualities, but the most apparent is their ability to fly. Their "wings" are leathery membranes stretched between the very much elongated four "fingers" of their front feet and extended back to the outer aspect of their hind legs. Another membrane extends from the inside of the hind legs to the tail, leaving the hind feet themselves free for gripping as the bat hangs upside down in its roost. The bat, then, is a hairy little creature suspended in the middle of its own leather umbrella. The thumbs of the forefeet are small, equipped with sharp claws and not connected to the membrane.

Bats have greatly enlarged ears which they keep meticulously clean. These ears are essential to their flight. As it flies, the bat issues a steady stream of high-pitched sounds at the rate of about 30 per second. The frequency of these sounds starts at approximately 30,000 cycles, the extreme upper limit of human hearing, and ranges upward to 60,000 cycles or higher. The squeaking done by a bat in its roosting site is on a much lower frequency and readily discernible by the human ear.

If a bat picks up an echo from one of its sounds, it instantly speeds up the rate of discharge until the signals are coming at 50–60 per second. The pattern formed by the echoes tells the bat of obstacles, their size, shape, and location. Bats can thus locate night-flying insects, and can fly through a maze

[31]

of wires, other bats, and endless obstructions without colliding. Block those
ears, and a bat is helpless, as it crashes into walls and anything else in its path.
They are *not*, however, blind, and those that fly by day may use their eyes to
some extent.

Amazingly, bats contract muscles in their ears to cut off their own signals
as they emit them, opening their ears to receive echoes. At a rate of 50–60
sounds per second, the muscular activity in which a bat must engage is really
remarkable. The perfection of this little flying machine is one of the true
wonders of the natural world.

Names and Range

Unfortunately, there is no really simple way of breaking the bats down
into groups while maintaining any degree of accuracy without using the
refinements of scientific nomenclature. The groupings we use here, then, must
be broad, sometimes rather arbitrary, but can suggest the fascinating field that
awaits the interested observer.

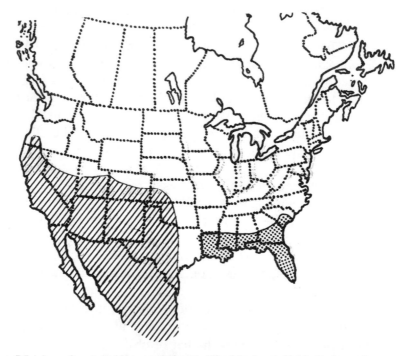

Mexican freetail (diagonal lines). Florida freetail (dotted area).

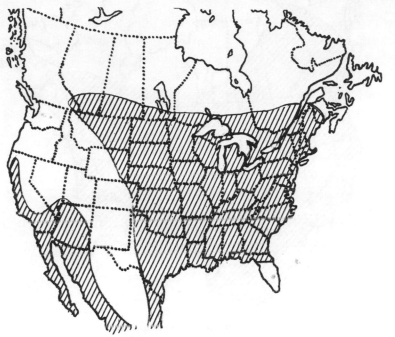

Red bat (diagonal lines).

Keen myotis (diagonal lines).

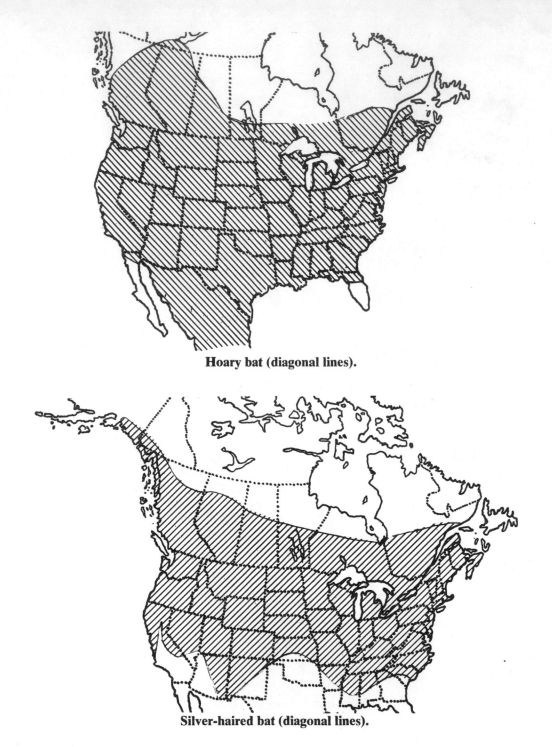

Hoary bat (diagonal lines).

Silver-haired bat (diagonal lines).

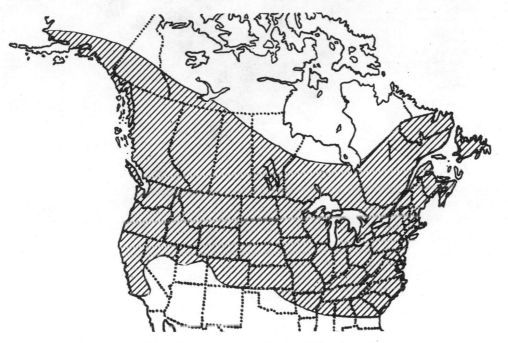

Little brown myotis (diagonal lines).

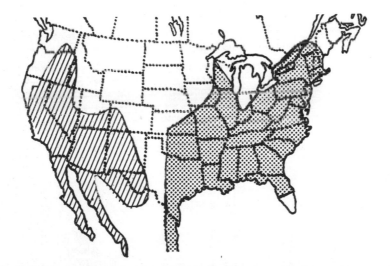

Western pipistrel (diagonal lines). Eastern pipistrel (dotted area).

The Principal Bats of North America

MAJOR GROUPINGS	REFINED GROUPINGS	COMMON NAMES	RANGE
Leaf-nosed bats		Leafchin or Peter's leafchin	Extreme southern Tex.
		Leafnose or California leafnose	Extreme southern Calif. and Nev., southern and western Ariz.
		Hog-nosed or long-tongued	Extreme southern Calif. and Ariz.
Typical insect-eating or plain-nosed bats	Myotis	Little brown myotis	Found in every state except La., Ariz., Fla. Found in Alaska and every province of Canada.
		Yuma myotis	B.C. to Mex., east through Wyo. and Tex.; skips Col. and Utah.
		Mississippi myotis or southeastern myotis	Fla., southern Ga., Ala., Miss., La., Ark., Mo., Ill., Ind., Tenn., Ky.
		Gray myotis	Ala., N.C., Tenn., Ky., Mo., Ark., Okla.
		Cave myotis	All of Southwest.
		Keen myotis	Labrador west through Dakotas, south to Ark., Ga., and S.C.
		Long-eared myotis	Western United States, east to Tex. and Dakotas, north to B.C. and Alberta.
		Fringed myotis	Western United States, east to S.D., north to Wash.
		Indiana myotis	New England toward Southwest to Okla. Misses Great Lakes region and Southeast.
		Long-legged myotis	All of western United States west of Kansas, north almost to Alaska; B.C. and Alberta.
		Small-footed myotis or least myotis	Northeastern United States, southeastern Canada.

The Principal Bats of North America (Continued)

MAJOR GROUPINGS	REFINED GROUPINGS	COMMON NAMES	RANGE
	Pipistrels	Western pipistrel	Western Tex. west to Calif., north to Wash.
		Eastern pipistrel	All of eastern United States west to Wis. in north, Tex. in south.
	Other plain-nosed bats	Big brown	All of United States, most of Canada south of tundra.
		Evening	Southeastern United States, north to Ind.
		Silver-haired	All of United States except Fla., La., Tex. Most of Canada south of tundra; into Alaska.
		Hoary	All of United States, most of Canada south of tundra.
		Red	All of United States, except N.M., Wash., Oreg., Ida., northern Nev. and Utah.
		Seminole (red)	Fla. west to Tex.
		Western yellow	Extreme southern Calif.
		Eastern yellow	Fla. west to Tex.
		Spotted	Southwestern United States
	Lump-nosed or big eared bats	Western big-eared	All of western United States north to B.C., east to Va. in central states only.
		Eastern big eared	Southeastern United States
		Pallid	Western United States, Mex. to B.C.
Free-tailed bats	Freetails	Florida or eastern freetail	Southeastern United States, north to S.C., west to Tex.
		Mexican freetail	Southwestern United States, north to Oreg.
		Big freetail	Western United States, south of Dakotas but north to B.C. in West.
	Mastiffs	Western mastiff	Southern Cal., Ariz., N.M. and Tex.
		Eastern mastiff	Southeastern Fla.

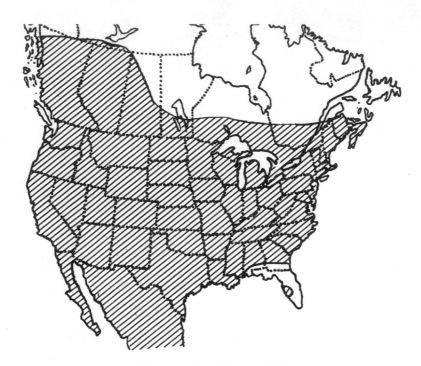

Big brown bat (diagonal lines).

Very roughly, the bats of the United States and Canada can be broken down as follows: American leaf-nosed bats, typical insect-eating bats, and free-tailed bats. The refinements of these groupings, the names that must be included, are so numerous that only a skeletal chart will serve our needs.

Appearance and Distinguishing Characteristics

The characteristics that separate the species of North American bats are many. They generally depend, however, on close examination. As a bat swoops by in the dusk, or flits through the cone of light thrown to earth by a porch light, only the most expert eye can focus quickly enough on fine details to make a distinction. In our section on observation we will discuss opportunities for close examination. The details outlined here will presuppose this close examination and not a mere glance of the creature on wing.

Distinguishing Characteristics of Major Groups of North American Bats

	LEAF-NOSED BATS	MYOTIS BATS	PIPISTRELS	LUMP-NOSED OR BIG-EARED BATS	FREETAILS AND MASTIFFS
Major Characteristics	Leaflike triangular piece of skin projecting up from tip of nose. Leafchin has leaflike flaps of skin on chin from ear to ear, usually warty. Tail to edge of membrane.	No projections on muzzle. Tail to edge of membrane but not beyond. Pointed tragus.* Fringed myotis has stiff hairs along edge of tail membrane.	Blunt tragus. Small size. Tail to edge of membrane.	Very large ears; two marked lumps on nose. Tail to edge of membrane.	Tail extends well beyond edge of membrane. Vertical wrinkles in upper lip. Mastiffs very large with broad ears that meet in middle.
Size (length in inches)	3–4	3–4	2½–3½	3½–4½	Freetails: 4 Mastiffs: 6.5
Color	Leafchin: reddish-brown; Leafnose: brownish-gray; Hognose: brown above, pale below.	Blackish-brown to reddish-brown. Great variations.	Western: pale smoky-gray to brown. Eastern: yellowish-brown to warm brown. Some grayish or blackish.	Western: buff-tan to brown. Eastern: cinnamon above, white-tipped hairs on belly.	Freetails: dark-brown to nearly black. Mastiffs: dark-brown, whitish or pale cream at base.
Habitat	Caves, mines, rock crevices; arid regions.	Caves, buildings, hollow trees. All over continent.	Caves, sheltered cliff crevices, buildings.	Caves, mines, buildings, hollow trees.	Rock crevices and buildings.
Flight	Well after dark.	Varies: daylight, dusk, after dark.	Dusk and just before sunrise.	After dark.	Freetails: dusk. Mastiffs: evening.

* The tragus is a fleshy prominence just in front of the external ear opening. It is large, sometimes nearly as long as the ear itself.

Habits

Bats vary greatly in habit. Some fly in daylight, others at dusk or dawn, and still others only in the dark of night. Some are found exclusively in remote caves, others in remote caves *or* behind the shutters of your house. Some hibernate while others migrate impressive distances. It is, obviously, very difficult to generalize and even more difficult to cover the entire field meaningfully. To overcome this difficulty, we will select one of our most common and widely distributed bats and tell its story. In effect, it is an ambassador for all the rest.

North America's little brown or myotis bat ranges from Alaska to Labrador, from southern California to Georgia. Every province of Canada, then, is populated and every mainland state of the United States except Arizona, Louisiana, and Florida.

The fact that this creature has managed to adapt to environments as different as southwestern desert and Arctic tundra, as Rocky Mountain fir forests and Georgia lowland swamps is proof in itself that it has a wholly successful way of life. While other creatures have come and gone, most far more impressive than this little nighttime shadow, the little brown bat has continued its unvarying way across hundreds of centuries and hundreds of thousands of square miles.

When evening comes, the pug-nosed little bat moves out from its daytime sanctuary and starts to hunt. Its beady black eyes are barely discernible among the folds of skin on its wrinkled face. They will have little use in the course of a night's hunting. The small, forward-pointing ears will seek echoes bounced off objects as small as night-flying insects. Echolocation will be the animal's sole guide throughout its hours of flight.

The flight of the little brown bat is not direct but undulating. It is rather like watching a stone skipped across a pond.

As it flits about, the bat gathers insects in its open mouth or in its tail membrane, which it controls like a scoop. As it flies across open water, the bat swoops low and dredges up water in its dangling lower jaw. It may make several passes across a pond or rain puddle before it has slaked its thirst. Throughout the night the creature will stay awing, satisfying all its needs until, in the predawn, it seeks the cover of its daytime hideaway. Some species of bat remain close to this cover all night, others travel many, many miles. In the course of one night's hunting a bat may consume more than half its own body weight in insects.

As it hunts, the bat is virtually unmolested. On occasion one may fall prey to an owl, and a sudden storm will claim some victims, but, for the most part, the life of the bat is quite uneventful.

Although their general appearance would seem to deny it, bats are clean. When a bat returns to its roost for its upside-down sleep, it will spend as much as thirty minutes cleaning itself before settling down to sleep. Wherever it can reach with its long, pink tongue will be thoroughly bathed. Frequently-moistened hind feet with their fingers free of the membrane will tend to the rest of the body. The fingers of the forefeet are quite useless, having been given over to the single task of supporting the flight membrane. The thumb of the forefoot, however, has a very important function. It twists around and around in the bat's ear, keeping the passage fastidiously clean. An ear blocked with dirt would spell doom to the echo-sounding night-flyer.

The daytime roost of the little brown bat can be anywhere from a cave to a church steeple. Hollow trees, attics, barns, abandoned outbuildings, garages, even niches behind house shutters will serve as well. The musky odor and telltale droppings beneath the perch are the signs to seek. Where large concentrations are found, the rustling and mouselike squeaking can be heard as the bats move about and change their positions.

When winter comes, with insects no longer available and weather extremes making flying hazardous, the bat, having at least doubled its weight since spring, will either hibernate or migrate. Some bat migrations are known to cover as much as a thousand miles. One way or another, by late fall, the bat has a layer of fat to see it through a winter's sleep or sustain it for a marathon flight.

Reproduction

A bat's life is a long one—ten to twenty years, depending on species. Accidents claim some, cave temperatures that drop below freezing take those that don't move in time, but bats are more apt to live out their full life potential than most small mammals.

Mating may occur two or even three times a year; in late fall, just before hibernation, in midwinter if the roost is warm enough, and again in spring. The birth, however, following a delayed fertilization where the sperm is held dormant within the female, takes place in the spring or summer after an actual gestation period of fifty to sixty days. Some births may occur in May, but June and July see the arrival of most baby bats.

When she is about to give birth, the female moves off to a "maternity ward" within the roost and switches her position so that she is hanging head-up by her thumbs instead of head-down. As the infant emerges, the female cups her tail membrane to catch it. She then licks it to help it free its wings and legs, which are stuck to its body.

The young bat is very large compared to its eventual size. It may weigh one fifth as much as its mother. Its eyes are closed for the first day only, and it is quite naked for the first several days. Within a week after its birth the baby bat is carried on the nightly hunts by the female; it grasps her fur and feeds at one of her two nipples. When it is too heavy to carry, it is left behind. In two or three weeks it is weaned and then may be fed on regurgitated food brought home by the mother. By the third or fourth week it is hunting on its own and is only five weeks away from full growth. Females mate at the end of their first summer, males at the end of their second. In some species multiple births occur, and the female does her best to care for all her young—up to four. Multiple births do not occur, however, in the little brown myotis bat, as far as is known.

Observation

A WORD OF CAUTION: Some species of bats, at least, are known to carry rabies and, indeed, may be the major reservoir of this dread disease in some areas. *Do not handle a bat that appears unable to fly. Never use your hands to pick up a bat found on the ground. Most bats will bite when first captured and handled.* Before entering a bat roosting site to study specimens, contact the Board of Health and inquire about local rabies conditions. *This is a very important consideration for the amateur observer.*

The thrill and fascination of watching a bat on the wing is real enough, and time spent afield at dusk or of an evening will present its opportunities. Little will be learned, however, about the strange appearance of these small mammals unless you seek their roosts. Your local museums or state conservation offices will tell you of good locations if you can't find some on your own. Seek dark, protected areas where wind and precipitation are not problems. Barns, attics, and caves are the first places to look. Be careful in caves; the fascination of a bouquet of bats overhead can be considerably dampened by a bad fall or the realization that you have lost your way. It will not take long to determine whether a cave is inhabited by bats or not. The strong, musky odor will be immediately apparent.

In some areas bat concentrations are huge, and local sources of natural-history information will lead you to them. Some such locations in the United

States are world famous. Ney Bat Cave, twelve miles southwest of Bandera, on Texas Route 16, is perhaps the greatest in the United States. Between twenty and thirty million bats live in this great cave, and the exodus of free-tails at dusk in summer is a natural wonder second to none. So prolonged is the flight that the last to leave meet the first returning. They pour from the mouth of the cave like a stream of smoke that is visible several miles away.

New Mexico's Carlsbad Caverns are home to several million bats, and it was their flights that led to the discovery of this great scenic wonder. Abandoned iron mines in New Jersey (within thirty miles of Times Square) and limestone caves in southern Missouri have great concentrations. Hundreds of such locations all over the continent offer wonderful opportunities for observation. Local sources of information will direct you to them. It is a fascinating nature-observation project.

Bat tracks.

5

The Armored Mammal: The Armadillo

THE ORDER OF MAMMALS known as edentates are primitive creatures with degenerate teeth. In the New World they are represented by the sloths and armadillos. The North American allotment is one species, one lone edentate on this whole, vast continent. Because it is so unique, it is worth observing. Fortunately, that is not a difficult assignment.

Names and Range

The nine-banded or Texas armadillo has a fairly restricted range: Kansas, Oklahoma, Texas, to Mexico; Arkansas, Louisiana, Mississippi, and New Mexico. In recent years, evidently, specimens were liberated also in Florida, and they are spreading throughout that state. There are reports from Missouri that the armadillo may become established there. The armadillo is a newcomer north of Mexico (it undoubtedly arrived in the United States well within historical times) and, like the opossum, is expanding its range northward.

Appearance and Distinguishing Characteristics

You are unlikely to mistake an armadillo for any other animal. Its nine-banded shell and long, tapering, seemingly segmented tail are quite distinct. A mottled brownish color overall, the animal has few hairs and these mostly on the unprotected underside. The entire forepart is encased in a single shield, with the movable bands starting in the middle of the back. The head has a donkeylike look to it with the two high, pointed ears. One large, immovable shield protects the head. The legs are short with five clawed toes on each hind

Armadillo (diagonal lines).

foot, four on each front. The two middle toes on the forefoot are particularly long and heavy, adapted for rapid digging. The overall length of the adult is about thirty-two inches, nearly half of which is tail.

Habits

The nearsighted little busybody we call armadillo lives almost exclusively on insects and arachnids. These it acquires by endless snuffling about in plant debris, by day as well as night.

It prefers to seek its food in low brush and foliage, in cactus patches, coarse grass, among scrub oaks and thorny thickets. Armadillos are common along highways through such areas and often fall victim to passing cars. They can probably adapt with ease to any area with a high ground-insect population and where prolonged cold spells are rare or absent.

The armadillo, when attacked, either rolls into a ball to protect its vulnerable underside (some observers don't believe the nine-banded armadillo does this), or runs at quite a startling speed. If in danger of being

Courtesy U.S. Department of Interior, Fish & Wildlife Service

The shy nine-banded armadillo in a lifelike situation. These are stuffed specimens.

overtaken, it digs in. The speed and facility with which an armadillo can burrow completely underground is really quite amazing. Even if you catch up with one before it has disappeared and catch on to its tail, you will have great trouble in dislodging it. Its shell and forefeet are more than strong enough to anchor it firmly in place.

Despite its speed, shell, and burrowing capabilities, the armadillo is regularly preyed upon by bobcat, mountain lion, wolf, coyote, and one or two other predators. Men hunt them throughout their range for their distinctly porklike flesh and their shells, which can be made into a variety of perfectly useless ornaments.

Reproduction

Armadillos mate in July and August, but the actual development of the young doesn't begin much before November. The young are born from February to April, after a gestation period of 120 days.

Strangely, the armadillo bears identical quadruplets, all of one sex. If the mother has "twins," she bears eight identical babies, again all of one sex.

The young are born in a burrow that can be as much as twenty-five feet long and many feet below the surface. The diameter of the opening is seldom much more than eight inches. Side chambers may be occupied by anything from rabbits to rattlesnakes. This should be kept in mind when thinking of reaching into a burrow to see who might be at home. A grass-lined chamber at the end of the burrow serves as the maternity ward. In areas where rock formations create natural caves, these may be used instead of burrows.

The young are born with their eyes open, and within a day or two are tottering after their mother. They continue to nurse for two months, well after they have started eating insects.

At birth the armadillo's skin is soft and flexible and shows the pattern its shell will eventually have. As the animal matures, its armor hardens.

If not taken by a predator or hit by a car, the armadillo lives four years.

Observation

Few North American mammals are easier to observe than the armadillo. They are very nearsighted and have poor hearing, and if their sense of smell is good, they seldom *focus* it on anything but the pursuit of food. If you are light on your feet, don't cast shadows directly in front of them, and don't move suddenly, you can watch an armadillo for hours—even follow it—without being noticed. If you are watching one armadillo, you are likely to be watching many. They are gregarious little animals, and as many as sixty may be found feeding in a small area.

Armadillos leave well-defined trails and make cone-shaped holes or rooted furrows as they dig after prey. In any scrub or low-brush area within their

Armadillo tracks.

range, unless it is an area so heavily trafficked by predators that they are hunted out, a short walk will turn one up. They are very sensitive to ground vibrations, and a light tread will increase your chances of success. Dusk and just after dark are especially good times to find them moving about. Hint: in the eastern parts of their range, look to pine forests.

Large populations will be found in Texas' Aransas National Wildlife Refuge and Louisiana's Lacassine National Wildlife Refuge. You will do nearly as well, however, in any wild scrub area within those states and several others.

6

The Great North American Bears

OTHER COUNTRIES, other continents may boast of great and exotic beasts, but no continent can match North America for bears. Terribly decimated in many areas by prejudice and overhunting, our bears still maintain respectable populations in others. Among them are the largest and the second-largest meat-eating land animals left on planet earth.

The observation of the North American bears is not an easy task. It requires a measure of dedication not required by most other animal groups, not to mention available funds and a hardy constitution. For most amateur observers the habitats of many of our bears are too remote to offer much of an opportunity for study. They are, however, so impressive, so much a part of our wildlife heritage that our careful attention is warranted.

Bears are extremely adaptable creatures and have been able to accommodate themselves to virtually every surface environment on our continent except the heart of burning sand deserts. They are found in semiarid regions just as they are in swamps, mountains, forests, on tundra, and open Arctic ice.

Names and Range

For our needs, there are four groups of bears in the United States and Canada:

Polar bears
Black bears
Grizzly bears
Big brown bears

The Polar Bears

Polar bears are Arctic creatures of barren rock- and ice-bound shores. Rare indeed is the polar bear that sees a tree, and equally rare is the citizen of North America who sees a polar bear in the wild. One word describes their haunt, *remote*.

In the summer, the white giant ranges far to the north, far at sea to hunt the seal on floating ice. Almost every year a few follow the seal herds southward when the Arctic night blankets the great polar region. Some have come as far south as the Gulf of St. Lawrence, and a few may reach the Gaspé Peninsula on rare occasions.

The Black Bears

Our most widely distributed bear is the so-called black bear. I pointedly say "so-called" because, as we shall see, in many parts of his range he is as often found wearing colors other than black. Black bears may be found from northern Alaska, above the Arctic Circle, to well down into Mexico. Every province of Canada is populated by them and most of the United States. In the few states where he is missing, he is so only because he has been driven out by hunting and the destruction of suitable habitat.

The Grizzly Bears

Grizzly bears are now western and northern animals for the most part. Very closely related to the big brown bears, they overlap their range. In the United States, grizzly bears are found only in Alaska, Idaho, Montana, Wyoming, Utah, Colorado, and New Mexico. Northeast Washington may have a few, and they are known to have disappeared from California in 1922. In Canada grizzlies range through the Yukon and Northwest Territories, British Columbia, and Alberta. Just how far to the east they range in the Far North is not known. There is no doubt that they range beyond the Arctic Circle and overlap ranges with the polar bears.

The Big Brown Bears

A number of close relatives of the grizzly bears are known collectively as the big brown bears. They have a very limited range: the southern shores of

Photo by Wilford L. Miller

Two grizzlies in Yellowstone National Park. Note the frosted look on the larger animal, higher up the slope. Note also how the profile differs from that of the black bear.

Alaska and the islands close offshore, the extreme southwestern corner of the Yukon Territory, the northwest shores of British Columbia, and a few of the adjacent islands.

Appearance and Distinguishing Characteristics

The differences between the four groups of bears are easy to distinguish, even through a pair of binoculars. A simple chart will establish these immediately.

The matter of coloring among bears can be quite confusing. The black bear may be intense black, various shades of brown, including cinnamon, of a bluish cast, or, on Gribbell Island, British Columbia, and in the area of Douglas Channel, quite distinctly white with a buff tint on the head. Still, its small size and Roman profile make it clearly a black bear, in any color.

The Four Groups of North American Bears

	POLAR BEARS	BLACK BEARS	GRIZZLY BEARS	BIG BROWN BEARS
Colors	White	Black, brown, cinnamon, blue, or white The face is always brownish, and a blaze of white on the chest is usual.	Yellowish brown, dark brown to almost black. Back hairs usually have white tips, giving a frosted or grizzly look. Intensity of color varies over body. Not uniform.	Yellowish to dark brown. Frequently with white-tipped hairs. Less grizzled than true grizzlies. Color more uniform.
Size				
Overall length:	7–8 ft.	5 ft.	6–8 ft.	8–10 ft.
Weight:	700–1,600 lbs.	200–500 lbs.	350–1,100 lbs.	To 1,500 lbs. or more
Height at shoulder:	3–4 ft.	2–3 ft.	3–3½ ft.	4–4½ ft.
Face	Straight Roman profile; nose black; head small on long neck.	Straight Roman profile; brown snout.	Dished-in profile.	Dished-in profile.
Major Distinguishing Characteristics	1. White color 2. Roman nose 3. Small head 4. Large size	1. Roman nose 2. No shoulder humps 3. Small size 4. Short, rounded front claws	1. Dished-in profile 2. Large size 3. Grizzled app. 4. Maned hump on shoulders 5. Front claws very long 6. Lack of uniformity in color over body and head	1. Dished-in profile 2. Huge size 3. Massive head 4. Slightly grizzled appearance 5. More uniform color 6. Short, stout curved claws

The massive size of the big brown bears distinguishes them from all other bears in the world. Up on their hind legs, they may tower twice the height of a tall man—as much as twelve feet. The biggest grizzly, although a very large bear by any standard, does not have the same bulk and height.

THE POLAR BEARS

Habits

The polar bear has given up his dependence on land. Far at sea, all summer he can be found on floating ice or swimming in the open leads between floes. He is a powerful swimmer. On ice an adult polar bear can reach a speed of twenty-five miles an hour, aided by his unique, nonskid sole pads. His endurance is great at slower speeds and he can walk for days on end.

The pelage of the great creature of the North is extremely dense, and only females heavy with young den up for the winter. Males, barren females, and females with cubs born the winter before hunt along the edge of the ice throughout the bleak Arctic night. No temperature extremes seem to bother them.

Courtesy Ontario Department of Lands & Forests

A great white bear accepts even the challenge of the low-flying plane from which this photo was taken, at Cape Henrietta Maria, Hudson Bay, 1963.

Courtesy Ontario Department of Lands & Forests

Polar bears at sea. This is when the great white animals are most vulnerable and are often shot from boats.

The female is indistinguishable from the male in color, although about one fifth smaller. Except for a brief mating season during the spring, adult males and females are strictly solitary. Several may be found together near a common food source like a stranded whale, but these are brief and accidental encounters.

The food of the polar bear consists of seals, fish, shrimps, mollusks, foxes, caribou, birds, lemmings, young walrus, and an occasional whale that is washed ashore or trapped in shallow water. On occasion polar bears do come ashore, and some grasses and roots are eaten. Seaweed is sometimes added to the diet, which is more nearly completely carnivorous than that of any other bear. The polar bear's only enemy besides man is probably the killer whale, although little is known about this matter.

Adult polar bears roar with great gusto. The young hum and whine. It is difficult to assess their intelligence, but they are probably quite as bright as the other bears. Their disposition is notoriously bad, and in captivity they cannot be trusted.

There can be little doubt that the polar bear is less afraid of man than almost any other species. Contacts with men are few, and although some polar bears will turn and run at the sight or smell of a human being, others will attempt to hunt him down as if he were a seal. Man-eating apparently does occur—if not often, at least from time to time. Since man in the Arctic invariably hunts the polar bear, there is a kind of natural justice in this.

The mighty polar bear has poor hearing but probably the best eyesight of the world's bears. His sense of smell is extremely fine. He is a fierce fighter, a masterful hunter using a combination of stealth and sudden bursts of speed. He is the second-largest meat-eating land animal in the world.

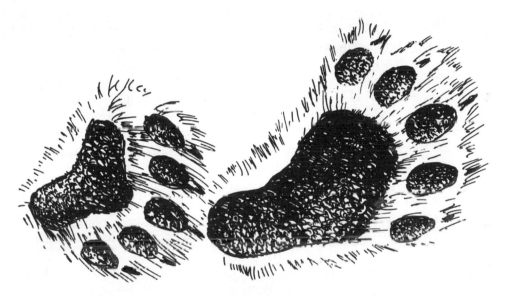

Polar bear tracks.

Reproduction

Polar bears breed when they are three or four years old. Females mated during the spring or early summer den up in ice caves after the Arctic night has fallen and deliver twins in late December or early January. The actual gestation is somewhat over eight months. The young are nursed in the hideaway until March, when they emerge and are taken directly to the water, where their schooling begins. Mother bears with cubs are particularly ferocious and take meticulous care in the preparation of their offspring for independence.

When a female has cubs with her, males keep their distance. The chances are that a male would kill and eat any cub he found unattended, and the females are particularly alert to this danger. The life expectancy of polar bears in the wild is reported as fifteen to twenty years, but in captivity they may live much longer.

THE BLACK BEARS

Habits

America's smallest bear is a very adaptable creature. Largely nocturnal near civilization, he can be found abroad day and night in undisturbed areas. He can be found anywhere from lowland, hardwood swamps to alpine meadows. He generally prefers heavily wooded areas and establishes a home range. Females most often hold their ranges to a ten-mile radius, but males will travel farther. These ranges are well defined, and legend has the animals clawing "boundary" trees to warn other bears off. The exact purpose of these clawed and bitten trees, which do exist, is not precisely known. Within his range, the black bear tends to use well-established trails and is a creature of habit. He is easily enraged by an interruption of his solitary routine.

The black bear's eyesight is only fair, but his hearing and sense of smell are very acute. If he suspects an intruder he will often go up on his hind legs and perhaps waddle comically for a few steps to get a better "reading." This has led to the misconception that bears wade into combat like hairy gladiators. Bears, in fact, travel on all fours and bite like dogs when forced into battle. They can, and do, however, strike out with their heavily clawed front feet.

Adult black bears make a variety of sounds: they grunt, squeak, roar, mumble, and moan; young ones whimper. They are strong swimmers, can run in bursts up to twenty-five miles an hour and, at least when young, climb trees well. Older bears are less adept aloft.

Contrary to popular belief, black bears do not truly hibernate. In the northern parts of their range they do den up for the worst of the winter in a self-made bed of grass, twigs, bark, and leaves. This nest may be in a hollow tree, cave, sheltered under roots or a fallen tree, or may be just a shallow excavation in a wooded area. They are frequently exposed to falling snow during their dormancy.

Profile of the black bear with his easily distinguished Roman nose.

This winter sleep of the black bear is deep, but his body temperature remains near normal. During a warm spell a bear may move around a bit and then return to his nest. In the southern parts of his range, during the winter the black bear takes naps for a few days at a time, even in Florida and Louisiana. Bears usually den alone, although on occasion a sow will allow her cubs of the previous season to hole up with her. During the summer, black bears have no permanent home but sleep in trees or on the ground whenever they get tired.

The food preferences of the black bears are varied. They readily eat a variety of grasses, berries and fruits of all kinds, seeds, nuts, tender under-bark, roots, insects, particularly ants and bees, honey, fish caught and found, frogs, rodents, birds, eggs, and carrion, even dead bears. Black bears are not great hunters, but some specimens will take fawns, and some few take to raiding domestic stock, with a particular passion for pigs. They have a great fondness for garbage dumps and will frequently raid camps and cabins. At times they can be very destructive and quite dangerous. They are diabolically clever at gaining entry to locked buildings, and many are the woodsmen and vacationers who have returned home and found a bear in the kitchen.

Bears are particularly attracted to carrion and will seek it out and roll in it before feasting. They also take dust and mud baths in hot weather.

Young bears are playful and inquisitive, but mature specimens are considerably less charming. They are not gregarious and are suspicious of any intruder, man and bear alike. When they do congregate briefly around a common food supply like a garbage dump, there is constant quarreling, and bitter fighting can break out, preceded by much snapping and nipping. Fascinating to watch, they tend to be decidedly disagreeable once past the first flush of youth.

Photo by Wilford L. Miller

Unusual photograph of a black bear sow nursing her twin cubs.

Reproduction

Black bears mate in June or early July, breaking the ritual of their solitary ways for the purpose. Gestation is around seven and a half months, and the young are born in late January or early February. Females mate in their third summer and generally have one cub the first time. Subsequent litters usually consist of two cubs; three are not uncommon, four rare, and, reportedly, five exceptional. They normally breed regularly in alternate years.

Black bear tracks.

The young are very small for an animal that may one day weigh several hundred pounds: six to eight ounces. They are blind, toothless, and covered with very fine hair at birth. At six weeks the eyes open and the teeth begin to cut through the gums. They weigh about two pounds at this time.

At two months, when they weigh about five pounds, the young leave the den and undergo strict training. The female nurses her cubs throughout the summer and constantly reprimands them for the slightest infraction of bear etiquette. The cubs may be turned out on their own after the first summer or kept until the following spring. When they first go on their own, they are confused and frightened and stay together for about two months. They drift apart by the time their playful mauling of each other starts to become disagreeably serious.

Males will kill and eat their own cubs (which they cannot recognize), and females with young in tow will attack any male that comes close. Not until her cubs have left her will a female show the slightest interest in a prospective mate, and even then her desire for his companionship is short-lived. Bears are not sociable, and any socializing nature forces on them is strictly for the one purpose of continuing the species. A female meeting her own cubs after she has once set them loose will be as short-tempered with them as she would be with a perfect stranger, or with her own mate after their romance is over. An adult bear is a suspicious crank.

THE GRIZZLY BEARS

Sad to report, the great grizzly bears are fast disappearing from the United States, except Alaska. Outside of Alaska and Canada there are only a few hundred of these fine animals left.

Habits

The great grizzly bear has one overriding concern in his life—food. Except at mating time, or just after emerging from his winter den, he is either eating, has just finished eating, or is about to start. Although classed as a carnivore, an eater of flesh, the grizzly, like all bears, is omnivorous. He grazes on grass, brouses on leaves, harvests fruits and berries with relish, and spices his meals with bark and numerous wild plants. He hunts rodents, particularly ground squirrels, and a variety of other mammals, lizards, snakes, and insects. He is an expert fisherman and has a particular passion for salmon. During the migration of the salmon upstream to breed, every brook and river in the range will have bears along the banks and up to their haunches in the swirling waters. The grizzly is a powerful swimmer.

Some grizzlies become expert at taking larger prey and will hunt elk, caribou, and deer. A small percentage takes to stock raiding, and farmers in the district may suffer great financial loss before the outlaw is killed. Unfortunately, the sins of a few have reflected on the many, and grizzlies are hunted down without mercy over most of their range outside national parks. It is a sad comment on our civilization that we have not found room for this spectacular, handsome animal.

Grizzlies, like all bears, rejoice in carrion and seek it out with their extraordinary keen sense of smell. Meat, stale or fresh, will be eaten by a grizzly any time it is available. They are known to be cannibalistic, and a cub that strays from its mother is likely to be killed and eaten if other adults are about.

Grizzly bears prefer mountainous terrain and alpine meadows. They range well beyond the timberline both in altitude and latitude. The Barren Ground grizzly and several others range over the Arctic tundra. Once common on the Great Plains, they have long since been driven up into the mountains and to the North.

Grizzly bears can be found abroad by day or night, although they tend to be nocturnal close to settled areas. Except in winter, the grizzly bear has no regular home. He wanders over his private range, which may be twenty miles or more in radius, and may have several "nests," hollow grass-lined excavations in which he will catnap after feeding. Sometimes home ranges overlap and bears coming upon each other either feign a ritualistic surprise and drift apart after making a woofing sound, or ignore each other completely. Adults cough, sniff, woof, growl, grunt, and roar to express their transient feelings. Cubs whine and hum. Within their home ranges grizzlies stick very close to well-worn trails and have the peculiar habit of stepping quite accurately into their own footprints.

Young grizzlies climb expertly, but adults, due to their weight, do not. Rarely will an adult even attempt to climb a tree. Their hearing is as keen as their sense of smell, but their eyesight is evidently quite poor.

The winter den of the grizzly bear is considerably more elaborate than that of the black bear. It is usually high up, often at the timberline. It is generally either a cave or a great excavation running twelve to fourteen feet into a hillside, often with the opening under the roots of a tree. It is lined with grass and leaves, and the opening may be plugged with branches dragged to the site for the purpose. Very often the opening will face to the north, probably to prevent an early thaw from flooding the cave.

They do not hibernate in the real sense of the word, but den up for a winter sleep. They can be disturbed and awakened with little difficulty, but they are dangerously disagreeable when this is done.

Reproduction

The female (and probably the male) grizzly breeds first between its third and fifth year. The courtship is a midsummer affair, and for just how long the animals relinquish their cherished solitude is not known. Estimates run from a few hours to all summer. In fact, male and female probably spend a month together off and on. They are playful and affectionate toward each other

Grizzly bear tracks.

during this idyllic period, but eventually separate, with the romance very much over. Like all bears, they are driven together by internal stirrings for the one purpose of procreation.

When winter starts to settle on the land, the female takes to her den. She caves up about a month earlier than the male. (In the South, males may not den up at all). With great care she seals the entrance and goes into her deep sleep. In late January or early February she awakens and gives birth to her cubs. There may be from one to four, but one or two are usual. She has undergone a gestation period of 266 days or more.

At birth the cubs are a little over eight inches long, covered with fine hair, blind and toothless. The solicitous mother wraps her great body around her infants and they begin to suckle.

In about ten days the cubs' eyes open. In a few weeks they start to move about the confined space. By April the female is ready to introduce her offspring to the world beyond the mouth of the cave.

Throughout the summer the female grizzly is concerned about two things other than her own stomach; the safety of her young, and their education.

They are playful little creatures, and she is often very strict. Their endless antics earn them many a severe cuffing. Any adult males approaching are driven off with vicious charges.

By August, the cubs weigh anywhere from fifty to eighty pounds. By the next fall they will weigh from two hundred to four hundred pounds. It takes from eight to ten years for a grizzly to achieve full growth, but they become parents long before attaining that mark.

Yearling cubs generally den up with their mother. Her breeding, then, is restricted to alternate summers. In the wild state the life expectancy probably runs from fifteen to twenty years. It is much greater in captivity, as much as thirty years or more.

THE BIG BROWN BEARS

Habits

These mighty bears are the largest meat-eating land animals left on our planet. Weighing as much as three quarters of a ton, they are impressive indeed.

The habits of this diurnal bear do not vary much from those of the grizzly except in certain details and in ways dictated by their coastal environment. They feed on mice, marmots, and other small mammals, berries, roots, grass, moss, sedges, and fish. Salmon is their favorite food and dead whales and seals washed ashore are attacked with obvious pleasure. Occasionally a big brown bear will hunt larger game and possibly take to stock raiding.

When the big brown bear first emerges from his winter den he remains high in the snow fields, eating lightly of what he can find in the wind-bared patches. His appetite grows from day to day, and he soon follows a well-worn trail down to the valley floor or out onto the beach in search of carrion. By midsummer he is back in the mountains, enjoying the brief profusion of plant and animal life that flourishes there. By late summer or early fall he is back in the lowlands for the salmon migration, where he feasts as at no other time of the year.

The great bears wade out into shallow water among the swarming fish. A deft blow pins the catch to the bottom. Occasionally a large bear wanders into deep water and snatches fish up in his jaws. Everything but the head and gills is eaten.

Big brown bears attack in defense of a food supply or to protect their cubs. They are majestic, solitary creatures, but they can become violently angry and charge in great leaping bounds while uttering a deep roar. Though they usually avoid man, they can be very dangerous if provoked in any way.

Reproduction

What has been said about the reproduction of the grizzly bear applies to the big brown bear as well. The young are very small, probably not much bigger than those of the grizzly bear, but they grow, of course, more quickly. Maturity, however, does not come sooner. There is very little difference between the reproductive habits of the grizzly bear and those of the big brown bear.

Big brown bear tracks.

Observation

A WORD OF CAUTION: *Unprovoked attacks on man by bears are not very common*. However, *all* bears must be considered dangerous at *all* times and the temptation to move close to unrestrained animals should be resisted. "A closer look" at an enchanting pair of cubs can provoke an attack by the mother.

If we had to characterize a typical bear, we would say he would run at the smell or sound of man. But to rely on any individual bear to be "typical" when your life could be at stake is foolish in the extreme.

Bears in national parks are, if anything, more dangerous than completely wild bears in that they have lost their fear of man. They often bite the hands that feed them.

Do not attempt to approach any bear at any time.

The observation of our bears is not an easy assignment. They are shy and retiring by nature and because they have been heavily hunted are easily driven off by the first sign of man.

We will begin with the polar bear; the other species will be discussed together.

Polar Bears

The rules of observation for the polar bear are fairly academic because few of us will ever have the opportunity to use them. Most of those of us who will ever see a polar bear in the wild will do so from a low flying plane or from the deck of a ship. Excursions by ship to the land of the polar bear are available through the Hudson's Bay Company in Winnipeg, Manitoba. The trip is long, however, and not inexpensive. No polar-bear sightings are guaranteed.

If you are ever on foot in the Arctic wastes, rely on your guide (you must have one!). Remember that polar bears, unlike all other bears of North America, have very keen eyesight but poor hearing. They are much more apt to observe you than you are them.

Black Bears, Grizzlies, and Big Brown Bears

The bear's sense of smell, as we have mentioned several times, is extremely keen. If the wind is blowing past you toward him, he will catch your scent. Once he has it he will be on his way, unless he is a "park" bear, in which case he may move in to see if a free meal is in the offing.

The bear's hearing, too, is very sharp. Your movement through the brush will be heard unless you are very careful. If he hears you and doesn't smell you, he may move around you in a wide circle until he has your scent; then he will be gone. You may never know that you were being studied—at least your sounds and smells were.

Equipped with poor eyesight, a bear will not notice you even at fairly close quarters if you are quiet, he doesn't get your scent, *and you don't move.* Even with poor eyesight a bear will notice movement, particularly if it is movement he is unused to. Human movement is different and will attract attention.

A good way to get to see bears outside our national parks and game refuges is with the use of a guide. A guide need not be an expensive professional but may be a local farmer with a free afternoon and no aversion to a few extra dollars. In bear country, stop at any gunsmith shop or hardware store and ask who can lead you to your quarry. A suggestion and a phone number will often be forthcoming. This is true over much of the United States and Canada. The help of someone thoroughly familiar with the area will save you a lot of endless tramping and a lot of frustration.

Getting to see the big grizzlies and particularly the big brown bears will prove to be a bit more of a problem. It will also be more expensive. For grizzlies you may have to pack into remote country and be gone for several days. Grizzlies living close to settled areas are much too shy to expose themselves and will work the area only at night. Big brown bears exist off the beaten track and seldom come near roads or settled areas. A professional guide employing a light plane or sturdy boat, or both, will be necessary. It is, however, a unique experience in natural history, and seeing the world's biggest meat-eating land dweller is something worth doing. A letter to the Alaskan State Department of Conservation in Juneau will start you off. Request a list of licensed guides.

If you are alone and do not wish or cannot employ the services of any kind of guide, how do you find bears?

(1) Contact the Department of Conservation of the state you will be in and ask for information about the distribution of bears in that state. Populations fluctuate, greatly affecting your chances for success. Some apparently good areas may have been hunted out and going there would be a waste of time.

(2) The time of day and season of the year are very important. If the range is fairly close to a populated area you will have little chance of success during daylight. Working through strange woods at night is difficult, so you had better try your luck at dusk. Garbage dumps in good bear country usually draw specimens around sundown. It is best to get there well before dusk, park your car, and sit quietly. Don't play your car radio. You may see quite a show from your front seat.

(3) In the northern states and in Canada you will see little bear activity

after late October or much before March. This varies, of course, with the
severity of the seasons and the peculiarities of local bear populations. In
extremely hot weather, bears will be less active during the middle hours of the
day. Morning, shortly after sunrise, and late afternoon into evening will be
your best hours in the southern and middle states. The hours of the long
shadows are the best bear hours.

(4) Find the bear's food and you will have a good chance of finding the
bear. Determine the weeks of the salmon run in areas affected and watch the
stream and river banks. You will see bears if there are any to be seen in the
area. Particularly seek out areas along the river where there are rocky
shallows, and where sand spits run out into the water creating shallows, pools,
and beaches. Deep water will not attract bears as much as sections of the river
affording easy access to the channel.

Determine what berries and wild or feral fruits grow in the area and find
out when they ripen. There is no sense in looking for bears very far away from
blueberry patches when the blueberries are ripe.

(5) Look for bear signs. In country where there is a good bear population, their trails will be well worn. You will find trees clawed and bitten. You
will find stumps and rotting logs clawed apart and strewn about where bears
have looked for grubs. You will find berry bushes trampled and broken where
they have gone after the ripening fruit. All these signs will tell you if there are
bears around.

It is next to impossible to generalize as to where you will find bears in
every state beyond stating once again that they prefer wooded areas. They do
work out into meadows, particularly at higher altitudes, to graze on the tender
grasses and succulent wild flowers to be found there in spring and early summer. In Louisiana, the black bear sticks almost exclusively to well-watered
bottomland and hardwood areas. In Texas, one state away, the same animal
will be found only in inaccessible mountain areas or in nearly impenetrable
thickets along watercourses. In California, black bears will be found in a
variety of timber and brush situations, while in Florida and Georgia they prefer deep swamps, where quicksand and rattlesnakes flourish. To be successful
in your quest for the elusive but fascinating bear you must obtain specific information from the local Department of Conservation. Many states have inexpensive booklets for sale that will answer just about all your questions about
local conditions. A little preparation and advance planning will increase your
chances a thousandfold.

There are wonderful opportunities to see semiwild bears in our national
parks and refuges. These bears are semiwild because they have lost their fear

of man and will wander in open sight while you photograph them to your heart's content. *They may not, however, be treated as domestic animals; they may not be approached or fed.*

The following national parks, wildlife refuges, and ranges have bears in varying populations and offer unique opportunities for observation:

The Bears in Our Parks and Wildlife Sanctuaries and Other Protected Areas
A Partial List

PARK OR SANCTUARY	STATE	SPECIES OF BEAR
Aleutian Islands National Wildlife Refuge	Alaska (Aleutian Islands)	Big brown bear
Arctic National Wildlife Range	Northeast Alaska	Grizzly bear, polar bear
Everglades National Park	Southern Florida	Black bear
Glacier National Park	Northwestern Montana	Grizzly bear, black bear
Kenai National Moose Range	Southern Alaska (Kenai Peninsula)	Black bear, big brown bear
Kodiak National Wildlife Refuge	Alaska (Kodiak Island)	Big brown bear
Grand Teton National Park	Northwest Wyoming	Grizzly bear
Little Pend Oreille Wildlife Range	Washington	Black bear
Moosehorn National Wildlife Refuge	Maine	Black bear
Mount McKinley National Park	South Central Alaska	Grizzly bear
Okefenokee National Wildlife Refuge	Southeastern Georgia	Black bear
Olympic National Park	Northwest Washington (Olympic Peninsula)	Black bear
Rio Grande National Forest	Colorado	Grizzly bear
San Juan National Forest	Colorado	Grizzly bear
Seney National Wildlife Refuge	Michigan (Upper Peninsula)	Black bear
White River National Wildlife Refuge	Eastern Arkansas	Black bear
Willapa Wildlife Range	Washington	Black bear
Yellowstone National Park	Wyoming–Montana–Idaho	Black bear, grizzly bear

There are also a number of scenic national and provincial parks in Canada with substantial stocks of native wildlife: Yoho, Kootenay, Glacier, and Mount Revelstoke in British Columbia, the many parks of Manitoba, Saskatchewan, and Alberta, notably Banff and Jasper in Alberta, and many other areas in British Columbia have large bear populations. Further information can be obtained from the organizations listed on pages 560–564.

7

Our Long-Suffering Wolves

No MATTER how intense your research, you will be hard put to find a four-legged animal about whom more nonsense has been written than the wolf. To surpass the wolf's unenviable record in this regard you almost certainly must turn to the unicorn or the Chinese dragon.

The word "berserk" comes from the old Norse *berserker,* which referred to a person who donned the skin of a wolf and engaged in excessive bestial fury. The Romans called such creatures *versipellis,* the English *turnskins,* the French *loup-garou,* while the Slovak peoples used the word *vrkolak.* In modern English, we say, quite simply, *werewolf,* or, in the language of the scientist, the Greek *lycanthrop.* What it all amounts to is that man, in the utter extreme of hateful bestiality, becomes a wolf, voluntarily or involuntarily, depending on how you like your nonsense construed.

When wolves of fiction are not luring men to assume their forms and rob graves with them, they are, of course, devouring humans in great numbers. When they can't get people to eat, they make their pursuit of animal husbandry impossible by killing every domestic creature in sight. Everyone *knows,* needless to say, that all wolves are "cruel," "bloodthirsty," "mean," "vicious," "treacherous," "savage," "hideous," and "ghoulish." (I have taken all of these words from descriptions of wolves that have appeared in print.) All of this, I am happy to say, is complete nonsense.

When wolves have not been put in a class with the witches of Salem, they have been envied and honored. The old Anglo-Saxon kings named themselves for these powerful predators (Beowulf, Wulfred, etc.) as did the American Indians (the Wolf Clan of British Columbia, Gray Wolf of the Plains Indians, etc.).

Strangely, the wolf is seldom recognized for what he is, nothing more spectacular than a fairly large predator, a member of the dog family. He is a fine parent (she, too), an efficient hunter, generally very peaceful and, in many ways, most admirable. As for being "cruel," "bloodthirsty," and all the rest of those totally human and therefore inapplicable adjectives—bosh! he is just hungry.

Names and Range

The wolves of North America are all closely related, and we shall review them here as a body. Wolves once ranged over most, if not all, of North America. Today they are still to be found from the Arctic barrens to Mexico, from the extreme eastern to the extreme western end of our continent. Except in the North, however, he is today able to survive only in very small pockets, and even in these he is being pushed toward extinction. Man's prejudice against the wolf seems almost inherent, and he is shot, trapped, poisoned, his dens are smoked and dynamited; he is even strafed from the air. His days, unhappily, are numbered.

Oregon *may* have some wolves; New Mexico and Arizona have small populations; Texas, possibly Oklahoma, Arkansas, Louisiana, Mississippi, Missouri, Wisconsin, Upper Michigan, northern Minnesota, and one or two prairie states are *reportedly* still populated with small numbers. A very small percentage of Canada's huge land mass, however, is out of the wolves' range even today. Alaska has a large, stable wolf population. In general, our wolf inhabits all of temperate and Arctic North America not denied him by man.

Appearance and Distinguishing Characteristics

The wolf, of course, looks rather like a large dog. He greatly resembles a German shepherd, but there are certain differences: His skull is broader, the ears are longer, his legs are longer, etc. A male may run up to sixty-four inches in length and stand eighteen inches or more at the shoulder. His weight usually runs between 75 and 100 pounds, but specimens have been taken as heavy as 150 pounds. Females run up to fifty-six inches in length, sixteen inches in height, with weights running from 60 to 80 pounds.

The sexes are not distinguishable by color, which runs from almost pure white to almost black. They can be all shades of gray or brown, yellowish, rusty red, or almost any combination of these colors. They are bushy-tailed, long-legged, and long-snouted, and have a tendency to appear lean and rangy. They are similar in appearance to the coyotes but, of course, much larger.

Photo by Dr. D. H. Pimlott, courtesy Province of Ontario, Department of Lands & Forests

Year-old wolf cubs near Algonquin Provincial Park's Lake Sasajewan Research Station. Algonquin Park has about one wolf per ten square miles.

Habits

The wolf is essentially a carnivore. Although he will certainly take carrion, he is a hunter and uses skillful pack tactics to gain his prey. Among the food he is known to take are deer, moose, caribou, musk-oxen, mountain sheep, elk, pronghorn, rabbits, prairie dogs, mice and other small mammals, birds, fish, insects, rarely vegetable matter and, unfortunately, domestic stock.

The wolf is a powerful animal better equipped with endurance than speed, although he is fast when really in a hurry. While he can certainly outrun a man, he has trouble overtaking healthy hoofed animals and relies on group cooperation. Unlike many predators he is not a solitary animal under normal circumstances and travels in a family unit. It is believed that he mates for life. A family group will consist of the parents, cubs of one or two litters, plus an occasional "auntie" or "uncle," a solitary animal that has been accepted into the unit as a part-time baby-sitter and hunting partner. Often one or more family units will join together and form the well-known "wolf pack." These wolf packs are temporary and usually occur under severe weather conditions or when following a migrating herd of caribou.

A wolf seldom walks; he trots. Unlike the coyote, who carries his tail low, the wolf carries his high. It is one way of telling them apart from a distance. He may be abroad at any hour of the day or night but is, as might be expected, nocturnal near settled areas.

The wolf is an extremely intelligent animal. He is generally very peaceful, seldom quarrels with his kind unless driven by severe hunger, and willingly accepts strangers, even greets them with fond play and much doglike tail wagging. He is very expressive and makes a great variety of sounds, and postures endlessly to make his wishes or emotions known. His howl is well known and takes many different forms to express various reactions and attitudes. The Indians and Eskimos who know him well say they can interpret this language, and indeed, there are so many demonstrations on record that it is difficult to discount them.

The extensive range of a wolf family may cover several hundred miles. They need broken country with highlands or plateaus cut by ravines and canyons and some wooded cover to be in perfect wolf country, but they are versatile and can tolerate a wide range of habitats if forced to it. Ideally they should have either dense cover where they can hide, or very broad open expanses where their speed and endurance will allow them to escape.

There is no doubt that wolves destroy thousands of hoofed animals in the United States and Canada every year. What is too often overlooked, however, is that most of the animals taken by wolves are feeble, old, or crippled. The wolf is the great thinner. He attacks a herd of migrating caribou and weeds out the poor specimens whose continued existence could only hurt the breeding stock. In most cases, a healthy hoofed animal can outrun a wolf and even drive him off unless he has hunting partners. Certainly, healthy animals are also killed by wolves, but no one has yet been able to demonstrate that the predation of wolves seriously impairs the existence of any wild hoofed animal species. The wolf is generally blamed for what man himself has done. (The only species ever known to wipe out another species is man.)

It cannot be denied that some wolves take to stock raiding and must be destroyed. Some few even engage in the very unwolflike behavior of slaughtering much more than they can consume. Such outlaws seldom last long, but a few have.

In one night in 1739, on a farm east of Hartford, Connecticut, General Israel Putnam lost seventy-five sheep and goats to one she-wolf. The famous renegade of South Dakota, the white "Custer Wolf," wasn't killed until 1920 and then only after the nation's top hunters had tracked him for years without success. His devastating raids on livestock made him the scourge of the

WHEN STRIVING TO
KEEP THE WOLF
FROM THE DOOR
REMEMBER THAT IT IS NOT ALWAYS

the lowest price that is the most economic; the vast superiority of

HOVIS

over any other bread, either brown or white, both in its bone and muscle making substances, secures for it the coveted position of the

"CHEAPEST & BEST."

Highest Awards at the Food and Cookery Exhibitions, London, May 1895 and 1896.

IMITATION IS THE SINCEREST FLATTERY.

The Public are Cautioned against accepting from Bakers spurious imitations of "HOVIS," which, having met with such unprecedented success, is being copied in many instances as closely as can be done without risk.

Purchasers are requested to see that all Bread supplied to them as "Hovis" is stamped "Hovis."

Apply to your Baker or Grocer for "Hovis" Flour for Home use, packed in bags of 3½ lb. and 7 lb.

If any difficulty be experienced in obtaining "HOVIS," or if what is supplied as "HOVIS" is not satisfactory, please write, sending sample (the cost of which will be defrayed), to

S. FITTON & SON, Millers, Macclesfield.
6d. or 1s. Sample on receipt of Stamps.

This advertisement from the *Illustrated London News* of 1896 shows the classical attitude toward the wolf. It was this ancient tradition of wolf hating that the settlers brought to the New World with them.

Plains country and made him one of the most famous wolves in North American history.

There can be no doubt that a large population of wolves in farming and ranching country would be intolerable. Early settlers suffered greatly from their predation, but now things have gone far over the other way. Unless more measures are taken to protect the wolf in parts of his range, he will soon be gone.

Reproduction

Wolves mate at two or three years of age, probably for life. The mating occurs in January or February, and after sixty-three days of gestation, anywhere from three to fourteen young are born. Six or seven are average.

This birth takes place from mid-March to mid-April, with the male standing guard nearby. Birth occurs in a well-concealed den that may be in a cave, a hollow log, or in an excavation into the side of rising ground. There is almost inevitably high ground nearby that can be used as a lookout point.

The pups are blind and quite helpless at birth, but on the ninth day their eyes open. It is about three weeks before they are taken out of the den and their training begins. Actually, training at the beginning amounts to little more than tolerance of play, which becomes progressively rougher. The first lesson learned is strict obedience, and although wolf parents are famous for their patience with their young, they are very intolerant of disobedience.

For months the young are never left alone. At first, the male alone goes off to hunt, leaving the female to care for the pups. He brings food back to her and, when the weaning process starts, he brings meat back to the pups in his own stomach. He swallows great hunks of meat at his kill and regurgitates it at the feet of the pups. At first the pups show little interest in meat as food but are encouraged to play with it like a toy until a trial bite starts them gnawing. Their lifelong passion for fresh and carrion meat is not long in developing.

After the pups are subsisting at least in part on meat, they may be left in the care of another adult who has joined the family unit. On some days, the female may go off to hunt, leaving the male behind as a pup-sitter.

Eventually, organized schooling starts. The play energy and rough-and-tumble attitude that are so natural to the pups are slowly and carefully channeled into a finely drawn hunting skill. The pups are taken along on hunting forays that grow longer each day. They are "ordered" to wait and watch as their parents make the kill. They are encouraged to try their own skill on small mammals and birds, but their first clumsy efforts are doomed to failure, and the pups soon become bored. Still, the training goes on at least

Photo by Dr. D. H. Pimlott, courtesy Province of Ontario, Department of Lands & Forests

Howling wolf, a sound never to be forgotten.

through the first winter and into the following summer. The young may spend up to two winters with their parents, and it is not uncommon to see cubs of two different litters tagging along after adults. Young wolves are probably subject to attack by eagles and bears but little else. Cubs attempting to tackle large hoofed animals before their skill has been developed are apt to be injured or even killed by sharp hooves and flailing antlers. The life span of the wolf in the wild probably runs from ten to eighteen years. Man manages to cut many such lives short, however.

All in all, the family life of the wolf as so often reported by trained observers is one of the most delightful in nature. The care of the young and the tolerance of the individual within the family group are most admirable.

Observation

Few animals will make it more difficult for you to observe their habits than the wolf. He will consciously strive to escape your notice and to keep far out of your way. His very keen senses and uncanny knowledge of what is going on within his range will make it almost impossible for you to surprise him. In the Far North, on the great tundra, they are less wary of man, but in any area where man has settled, the wolf will avoid contact. Yet, a few hours' drive north of most big Canadian cities will put you into wolf country. To observe him, it will be skill against skill, and the chances are his will be greater.

The ideal way to see wolves within the sub-Arctic-to-temperate regions is with the use of a professional guide. Bait is used to attract wolves, but great skill is needed to keep the man-smell off the bait and away from the area. Special potions are mixed that reputedly attract wolves and mask human odors. There are dozens of formulas requiring many noxious ingredients.

Wolves are attracted to carrion, and meat that is high makes excellent bait. Many wolves, however, will assiduously avoid any bait that is offered because they have come to learn that such gratuitous offerings generally mean strychnine or a steel trap. Unless you have blind luck, you will almost certainly need a guide and a hardy constitution. A great deal of wolf-spotting today is done with light planes from the air. There are bush pilots all over Canada who will hire themselves out for this purpose. On foot or in the air, a good pair of binoculars is required equipment.

Here are a few areas within the United States where wolves may sometimes be seen:

Seney National Wildlife Refuge on Michigan's Upper Peninsula. Sightings rare.

Kenai National Moose Range at the west end of the Kenai Peninsula on Alaska's south coast. Sightings extremely rare.

Mount McKinley National Park in south-central Alaska. Fair population.

Superior National Forest, northeastern Minnesota. Rare sightings.

Glacier National Park, northwestern Montana. Rare sightings.

White River National Wildlife Refuge, eastern Arkansas. Rare sightings within the boundaries of the refuge, but some wolves believed living about a hundred miles to the south in the Tensas Swamp.

Arctic National Wildlife Range, northeastern Alaska. Many wolves in this vast Arctic tundra wilderness. Not exactly a weekend trip but the best place in North America to see wolves.

In Texas, the so-called red wolf still reportedly survives in some thirty counties in the southern, central, and eastern parts of the state—as far north as Clay and Young counties, as far west as Pecos, and in Newton County up to the Louisiana state line.

In North Dakota, rare sightings of the so-called buffalo wolf. Probably strays from Canada.

In Missouri, a few red wolves are reported to be surviving in the Ozark Highlands in the east-central portion of the state.

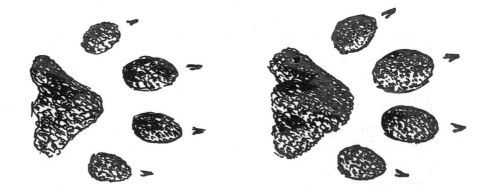

Wolf tracks.

8

Symbol of the West: The Coyote

Although the coyote was originally bright green in color, he longed to be a beautiful shade of blue. He went to a bluebird and asked for advice. The bird told him of a magic lake and said that if the little wolf would only bathe in its waters, he would emerge as blue as the sky. The coyote did as he was told and was delighted to see that the bird had spoken well. He trotted off as proud as he could be in his bright-blue coat. After a few minutes he turned to see if his shadow was blue as well and in so doing stumbled over a rock and rolled in the dust. When he got up, he was the dull color of the dry earth. . . .

In that simple little folk tale the coyote, the great trickster of Indian legendry, has the tables turned on him for a change. The legend has been adapted from one of the tales related in Frank Dobie's *The Voice of the Coyote*.

The coyote's name comes from the Aztec word *coyotl* while his Latin name means "barking dog." According to an Indian legend, he will be the last animal on earth. There are many ranchers and farmers who would tend to agree with this belief, having been exposed to the little prairie wolf's sly ways. First, last, or always, the yapping howl of the coyote at sunset, at full moon, and at sunrise is truly the song and symbol of the American West. Fortunately, it does not appear as if it will soon be gone from our land. Where the great wolves have failed, the little coyote has succeeded. He regularly outwits man and survives despite all efforts to kill him off.

Names and Range

There is a great deal of discussion as to where the coyote lives and where he doesn't. He regularly interbreeds with domestic dogs and the so-called "coydog" causes a great deal of confusion. In general, coyotes in the United States are found throughout the greater part of all the states west of the Mississippi River except in Arkansas (some possibly remain in the extreme northwest section of that state) and Louisiana. East of the Mississippi River they are found in Wisconsin, Michigan, Illinois, and Indiana. They crop up from time to time in most eastern states.

In Canada only the easternmost provinces are free of this little wolf, and probably that assumption will go by the boards in due time. The coyote is forever extending his range as he follows man's domestic stock and game animals. He did not appear in Alaska before 1900, but today he is abundant in many areas as far north as Point Barrow. There are large populations in the Matanuska and Copper River valleys and on the Kenai Peninsula.

Although more than 125,000 are killed each year in the United States alone, the coyote holds on. He is sly, tricky, and tenacious. He can adapt himself to almost any surface environment on our continent and thrives on almost any food. As long as he retains these characteristics, he will be found just about everywhere. Certain areas will continue to have very heavy populations while others will continue to consider the little doglike animal a rarity. One way or the other, the coyote is here to stay.

Appearance and Distinguishing Characteristics

The coyote looks like nothing so much as a small German shepherd. He runs between forty-two and forty-eight inches in length, his full, flowing tail accounting for a good part of that—about sixteen inches. His weight normally runs between thirty-five and forty pounds. As compared with both the wolf and the shepherd, his tail is fuller, the ears are more erect, his nose and legs more slender. (The shepherd's tail has a slight curl.)

His hair is coarse and grizzled and runs from buff-gray to black, frequently with a yellowish tinge on the muzzle, on the ears, and often on the outside of his legs. The tip of the tail is almost always darker, generally black. A white flash is on the underside of the tail near the base, and on the throat. Actually he is most variable. As mentioned in the preceding chapter, when you see a doglike animal loping along, look to the tail. The wolf carries his high, the dog often straight out back, and the coyote low. This is not an infallible rule but one that can give a good indication in most cases.

Photo by Wilford L. Miller

North Dakota coyote singing his eternal song.

When seen loping alone, the coyote gives the impression of effortlessness. He has an easy flowing movement and it almost looks as if his feet weren't touching the ground. With his slender legs, he is really a very delicate little animal.

Habits

One word describes the coyote: sly. In Mexico, the expression *muy coyote,* when applied to a human being, means he is shrewd and crafty, a good businessman. The coyote is a good businessman indeed!

Found from sea level to over ten thousand feet, the coyote has adapted to every situation man has forced upon him. He was almost surely an open-plains animal originally but has long since learned how to get along in many different environments. His home range may be limited to a few square miles in some areas and may extend to twenty-five or more in others. There may be a seasonal variation in this as well. In some Western metropolises he has been discovered successfully raising his family within the city limits. Like his big cousins, the wolves, he lives in a family unit. Occasionally, family units may join, but these packs are temporary. Generally, it is father, mother, and the cubs of the current year.

Señor Coyote capitalizes on the curiosity of other animals and has been known to take prey by playing dead and suddenly springing to life when some unsuspecting bird or small mammal came to investigate the carcass.

The food of the coyote consists of just about everything that he can swallow. He is a great garbage pail and will take carrion anytime he can find it. As a hunter he takes birds, eggs, snakes, lizards, grasshoppers and other insects, mice and other small rodents, the young of larger game animals and domestic stock, weak and helpless larger animals, again including domestic stock, any unprotected fowl, and he even delights in some vegetable matter. He has a passion for ripe melons, particularly watermelons, and often raids truck farms. Agriculturalists decry his uncanny way of picking only the best melons in a patch. Tomatoes and just about every other crop have been raided, and certainly, in farming areas, the coyote is a full-fledged pest. The farmer who loses colts, calves, ducks, hens, watermelons, and peaches to the same animal can't be blamed for investing in a few steel traps.

Since he tends to live near human habitations much of the time, the coyote has become nocturnal. Where man is scarce, he will be found abroad at all hours. He has a very distinctive yapping howl that is a delight once the eerie shock of hearing it for the first time is past. He sings to the sun, to the moon, to his own kind, and to himself.

As pointed out earlier, the coyote does interbreed with domestic dogs, and the resulting pups can make good pets. They are not sterile and can in turn reproduce with either dogs or other coyotes. There may be more coyote in many of our domestic dogs than we realize. The coyote himself, technically, is a small wolf. A small wolf and a large coyote could easily be confused.

Reproduction

Coyotes, after the manner of wolves, probably mate for life at about two years of age. The breeding occurs between January and very early May. Gestation is from 60 to 63 days, and the litter may run from three to nineteen young. Six or seven are apparently usual.

The mated pair prepare for the coming of the young, usually from April to June, by digging a den or enlarging one already made by another animal, frequently a badger. The chamber may be anywhere from two to six feet underground, and there usually will be an escape hatch off to one side. In areas where rock formations form natural caves, these will be used rather than holes in the ground. In wooded areas, coyotes have even been known to nest in hollow trees. Where a large branch dips down low, the den may be many feet above the ground. Here again, the coyote is a most adaptable fellow.

At birth the little coyotes are blind and helpless. Their eyes open after about nine days. At the end of eight weeks they are fully weaned and are eating meat brought home to them by their parents in the form of small mammals and birds. If the parents made a good-sized kill, they swallow hunks of meat and retch it up for their cubs just as wolves do.

After about ten weeks, the pups start hunting as a group with their parents. Their training is very carefully managed by the attentive elders, and the young are soon able to hunt on their own. By the late fall the cubs drift away, before the home hunting range fails the now expanded population. It is rare, evidently, that a cub remains with its parents through a winter. The cub often must travel very far before he can find and establish a range of his own. It is during these "migrations" that the cubs are most vulnerable and many are killed off due to their lack of experience.

Observation

A characteristic of the coyote is that if you don't want to see him you will, and if you do want to, you won't! He is one sly fellow, and you will see him best with professional help, or with luck. At any rate, be sure you have binoculars and patience at hand. You will need both.

In the states east of the Mississippi River the coyote will be hard to find.

Mature coyote in winter coat.

Coyote tracks.

The dense human population has forced him into being even more sly than in the West, and you will catch only a fleeting glimpse of him as he disappears into the bushes. Even that will depend on your measure of luck, not skill. The chances are you will never be quite sure whether you have seen a coyote or a dog.

In the Western states, where he is abundant, you may see him at a great distance if you keep your silhouette off the skyline. He is often spotted (and hunted!) from light planes. Almost any rancher will know where he can be found. He can be baited unless he has had a few near-misses, in which case he is usually too cautious to be caught napping a second time. Unhappily, there are organized coyote hunts in ranching areas, and many animals are turned out and destroyed.

In almost any wildlife refuge, any area at all where there is a good supply of small mammals and ground-nesting birds and where hunting is not permitted, the coyote will show up sooner or later. In many such areas he is kept under strict control by game wardens far more interested in protecting endangered species than the ubiquitous coyote.

In states like California, Texas, New Mexico, Arizona, and South Dakota, the little wolf from the prairie country can be found in all life zones, including suburban back yards. Surprisingly for such an alert animal, some are killed by cars, and Easterners driving along the open highway mistake their small carcasses for those of domestic dogs.

There are areas where coyotes are protected. Among these are:

RESERVE AREA	LOCATION
Bear River Migratory Bird Refuge	Delta marshes of Bear River and Great Salt Lake, Utah
Desert Game Range	Southern Nevada
Glacier National Park	Northwestern Montana
Hart Mountain National Antelope Refuge	South-central Oregon
Kenai National Moose Range	Western Kenai Peninsula, southern Alaska
Laguna Atascosa National Wildlife Refuge	Near Port Isabel on Texas' south coast
McNary Wildlife Refuge	Columbia River Valley, Washington
Monte Vista Wildlife Refuge	South-central Colorado
Mount McKinley National Park	South-central Alaska
National Elk Refuge	Western Wyoming
Quivira Wildlife Refuge	Kansas (southeast of Great Bend)
Santa Ana National Wildlife Refuge	South Texas—banks of Rio Grande
Seney National Wildlife Refuge	Michigan's Upper Peninsula
Wichita Mountains Wildlife Refuge	Southwestern Oklahoma
Yellowstone National Park	Northwestern Wyoming

9

Look to the Tip of the Tail: Our Graceful Foxes

SEVEN HOUNDS were hot on the trail of the red fox as it bounded up the hillside toward the edge of the cliff. It dodged and swerved endlessly as it coursed through the underbrush. As it reached the edge of the drop-off it stopped in front of a bush that masked the edge and stood there panting; in full, open sight it waited for the dogs. They burst through the brush at him but he held his ground until the very last moment and then swiftly stepped aside. All seven hounds plummeted over the cliff to their deaths. That is our fox. He is also the wild, little dog that will run out onto thin ice and wait there until his heavier pursuers, driven to a fury by his appearance in the open, dash after him, crash through the ice and drown. He will take to a wooden fence when being pursued and hop from fence post to fence post, or from rock to rock along a stone wall to break up his trail.

Our graceful, dainty little foxes are experts in survival tactics. Unfortunately, men with traps and poisons often outwit the little ghostlike creatures, and in some areas their survival is endangered. One publication issued by the United States Government gives the following advice:

> If it is not desired to know the number or size of the pups, they may be gassed in the burrow through a 6-foot piece of hose, one end of which is attached to the exhaust pipe of an automobile and the other put down into the den. All burrow entrances should be closed and the motor allowed to run for 15 minutes with the carburetor set for a rich mixture.

In the face of such fine, clear-cut, technical advice, the fox is at a disadvantage.

Names and Range

The United States and Canada are enriched by the presence of four different kinds of foxes.

Our most common and widespread fox is Reynard—the red fox. He is found from the Arctic to the Mexican border. In all of Canada only the western edge of British Columbia, a few islands off the east and west coasts of the mainland, and the highest Arctic regions are lacking this wily little animal. In the United States, only the deep Southeast, parts of the Great Plains, and some parts of the Southwest and Rocky Mountain states are without any red foxes, and although in many cases only part of a state will be populated, Florida alone is without any red foxes at all. Alaska, with its normal extension of western Canadian fauna, is inhabited throughout, including many of the countless small islands that sentinel its coastline.

Most closely related to the red fox are several kit or swift foxes. The smallest of our foxes, they range throughout the arid Southwest up across the Plains east of the Rockies to southern Alberta and Saskatchewan.

The animals known as gray or tree foxes have a vast range, covering all of the eastern half of the United States, all of the Southwest, and up the Pacific Coast to southern Washington. Here again, most states have at least some along one border or another, and no more than three of four states have none at all—probably Idaho, Montana, and North and South Dakota. A few cross over into Canada, but these only from extreme southeastern Saskatchewan eastward, for the gray fox is a warm-climate animal, ranging down through all of Mexico and Central America.

Our last fox is the distinctive Arctic fox, and in the United States he is found only in northern Alaska. Very common in the northern reaches of Canada, the greatest concentration of this unique creature is in the Northwest Territories. The Queen Elizabeth Islands and District of Franklin, those countless islands and frozen bits of land between the Canadian Mainland and Greenland, are blanketed with the diminutive footprints of this beautiful and valuable furbearer.

Appearance and Distinguishing Characteristics

All of our foxes are small, smaller by far than the coyote. They are distinctly doglike, with their elongated, pointed muzzles, their erect, forward-pointing ears. They are dainty and light-footed. And one peculiarity distinguishes them from all our other wild canines, even when confusion may cover other identification points: the pupils of the fox's eyes are elliptical when contracted, while those of domestic and other wild dogs are round. This,

Photo by O. J. Murie, courtesy U.S. Department of Interior, Fish & Wildlife Service

A quiet moment in the life of a young kit fox.

however, requires rather close examination, and we must rely on somewhat grosser points of identification when we catch a fleeting glimpse of a little, doglike animal disappearing into the roadside brush.

A simple chart best presents the distinguishing characteristics by which we can identify major groupings. For our foxes, these differences are:

The Foxes of North America
(Major Groupings)

| | COLORATION | | | | | |
GROUP	UPPER PARTS	UNDER PARTS	TIP OF TAIL*	WEIGHT (*Pounds*)	LENGTH (*Inches*)	HABITAT
Red	Reddish, black, or mixed	White	White	8–14	36–41	Open, timbered, and farmlands.
Kit or Desert (Swift) †	Yellowish gray	White (throat)	Black	4–5½	24–32	Brushy, prairie, and desert lands.
Gray	Grizzled gray	White to ashy gray	Dark gray to black	7–11	32–45	Lightly timbered, brushy, and swampy areas in the warmer regions.
Arctic‡ *Summer*	Dull brownish to slate	Yellowish white	Same as body color	7–15	31–36	Arctic tundra above tree line.
Winter	White or slate-blue	White or slate-blue	Same as body color			

 * This is the easiest way to distinguish our major fox groupings. It is particularly valuable since the color phases (reddish, black with white grizzling, or a mixture or "cross" in the red fox) and the great variety of shadings in the kit and gray foxes can lead to confusion. The tail of the red fox, no matter what its color phase, *always* has a white tip; the tail of the kit fox, no matter what its color phase, always has a black or very dark gray tip *without* black guard hairs along the top; and the tail of the gray fox, no matter what its color phase, always has a dark-gray or black tip with a line of very dark to black guard hairs from the tip to the base. Guard hairs are long, wiry hairs that stick out of the regular fur.

 † The kit, desert, or swift foxes can be readily distinguished by their very long ears.

 ‡ The Arctic fox has very short, rounded ears.

Habits

Our common red fox, a denizen of open woodlands, brushy country bordering on marshes and swamps, treeless mountain slopes and even suburban areas, has learned how to live with man, or rather, *despite* man. He is wily and bright and owns an endless bag of tricks. He is not particularly fast (although spurts of twenty-six miles an hour have been reported), so he compensates with very sophisticated escape tactics. He doubles back on his trail, takes to water, hops along fences and stone walls like a circus performer, and goes underground to escape his pursuers. His underground tunnels may have many exits, as many as twenty-seven, as in one recorded case.

Unfortunately, Reynard has many enemies. Bobcats, lynx, mountain lions, wolves, coyotes, bears, and golden eagles join man and domestic dogs in the hunt. Somehow, though, Reynard holds his own. He seems to enjoy living near farmlands, and as man has cleared forest areas, he has actually increased the red fox's range. Although trapped, poisoned, and shot as a predator, hunted down for his valuable fur, and run down for sport, the red fox, of all our foxes, seems to be holding on most effectively. His sharp ears and very bright, alert nature enable him to survive where all other wildlife of his size and huntable nature has vanished.

Very much in favor of the red fox is his ability to survive on a wide variety of foods. Among the foods relished by him are mice, rabbits, rats, ground-nesting birds, eggs, snakes, lizards, insects, fruit and berries of all kinds, grasses, and even clay and gravel in small quantities, probably to get vital minerals. In the winter he is far more carnivorous than at other times and he will even take on porcupines, using his deft paws to roll them over so that he can get at their unprotected underparts. He will take carrion of all kinds and, unfortunately, is a terrible barnyard thief. His habit of making off with ducks, geese, and chickens hasn't endeared him to agricultural America and Canada. He will even take young lambs and pigs, given half a chance.

Raids on henhouses can be very destructive, and some foxes, it must be admitted, will kill far more than they can possibly carry off. This very unfortunate characteristic, it should be explained, does not come from the animal's being "bloodthirsty" or any other such inapplicable human charac-teristic, but from the fox's habit in the wild of killing as much as is at hand and storing what he cannot eat. The fox is very fond of his meat "high," and stores his surplus until it is delightfully ripe. When suddenly confronted with a hutful of squawking but vulnerable chickens or ducks, the fox cannot think ahead to the inevitable fact that he will be lucky to get away with even one victim— with farmer, shotgun, and dogs at his heels.

In all fairness to the fox it should also be noted that when his den is discovered, the debris of domestic animals found around the entrance is not a fair measure of his destructiveness. Foxes, fond as they are of carrion, work

Courtesy U.S. Department of Interior, Fish & Wildlife Service

A half-grown gray fox, photographed in Alabama.

along highways at night and collect the victims of automobiles. Many domestic fowl wander in front of cars speeding by farms and finally end up as suppers for local fox families.

Reynard is not a hibernator. He works his range in winter as well as summer but extends that range as the pickings thin out. During the summer, a fox can usually feed himself and his family in a range not exceeding one mile in radius. In winter, when he is on his own, he may range over twenty square miles or more just to feed himself. During cold weather he may lay up for a day or two in some sheltered spot when the weather is at its worst. He daintily covers his delicate black nose and sensitive paws with his bushy tail.

The fox will hunt when he is hungry—night or day. Like almost all predators, though, he finds working at night a great deal safer near human settlements. Nonetheless, when a fox is hungry enough, he will take incredible chances, and many farmers have turned around to see a fox making off with a chicken that was only moments ago feeding a few yards off. His sly stealth as a hunter is as infuriating as it is destructive.

If you are lucky enough to be able to watch a fox in the daylight, you will probably see him hunting, as this is virtually his full-time occupation. He uses several techniques. You may see him wriggling along very close to the ground as he works toward unsuspecting prey. A sudden rush and a quick snap of his jaws will conclude such tactics. Then again, you may see him perform a little dancing ritual in a meadow. You will see him stiff-legged and bouncy as he dances around some invisible victim. Suddenly he will dart with his nose to the ground and make off for cover to enjoy his meal in peace. He is either disturbing the nest or burrow of a field mouse or similar small rodent or gaining the advantage over a snake when you see such rituals in operation. Generally, though, the fox is a "rusher and pouncer." Like the coyote he will play dead and suddenly come to life and seize some curious spectator who couldn't resist a closer look.

The fox is an extremely graceful animal. He walks on his toes and, when traveling at high speed, appears to glide over the ground effortlessly. Twelve to sixteen inches of his thirty-six-to-forty-six overall length is graceful-flowing tail, which characteristically floats out behind as he streams along busy at the business of staying alive in a hostile world.

The male red fox yelps and the female yaps, that is about the best way to describe it. It takes an expert to distinguish between the two, but the call of either is quite different from that of the coyote or domestic dog and nothing at all like that of the wolf.

The slightly smaller gray or tree fox is very much like the red fox in most ways. His hunting prowess, his food habits, and his enemies are the same. He is generally considered less sly and is apparently more easily trapped. He is a good fighter, though, and domestic dogs, unless hunting together, are in for a good scrap if they take a gray fox on in single combat. Unfortunately, gray foxes, like all of our foxes, are reservoirs for rabies, and pets should be discouraged from fighting with them. A bite from a fox can be deadly dangerous to any other mammal—including man.

The gray fox tends to be more nocturnal than the red, but he will hunt during the day, particularly in the late morning and early evening, if he is hungry enough.

One thing that distinguishes the gray fox is his habit of climbing trees. Grays are very adept at this, and they add the practice of scrambling up a tree and lying low along a leafy branch to the red fox's bag of escape tricks. It is particularly confounding to dogs, and a gray being pursued will do it sooner or later.

Very closely related to the red fox, but easily distinguishable from him, are several kit, desert, or swift foxes. They have extremely long ears and are considerably smaller in overall size. They favor arid and semiarid regions and spend much more time underground than any of the other foxes. They are extremely shy, almost totally nocturnal, and are seldom seen in the open. They live almost exclusively on kangaroo rats and pocket mice, which they hunt across the desert wastes in the dead of night. This grayish-yellow little dog, smallest of our foxes by far, is also our most enchanting. He is not very bright, however, and easily succumbs to man and his ways. As desert areas are irrigated and claimed for agriculture, the kit fox will go. He is only safe when man is not near, when the moon shines on discarded wastelands. He cannot adapt as can the red and the gray. Happily, there are still vast areas in the United States not claimed by man. On moonlit nights, the call of the kit fox can still be heard. This call sounds much more like the chattering of a squirrel than of a member of the dog family. A close relative, the Plains swift or long-eared fox ranges north of the desert lands onto the prairies, but he, too, may soon be in serious trouble.

The grizzled gray fox is still a common sight in many parts of the United States. Although his fur is not as coveted as that of the Arctic and red foxes, he is losing ground to poisons and traps set for him as well as for other barnyard pests. He will probably go long before the more clever red.

Photo by Wilford L. Miller

A red fox in North Dakota with his cottontail-rabbit prey. Note the lush winter coat on both animals.

Far to the north and easily distinguished from all other foxes is the Arctic fox. Dull brownish and gray in summer, he changes his colors for the winter. By the time the snow covers the ground, he is either pure-white or slate-blue.

Although he comes as far south as the Aleutian Islands, the Arctic fox is a creature of the far, frozen North. He hunts lemmings, birds, the Arctic hare, and takes birds' eggs in the summer. In the winter he is a great scavenger, cleaning up after wolves and polar bears. A stranded whale will feed many foxes for a whole year.

The fur of the Arctic fox is valuable, and trapping them is a major industry among the Eskimos. The range of the little white fox is so vast and reaches into such inaccessible areas that they will probably survive indefinitely. These same characteristics make it doubtful that most of us will ever see one in the wild state.

Reproduction

Foxes mate when they are about a year old. The joining usually occurs in January or February, when the females come into their extremely abbreviated period of heat. There are relatively few days in the year when a female may be bred, and when the critical season approaches there is a great deal of squabbling and open fighting among the males. Solitary throughout most of the winter months, males start seeking out an unattached female early in January preparatory to remaining at her side until late in the fall, when they will again go their own ways.

The gestation period runs from 50 to 53 days on the average, and during this period the vixen becomes progressively more irritable. She prepares her

Red fox tracks.   **Kit fox tracks.**

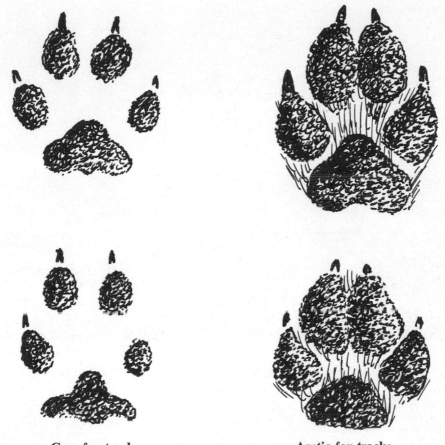

Gray fox tracks.   **Arctic fox tracks.**

den, which may be used year after year. She prefers to take over the burrow of a woodchuck or porcupine but may excavate her own in loose, sandy soil, frequently on the south side of a hill. Natural rock shelters are sometimes utilized, and hollow logs are common den sites for the gray fox. The gray fox also nests in hollow trees, and where the branch structure allows reasonable access the nest may be many feet above the ground. Dens dug into soil or enlarged from other burrows may be as much as seventy-five feet in length and have a great many side chambers for food storage and for the transfer of young once an old chamber becomes too soiled to inhabit. Many exits are often provided, ten or more not being too uncommon. Fence rows, meadow and brush areas at the edge of timber are likely sites.

Photo by Victor B. Scheffer, courtesy U.S. Department of Interior, Fish & Wildlife Service

A red fox in the black phase. Photographed in the Pribilof Islands.

The tunnel entrance normally lacks the earth mound common around the burrows of other animals. Fox hair will generally be found imbedded in the walls near the tunnel mouth. The burrow soon takes on a mild skunky smell, and debris will litter the area around the main opening. Well-defined trails will merge as they approach the den site. The den of the fox is quite distinct and easy to identify by these means.

Anywhere from one to ten kits may be born, four to six are average. While the female is nursing her young, the male works very hard to feed her as well as himself. He beats a steady path to her door with all sorts of food. The well-furred kits weigh from 2½ to 4½ ounces at birth and are blind for the first ten days. By the end of the fourth or at least by the middle of the fifth week the kits are out of the burrow, playing under the careful scrutiny of their parents. By the end of their tenth week, sometimes as early as their eighth, the young are weaned. They are taken on hunting trips and trained very carefully in the ways of the fox. They are taught to escape detection and to escape pursuit if detected. The family remains together until late fall and then separates. Whether or not the same males and females always or even ever rejoin in subsequent breeding seasons is not clearly understood. All foxes, however, are generally solitary throughout the winter or at least until January. The kit foxes apparently breed and litter somewhat earlier than the other species. Little is known about the family life of the Arctic fox. The life expectancy of a fox in captivity usually runs from ten to twelve years. It is almost certainly much shorter in the wild. Any fox who could escape his enemies to survive for a full decade would be exceptional indeed.

Observation

There is virtually no area except downtown city streets in all of the United States and Canada where foxes of one kind or another may not be found. They are in every state, in every province, in high Arctic wastes, lowland swamps, plains, mountains—just about everywhere. You will find only strays above the snow line in otherwise temperate areas, where mountains create small pockets of Arctic conditions, and in the center of the real burning-sand deserts; but every other surface environment has a population, if not in one location, then in another, similar one, not too far off. Still, you will not be likely to stumble upon a fox in the open waiting for you. The fox has been too heavily hunted, has been too persecuted for such carelessness. Unless you are very lucky, you will really have to look for your fox in most areas.

A likely place to look is around a den site between March and May. The kits are out of the den by then for at least a part of each day, and the male will be traveling back and forth with food for his mate and for the kits about to be weaned.

Ideally, look for travel ways, regular trails leading from a good hunting area to a relatively undisturbed area where a den would logically be placed. Foxes, like all wild dogs and bears and most other wild animals, tend to follow established trails. Look for tracks in mud, dust, or late snow patches. Look for hair stuck to fence posts, logs and trees, and to burrow walls if you locate one. Pick a perch up out of the way and wait quietly. At dusk, at dawn, and perhaps at any hour, you may be lucky enough to see some fox traveling to and fro. If you have access to a dead animal, place it near a trail; the higher it gets, the more likely it is to attract some attention.

In areas where you suspect fox traffic, watch (with your binoculars) for movement along hedges, fences, bushes lining streams, and other places where a fox will feel comfortable with cover close by. Remember, you are a human being with the dread man-smell about you. The fox cannot know that you are out to look and not to touch. In his automatic estimate you are his deadly enemy, and he will use every one of his remarkable talents to avoid detection. Fox-spotting is a delightful game of wits.

Foxes long resident in areas where hunting them is forbidden tend to be less shy. They even approach campsites to look for nourishing debris, and very quiet and patient people in these game preserves are rewarded by seeing these wonderful little wild dogs go about their business. (*See* pp. 102–103 for a listing of some of the areas where you may be rewarded.)

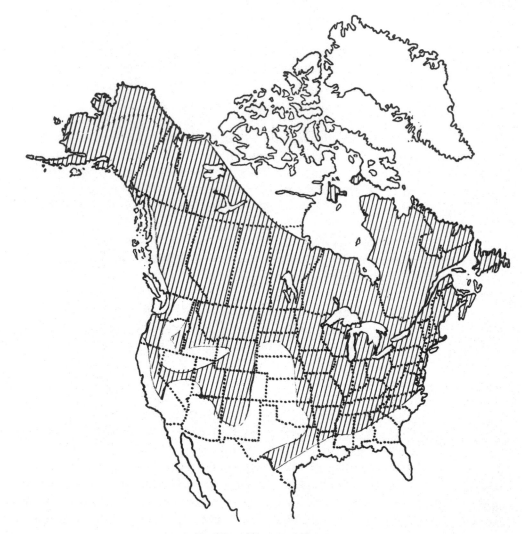

Red fox (diagonal lines).

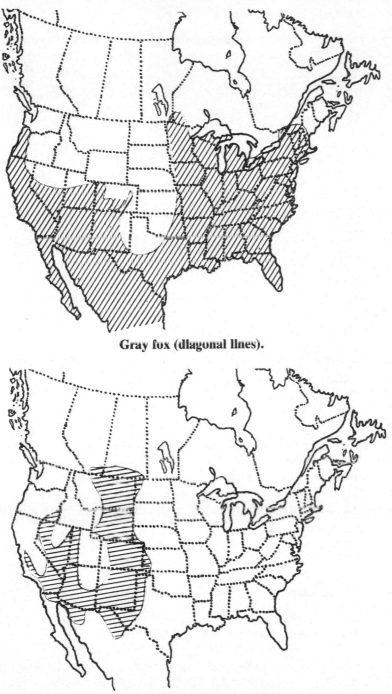

Gray fox (diagonal lines).

Kit or swift fox (diagonal lines).

The United States

AREA	LOCATION	FOX TYPE
Aleutian Islands National Wildlife Refuge	Alaska offshore	Arctic (blue phase)
Arcadia Wildlife Sanctuary	Central-western Massachusetts	Red
Arctic National Wildlife Range	Northeast Alaska	Red and Arctic
Bering Sea Wildlife Range	Alaska—Islands in Bering Sea	Arctic
Carolina Sandhills Wildlife Refuge	South Carolina	Gray
Chincoteague National Wildlife Refuge	Assateague Island off Maryland and Virginia	Red
Desert Game Range	Southern Nevada	Kit and gray
Everglades National Park	Southern Florida	Gray
Glacier National Park	Northwestern Montana	Red
Ipswich River Wildlife Sanctuary	Northeastern Massachusetts	Red
Isle Royale National Park	Lake Superior	Red
Kenai National Moose Range	Kenai Peninsula, Alaska	Red (rare) and blue Arctic
Moosehorn National Wildlife Refuge	Eastern Maine	Red
Morton National Wildlife Refuge	Long Island, New York	Red and gray
Mount McKinley National Park	South-central Alaska	Red
Savannah National Wildlife Refuge	Georgia and South Carolina	Gray
Sespe Wildlife Preserve	Southern California	Gray
Wichita Mountains Wildlife Refuge	Southwestern Oklahoma	Gray
Yellowstone National Park	Northwestern Wyoming	Red

In addition to those listed above, there are dozens of state parks, wildlife refuges, and private sanctuaries. Some such areas exist in every state.

Canada (All National Parks)

AREA	LOCATION	FOX TYPE
Banff	Southwestern Alberta	Red
Cape Breton Highlands	Northern Nova Scotia (Cape Breton Island)	Red
Elk Island	Central Alberta	Red
Fundy	Southern New Brunswick	Red
Georgian Bay Islands	Forty-two islands in Lake Huron	Red
Glacier	Southeastern British Columbia	Red
Jasper	Western Alberta	Red
Kootenay	Southeastern British Columbia	Red
Mount Revelstoke	Southeastern British Columbia	Red
Point Pelee	Southern Ontario	Red
Prince Albert	Central Saskatchewan	Red
Prince Edward Island	Prince Edward Island	Red
Riding Mountain	Southwestern Manitoba	Red
St. Lawrence Islands	Southeastern Ontario	Red
Terra Nova	Northeastern Newfoundland (Island)	Red
Waterton Lakes	Southwestern Alberta	Red
Wood Buffalo	Northern Alberta and Southern Northwestern Territories	Red and Arctic
Yoho	Southeastern British Columbia	Red

In addition to the above, there are a great many provincial parks and wildlife refuges within which red and Arctic foxes may be found.

10

The Jaguar: Greatest New World Cat

YOU WILL PROBABLY never see a jaguar outside a zoo. This cat, the largest and most formidable in the entire Western Hemisphere, is rare north of Mexico and extremely shy.

If you happen to be one of the dozen or so people who *may* see a wild jaguar north of the Mexican border in the next fifty years or so, cherish the experience well. If you happen to stumble upon one, keep your distance; the jaguar, though breathtakingly beautiful, is not a friendly animal.

Names and Range

El tigre to the Mexicans, the jaguar is far more common in their country than ours. From Mexico he ranges southward through Central and South America, all the way to where Antarctic winds and fog bathe the southernmost shores. He gets bigger as he goes south, reaching his greatest size among the four-hundred-pound giants of the Brazilian jungle.

There are rivers in Mexico that run north and south. The banks of some of these are lined with heavy growth, deep, impenetrable thorn thickets. These chaparral regions constitute the only environment in the United States in which this jungle cat can really feel at home. These thickly overgrown river bottoms are the jaguar's secret highways into our Southwest. The Yaqui, Sonora, Santa Cruz, San Miguel Rivers and Sonoyta Creek, to name a few—these are the pathways that lead from our country to the jungle lands of Spanish-speaking America. Since the great spotted cat also ascends mountains to an altitude of seven thousand feet (but that rarely), some mountain chains may serve as links as well.

Today the jaguar can be found, but only rarely, in Texas along the Mexican border, in southwestern New Mexico, and southeastern Arizona. Since 1885, forty-five have been killed in Arizona; thirty-seven since 1890. Recent records from that state are: 1961—Pima County; 1959—Pima County; 1959—Patagonia Mountains.

Appearance and Distinguishing Characteristics

It is virtually impossible to confuse the jaguar with any other animal found in this hemisphere. His six-to-seven-foot overall length immediately distinguishes him from the spotted ocelot, with which he shares part of his range, his twenty-eight-inch shoulder height and weights approaching 200 to 250 pounds even distinguish him from the smaller, much lighter African and Asiatic leopard.

The jaguar has a heavy chest, very broad and full, and powerful hindquarters. His tail is quite short; this is because he seldom climbs trees and doesn't require the balancing mechanism exhibited by the tree-climbing, long-tailed mountain lion whose range he also crosses.

The base color of the jaguar is buffy-yellow or tawny and he is marked with rosettes (*not* spots like the leopard)—rings of deep rich brown or black, often with a spot in the middle. His tail is heavily marked with black, especially near the tip, and his pale-yellow or even white belly is similarly rich with rosettes and spots. A melano, or black phase, is not too uncommon in parts of Central and South America, although I know of no reports from the United States.

Although the jaguar of Brazil's rain forests may be much larger than any found in this country, our jaguar is still a big cat, built something like a not too small lion. His size, the spotted and rosetted coat, the small, rounded ears and rather abbreviated tail are what distinguish the jaguar in North America To the occasional rancher who loses his stock to the hunting prowess of this great predator he is a menace and a nuisance. To those of us who may dream of being one of the lucky few to see him about his very secret ways, he is a vision of what the world must have been like long, long ago.

Habits

The jaguar has no enemies except armed men. So many travelers have described his demeanor as "arrogant," one can't help but believe that the jaguar knows it. Where he treads, all life must part and make silent way.

The jaguar will take carrion and often buries part of his kill. He will frequently lay up near a kill to guard it between meals.

Photo by Karl Weidmann

A magnificent study of the powerful jaguar at a moment of repose.

As a hunter he relies on stealth, ambush, surprise, and strength. His great weight propelled forward by those immense hindquarters will drag almost any animal down. His sharp claws and powerful bite can put an end to any struggle. Peccaries, deer, birds, snakes, turtles, fish, coatimundis, armadillos, jackrabbits, coyotes, dogs, squirrels, and small animals of all kinds know the terror of being stalked by this jungle cat. He has a great fondness for sea-turtle eggs and will dig them up along beaches. Unhappily, and this is one reason we shall probably see him only in the zoo, he is a terror with livestock. Horses and cattle are among his favorite foods, while pigs, sheep, and goats are also taken. Farmers and ranchers who depend on these animals for their livelihood find his presence intolerable. The destruction he wreaks is legendary throughout the lands he travels.

It can be assumed that the jaguar establishes a home territory and guards it well. Nonetheless, he is a great traveler, and that is the only reason we find him within our borders at all. He is extremely fond of water and will often play in warm and shallow pools during hot summer days. He will wander out into streams and ponds to hunt for fish, which he *reportedly* flips up onto the bank with his paw. He swims very well and will not hesitate to cross even a wide river if pursued or if lured by the prospect of something good to eat.

Reproduction

Observations on the family life of the jaguar in the United States are few. He breeds in December and January, relinquishing his usually solitary ways for that purpose. Gestation is reported variously from 93 to 110 days, and the two to four cubs are born in April or May.

The birth occurs in a rocky cave or extremely dense thorn thicket where interference is unlikely. Any intrusion at all would be greeted with a violent display.

The cubs are more spotted than their parents, and much woollier. Their eyes are closed and they are as helpless as might be expected. Within six weeks, however, the cubs are as large as house cats and ready to follow their parents on the hunt.

When the cubs are born, the male keeps away. The female's disposition is very short at first, and any attempt at familiarity by the male would be greeted with flying claws and savage lunges. After the first hectic days have passed, the mother becomes somewhat more tolerant and the male sets about feeding her while she nurses the litter. When the schooling of the cubs starts, the burden of the education rests mostly with the female. When the cubs are about a year old, they drift away. The mated pair may stay together or separate, leaving it to chance that they will one day meet again.

Jaguars are quite long-lived, and zoo specimens, at least, have approached twenty-five years. Such longevity would probably be quite unlikely in the river bottoms of Arizona.

Observation

There is no question about where you go to find the jaguar; where you go, that is, in the sense of what states you fly, take a train, or drive to. Beyond that, it is all an open question.

Jaguars are hunted by professionals, or at least by experts, using dogs, bait, long periods away in the brush, and great tolerance for rough living. A jaguar was spotted on a highway outside Tucson not many years ago, but that kind of luck tends to be unreliable for the nature observer with limited time at his disposal.

Theoretically, you should go to the spot where a river from Mexico emerges into Texas, New Mexico, or Arizona and follow the stream wherever it takes you. You should carefully inspect its banks for tracks, look for caves and natural shelters, and poke through every chaparral patch you encounter. Sooner or later you might come upon a jaguar. You are more apt to come upon a great many rattlesnakes.

Realistically, unless you are a dedicated outdoorsman with the funds to invest in a professional guide and a pack of trailing dogs, you will see a jaguar only with pure luck working for you. He is a predator with a price on his head and is very, very alert to his surroundings. His hearing is good, his protective coloration near perfect, and even if you pass close by a jaguar, you will know it only if he decides to let you.

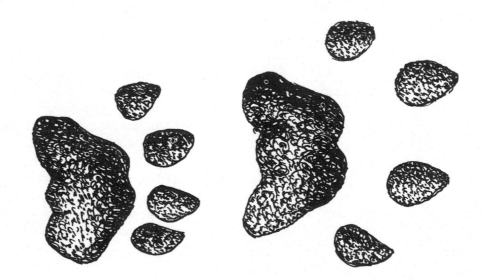

Jaguar tracks.

11

The Little Spotted Cats:
The Ocelot and Margay

TWO OF THE MOST BEAUTIFUL MAMMALS in all of North America are unfortunately so extremely rare and so limited in range that few people will ever chance to see them in the wild. Ocelots are common in some large pet shops, but nowhere else within the United States. The margay, however, is very likely no longer within our borders at all.

Names and Range

The ocelot, or *tigrillo,* still appears from time to time within the United States. Like the jaguar, this beautiful little cat is a visitor from Mexico and Central America, where he is quite common. Also known as the tiger cat or leopard cat, he still may appear in any one of fourteen different counties in southern Texas or in extreme southeastern Arizona. In 1943, one was seen in Arizona's Yavapai County.

The margay, a kind of miniaturized ocelot, is another story. No one knows for certain that there have been any in the United States in many decades. Back in the mid-1800's one was reported from Eagle Pass in Texas' Maverick County. They have not been reported from any other area, and it would seem likely that they are now gone from our land altogether.

Appearance and Distinguishing Characteristics

The ocelot can reach forty pounds in weight, although twenty-five is more likely. Generally they are about twice the size of a large house cat, but can be forty-to-fifty inches in length, nearly half of which is tail.

Photo by Sy Merrill

The pet margay cat of Sy and Meg Merrill of New York City. Few people have the skill and patience to raise one of these energetic and nervous cats properly.

The ground color of the ocelot's coat is usually a warm gray to buff, marked with black or rich brown blotches. It is hard to say whether an ocelot is spotted or rosetted, but whatever you may wish to call them, they are irregular. Not only are no two ocelots marked alike, even the left and right side of a single animal will be very different. This is, of course, just about universally true in the animal kingdom. The spots frequently have light buffy centers, making them appear to be rosettes; again, they will form into bars and stripes. There are usually such bars about the back and top of the head. They frequently appear on the shoulders and sides as well.

In brief, the ocelot is a beautiful little blotched cat with a small head, large eyes, and short, rounded ears.

The margay is very similar to the ocelot, but somewhat smaller. He probably doesn't exceed, at his maximum, the average minimum length of an adult ocelot. His coat is very much like that of the ocelot, and in fact it is extremely difficult to tell them apart without an expert's consultation.

Habits

Not very much is known about the habits of the ocelot in the United States, and what is claimed as knowledge is usually information borrowed from writings on the Mexican specimens. Nothing at all is known about the margay in the United States.

We do know that ocelots climb and swim extremely well. They are almost totally nocturnal, so much so that some writers suggest that they will not even hunt on a moonlit night.

For obvious reasons the ocelot inhabits the most densely thicketed and most remote regions. He is small enough to be able to use passages beneath thorn tangles that eliminate traffic by any pursuer. He keeps to the dense chaparral and to himself.

The ocelot feeds on small mammals, birds, reptiles, and domestic poultry. He will take to a tree to catch a bird on its perch. It is reported that he will enter hen houses on stormy nights and carry off a number of victims. He is more apt to remain rather far away from man's works, however.

They are apparently good little hunters, and since they often hunt and travel in pairs, they use a cooperative tactic of sorts. Reportedly, the mates chat with each other and give each other signals while hunting, using a very catlike meow.

New York Zoological Society Photo

The ocelot or tiger cat, an occasional visitor to the American Southwest. A combination of beauty and deceptive calm.

Reproduction

Some authorities claim that ocelots may bear cubs in any month of the year. Others state September to November as the season for parturition. The gestation period is not exactly known, although it is probably upward of eighty to a hundred days.

The den is usually in a rocky cave or hollow tree. Small twigs and leaves are chewed and arranged into a comfortable bed. Both parents probably attend to the all-important education of the young, which apparently always number two.

The cubs are helpless and blind at birth, and their care and training are probably very similar in general outline to those of the other cats we will be discussing.

Observation

Seeing an ocelot in the wild, one that isn't in a trap at least, once again requires luck and little else. Since they are extremely shy, almost completely nocturnal, very remote and quite rare, the odds are somewhat against the observer. Besides, their beautiful coat provides superb protection in the brush they seldom if ever leave.

Letters to the wildlife agents in the various southern counties of Texas and Arizona may reveal spottings recent enough to inspire an effort to track one down. It is much more likely that any reports received will be rife with qualifications, such as "reported," "last thought," etc.

For the very persistent, the Santa Ana National Wildlife Refuge along the bank of the Rio Grande in southern Texas is three square miles of original South Texas brush and hardwood growth preserved hopefully for all time against exploitation and destruction. The ocelot is protected in this refuge and is known to exist there. There at least is a small unit of land on which we know there are ocelots. If you can't see your ocelot there, in three square miles of mapped land, imagine what your chances are of seeing one in the hundreds of square miles of chaparral country where we can't even be certain they exist! Information about Santa Ana can be obtained at the refuge headquarters in the Post Office building in the town of San Benito, Cameron County, seventeen miles from the Mexican border.

Ocelot tracks.

12

The Third Visitor: The Jaguarundi

WE HAVE a third visitor from the forests and junglelands of Mexico and Central America. This, the least-known cat in North America, is seldom seen—not only because he is relatively rare and very limited in range within the United States, but because he is shy in the extreme and very uncooperative in his choice of habitat.

Names and Range

He has two color phases, red and gray, and is known by many names: cacomitl, eyra, red cat, gray cat, otter cat, weasel cat are a few—he is the jaguarundi, the cat nobody knows. You can live your entire life within his range and never so much as catch a glimpse of him. Few Americans even realize he exists within our borders.

He can be found only in two states, Texas and Arizona. In 1944, one was spotted in the southeastern Arizona county of Santa Cruz. In Texas he is found only in the extreme southern tip: Cameron, Hidalgo, Starr, and Willacy counties. His range is even more limited, then, than that of the much larger and far more spectacular jaguar.

Appearance and Distinguishing Characteristics

The jaguarundi is very long-bodied and short-legged, with a small, flattened head. His tail can be nearly 50 percent of his length.

This slender little feline can be anywhere from thirty-five to fifty-four inches long and will usually weigh from fifteen to eighteen pounds. He is about twice the size of a house cat at full maturity.

His color tends to be more uniform than that of any other cat in this hemisphere. In the red phase (once thought to be a separate species and called eyra) he is rusty all over, somewhat paler underneath. His lips and throat will have a splash of white, and his back will be sprinkled with some black-tipped hairs. He has a lighter undercoat, and when he is angry and his coat bristles, this coat will show. He literally pales with anger.

In the gray phase he presents a grizzled or salt-and-pepper appearance. Yet, he does have a uniform smoky look without differentiation when seen from a distance. In winter his coat is darker. Both the red and gray phases may appear in the same litter.

Habits

The jaguarundi is a nervous animal. He is very alert, very active, extremely sensitive to any movement around him. His hearing is particularly good. He moves silently along well-worn trails in the thickest cactus and thorn country and because of his low silhouette can negotiate difficult passageways.

This strange little predator takes a variety of small mammals, the kinds he can run to ground amid the thorn tangles. Included are rabbits, rats, and mice. He climbs extremely well and will slink along branches like a ghost to take small birds and larger ones when he can overpower them at water's edge. He swims well and is said to take fish, frogs, crayfish, turtles, and turtle eggs. He may very well dine on an occasional snake or lizard, but it is not known for certain that he does.

The jaguarundi is not gregarious and does not make a good pet. He is too tense and high-strung for anything but the life he leads—as a silent shadow in the impossible, thorn-lined runways along the muddy, secret waterways of the Mexican border country.

Both young and adults make a chirping sound like a small bird. Adults can growl and spit quite convincingly. He moves about by day as well as by night, and since his habitat is so remote and forbidding, he hasn't had to adjust to a night life as have so many other predators.

Much of the territory now claimed by the jaguarundi is being cleared and reclaimed for agriculture, suburban living, and recreation. It won't be long before the thorn jungles are gone from this land; with them will go the already rare little "otter cat," the feline few people know.

Reproduction

Very little is known about the family life of this little cat. Young have been reported at all seasons, and possibly they will breed at any time of the year. It is likely, though, that there are two breeding seasons, spring and fall. The young are said to weigh about eight ounces at birth, but the number in the average litter is not known; three has been suggested.

Since the survival of the jaguarundi depends on his hunting prowess, it can be assumed that the young are meticulously educated, and their care is probably as intense as that of other cats. They probably mature quickly and leave their parents as soon as they are able to catch their own mice and rats.

Observation

Hunters and game wardens in the isolated areas where the jaguarundi are found may have secret information about where you might catch sight of one, but aside from that these retiring little animals will be very hard to find indeed. Few people have seen them, largely because they live in country in which it is all but impossible for a man to move about quietly. Thorns catching onto clothing and the necessity of cutting or moving vegetation aside in order to make way will alert them to your presence and give them ample opportunity to disappear into their secret tunnels beneath the thorn growth long before you can get close. If you ever manage to spot a lone specimen in the wild you will be rewarded by having accomplished one of North America's most difficult wildlife observation projects.

Jaguarundi share the Santa Ana National Wildlife Refuge with the ocelot. In this three-square-mile area you will at least have *some* chance of seeing these two extremely rare wild cats. Even in this controlled area, however, luck will have to be on your side. A lot of thorn and cactus can grow in three square miles!

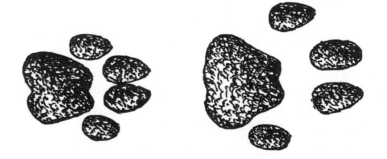

Jaguarundi tracks.

13

The Mysterious One:
The Mountain Lion or Puma

NATURALIST Bruce S. Wright calls him *"The Ghost of North America."* Stanley Young and Edward Goldman refer to him as "the 'lyric soprano' of the wild felines." Frank C. Hibben quotes a hunter as calling them "the 'Cains' of the animal world." Professional hunter Elmer Keith says he is "the most adept still-hunter on God's green earth," while other writers refer to him as everything from a coward to a man-eater. The mountain lion is *the* most controversial large mammal in North America with the possible exception of the wolf.

Names and Range

The popular names by which the mountain lion is known are as numerous as the scientific. Among them are cougar, puma, panther, painter, catamount, brown tiger, red tiger, American lion, king cat, silver lion, mountain screamer, purple panther, and as many more again.

Today, as for uncounted thousands of years, the mountain lion ranges from well up in Canada to almost the southern tip of South America. He has adjusted successfully to virtually every surface environment on the two continents except true desert and Arctic conditions, and few areas have not known the night cry of this stealthy cat at some time in history. The big difference between "then" and "now" is that the mountain lion is now extinct over most of the northern parts of his range. Few areas in the United States and Canada can boast of any mountain lion population at all. Man and

Photo by Wilford L. Miller

The mountain lion in Colorado, a typical pose.

mountain lion just don't get along together. Man, quite characteristically, has been the aggressor.

In many areas from Mexico on south this great cat, largest of the New World unspotted cats, is still to be found in something like his original numbers. We also know or at least believe that he still exists in at least nineteen Texas counties and in Louisiana, Mississippi, Alabama, Florida, Arizona, New Mexico, California, Nevada, Utah, Colorado, Wyoming, Montana, Idaho, Oregon, and Washington. In Canada he can still be found in British Columbia and Alberta. All that is fairly certain. Now, here is where the mystery starts: How about reports from southern Saskatchewan, Ontario, Quebec, New Brunswick? What of persistent reports from Maine, Vermont, New York, Michigan, Wisconsin, and Minnesota? Has he moved out of Florida back up into Georgia? What about Pennsylvania?

It does in fact seem as if the mountain lion were again expanding his range. He may be moving back into areas where he hasn't been seen or heard in a century, and there is an explanation for it all.

The mountain lion did not disappear only because he was hunted; he disappeared from most parts of his range in large part because his food, the deer, was hunted. When the deer herds were thinned out, the great predator vanished. Now, with game-control measures in effect just about everywhere, the deer herds are back, and so may be the mountain lion. This cat will never again wander over what is now Boston Common as he once did, and he won't return to his former hunting ground in the area surrounding Times Square. He may, however, soon be found in areas long since denied him. Strangely enough, most people will probably never know the difference. Unless you stumbled across his kill or happened to catch an accidental glimpse of him at dusk, you could live very close to a mountain lion family and never know you had such fascinating neighbors.

Appearance and Distinguishing Characteristics

You are not likely to confuse a mountain lion with any other wild mammal on this continent. His average length is between six and eight feet. Height at the shoulder runs 25 to 30 inches, generally, and weights at maturity run from 80 to 225 pounds. The preponderance of smaller cats taken by hunters is explained by the fact that young and immature specimens are usually the ones shot.

He is usually tawny to grayish in color, with lighter areas on the throat, belly, and inside of his legs. This ground color varies with his habitat; specimens from semiarid regions are lighter than woods or jungle specimens. (Melano specimens have been reported but are apparently *very* rare.) There are blackish markings on the tip of his tail, in back of his ears, and on the sides of his muzzle. His head is rather small and his body long and lithe. The tail is very long and distinctly cylindrical. He has clear yellow eyes, prominent whiskers, and a great, easy grace about him.

Photo by Wilford L. Miller

A mountain lion kitten in Glacier National Park.

This smooth-flowing, great tawny cat is *the* big cat of the United States and Canada, our greatest predator and quite legitimately the symbol of all our wildlife. For many reasons, nature could give us no finer gift than to return this wonderful creature to our wild places, where he belongs. His return to many areas would stand as a beacon and a monument to an awakening populace who had at last made up its mind to preserve some of the heritage that made this great land a place of beauty and plenty before a few generations of myopic men decided that only what they themselves could build was worth saving.

Habits

The mountain lion, like most cats, is a secretive animal. His is a world apart, a world of stealth and quiet. He is definitely territorial and will defend his established range with violence if necessary, particularly at courtship time.

He is also far-ranging and may hunt in a radius of thirty to fifty miles. He is active all year and is a creature of habit, using familiar trails in search of prey. In areas where man intrudes, the mountain lion moves about more at night, but by nature he will hunt day and night if undisturbed.

He climbs extremely well even when full grown and will take to trees if pursued. This is his undoing, since most of them that are killed by hunters are shot out of trees after being chased there by dogs.

Few habitats exclude him. He has a particular fondness for elevated areas with some wooded cover and for rocky ledges that enable him to survey the area and remain hidden. He does, however, do well in semiarid areas and can be found from the cactus country of the Southwest to the great swamps of the Southeast. He readily takes to water and will swim a river or search in the shallows for food.

He is a master hunter and stalks his prey with complete silence. He can approach grazing deer to an astonishingly close distance before making his rush and leap. A single bite by a mature cat at the base of a deer's skull will kill it outright. Younger cats will disembowel a deer as it makes off in panic with the hunter clinging to it. Some mountain lions certainly, and perhaps all from time to time, use the ambush technique and fall on prey from trees and ledges. Generally, though, he is an active hunter, stalking and leaping. This uncanny skill makes him a tough project for the nature observer. It is very hard indeed to stalk an animal whose very life depends on his own mastery of that art.

The mountain lion's major source of food is the deer, especially the whitetail and mule deer. Some elk, mountain sheep, pronghorns, and perhaps moose (but these rarely) are taken, and all small mammals and birds figure in the diet, but deer are the staple. Fish, frogs, and other odds and ends are eaten occasionally, particularly by young specimens. Sad to say, the mountain lion also takes domestic stock. In some areas predation on horses, sheep, and pigs became so great in the last century that the great cats had to be hunted down and destroyed. It became impossible for some ranchers and farmers to raise colts at all. Most ranchers will never forgive the mountain lion for past sins, and he is hunted today as he was a century ago. (One of the many scientific names given him translates from the Latin as "horse killer.")

Although there are exceptions, the mountain lion is not generally a wasteful killer. He kills one animal at a time and covers what he can't eat to return again and again until there is little or nothing left. He is not particularly keen on carrion and will take, on the average, a deer or an equivalent

Photo by Wilford L. Miller

The graceful line of the cat. Note the full winter coat.

weight in smaller game every week. Since, as we shall be seeing, females keep their cubs with them until nearly full grown, kills will be made more often in an area where young are being raised. It takes a lot more meat than can be found on one deer to feed a lion and her cubs for a full week.

The sounds made by the mountain lion have been the subject of endless controversy. Actually, they make a great variety of sounds; they hiss, spit, growl, snarl, grunt, roar, and scream. Their long, drawn-out, high-pitched scream has been likened to that of a woman in mortal terror. It has also been described as resembling a train whistle. This last sound is rarely heard and may be tied in with certain courtship rituals. Some animals may be more prone to use it than others.

Females apparently have a wilder disposition than males, and when young are around, they can be particularly fierce. There have been many reports of attacks on man down through the years, and there can be little doubt that some have occurred from time to time. The mountain lion is not a man-eater by nature, but there are conditions under which an attack will occur and even cases where humans have been partially eaten. Most reports, however, have undoubtedly been greatly exaggerated—if not entirely fabricated.

Mountain lions are subject to rabies, and there are one or two cases on record of rabid animals attacking humans. These cases suggest that other unprovoked attacks may have occurred for the same reason. Another cause may be that the young, when they are finally cast off by the mother, often come close to starvation. During their first weeks and months on their own they have trouble providing for themselves and then will take livestock. Many stock-killers, when hunted down and killed, have turned out to be immature animals in very poor condition. Similarly, a number of the attacks made on men were made by young, half-starved cats obviously on their own for only a short time.

Very few mountain lions, certainly, care to come close enough to man to attack him. They are shy, retiring, and very much too intent on self-preservation to approach man in any but the most unusual circumstances. There have been attacks, however, and some of them unprovoked. To think of the mountain lion as harmless is to ignore or deny his size, strength, and skill as a predator.

Reproduction

Mountain lions breed first at two or three years of age, at least this is the case with the females. Mates are together for a short time, and the breeding may occur at any time of the year. It is thought that some pairs are monogamous and rejoin every second or third year from neighboring ranges. Gestation is variously reported from 90 to 104 days. Birth takes place in a secluded area in natural formations or in heavy wooded growth. Caves are sometimes used, but rocky ledges with sloping cover seem to be preferred. Occasionally a hollow log, or even an underground burrow that has been taken over and enlarged, will be used. A nest under thick brush will do where natural formations are not at hand.

The young may be one to six in number, although the usual is two or three. At birth they are blind, buffy, spotted, have a ringed tail, and are helpless. They weigh anywhere from half a pound to a pound. At ten to fourteen days, the eyes open. They grow rapidly and may be weaned any time after five weeks, usually before three months. At six months, the cubs weigh 30 to 45 pounds. By this time they have lost the spotted coat and resemble their tawny mother. A female may keep her cubs with her for as long as two years, and woe to the male that tries to get close during this time. The male mountain lion will occasionally kill and eat a cub, and the very aggressive female is terribly harsh toward any male that attempts to approach her cubs.

As the cubs grow, the female teaches them to hunt and kill. Still, the task of feeding the cubs falls on her, and she must kill more often as the weeks pass. As the cubs start to approach maturity, if the female has kept them around that long, she will no longer allow them to feed at her kill until after she has fed. She will drive them off to wait their turn. They are very rough, and when she finally lets them at the kill it is soon torn up and spread around. In captivity, mountain lions have lived as long as sixteen and eighteen years. Where hunting is good and man not persistent, wild specimens may do as well.

Observation

As Olaus Murie put it, "This American lion . . . is so secretive that the sight of one in the wild is a rarity, and a choice experience." Only by accident will you spot a mountain lion in his natural environment unless you are on horseback, using expert guides, and running the cat on a hot trail with specially trained dogs. Then you may eventually see a very angry cat high in a tree. To stumble across one on foot is one of the most unusual and most rewarding experiences in wildlife observation on this entire continent. Few people have it.

As we have seen, the mountain lion's life is one of stealth and secret ways. He is keenly attuned to his environment and is apt to follow you while you think you are following him. He seems to be quite concerned about strangers on his range and many times has been reported following people on foot. Since attacks are rare, even in these cases, we can assume that there is some curiosity involved.

If, by some incredible good fortune, you should discover a mountain lion den occupied by a female with young cubs and therefore reduced mobility, use care in approaching too closely. This usually quiet cat can become violently angry and be a terrible antagonist if aroused. Anyone seriously interested in seeing a mountain lion in the wild is urged to engage the services of a professional, or at least of an expert hunter.

There are a few places where mountain lions are protected, and here they can on occasion be spotted by the very, very patient, very quiet observer with plenty of stamina. At best it is a long shot, however, and the following list in no way suggests that mountain lions are waiting around to be looked at as in a zoo. For the record:

Big Bend National Park, hugging the Mexican border along the Rio Grande in Texas, has a few. They cling to the most inaccessible country and will be extremely hard to find.

Photo by Wilford L. Miller

A magnificent animal in magnificent country!

Everglades National Park in southern Florida has a few. They are occasionally spotted, but even the most deliberate search is unlikely to succeed unless many weeks are dedicated to the project. To find a few cats in 2,347 square miles of swampland is indeed like searching for a needle in the haystack. And, unlike the proverbial needle, the mountain lion won't sit around waiting to be found.

Glacier National Park in western Montana has a mountain lion population, but it also has 1,583 square miles of wilderness for them to hide in.

Jasper National Park is one of Canada's glorious sanctuaries in the western provinces. Located in western Alberta, on the British Columbia line, it has and protects some of these cats. Here, again, they are there but very hard to find.

Kaibab National Forest on the north rim of the Grand Canyon in Arizona has a few—very few. They have been overhunted and are extremely shy. Chances of spotting them are slight.

Kootenay National Park is another one of Canada's scenic wonders. Situated in southern British Columbia, it can boast of some mountain lions, but no guarantees are given the short-term visitor.

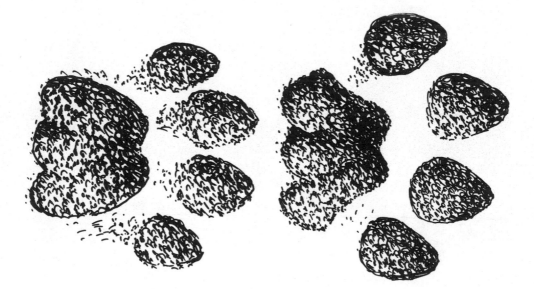

Mountain lion tracks.

Olympic National Park in northwestern Washington, on the Olympic Peninsula, has a few. They are listed as rare and are seldom seen.

Sequoia and *Kings Canyon National Parks* in central California have some mountain lions left. In all of California's 158,693 square miles there are an estimated six hundred mountain lions. Some of them live in the 1,314 square miles within the boundaries of these two parks.

Waterton Lakes National Park in southern Alberta still has some specimens left. They seldom reveal themselves, however, but their sign is spotted from time to time.

Zion National Park, 223 square miles in southwestern Utah, has some left, but the country is so rough that they will have endless opportunities to hide long before you can come close or will even be aware of their presence.

14

Lamps in the Night:
The Lynx and Bobcat

Names and Range

In North America there are two species of wild felines properly called lynx and bobcat. A number of their common names overlap, just as do their ranges. The lynx is variously known as lucivee, *loup-cervier,* wildcat, catamount—along with the bobcat and mountain lion—and there are many more names derived from various Indian dialects and from French, English, and Scottish words. The bobcat is variously known as lynx cat, wildcat, bay lynx, red lynx, tiger cat, and catamount. We have, then, three cats known as catamount, all of them at least in part forest and mountain animals. Whether catamount comes from the Spanish *gatomonte,* meaning "mountain cat," or is a contraction of "cat-of-the-mountain"—another name by which they are known—cannot be determined. Here is one very good example of why the scientific names are absolutely essential if any sense is to be made of the study of wildlife.

The lynx is a cat of the northern forests. He ranges from far western Alaska (he is the only wild feline in our forty-ninth state) across all of Canada to the eastern Maritime Provinces. He blends his range with that of the bobcat in the northern United States, reaching right up to the Arctic Circle.

Our bobcat appears in southern Canada, throughout the entire United States, and southward into Mexico. Still, his range is but a fraction of that enjoyed by the mountain lion. There are probably no states within the original forty-eight in which the bobcat does not occur today. He is rarer, to be sure,

A typical bobcat—power, stealth, and skill. Note the lack of ear tufts and the spotted belly.

in the open Plains states than in the forested margins of the Northwest and Northeast, but his range is expanding, and man's activities help more than harm him.

As man clears land for agriculture, he increases the number of habitats suitable for small rodents. Rodents, certainly, are more common on farmlands and in brush areas than in deep forests, and bobcats, largely dependent on rodents for food, follow in ever-expanding numbers. Our western bobcats prefer canyon habitats where piñon, mountain mahogany, manzanita, sagebrush, and juniper grow. In the Southeast bobcats flourish in the deciduous forests with their weedy areas and in swamps with grassy borders. The so-called magnolia climax forests are rich in rodent life, and here the bobcat can survive amid plenty. The southern canebrake regions and hummocky swamps are also to his liking, and he gets along very well indeed in our arid Southwest. Occasionally, the bobcat ranges above 6,000 feet but never above 12,000.

The bobcat, our most common wild feline, is a very versatile fellow. However, where boreal conditions exist and the snow is deep for long months at a time, he relinquishes the range to his very close cousin, the Canada lynx. Between them they have neatly divided our continent in half. Where their ranges overlap they apparently live in mutual respect.

Appearance and Distinguishing Characteristics

Most people, seeing either a bobcat or a lynx alone, could not say for sure which it was. While they are similar in many ways, when seen side by side the many differences are immediately apparent. A moment's attention to the chart on page 131 will clear up the mystery and make confusion less likely in the future.

Habits

There is an old saying used to describe a particularly tough individual: "He can lick his weight in wildcats." Actually, the man who could do that hasn't been born and probably never will be, for our wildcat (whether you define him as a lynx or a bobcat) is a tough customer. A man would have far more than he could handle faced with even fifteen or twenty pounds of angry bobcat unless he were well armed. An angry, hissing, snarling wildcat is about as awe-inspiring a sight as there is in nature. He moves like a coiled spring, lashes out, rolls over, bringing his four heavily armed feet into play, and bites with a slashing, ripping movement.

Both cats will hunt by day and by night. In cases where man puts up his dwellings close to a hunting range, the local cats will shift their habits to move about more by night.

The noises made by our wildcats are legendary. The caterwauling of the males during the breeding season is a source of endless annoyance to people living near a range. They also hiss, growl, snarl, and scream after a fashion. Generally silent or nearly so, they can be very noisy and unpleasant from January through March, when their mating usually takes place.

Both animals have very keen eyesight and hearing and a fairly good sense of smell. The differences in their diets are the result of local availabilities, for both are almost entirely carnivorous. Only rarely has any vegetable matter been known to be consumed, and it is certain that neither animal can exist on anything but meat.

Both will take any small rodent and indeed do whenever the supply is available. Birds are taken regularly, and the bobcat will take snakes and lizards. Even grasshoppers and beetles are consumed from time to time.

	BOBCAT	LYNX
Tail	SHORT—black only on top of tip—white or tan on very tip and generally striped with black or deep brown.	SHORT—tip all black. Shorter than bobcat. Not striped.
Feet	Relatively small and NOT heavily furred.	VERY LARGE—"built-in snow-shoes"—and heavily furred.
Size	15–25 lb. (up to 43 lb. on record, but rarely). 25–30 in. long, 20–23 in. at shoulder.	20–40 lb. usually. 32–36 in. long, 24+ in. at shoulder.

The lynx is a larger cat with appreciably longer legs.

	BOBCAT	LYNX
Ears	Grayish—white on back, small or absent ear tuft.	Gray, with long pointed black tufts.
Ruff or "sideburn"	Present and sometimes quite prominent.	Always very prominent.
Fur	Varies with habitat and season but generally rather short. Silky.	Longer and thicker than bob-cat—very soft and full.
Coloration	Varies with habitat—darker in heavily wooded areas of both North and South than in Plains and arid areas. Basic cream buff with reddish and various gray and brown tones. Markedly dappled with spots and other dark markings. Has spotted belly.	Varying ground colors as with bobcat but with few spots. Does not have spotted belly.

In general, coloration is so variable with both the lynx and bobcat that the major distinguishing characteristic is the lynx's less spotted, less marked fur. Both have very soft and silky fur, not at all wiry as it would appear from a distance. Melano and albino specimens occur.

	BOBCAT	LYNX
Eyes	Large and yellow. Elliptical when contracted.	Large and yellow. Elliptical when contracted.

Deer and other large game are taken occasionally, but the victim is generally young, old, or sick. In heavy snow, the lynx—because his broad, heavily furred feet enable him to walk on top of the snow—has little difficulty

Courtesy U.S. Department of Interior, Bureau of Biological Survey

A bobcat kitten in Idaho. Note the prominent body and face markings. They will fade slightly as maturity is reached.

bringing a deer down as it flounders in a drift. Bobcats will drop from overhanging trees and take large game as well, and there can be little doubt that either animal will take almost anything it can get in the way of fresh meat.

Unfortunately, both cats take livestock. The bobcat lives closer to agricultural areas and so is more often a culprit than his rarer woodland cousin. Sheep and goats are taken, as are calves and colts. In some areas, particularly in the Southeast, a bobcat will develop a liking for domestic swine and raids will occur regularly. Chickens, ducks, and turkeys are also taken. Full-grown specimens of larger domestic stock are rarely taken.

Rodents are the staple item in the diet of the bobcat, and because of this he is extremely valuable to the farmer. There can be little argument that an individual cat that takes to raiding the farmyard three or four nights a week should be eliminated, but these cats as a group do far more good than harm. Although they do take some deer and some game birds and eggs, it has never been demonstrated that they reduce the stock to any marked degree. They probably do more good than harm where deer are concerned, just as wolves do, by eliminating the weak specimens from the breeding stock. A controlled bobcat population probably results in an increased deer population.

The lynx has the varying or snowshoe hare as his diet staple. This small rabbit exists everywhere the lynx does.

Like all cats—like virtually all predators, for that matter—both the bobcat and the lynx seek anonymity as the ideal way of life. The less they have to do with man, the better they like it. The bobcat is willing to accept the benefits that man gives him—forest clearing and farmland and therefore expanded range, plus an occasional farm animal—and the lynx is willing to pick man's traps clean of their easy-to-be-had victims, but direct association with man is never pursued. Both cats, although great fighters and often extremely short-tempered, run when man is near. Both are easily trapped and hunted, but neither seeks the company of man for any reason whatsoever.

Both cats are territorial and, if the food supply is good, neither will wander. If the available supply of rodents thins out, they will expand their range as far as necessary to care for their needs. If things get too bad, they will move off to a new range. In general, because of their small size, they can satisfy their needs on any range once established, unless it is seriously interfered with by man, and these ranges are generally small. A few thousand square yards around a den site will usually keep a bobcat happy for a long time. A range, however, depending on its richness, can be four or five square miles. Naturally, it will be larger in winter, for these cats hunt the year round. Both cats scent their ranges and claw trees. Whether either or both of these practices is for the purpose of boundary marking is not clear.

The lynx and the bobcat are creatures of habit. They use established trails, have favorite ledges and tree branches for sunning themselves, and use the same den year after year. This often leads to their downfall, since hunters need only to run a cat once or twice with or without dogs to learn their routes. All they must do the next time is start the animal from its den site and then set themselves up on the route and wait for the cat to run its circular course and head for home. The hunter and his gun will be waiting. It is an old trick but one that works with the bobcat and the lynx.

There is some suggestion that the lynx is more gregarious than the bobcat and congregations have been reported. It is also suggested that the lynx spends more time with his mate and helps to care for the young. None of this is quite clear, however.

Reproduction

Bobcats, and presumably lynx, breed sometime after their first year. Breeding and therefore the birth of the cubs may occur in any month, although the height of breeding activity occurs between January and April. Gestation is from fifty to sixty days, and the litter size varies from one to five; two or three are most common. Most births apparently take place in April or May, and it is suggested that some females may have two litters a year. Births seldom if ever occur in November, December, or January, when hunting is at its worst.

The young are well furred and spotted at birth. They weigh about twelve ounces and mature very quickly. There have been some reports of lynx born

New York Zoological Society Photo

The squat, powerful Canadian lynx. Note the size of the enormous feet and the dark ear tufts.

with their eyes open, but generally, if not always, both bobcat and lynx cubs are blind for at least three days and often as long as nine or ten days after birth.

Weaning is usually completed shortly after the second month, but some cats may keep their young nursing for as long as three. This may vary from individual to individual, or over different range conditions. Young born in the spring remain with their mother until the fall and then move off to establish their own ranges. There are conflicting reports as to whether the father contributes to the care of the young. Some reports have the male killing cubs and being driven off by the female. Others have the male bringing fresh kills to the mother and her nursing young. In the absence of clearly defined facts, we can assume there is some latitude among individual animals. There is little doubt that the female carries most of the burden.

Den sites vary greatly. They are most commonly observed occurring under logs that are overgrown with brush or vines. Root depressions and decomposing windfalls are also likely sites, as are small rocky caves and recesses in limestone or sandstone formations. Almost any natural cover is apt to be utilized. Bobcats have been found with their nest and young under farm buildings. They must have found their nighttime "shopping" trips very convenient in such cases. Occasionally bobcats will set up housekeeping within city limits.

It is believed that the bobcat can breed with the domestic cat, and there are records that *appear* to substantiate this belief. In captivity the bobcat and the lynx will live fifteen years. Life in the wild is undoubtedly more abbreviated in most cases.

Observation

You are more apt to see a bobcat or a lynx than any other wild feline in the United States and Canada. They are our commonest cats, and the range of the lynx is shrinking while that of the bobcat is expanding. The lynx, too, prefers more remote regions, while a bobcat will set up housekeeping at the wooded end of the back pasture. Both cats, however, maintain respectable populations and are rare only very close to cities and in the open prairies and Plains states.

It is, as we have often seen in this book, characteristic of all big game left on this continent to be very common in some areas and rare in others, although the habitat opportunities appear to be the same in both. This is, of course, due to man and his unending interference with the natural order of things. It is necessary in a serious wildlife observation project to seek local advice. If you are out to find bobcat tracks, if you are away from home and want a chance at spotting one of these dramatic little animals, ask for specific *up-to-date* information from local wildlife conservation organizations, state,

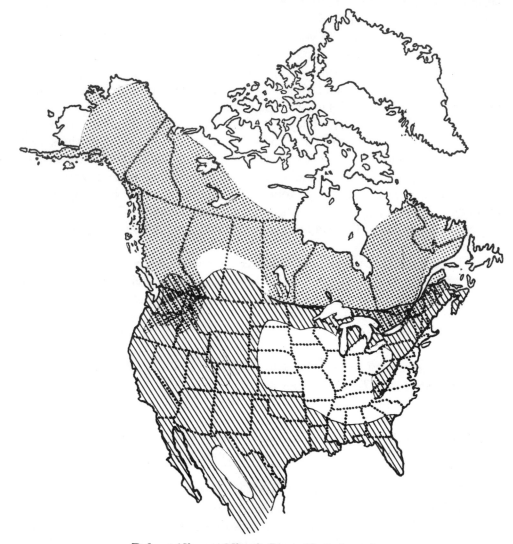

Bobcat (diagonal lines). Lynx (dotted area).

federal and private. Seek information from local farming and ranching groups, 4-H Clubs, and sporting groups. You can always resort to the gunsmith and small-town hardware store.

Although nowhere near complete, the following list will give you a few areas in which to look. Within these parks and refuges the animals cannot be hunted or trapped. Their natural food is left alone as well, so the populations maintain themselves at something like a constant level.

A WORD OF CAUTION: A bobcat or a lynx may look like an overgrown, short-tailed house cat to you, but he is most definitely not to be stroked! If

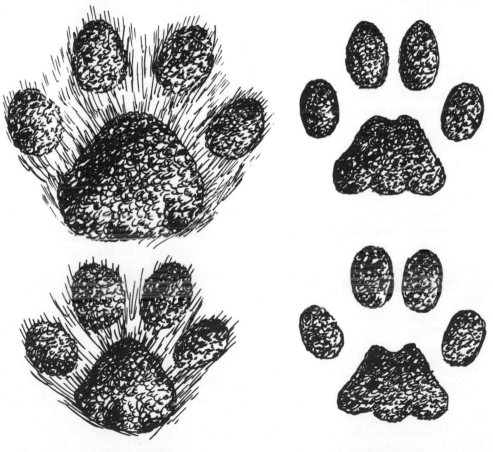

Lynx tracks.   **Bobcat tracks.**

Some Areas Where Bobcat and Lynx May Be Found

PRESERVE	LOCATION	ANIMAL
Banff National Park	Southwestern Alberta	Lynx
Cape Breton Highlands National Park	Northern Nova Scotia	Lynx and bobcat
Carolina Sandhills Wildlife Refuge	South Carolina	Bobcat
Everglades National Park	Southern Florida	Bobcat
Fundy National Park	Southern New Brunswick	Bobcat and lynx
Glacier National Park	Northwestern Montana	Bobcat
Jasper National Park	Western Alberta	Lynx and bobcat
Kenai National Moose Range	Southern Alaska	Lynx
Kootenay National Park	Southeastern British Columbia	Lynx
Laguna Atascosa National Wildlife Refuge	Southern Texas	Bobcat
Loxahatchee National Wildlife Refuge	Southeastern Florida	Bobcat
Monte Vista Wildlife Refuge	South-central Colorado	Bobcat
Moosehorn National Wildlife Refuge	Eastern Maine	Bobcat and lynx
Mount McKinley National Park	South-central Alaska	Lynx
Okefenokee National Wildlife Refuge	Southeastern Georgia	Bobcat
Olympic National Park	Northwestern Washington	Bobcat and lynx (?)
Prince Albert National Park	Central Saskatchewan	Lynx
Riding Mountain National Park	Southwestern Manitoba	Lynx
Santa Ana National Wildlife Refuge	Southern Texas	Bobcat
Savannah National Wildlife Refuge	Georgia and South Carolina	Bobcat
Seney National Wildlife Refuge	Michigan's Upper Peninsula	Bobcat and lynx (?)
Terra Nova National Park	Northern Newfoundland	Lynx
Waterton Lakes National Park	Southwestern Alberta	Lynx and bobcat (?)
Wichita Mountains Wildlife Refuge	Southwestern Oklahoma	Bobcat
Yoho National Park	Southeastern British Columbia	Lynx and bobcat (?)

you tree one or encounter one in a cave, back off. When cornered or trapped, these wild felines can be very tough customers.

There are dozens of state and provincial parks and refuges as well where bobcat and lynx roam unmolested. Farms and ranch lands over both countries have populations, as do even suburban areas. No matter where you are in the United States or Canada, you are not very far away from a bobcat or a lynx. Even in Times Square you are no more than thirty to thirty-five miles from a den site. It is safe to say the bobcat will be the last wild cat and perhaps the last great predator to go in North America. Long after the bears and wolves, even the coyotes have been eliminated, the bobcat will still sit high on his perch overlooking a highway watching the cars roll past. And, when he tires of watching, he will stretch, yawn, and slip back into the dusk at the edge of the wood just as he has for hundreds of thousands of years.

15

The Masked Bandit: The Raccoon

HIS SCIENTIFIC NAME is *Procyon lotor*—meaning "before the dog" (*Procyon*) and "a washer" (*lotor*), while his common name apparently derives after a fashion from an Algonquian word (*äräkun,* or perhaps *äräkunem*), meaning "he who scratches with his hands"; the French Canadians call him *raton,* but, for it all, he is just a plain old raccoon or coon, one of our most common small mammals.

Names and Range

The raccoon is to be found from the southernmost reaches of Central America to the southern parts of every Canadian province adjacent to the United States. He is in some part of every one of the original forty-eight states. Resilient to change, versatile in diet, and sturdy in his determination to outwit every enemy, natural or unnatural, our raccoon is *the* mammal you are the most apt to see in a nighttime stroll in about 95 percent of the woods and brush of the United States and in the southern woodlands of Canada from the Atlantic to the Pacific Ocean.

Appearance and Distinguishing Characteristics

One word describes the raccoon: *robust*. Six to twelve inches at the shoulder and with an overall length of twenty to forty inches, he may weigh from three to thirty-five pounds! He is compact, rugged, built close to the ground, and a terrible scrapper when pushed too far.

His coat is shaggy with long, coarse guard hairs and a luxurious soft underfur. His color ranges through the grayish and brownish buff tones, often suffused with yellow or orange, and is heavily sprinkled with black on the tips of the guard hairs; it can best be described as "grizzled gray." The distinctive black face mask is always present and marks him immediately even in a fleeting glance. Three odd colors are known: red, albino, and melanistic. Apparently none of the three is particularly rare. The author has seen one specimen that was distinctly pale *gold!*

The tail of the raccoon is as distinguishing as his bandit's mask; it is very bushy and from eight to twelve inches long with alternating rings of yellowish white and black. There are generally from four to seven black bands.

His snout and ears are pointed and his dark little eyes very bright and alert. He has a smart look about him that accurately reflects his personality. His feet are long and slender and have naked soles. There are five toes on each with short, curved claws. He is extremely adept with his forefeet and can readily handle very small objects with his "hands."

Habits

The raccoon is into everything. He is a curious, meddlesome little nighttime thief who apparently is well aware of his powers of survival. Your approach won't panic him, and if he doesn't find you particularly interesting, he will shuffle off in his bearlike, flat-footed manner and look for trouble elsewhere. If you live in the suburbs of many of even our largest cities and have a savory garbage can, he will be a nightly caller. If you are on a camping trip or live on a farm, you can expect to share at least part of your wealth with him. His sense of touch is very sensitive, and his ability with traps, locks, windows, doors, and what-have-you is legendary.

Raccoons are territorial but have very limited private ranges. An area a mile in diameter will satisfy him, for he can adapt to almost any situation below six thousand feet in altitude. He is equally at home in the desert country of our Southwest as along the beaches of Maine, where he hunts for clams. In some areas the population becomes very thick, and there will be at least one raccoon to every four or five acres. There have been times when the population in certain areas exceeded an animal per acre. For their fur, their flesh, and for their gamy, sporting qualities they are killed by the hundreds of thousands every year. An unfortunate number fall victim to automobiles, and there are few areas in the United States where they aren't seen beside the road every night except in the worst of the winter.

The raccoon likes partially cleared land near broad-leafed trees. He will always be found near streams and lakes when any are present and is very

Courtesy Province of Ontario, Department of Lands & Forests

Ontario raccoon caught hunting his dinner in daylight.

common in most woody or swampy areas. He generally feeds along the water's edge and swims very well. He is strictly nocturnal unless disturbed during the day and takes to trees with great skill. The report that raccoons won't eat unless they can wash their food is not true. They will readily devour any morsel with gusto, washed or not.

The raccoon is truly omnivorous. You name it, and he eats it. Nuts of all kinds, all sorts of berries and fruit, seeds, corn in milk, honey, crayfish, crabs, clams, oysters, frogs, fishes, mammals, birds, reptiles, insects, chickens, ducks, alligator and turtle eggs, eggs of all kinds, domestic and otherwise—all these figure in his diet. He is a terrible barnyard pest. Delightful as he is, he can be a nuisance when his nighttime hunting trips bring him to the threshold of the chicken coop or the corn crib.

The raccoon has few enemies besides man. Eagles, owls, and certain weasels prey on the young. Although a scrappy fighter himself, even a full-grown boar coon is no match for our lightning-like weasels. Trailing dogs have been severely mauled by coons, and reportedly some coon will drown a pursuing dog by taking to the water and latching onto the dog's head when it comes in after him. He is said to be able to hold the dog under.

The sounds made by the coon are endless. In the words of various observers, he snorts, hisses, purrs, barks, growls, screeches, snarls, whines, churrs, chatters, trills, chuckles, and makes a peculiar owl-like hoot and whistle. None of these sounds has any great carrying power.

In the South, raccoons are active the year round. In the North they sleep part of the winter away in a hollow tree, under some roots, or even in a cave. It is often reported that they will den up in groups for a winter's sleep. During mild spells they may emerge, and their tracks can be found in the snow just as they can in the mud along local stream banks during warmer weather.

Photo by Wilford L. Miller

Three North Dakota raccoon young ready to face the uncertain world.

From early March on the raccoon molts. By the end of May he is usually in his lighter summer coat. In October his coat begins to thicken again, and by early November his full, luxurious winter coat is ready for the worst nature has to offer. This rich winter pelage has made the raccoon prey to several centuries of trappers and before that to thousands of years of Indian hunters. The annual harvest of raccoon fur is still a valuable commodity.

Reproduction

The raccoon is promiscuous. Females breed at ten to twelve months, males a little later. The joining usually occurs in February or March in the North, somewhat earlier in the South. Since the well-furred young are born well into the summer, it can be assumed that males move off and find new mates throughout the spring. Gestation is sixty-three days, and litter size varies from two to seven, with four being average and usual.

The den is generally located in a hollow tree, upright or prone. Excavations under a root system will be taken over and enlarged and other natural formations are taken advantage of according to the peculiarities of individual

Raccoon (diagonal lines).

animals and local problems and pressures. One raccoon may have several dens and may share some of them with other specimens in the area.

At birth, the young weigh about two and a half ounces. The face mask appears in ten days, the tail rings in nineteen. At forty days, when the young weigh about a pound and a half, they start taking some solid food. At ten weeks they start making the nightly rounds of the hunting range with the mother and are taught the ways of the raccoon. The mother is solely responsible for their feeding and education. It is an uncertain world even for the raccoon with his endless bag of tricks, so any cub who loses his mother to a car, trap, or gun before early November, when his education is completed, has a poor chance of surviving for very long. It is during this period that the young coon is most vulnerable, for as he moves around he is hunted by birds of prey as well as cars. It is safe to assume that most litters are thinned out before maturity. Some captive raccoons have lived to be fourteen years old, but this is surely unusual. Seven is more likely.

Observation

The raccoon is so common, so widespread, that it really isn't necessary to list parks in which he may be found. If you live in New York City, look in the northern Bronx and on Long Island; if you live in Chicago or Detroit, go out to the suburbs; if you live in Cleveland, look in Shaker Heights. The raccoon is everywhere, including city parks and farm kitchens. He is a night creature

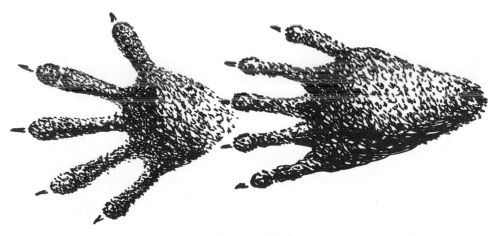

Raccoon tracks.

and will be shy where he is hunted. Where men don't pursue him with rifles and dogs, he will be curious to the point of being a pest.

You can lure a raccoon with any shiny or tinkly object hung from a string. You can bring him to your doorsteps or window sill with a variety of savory morsels. The stronger the smell, the farther you will draw them. Look to stream and river banks in the first four hours after sundown. Walk along quietly with a flashlight handy, or drive along very slowly with your headlights on high. There are few parts of rural America where you won't turn up a raccoon every spring, summer, and fall night of the year. In the opinion of the author, the fact that he provides children everywhere with an opportunity to see a fairly good-sized mammal in the wild makes him even more valuable than his fur. His ways are quaint and his personality engaging. He makes a good pet when he is young (although highly destructive if left unattended) but tends to be somewhat unreliable when mature. Raccoons bite very well.

16

The Coatimundi

Names and Range

Depending on where you come from you may call him coatimundi, coati, choluga, chula, or pisote. If you are adept at Latin, you can translate his scientific name (*Nasua narica*) as "the nosy one."

The coatimundi is a visitor from south of the border. He ranges in Texas from Brownsville to the Big Bend region of the trans-Pecos, showing up from time to time in Aransas, Brewster, Cameron, Maverick and Uvalde counties. He also inhabits pockets in the southern parts of Arizona and New Mexico. Señor Chula is a sometime resident in the United States and adds a delightful little wildlife vignette to our natural scene.

Appearance and Distinguishing Characteristics

The coatimundi is a raccoonlike carnivore, but he is more slender and has a much longer snout. That slender, flexible snout projecting well beyond the lower lip is a major distinguishing characteristic. Rather piglike, it is seldom still, constantly twitching as its owner thrusts it endlessly into every nook and cranny looking for something to eat.

The coatimundi has a very long tail (up to two feet or more), with six or seven indistinct bands. His ears are short, and his color is a grizzled yellowish brown. His snout, the areas around his eyes, and the insides of his ears are white. He has a dark-brown band across his snout between his eyes and whiskers. His lower legs and the tops of his feet are blackish brown and his underparts generally pale buff, becoming almost white under his chin.

The coati may weigh anywhere from ten to twenty-five pounds, may be thirty to fifty inches long overall, and will stand from eight to twelve inches at the shoulder. The male is considerably larger than the female.

Habits

The coati is essentially diurnal but is seldom abroad at the height of day, being at his active, curious best during the early morning hours and toward dusk. He sometimes hunts or forages at night as well, since his appetite is virtually unappeasable.

The food habits of the coati are not too well known. He will take lizards and snakes, insects and other invertebrates, roots, fruits, nuts, and eggs. Like the raccoon he is something of a traveling garbage can.

The coati apparently has quite a vocabulary, for different observers have accused him of hissing, spitting, chittering, whimpering, grunting, screaming, and snorting. He probably expresses himself in all of these ways, since he is very gregarious, and social animals generally require a vocabulary. Bands of ten to twenty are reported, and only the old males are solitary in their habits.

This southern visitor is both terrestrial and arboreal and will be found snuffing about ground debris for lizards as often as working along high branches for birds' eggs. He likes rocky canyons that enter the mountains from the lowlands and seems to prefer areas that are not too heavily wooded. Almost any woodland area in extreme southern Texas, however, is a good place to look.

Coatimundi.   Coatimundi.

The coatimundi swims well and will not hesitate to take to water. He is flat-footed and either shuffles or gallops along, depending on his immediate needs. He uses his long, slender tail as a balance when climbing and carries it in a variety of positions to express his moods.

Reproduction

The breeding habits of the coatimundi are not well known. They apparently mate in early spring and deliver their litter of four to six in late spring or early summer after a gestation period of approximately eleven weeks. A rocky niche is generally used for a den site, and the female does the feeding and educating. The mother is an attentive parent, and the communal habits of the animal may indicate some cooperation between females with young. There may be coatimundi baby-sitters.

Observation

Look to canyons. If the canyon starts in the lowlands with brush and wooded areas and extends into mountains where there is a lot of rocky shelter, you have a chance. If there is a stream running through the canyon, all the better. Move quietly, very quietly, into the canyon (without the sun at your back to throw disturbing shadows) around dusk, or just after dawn, and you may get to see not one but a whole band of coatimundis. Stop frequently and listen; their chittering, fussing, and chattering may help you locate them.

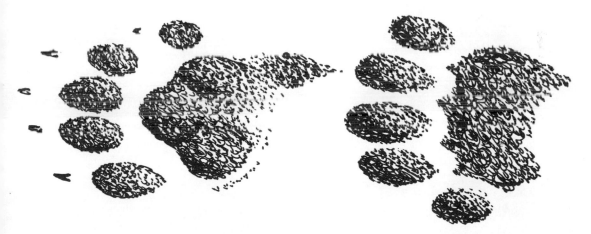

Coatimundi tracks.

Bands are frequently very vociferous as they discuss the various coatimundi social problems among themselves.

Confine your search to those few Texas counties listed and to southwestern New Mexico and southeastern Arizona. Ask locally for information on recent sightings or known coatimundi hangouts. This is one of the more intriguing nature observation projects. The subject animal is not so rare as to be impractical for even the amateur observer, yet rare enough to be an interesting challenge. Most people don't even realize he is to be found in the United States.

With the help of locally acquired information available from state agencies in the three states, the search for this nosy, busy little carnivore is a practical project for the nature observer traveling in the Southwest. It is not, however, a project to which you can casually assign a single afternoon. There will be some footwork involved and not just a few hours in some dry, rather rough country. It is well worth it, however.

17

The Ringtail or Cacomistle

Names and Range

This small carnivorous mammal has the most astounding collection of misnomers attached to him. His scientific name means "clever little fox," but he is not even related to the fox. He is commonly known as ring-tailed cat, miner's cat, coon cat, band-tailed cat, mountain cat, civet cat, and squirrel-cat. He is not related to the cats, the squirrels, or the civet. He *is* related to the raccoon but comes close namewise only when known as raccoon fox! To keep the record straight, he is also called babisuri, bassarisk, bassariscus, caco-mixtle, and tepemaxtle. Thank heavens for our system of scientific names, for wherever he is found, to people "in the know" he is *Bassariscus astutus*.

The ringtail ranges north from Mexico into central Texas and thence west and north. He is found in New Mexico, Arizona, from California to southwest Oregon, in parts of Nevada, Utah, and western Colorado.

Appearance and Distinguishing Characteristics

By stretching a point just a little bit you can see where the ringtail is related to the raccoon. He is, however, very much smaller and more slender with a far more resplendent tail. He has a broad head, a sharp muzzle, and big, round, alert ears. He is about six inches tall at the shoulder, from twenty-five to thirty-two inches long (half of that tail), and weighs a dainty two to three pounds. He has big, bright eyes set off by white spectacles.

The sleek little ringtail has a fluffy, lustrous coat that has a basic light brownish-gray ground color. His back is frosted with dark-tipped guard hairs and he blends to white underneath. All in all, he is a most attractive little creature.

A pair of young ringtail cats in Texas.

His handsome, distinguishing tail has alternating white and black rings; about fourteen in all. The tip is black, and the black rings are actually incomplete; they do not close on the underside. The tail, a precise balancing mechanism, is densely furred and somewhat flattened.

Habits

The ringtail is not uncommon in most parts of his range. He is, though, small and strictly nocturnal, so relatively few people know him. At altitudes up to six thousand feet, particularly on rocky, bush-covered slopes, he maintains himself in rather splendid isolation from man. In California, he seeks slopes where the blue oak and Digger pine grow. He also is common in the pine woods of many Texas counties.

This busy little night person is a great leaper and climber. Catlike feet with sharp claws enable him to scale even building walls, and agile leaps of ten feet are not unusual. He will sometimes take up dwellings close to man, in ruins and even within city limits. These are unusual occurrences, however.

He eats just about everything. Rodents, bats, lizards, birds, toads, frogs, nuts, corn, and insects all play a part in his diet. He loves certain fruits and will seek figs, dates, oranges, cacti fruit, mandrone, manzanita, cascara, blackberries, hackberries, persimmon, and mistletoe. He loves acorns. This variety in diet has enabled him to expand his range from southern Mexico to southern Oregon.

The ringtail makes a sharp metallic squeak when young but this gives way to a variety of barks, snarls, and even screams as he matures. He is not a noisy animal generally, but when attacked by his enemy, the owl, he can set up quite a racket.

Reproduction

The breeding habits of the ringtail are imperfectly known, to say the least. The young (from one to five, usually three) are born, according to most

Ringtail cat (diagonal lines).

reports, in May or June. Gestation *may be* from forty to fifty days, but that is more speculation than established fact.

At birth the kits are blind, toothless, and deaf; they are covered with a white fuzz with dark skin pigment showing where the black tail bands will eventually be.

The young are weaned early, at about three weeks. The eyes open some time after that—probably at thirty to thirty-five days. At seven to eight weeks the young start hunting with the parents, and at four months they are on their own. The father apparently makes some contribution to the care of the kits.

The den site is generally in a tree, near water. The entrance hole is very small, and the chamber is moss- or grass-lined. Occasionally rocky niches and caves are used, as are ruins and stone walls.

Captive ringtails have lived as long as eight years, but that is surely an outside figure.

Observation

Despite the habitat preferences given above, the ringtail will actually be found in a variety of situations within the boundaries of the eight states in which he occurs. He likes berries and fruit, as we have said, so look to the

Ringtail cat tracks.

orchards at ripening time. He will be found moving about under orange trees in the dead of night and has an absolute passion for fresh, ripe dates. Corn will attract him, for he not only can get vegetable matter there but also a choice selection of corn-fattened rodents, of whose flesh he is very fond.

During the day the ringtail will often select a branch high in a tall tree and sleep in the sun. You may see his tail hanging down with its bold stripes visible.

On slopes below six thousand feet where the blue oak and various pines grow, pick a moonlit night and sit out quietly on a high point with a good view. You may see your ringtail making great leaps from rock to rock, his tail delicately balancing him in midair.

He is the darling of many conservationists, and state, federal, and private agencies concerned with the preservation of our invaluable wildlife will be able to help you locate local ringtail populations once you have convinced them that your intentions are strictly friendly. He is worth pursuing, and a tick mark beside his name on your lifetime checklist is a thing of pride and joy.

18

Arboreal Lightning: The Marten

THE MARTEN, the first of the weasels or Mustelidae we will discuss, is one of our more valuable furbearers. Unfortunately, he is too valuable for his own good and has been pushed close to extinction over much of his range. Now protected in many areas, hopefully he may be on his way back.

Names and Range

Marten, pine marten, American sable, Hudson Bay sable—these are some of his many names. The word marten, *martre,* or sable appears in just about every one of them, so there isn't too much confusion. He is related to the very valuable Russian sable.

At one time the marten was found in most of the coniferous forests of the United States from the Atlantic to the Pacific. Today his range is much reduced. Still found in every Canadian province and throughout Alaska, all the way to the northernmost tree line, he is found in the United States only in Maine (rare), Vermont and New Hampshire (very rare), in small numbers around the Great Lakes, and in Wyoming, Montana, Colorado, Arizona, New Mexico, California, Washington, Oregon, and Idaho. He may be making a comeback in upper New York State and may indeed be reappearing right down the back of the Adirondacks as well as the Rocky Mountains. He is more common in the northwestern United States and in northern and western Canada than anywhere else.

Appearance and Distinguishing Characteristics

The ceaselessly active, lightning-fast marten is a handsome little weasel. He has a small head with large, bright eyes and broad, alert ears. His valuable

The marten is ever alert for prey and for his own safety.

fur ranges from almost blond to almost black, but basically he is a warm lustrous brown, blending to lighter orangy underparts. He has a distinctive light area on his throat while his legs, paws, ears, and tail are quite dark. His back is rich in glossy guard hairs, and he is blessed with an almost sinfully soft and luxurious undercoat.

The marten is from twenty-four to thirty inches overall, about a third of that being bushy tail. He seldom weighs more than six pounds, often less.

He has five toes on each foot, and they are well clawed. In the winter his feet are well furred between the toes.

Habits

The marten is greased lightning aloft. He has a passion for red squirrels and chases them from branch to branch until he finally makes his kill. Once he takes off after a squirrel, it has little or no chance for survival. He can climb and leap at least as well as his prey and often better. He spends most of his time in the trees during the summer but scurries about in the snow during the winter. Except during the very worst days he hunts all year round.

The marten is both nocturnal and diurnal and can best be seen late in the afternoon, if he can be seen at all. He is alert, hyperactive, and extremely agile. He is a powerful fighter and is given to much quarreling with his own kind when encounters occur. He is strictly a solitary animal.

Few animals are fast or strong enough to prey on the marten. At various times and in various places the fisher, a larger weasel and closely related, the lynx, the great horned owl, and the golden eagle have all been suggested as foes. Actually the marten's fur and his curiosity are his two worst enemies.

Martens are easy to trap. They can be lured with a wide variety of scents, including cheap perfume, and will investigate any bright, shiny, or tinkly object. Carrion, fish, and assorted high meats will draw a marten into a trap. If he is released, he is apt to be caught again and again by the same device. For such an alert little creature he is a dreadful dunderhead when it comes to man's mechanical contrivances.

During the winter the marten is generally found at altitudes from 4,000 to 7,000 feet, from 7,000 to 13,000 feet in the summer, well above the timberline. He prefers deep evergreen forests and moves out of an area as soon as man moves in. Heavy lumbering has done as much as trapping to reduce his numbers.

Besides red squirrels, the marten hunts birds, mice and other small rodents, frogs, snakes, fish, rabbits, and he will also take carrion. He buries what he doesn't eat and returns for subsequent meals. He loves birds' eggs. His diet is not restricted to flesh, although he is essentially a carnivore, and he will eat berries, honey, and pine-cone seeds. In different areas he is reported as particularly fond of mountain-ash berries, blueberries, huckleberries, and honey.

Where there is a good population, well away from settled areas, there may be as many as three pairs of martens per square mile during the brief breeding season. A marten may travel ten or more miles in a single hunting foray. He is a restless hunter and is extremely alert as he moves about. If on the forest floor, he will dart about gazing into holes and under bushes, keeping one eye on the trees overhead. If he spots something aloft he is up the tree in a flash and it is soon over. Martens variously squeal, squeak, growl, snarl, scream, whine, and chuckle, depending on their age and mood. The chuckling sound is apparently reserved for females at mating time. A chuckling female marten appears to be just about irresistible.

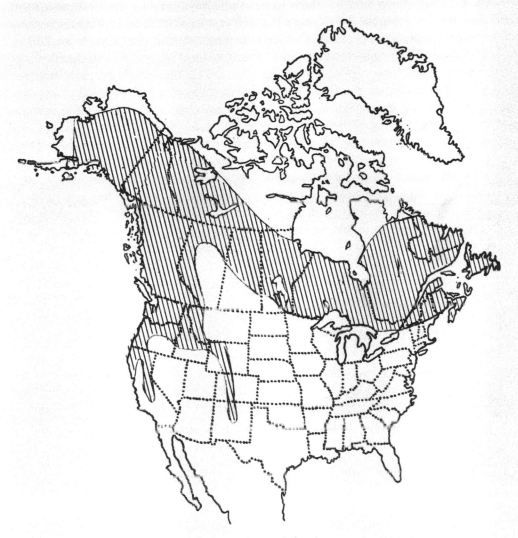

Marten (diagonal lines).

Reproduction

Martens have a very brief mating period. Early in July the male runs about, rubbing his rather powerful scent glands against tree trunks, fallen logs, and rocks. The female picks up the scent and begins her chuckling. They have about fifteen days in which to meet and consummate their romance, and then it is over for the year. There is a delayed implantation in the female, and the young aren't born until the following year, after a period of from 220 to 265 days. The young are generally born from mid-March to mid-April.

When the time to bear her young approaches, the female prepares a grass- and moss-lined nest in a hollow tree, occasionally in a burrow, and rarely in a cave or rocky niche. She has remained solitary since parting from her mate the summer before.

The young are covered with a pale-yellow fuzz at birth and weigh from half an ounce to an ounce. They are one to five in number (three or four is average) and are blind and helpless. They nurse for at least six weeks, and their eyes do not open until after the first thirty-eight days. They remain with their mother for about three months, in which time they must learn everything a marten needs to know to survive. By early July they are on their own. Captive specimens have lived as long as seventeen years, but that seems to be an extreme figure.

Observation

Martens are not easy to spot. A checkmark next to their name on the list at the end of this book will be the result of a great deal of patience and not just a little luck.

You will have to move into deep evergreen forests at an altitude of over four thousand feet at least, well away from any human habitation, if you hope to see your marten in the wild. Set yourself up in a well-concealed observation post in the early afternoon and stay put, *and quiet,* until dusk. You may be lucky. The odds of stumbling across one when you are moving about are very slim indeed. If you are sitting and waiting and there are birds around, listen to

Marten tracks.

them. If a marten comes prowling around they will put up quite an uproar. They will scold him from a safe distance, however.

Many western parks have a marten population. The following is a *partial* list of where some may be found.

Banff National Park	Southwestern Alberta
Cape Breton Highlands* National Park	Northern Nova Scotia (Cape Breton Island)
Glacier National Park	Northwestern Montana
Jasper National Park	Western Alberta
Monte Vista Wildlife Refuge	South-central Colorado
Mount McKinley National Park	South-central Alaska
Prince Albert National Park	Central Saskatchewan
Red Rock Lakes National Wildlife Refuge	Southwestern Montana
Waterton Lakes National Park	Southwestern Alberta
Yellowstone National Park	Northwestern Wyoming
Yoho National Park	Southeastern British Columbia

* Possibly the best marten-observing area in the East. The 167-mile drive along the Cabot Trail is a glorious adventure, with eagles overhead and groups of unconcerned deer by the sides of the road. You will have to park your car and do a lot of hiking, though, if you want to see your marten. He will not come down to look for you. (Also look to the wilderness areas on the Gaspé Peninsula.)

19

Vanishing Furbearer: The Fisher

Names and Range

There is a rare animal in the United States and Canada variously known as fisher, pekan, black fox, fisher-marten, Pennant's cat, and black cat. He is not related to either the cats or the foxes but is pure weasel, in fact nothing more than a large marten. No one knows for sure just why he is called fisher, because, if anything, fish plays a smaller role in his diet than in those of the other weasels.

The original range of the fisher probably went as far south as South Carolina, but that was long ago. Trapped for his extremely valuable fur, his range has been reduced until it now includes only parts of each Canadian province, the northern woodlands of the United States including a few in New England and New York, a few just east of the Great Lakes, and some in Oregon, Washington, Idaho, Montana, California, and southern Alaska. Nowhere is he common.

Appearance and Distinguishing Characteristics

The fisher looks like a large marten or a small, stumpy fox. He is short-legged, has round ears and a bushy tail. He may be as much as thirty-six to forty inches long (about a foot of that is tail) and can weigh up to twenty pounds, although eight to twelve is average. The male may be twice the size of his mate. Colors run from grayish or dark-brown to almost black. The feet and the tail tip are always black or nearly so. There is an overall distribution of white-tipped guard hairs that impart a characteristic frosty look. These hairs may be dense on head and shoulders, giving an almost gray cast. The

A large adult fisher overlooking Ontario's Wanapitei River.

underfur is extremely silky, and the guard hairs long and glossy. The pelt of the female, although much smaller, is far more valuable than that of the male. This is unusual among our furbearers.

As we shall see, the fisher is an extremely fast and agile creature. Glimpses of him will be rare and fleeting at best. Under the conditions in which he may be spotted for a second or two, the fisher will be hard to distinguish from a marten or even a mink. There will be little opportunity to study the animal as he moves about in one of the few dense forests where he may still be found.

Habits

In all of the United States and Canada only between eight and nine thousand fishers are trapped each year. Compare this to the fact that close to two hundred thousand mink were taken in Louisiana alone in one recent year, and you can see where the fisher now stands. He is *rare*.

The fisher has a fondness for dense spruce forests, and if they occur between 3,500 and 7,500 feet above sea level, he likes them even better. He will also be found in the lowlands, however, and often near water—as long as there is dense forest land for him to hunt and live in. He is arboreal *and* terrestrial, and whether he is more one thing than another is not clearly demonstrable. It may depend on local variations or individual peculiarities. He is, on land or aloft, extremely agile and very, very fast. A marten can run rings around even a fast squirrel, and a fisher can do the same to a marten. When hunting he is little more than a blur as his sinuous body darts in and out of shadows and light patches. He is capable of prodigious leaps.

The fisher is a strong swimmer but does not take to water as readily as some of his weasel kin. He is nocturnal by nature but does occasionally hunt by day, particularly during the midwinter months. He is not a hibernator but will lay up for several days if a storm is harassing his forest home. He establishes a large private range that can be ten to twenty miles in diameter. It may take him a full week to make a circuit of his territory, and he always does it alone. The fisher is a solitary fellow.

The adult fisher has a peculiarity of behavior that is often reported. If he is coming down a tree (head-first, as is his nature) and sees an intruder, he pounds his forepaws against the tree trunk while hanging on to the bark with his hind feet only. Whether this is to warn young secreted within a hollow in the tree (and therefore the work of a female only) or is some kind of a woodland challenge is not clear.

If a fisher is on the ground when encountered, he puts up quite a show. There is the arched back, the lashing tail, the bared fangs, and the explosive screams and hisses. He has no particular sounds that help in identification; just the usual collection of snarls and hisses. As a fighter the fisher knows no peer. Reputedly he can take a bobcat or lynx to task and is supposed to confound big dogs with his feisty nature. If pushed to the limit, the fisher can demonstrate his kinship with the skunks by releasing a disagreeable musk.

Courtesy Province of Ontario, Department of Lands & Forests

A coiled spring: a fisher on the alert.

The diet of the fisher is rather what one would expect: porcupines, other weasels, rabbits, hares, marmots, beavers, wood rats, birds, mice, raccoons, an occasional fish that did not require real fishing (a spawned-out salmon, for example), and anything he can steal from traps in the way of bait or trapped animals. There are some claims that a fisher can kill a deer. That is a tall order for an animal that will generally weigh under twenty pounds, usually under fifteen.

What the fisher doesn't eat he buries for later use. He will dine on carrion, some he has planted himself or some he comes upon in the course of his travels. He eats nuts and berries but is essentially a meat-eater.

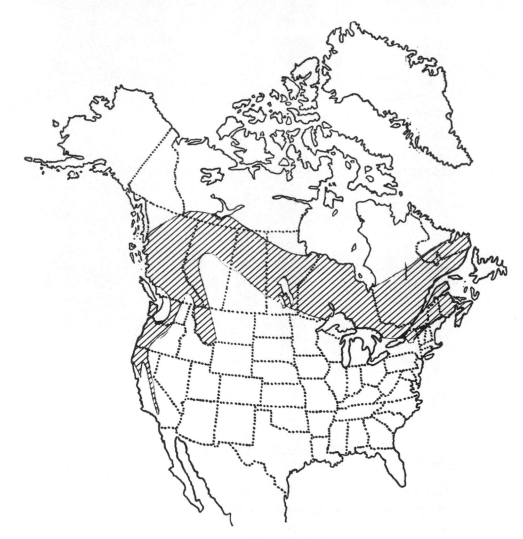

Fisher (diagonal lines).

A diet staple of some significance is the porcupine. The fisher deftly flips such prickly prey over and has a go at their soft, unprotected underbelly. It requires speed and accuracy, but this is well within the fisher's bag of tricks. He is valuable to forestry interests because of the number of porcupines he takes each year.

Reproduction

The fisher breeds first at about two years. A few days after a female delivers her young (usually in April), she leaves them alone and seeks out a mate. She churrs and chuckles until he is enchanted enough to participate, and then she hastens back to her litter. *It takes her more than fifty weeks to produce her cubs!*

Actually, there is a delayed implanting within the female, and it is many months after breeding before the real gestation starts. Her cubs appear just about a year after breeding.

The cubs (one to five, but usually three) are born in a grass- and moss-lined den in a hollow tree, in a fallen log, or in a rocky shelter. They are blind

Fisher track.

and hairless and must nurse for seven weeks before accepting solid food brought to them by the mother. At three months they start hunting with their mother, and at six months they are on their own. Their education is brief but apparently effective.

Observation

Without a great deal of luck, the fisher will be one of the last names you can check off on your lifetime observation list. They are hard to find; they are rare; they live in deep forests; they are largely nocturnal; they are shy and secretive, and they are very, very fast. Everything is against the observer.

With a lot of patience, with good eyesight and a great deal of determination, you may see your fisher in one of the following places. This is only a partial list:*

Algonquin Provincial Park	Ontario
Banff National Park	Alberta
California:	Trinity, Tuolumne and Tulare counties
Gaspé Peninsula:	Interior wilderness areas
Jasper National Park	Alberta
Wood Buffalo National Park	Alberta
Yellowstone National Park	Wyoming

There are, of course, many hundreds of wilderness areas where great spruce and other evergreens grow. Here, hidden in small and secret places, the fisher lives his solitary life. He is a wood nymph and a demon, a luxurious, fearsome predator whose fondest desire is to never be seen by man. Perhaps that is what makes him such an intriguing project for the nature observer. Try at dusk, try in deep woods, try alone in a very quiet, patient mood, and you might have success. Keep your eyes on fallen logs and low-hanging branches over trails used by small mammals.

* They are also beginning to appear in respectable numbers in the Adirondacks.

20

Our Three Weasels

Names and Range

Very closely related to the mink, the subject of our next chapter, are our three kinds of weasels: the least or mouse weasel, the ermine or short-tailed weasel, and the long-tailed weasel. They are also called stoats, ferrets, and the French *belette.*

The long-tailed weasel can be found in all of the original forty-eight states, most of Mexico, and all Canadian provinces adjacent to the United States. The short-tailed weasel is to be seen throughout all of Canada and Alaska, even beyond the Arctic Circle. He is found in most of the northern half of the United States. The least weasel ranges from northwestern Alaska to North Carolina. He is not found in the Northeast or the Southwest.

Appearance and Distinguishing Characteristics

Weasels in general are slender, long-bodied, short-legged little bundles of fury. They have very small heads, barely thicker than their necks, with low, rounded ears. They have small dark eyes and a luxurious pelt. The undercoat is extremely soft, with numerous guard hairs that are long, hard, and glistening. The chart on page 170 presents the major distinguishing characteristics.

Habits

In habits the three weasels are quite similar. They are hyperactive, hyperaggressive little demons without, it would seem, any fear mechanisms. The males are larger, but the sexes are colored alike, and act alike. They

	LONG-TAILED WEASEL	SHORT-TAILED WEASEL	LEAST WEASEL
Overall Length	13–18 inches	8–13 inches	7–8 inches
Tail Length	4–6 inches	2¼–4 inches	1–1½ inches
Weight	6–9 ounces	2–4 ounces	1–2 ounces
Summer Color	Various shades of brown above to yellowish white on underparts: BROWN FEET. No whitish line down inside of hind legs.	Various shades of brown above to white underparts and WHITE FEET. White line down inside of hind legs connecting white underparts with white toes.	Various shades of brown above and white below. WHITE FEET.
Winter Color	All white* except tip of tail, which is distinctly black (ermine phase).	All white* except tip of tail, which is distinctly black (ermine phase).	All white* with NO black tail tip; occasionally some black hairs but no distinct black tip.
Notes:		Largest specimens are found in the East and North, smallest in West.	This is the world's smallest living carnivorous mammal.

* The weasels in the southern parts of their range do not turn white in the winter.

characteristically lope along with their backs arched and their tails streaming out behind, straight and slightly elevated. They seldom walk, and when really in a hurry take little leaps. They swim well but are not basically water animals. They can all climb well, but the long-tailed weasel spends less time aloft than the short-tailed species. The least weasel spends most of his time on the ground.

They are speedy, agile little creatures, all with a great deal of suspicion and curiosity. They are often described as "bloodthirsty" because of the frequency and relentlessness of their hunting forays, but that really isn't a fair word. They are just always hungry and often kill much more than they can eat. They store the surplus but are so active that they continue to kill, seldom eating all they have stored before it is far too high. They will eat some carrion but only that which they themselves have killed and stored.

They are capable of putting up a perfectly horrendous fight when attacked

Photo by Wilford L. Miller

Photo by Wilford L. Miller   *Photo by Wilford L. Miller*

Three views of the long-tailed weasel: summer, transitional (mid-October), and winter.

Long-tailed weasel (horizontal lines). Short-tailed weasel (vertical lines). Least weasel (dotted area).

and are not afraid to take on anything from mouse to man. They bite like a sewing machine and discharge a really foul musk when attacked. It is at least as bad as that of the skunk, but they do not have their cousin's ability to spray. The musk is (perhaps) meant to mark ranges and to attract mates, it is not a weapon, and they do not use it on each other even in really bad brawls. Despite their speed, smell, and prodigious strength, they are preyed upon. Among their enemies are eagles, owls, hawks, mink, marten, fisher, bobcats, and lynx.

Their sense of smell is very well developed, and they hunt by scent. Once homed in on a hot trail, they move like lightning until the moment of truth when a single bite at the base of the skull brings their victim to earth. The weasel hangs on until the struggling stops. In the case of larger mammals, the weasel will ride it like a bucking bronco, hanging on with teeth and claws.

They are solitary little animals. If hungry they will hunt at any time of the day or night. They all establish home ranges which vary in size from a few hundred yards to many miles, depending on the available food supply. The least weasel prefers grassy or brushy areas and open woodlands. The others can be found in almost any environment within their range up to ten thousand feet, except deserts away from water. Farmlands, suburbs, prairies, woodlands, swamps, all of these areas know the long-tailed and many the short-tailed weasel.

The weasels are strictly meat-eaters. Small rodents constitute the diet staple, with birds, eggs, reptiles, amphibians, insects, and worms all having a part. The least weasel lives almost exclusively on mice. Unhappily, the larger weasels also raid henhouses, and a single animal can just about wipe out a full house in a single evening. Such raids are costly, certainly, but the weasel is more often the farmer's very good friend, being the highly effective, animated mouse trap that he is. His mousing ability will put any cat to shame.

The noises made by the weasels are seemingly endless; they bark, shrill, shriek, hiss, snarl, and make peculiar *took-took-took* and *choo-choo-choo* sounds. Their voices, except when they are violently, explosively angry, have little carrying power. They are so high-strung that they can die of excitement, at least in captivity. Their metabolism rate is very high.

Reproduction

There appears to be some variation in the breeding habits of these interesting little animals, which may be accounted for by differences in range, subspecies, or geographical races. In general, however, they all make neat little nests lined with feathers, mouse and rabbit fur, and other debris from their past conquests. These dens may be found in stumps, logs, under roots, underground in a rabbit burrow, in rock piles, old foundations, under barns, in mouse burrows, in piles of rotting vegetation, or almost any other sheltered, relatively undisturbed area.

The least weasel appears to breed in almost any month, the two larger cousins in July or August. In the cases of the long- and short-tailed weasels, gestation is very, very long. It is suggested that it runs from 205 to nearly 340 days; the average is given as 279. Actually, there is a long delay in fetal development after the first fourteen days, and most of it occurs in the last four weeks before birth. The young are generally born in April or May. Litter size varies considerably: least—three to ten; long-tailed—four to nine; short-tailed—four to thirteen.

The young are very small in size, those of the long-tailed, the largest weasel, weighing one ninth of an ounce or less. By the end of the third week the summer fur grows in on the downy little spots of life, and they start on some solid food. The eyes open at about five weeks, and weaning is completed at about the same time. At seven or eight weeks they are hunting and nearly ready to go on their own. Females born in the spring mate the same fall. Males may wait until the following year. Captive specimens have lived as long as four and five years, quite a long time for an animal that lives so very fast.

Observation

The weasels, particularly the long-tailed, are so widespread and live in such a variety of environments that it is easier to say where not to look than to list the likely places to start your search. Actually, weasels are hard to find, in the flesh at least, because they are so small and active. Any place where

Weasel tracks.

rodents abound and any place not too far from a water supply is a likely place to set up your looking post and take out your field glasses. The very early morning hours and dusk will be the most rewarding times of day unless you have exceptional night vision.

The brushy areas lining farmlands are likely spots, and areas around corn cribs, where mice are plentiful, are often productive. Also look along fences grown up with weeds.

21

Symbol of Luxury: The Mink

Names and Range

Our minks range from southern Alaska across all Canadian provinces to the far North. All of the original forty-eight states have some at least, although few, if any, occur in arid areas of the Southwest. Throughout the United States he is known as mink (although sometimes confused with the true weasels, otters, martens, fishers, and even the ferret); in French-speaking regions of Canada he is known as *vison*.

Appearance and Distinguishing Characteristics

The average wild mink measures from twenty to twenty-six inches in length (seven to nine inches of that is tail) and weighs from one and one-half to three pounds. The basic color is a dark, rich, even chocolaty brown to almost black, often with a white chin or chest patch and occasional scattered white spots on the underparts. The tail is somewhat bushy and the coat is lustrous, durable, and truly one of the most beautiful in the world. It is at its best in November, when the long, dark guard hairs glisten like metal.

On rare occasions exotic colors (albino, etc.) occur in the wild, but the popular pastels, whites, lavenders, silver-blues, etc. are farm-raised pelts achieved through generations of cross-breeding and mutations. Minks have been bred in captivity since 1866, and the million that are still trapped wild annually are supplemented by five million domestic pelts harvested each year. These six million pelts barely meet the demand, so popular has this fur become.

In general the mink looks like the weasel he is. He has small, rounded ears and beady eyes. His neck is not as long as that of the true weasel, but it is still sinuous and the head is quite small. The legs are stumpy and the claws sharp.

Habits

The mink is a solitary, fiercely aggressive, short-tempered little creature, semiaquatic by nature. He hunts by day or night and tracks his prey by scent.

This lustrous furbearer is seldom found far from water, and he swims extremely well. He likes back-country wilderness areas and woodland brooks but will be found on ocean beaches, within city limits, and in brackish marshes. He likes reeds and rushes along small water courses but will range far when prey is in short supply. In the winter he can be observed crossing open ice, since his coat does not change color.

Photo by Wilford L. Miller

Who says mink don't climb trees?

Neither ice, snow, wet, nor low temperatures interfere with a mink's endless preoccupation with hunting.

The mink is territorial by nature, but the males often wander far afield. When males meet, a perfectly terrible fight is likely to ensue, particularly at breeding time. These fights often result in one or more dead minks.

Although they are extremely fierce fighters, minks are preyed upon by bobcats, lynx, hawks, owls, and larger members of the weasel clan. When angry, minks variously screech, hiss, bark, and snarl. When contented they purr and churr. Like all weasels they have powerful scent glands but do not have the skunks' ballistic talents. They are intermink communication devices and not primarily weapons.

Minks hunt muskrats, birds, mice, snakes, frogs, fish, insects, rabbits, clams, mussels, and a variety of other small prey. They are wanton killers and take everything in sight. They store what they don't eat but usually keep right on killing, leaving their larder to rot or to be taken by another animal. A mink in the henhouse can spell great financial loss to the poultryman.

Reproduction

The polygamous mink mates between January and March, giving up his solitary ways for the event. A den is prepared in almost any sheltered area near water. A muskrat hole in a stream bank may be taken over, an area under a root system, a hollow log or tree stump—any such area will do.

Mink (diagonal lines).

Frequently the nest will be neat and grass-lined, but not all lady minks are good housekeepers, and animal debris may litter the inner chamber.

The gestation period varies from 39 to 76 days and the young, usually four to eight in number, are very small, about one fifth of an ounce each. At birth they are covered with white down and are blind. The eyes open in about five weeks and the weaning process is completed in eight or nine. Minks are full grown at five months. Captive specimens have lived ten years, but it is a rare mink that will achieve a decade in the wild.

Observation

Minks are found near water: ocean front, broad river, lake, pond, marsh, swamp, stream, lowland and mountainside. They like cover near their water and will seek out reedy or bushy stream banks. They like smaller streams where possible and love windfalls best of all. Find a tree or mass of vegetation cluttering up a stream, and you have found perfect mink country.

Minks generally shun open spaces. Nevertheless, give a mink reason enough and he will be more than happy to act out of the ordinary in return for a meal. I have watched a mink cross over two hundred feet of open, barren rock at Rockport, Massachusetts, to steal some frozen squid I was using as

Mink tracks.

bait. This in broad daylight, and the bait not a dozen feet from where I sat fishing.

If we were to list the national parks and wildlife refuges where mink are found we would list nearly every one in the United States and Canada. You need not travel far to find your mink unless you live in desert country.

Look to your local watercourses, the smaller and more sheltered, the better. Look for weedy banks, look for streams with a lot of vegetable debris where little isolated pools are formed, fed in between by trickles. Look to areas where muskrats, other small rodents, and water birds may be hunted. Look day or night, be very patient, and, unless an area is hunted out, you will see your mink. As valuable as he is, he is not in the least rare in many, many parts of his range. He is one of our most valuable furbearers and one of our most common weasels. It is a wonderful feeling to check his name off your lifetime checklist. Doing so will be the result of quiet waiting. Remember, he is first and foremost a predator and has a very high rate of metabolism. He is always looking for prey. Anticipate his needs and you will see him at his full-time occupation—hunting.

22

The Rare One: The Black-footed Ferret

THE BLACK-FOOTED FERRET is one of the rarest mammals in the Western Hemisphere and, indeed, probably in the world. Known to science only since 1851, he may soon be gone forever. In the little over a century since white man first learned of his existence he has managed to bring him to the very edge of extinction. His loss, like that of any animal species, will be a sad one. Although reports are few, the ferret can still be said to live over the broad expanse of the Plains states east of the Rocky Mountains. However, nowhere within this vast area is he common.

Appearance and Distinguishing Characteristics

This large and elusive weasel can be as much as two feet long, including five or six inches of tail. Slender as he is, he will seldom weigh much more than a pound and a half. He is a pale yellowish-brown to a buffy tone and has a black mask over his eyes, a black-tipped tail (the black tip accounting for one third of tail), and, of course, distinctive black feet. His legs are short, his neck very long and slender, and his ears rounded. His cheeks and the sides of his upper lip are white or almost so. A true weasel in habit and appearance, there is yet something different about him, a touch of elegance and mystery. Maybe it is the knowledge that he is so rare that makes him so attractive.

Habits

From all indications, the black-footed ferret was not common in historical times. As a result not too much is known about him. He apparently lives almost exclusively on prairie dogs and is seldom if ever found far from their

towns. He may dine on other small mammals as well, but too little is known to warrant a definitive statement.

Rare though he may be, and well worth any efforts to preserve, the ferret is still a weasel and as such is bold and aggressive. He is largely nocturnal from most reports but has been seen hunting during the daylight hours. He is inquisitive and restless and will fight viciously if caught. He hisses and spits rather like a cat. Although a prairie animal, he has been found at altitudes up to 10,500 feet in the Rocky Mountains. Wandering over a large area in his endless quest for food, he is characteristically seen sitting up on his haunches and craning his neck near a prairie dog town. Occasionally he is spotted sticking his head up out of a prairie dog's hole.

Like all weasels he has powerful scent glands but uses them for attracting mates and not as weapons. Larger predators that prey on the prairie dog may kill some ferrets as well, but they surely have a tough fight on their hands when they take on the assignment.

Reproduction

Relatively little is known of the breeding habits of this rare weasel. The young are apparently born in June or July, and almost certainly the event occurs in a preempted prairie dog burrow. Three to six are reported as average litter size.

The eyes of the young are reportedly open at three weeks, and in true weasel fashion they probably mature rapidly and get off on their own by ten or twelve weeks. This animal is solitary and probably tends to be rather disagreeable.

Observation

The first step in looking for a black-footed ferret is the purchase of a good pair of binoculars. The second is some suntan lotion because you are going to spend a long time sitting out in the open just waiting.

In seeking the ferret, look first for a prairie dog town. Here and perhaps here alone will you have an opportunity to see your ferret for a brief moment or two and join the ranks of the lucky few. In Wichita Mountains Wildlife Refuge in southwestern Oklahoma, in many areas in the South Dakota and Wyoming part of the Plains, particularly near Devils Tower National Monument in eastern Wyoming, you may have your chance.

Specifically, locate and become familiar with your prairie dog town. Once you are familiar with it, go there *before* sunup, the earlier the better, and pick a good vantage point. Take along something comfortable to sit on. As the sun comes up, slowly and systematically scan the whole town. Watch for an animal longer and more slender than the prairie dog moving from burrow to burrow. If you see a number of animals sitting upright on their haunches, observe them one by one, slowly and carefully. One of them may be a ferret but he can be easy to pass over since his position and stance from a distance resemble those of his prey.

If you do see a ferret, and are sure that you do, report it to a local museum. They will be interested to know of your sighting. If you fail to spot a ferret during the early morning hours, try at dusk. The chances are you will have to make many, many trips before you spot the ferret. The possibilities of your success are, though, very thin indeed, and the name "black-footed ferret" will almost surely be the last one you tick off on your lifetime checklist.

Black-footed ferret tracks.

23

Evil Spirit of the North: The Wolverine

Names and Range

From the Arctic Circle to the northernmost corners of our northwestern states, the wolverine, glutton, glouton, carcajou, Indian devil, or skunk-bear has earned a uniformly evil reputation. He is found in Alaska, the Northwest and Yukon Territories, throughout British Columbia, and rarely in northern Washington and in a few places in California. He extends all across northern Canada to the Atlantic Ocean but has not been seen in the northeastern part of the United States within the memory of living man.

Appearance and Distinguishing Characteristics

He is a weasel but barely looks the part. He resembles more a cross between a skunk and a bear. He smells like the former. The largest of the land weasels, he may measure up to forty-one or more inches in length, but three feet is closer to average. He has a seven-to-nine-inch tail and stands as much as fourteen inches at the shoulder. He generally weighs between twenty and thirty-five pounds, but fifty-pounders are supposedly on record.

The wolverine does in fact look like a small bear with a bushy tail. He is dark-brown to black in color, with a paler head and two yellow stripes that start on each shoulder and meet on the rump. He is squat, shaggy, heavy-bodied, and has big feet. His head is broad, his jaws are extremely powerful, and his ears rather small and rounded. His back is arched and his claws are long and curved. He has none of the sinuous grace and ease of the other weasels about him. He is the ugly duckling of the weasel tribe.

Habits

If the other weasels ever grew to be as big as a wolverine, they would probably act in much the same way he does—terribly. Actually, of course, there is nothing at all terrible about the wolverine, and he has done nothing more than adapt most successfully to his rugged environment. He is, however, notoriously destructive to man's property and enterprises. He has a perfectly astounding appetite.

The home ranges of the wolverine are the tundra, forests, and mountains of the Far North. He is a solitary hunter who can, despite his size and ungainly appearance, climb very well. He has often been reported as dropping on prey from overhanging branches.

Courtesy U.S. Department of Interior, Fish & Wildlife Service

A freshly live-caught adult wolverine in the vicinity of Auke Bay near Juneau, Alaska.

Hunting all hours in all seasons, the wolverine takes birds, any mammals he can overpower, amphibians, fish, berries, and anything he can steal from man. He loves carrion. He reputedly takes sick and old caribou (and young), mountain sheep and goats, deer bogged down in deep snow, and, it is reported in several places, moose. Since the moose is up to six times as tall at the shoulder and weighs as much as thirty-five times as many pounds, it is difficult at best to see how this is accomplished. Even with qualifications about the very large wolverine and very small moose it is hard to understand.

It has been observed that a hungry wolverine can drive other predators from their prey. Even wolves, bears, and mountain lions are supposed to retreat before his fury. His powerful jaws and evil musk may both play a role in such displays. He is not a fast animal but a terribly dogged one. He wears other animals down through tireless persistence.

The wolverine is best known, perhaps, for the havoc he plays with human residents of the Far North. He follows trappers, stealing their bait, destroying trapped animals, and burying their traps. When they are away from their cabins he breaks in and wrecks everything in sight. (How much of this is just plain "playfulness"?) What he cannot eat or break he fouls with his musk. He tears windows and doors apart, smashes furniture, fouls bedding, eats snow-shoes, and can destroy a food larder intended to see the cabin owner through the winter in a matter of minutes. Little wonder he is so beloved! His reputation for being an evil spirit comes in part from the fact that he is all but impossible to trap. A few are caught each year, however, and their fur is valued as trimming for foul-weather gear. It doesn't freeze up with moisture.

Reproduction

Wolverines apparently breed in February and March and give birth from May to July after a reported but unsubstantiated sixty-day gestation period. The one to five woolly babies are born in a nest of leaves under a rock pile or in almost any sheltered cranny or hollow log. They stay with their mother until the fall and go their own ways when about two thirds grown. They nurse for eight or nine weeks. Captive specimens have lived for as long as thirteen years.

Observation

The best and perhaps the only reliable place to look for the wolverine in the original forty-eight states is in California. A small number still live along

Wolverine (diagonal lines).

the timberline on both sides of the crest of the Sierra Nevadas. Search from
Lake Tahoe south to the Kern Gap, between five to thirteen thousand feet up.
Look to Mount Lyell in Tuolumne County. A few may still be found from
time to time in northern Washington. California is a more likely hunting
ground, though.

In Alaska many wolverines still live in the Aleutian Islands National Wildlife Refuge, the twelve-hundred-mile belt of islands from Umnak just off the tip of the Alaska Peninsula to Attu in the West. They may also be found in the 3,214 square miles of the Kenai National Moose Range on southern Alaska's Kenai Peninsula and in the 3,030 square miles of Mount McKinley National Park in south-central Alaska.

In Canada, the wolverine is found across the North, with specific recent sightings in British Columbia's Kootenay National Park, and Alberta's Banff, Jasper, Waterton Lakes, and Wood Buffalo National Parks. Terra Nova National Park in northern Newfoundland has some as well.

It is difficult to tell how one should go about looking for a wolverine. They are constant and restless travelers, always hunting, always looking for carrion. They inhabit rocky, forested, and tundra areas and are alert and resourceful. It is really a matter of luck, unless you want to spend a great deal of time in one wilderness area, becoming thoroughly familiar with the local ecological scheme and the inhabitants that make it work. Don't bother asking

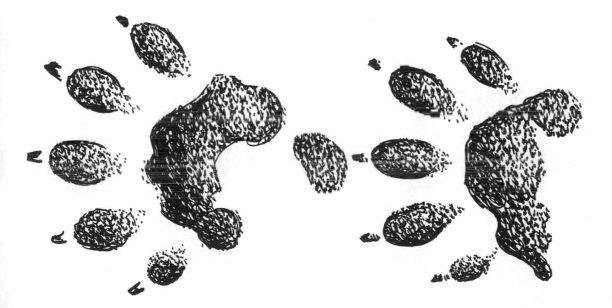

Wolverine tracks.

local trappers. If they could tell you where to find a wolverine, they would have shot it long ago.

In most parts of his range the wolverine has become rare to absent. Only in far northern Canada and in Alaska's many and extensive wildernesses is he still to be found. Few people have seen them in the wild. The pleasure and excitement of that adventure is reserved for the most hardy and persistent.

24

Freshwater Clown: The River Otter

IF CERTAIN private interests had their way, we would soon lose one of the most engaging of North American mammals and the most delightful member of the weasel clan. The river otter, long hunted for his beautiful and durable fur, is now protected in many areas and may well survive predatory man, albeit in reduced numbers. (But only if the pollution of our inland waterways is brought to a stop almost immediately!) He is one animal we simply can't afford to lose.

Names and Range

The river otter ranges through all Canadian provinces far to the north, throughout most of Alaska except the extreme northern coast, and is found in some part at least of each of the original forty-eight states. He is to be found in areas with suitable habitats where man has not made otter life impossible with his traps and vile pollutions.

The river otter is also known as the common otter, land otter, and Canada otter.

Appearance and Distinguishing Characteristics

In one deep breath, the river otter is a large, elongated, streamlined, cylindrical aquatic weasel with a stout neck, small eyes and ears, a broad, flattened head, a conspicuous nose pad, prominent whiskers, and a perfectly delightful way of life and attitude toward it. If that doesn't paint enough of a picture, he has short legs, webbed feet fore and aft, a long, heavy tail flattened on the bottom and tapering from a thick base toward the pointed (almost)

The wonderful, sleek bundle of fun and fury, the river otter—good-natured dynamite.

tip. (That tail can be as much as eighteen inches long.) The dense oily underfur of the river otter is set off by glossy guard hairs, and together the two "furs" constitute one of the most luxurious and lasting of pelts. The color goes from dark-brown to nearly black above with pale-brown to gray underparts. The animal looks particularly dark when wet. The muzzle and throat are silvery. Rare albinos have been recorded.

Males are larger than females, and lengths run from thirty-five to fifty-five inches overall. Weights recorded are generally from ten to thirty pounds. Extreme weights of fifty pounds have been noted. The river otter's eyes are located near the top of his head to facilitate his seeing while cruising along almost totally submerged.

Habits

The river otter is beautifully adapted to life in the water. His fur is ideal for a life spent wet and dripping, his ears and nose seal tight when he dives, and his body shape could well be the envy of marine engineers. He can swim a

River otter (diagonal lines).

good quarter mile underwater and can remain submerged for three to four minutes. On the surface he can easily maintain a speed of six miles an hour.

Characteristically, the otter swims in one of three ways: he either cruises along with his head partially exposed, undulates like a dolphin, or swims underwater, coming up for air five or six times to the mile. He constantly frolics in the water and will play with a hanging branch or a clam shell for hours. He invented water polo and loves rapids.

Otters often travel in a family group, and the range may cover fifty to a hundred miles of shoreline. They are largely nocturnal but will be seen abroad during the day when not disturbed. They are active, very active indeed, all year long. They are graceful, powerful animals and a joy to behold.

The hearing and eyesight of the otter are nothing to brag about, but his sense of smell is extremely keen. He hunts fishes, crayfish, frogs, salamanders, snails, clams, snakes, turtles, birds, some small mammals, the larvae of aquatic insects, and earthworms. His food demands are large and constant, and his rate of digestion is very rapid.

The otter variously chirps, chuckles, grunts, growls, snarls, whistles, screams, caterwauls, and exhales his breath in explosive bursts. He is a fierce fighter when he has to be and has a particularly powerful bite. He has scent glands that don't begin to challenge those of the other weasels, and he uses them to mark the boundary of his family's range. When captured young he makes a perfectly delightful pet.

In the water the river otter paddles primarily with his hind feet and sculls with his tail. He has a distinguishing loping gait on land.

He is as playful on land as he is in the water. He romps and wrestles, plays tag and hide-and-seek, and is always up to some trick when not seriously looking for something to eat. He is most famous, of course, for his slides, and he does indeed have an absolute passion for steep banks. In the summer a group will wet a mud bank down with their soaking fur and slide again and again until the slope is slick enough to send them plunging into the water at great speeds. They do the same thing on icy banks and slopes. When traveling overland on snow and ice, an otter builds up speed, folds his legs up out of the way, and slides on his belly. He can hit fifteen to eighteen miles an hour overland in this fashion.

Reproduction

The breeding habits of river otters vary somewhat from place to place, but they follow one general pattern. They breed in the winter or early spring (December to April) and deliver their one to five (usually two to four) young after ten to thirteen months of delayed development and true gestation—from January to May. They remate immediately after the young are born.

The young are born in a secluded den usually taken over from some other animal. A burrow under a river bank is a favorite spot, but excavations under a root system, a spot under a rocky ledge, and other similar hideaways are used. In the summer these dens will have openings in the air. In the winter openings will be underwater. Otters have lived nineteen years in captivity.

The half-pound kits are fuzzy and toothless, and their eyes remain closed for about thirty-five days. They remain in their den for ten to twelve weeks before venturing out with their mother and aren't weaned until four months old.

Strangely, the kits cannot swim and even show a reluctance to enter the water. Eventually their mother gets them in and supports their bodies while they learn to do that which one day they will do better than almost any other mammal in the world. Only the true marine mammals exceed their aquatic skill.

Observation

There are many animals on this continent rarer and more dramatic than the river otter, but none will give you greater joy in the observing of natural ways. If you are lucky enough to spot some at play, be prepared to spend

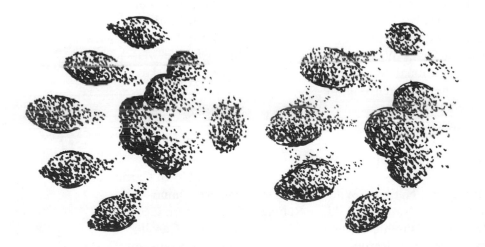

River otter tracks.

hours watching their antics. Certainly, they will be the ones to break off the relationship. You will probably regret not being able to take them home with you.

Look first for a body of water, preferably a stream of fair width. A stream that has high, sheltered banks, small pools, and some fast-flowing water between will be ideal. Look for regular "pulling-out" places and rolling spots where otters leave their distinctive marks. Look, of course, for slides and keep your fingers crossed that the playground is in use. You will occasionally find cross-country paths used by otters moving between separate bodies of water. Do not overlook marshy areas, for these, too, are favorite haunts.

There are many hundreds of areas in the United States and Canada where river otters may be observed. The following list provides only a brief indication of the opportunities.

Arcadia Wildlife Sanctuary	Central-western Massachusetts
Cape Breton Highlands National Park	Northern Nova Scotia
Cape Romain National Wildlife Refuge	Coastal South Carolina
Clarence Rhode National Wildlife Range	Western Alaska
Delta Wildlife Refuge	Southern Louisiana
Everglades National Park	Southern Florida
Fundy National Park	Southern New Brunswick
Ipswich River Wildlife Sanctuary	Northeastern Massachusetts
Kenai National Moose Range	Southern Alaska
Lacassine National Wildlife Refuge	Coastal Louisiana
Loxahatchee National Wildlife Refuge	Southeastern Florida
Mattamuskeet National Wildlife Refuge	Eastern North Carolina
Moosehorn National Wildlife Refuge	Eastern Maine
Okefenokee National Wildlife Refuge	Southeastern Georgia
Pea Island Wildlife Refuge	Off North Carolina
Rainey Wildlife Refuge	Southern Louisiana
Red Rock Lakes National Wildlife Refuge	Southwestern Montana

Sabine National Wildlife Refuge	Southern Louisiana
St. Marks National Wildlife Refuge	Northern Florida
Santee Wildlife Refuge	South Carolina
Savannah National Wildlife Refuge	Georgia and South Carolina
Seney National Wildlife Refuge	Michigan, Upper Peninsula
Swanquarter National Wildlife Refuge	Eastern North Carolina
White River National Wildlife Refuge	Eastern Arkansas
Yellowstone National Park	Northwestern Wyoming

_____ 25

The World's Most Valuable Furbearer:
The Sea Otter

IN 1938, one of the most exciting zoological events of our century occurred off Carmel, California. A band or pod of sea otters was discovered. It had long been assumed that man had destroyed this animal—the world's most valuable furbearer—in the last century. Today, the animal is protected everywhere, and it is against the law to so much as own a piece of a pelt without a special license. It now appears that the small number left in the world will be saved. The lives of all nature lovers are enriched by this fact.

Names and Range

Sea otter, sea beaver, _kalan,_ or the Eskimo _amikuk,_ whatever he is called, he is a weasel, the most impressive of the tribe.

Today, the sea otter in our hemisphere may be found only off southern California and around southern Alaskan and Aleutian Island waters. In the Old World he is still to be found near the Kamchatka Peninsula of the northeast Soviet Union and the Kurile and Bonin Islands.

Appearance and Distinguishing Characteristics

A sea otter may be as much as sixty inches in length, although forty-five is nearer to average; he weighs anywhere from twenty-five to eighty pounds. He has a supple body, short legs, and is long and powerful, with flipperlike webbed feet. He has a flattened head, a broad snout, small ears, and a short, stout tail. His inch-long, thick, velvety coat is the finest in the world. It is more

Courtesy U.S. Department of Interior, Fish & Wildlife Service

A good close study of an adult sea otter on Amchitka Island, Alaska.

durable than any other known fur and is magnificently lustrous. In color he ranges from reddish brown to almost black. His head and neck are in gray and yellow tones, and his white-tipped hairs give him an overall frosted look. Once very plentiful, he was slaughtered for this magnificent fur by the tens and hundreds of thousands. His fur remained for centuries the mark of royalty in the Orient. The slaughter off our shores ran from 1740 to 1911, when an international halt was called to the killing in the form of a binding treaty that is still in effect.

Habits

Today there are probably no more than 25,000 to 30,000 sea otters left in our hemisphere. Most of these are found in the Aleutians, with about a thousand still to be found off southern California.

The sea otter is truly a marine-adapted mammal. He spends most of his life offshore within a mile of rocky mainland and island coasts, and even

Photo by Robert D. Jones, Jr., courtesy U.S. Department of Interior, Fish & Wildlife Service

An adult sea otter in a characteristic pose, floating on his back in the sea.

breeds and gives birth at sea, according to the best available knowledge. (He comes ashore in rough weather, and the Alaskan animals seem to come ashore more often than their Californian counterparts.) He is playful and gregarious, although males are quarrelsome and sometimes engage in fierce fights, especially around breeding time. The pods are most active during the day, although they are seen moving around on bright moonlit nights. When they sleep they seek thick kelp beds and anchor themselves in them by wrapping strands of the seaweed around their bodies while floating on their backs. They are seldom found far from a kelp bed, to whose thickness they retreat at the first sign of a killer whale, their chief and perhaps only real enemy. Sharks are believed to take some.

When not in a hurry, the sea otter swims and floats on his back, often shading his eyes from the sun with his front paws. When in a hurry, he can swim very well indeed, sculling with his tail as he goes. He can dive to an estimated three hundred feet (but seldom does) and can remain submerged for four to five minutes. He really prefers shallow water, ten to seventy or eighty feet. His vision is only fair, but his sense of smell is believed to be highly developed. He generally exhibits little fear of man, and this trait contributed to the indiscriminate slaughter by fur hunters in the past.

The sea otter eats three main meals a day, it is reported, with snacks in between. Off California he eats some abalone, but in all parts of his range seeks sea urchins, mollusks (particularly blue mussels), crabs, and fishes. He has the engaging habit of floating on his back with a small stone brought up from below on his chest. Against this anvil he smashes his shellfish prey and dines daintily on the pieces at his leisure. In a very real sense this is a rare instance of an animal using a tool.

Reproduction

Sea otters probably don't breed much before they are three years old. The single (rarely two) young are born after an assumed gestation period of eight or nine months, usually in April or May. The courtship as well as the actual mating and birth occur at sea. The pups or kits are born with a full set of teeth, completely furred, and with their eyes open. They may be as much as seventeen inches long and can weigh up to three and a half pounds.

The mother, solitary at this time, is extremely affectionate and protective of her young. She constantly cuddles and plays with her pup and nurses him while floating on her back, holding him on her chest and belly. Pups swim well, but in time of danger she takes him under her foreleg and dives. Pups are started on soft food at about six months but may not be weaned until a year or more time has passed. Since females have been observed with pups of two ages, it is assumed that some young remain with their mother for well over a year. Full growth is not achieved until the animal is four years old. It is not known how long the sea otter lives, but some suggestions have been made that eight to ten years would be the extreme.

Observation

The sea otter is most often seen in our hemisphere off Carmel, California (look in Point Lobos Reserve), and around Amchitka Island in the Aleutians. There are other small islands off southern Alaska and in the Aleutian chain where some may be seen, but they are rare and hard to find without professional help.

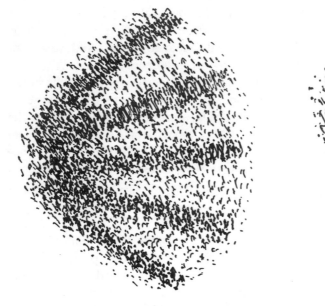

Sea otter tracks.

Good binoculars—or, better yet, a spotting scope—is an absolute necessity, and lots of patience. The reward, though, of seeing one of the most interesting animals in the world is great. This animal, don't forget, was a prime motive in the Russian exploration of our northwest coastline.

Keep your eyes on offshore kelp beds. You may think you are going blind as you try to distinguish an otter's head from a piece of floating kelp, but you will learn in time to recognize the objects even though they are a mile away and the sun is reflecting off the water. Your chances of seeing these animals are not too good, but enough time spent at it can pay off. If you choose to paddle a boat out offshore, listen for a clicking, tapping sound. That may be the sea otters cracking seashells on their belly-borne stone anvils.

When you mark the sea otter off your lifetime checklist you will have seen an animal that only a few years ago was on the very edge of extinction, an animal that inspired an era of exploration, and an animal that wears the world's most magnificent fur coat. If you see a specimen off Carmel and another in the Aleutians, you will have seen the two living subspecies in the New World.

26

The Unmolested: Our Four Skunks

Names and Range

Basically, there are four different kinds of skunks in the United States and Canada: the striped skunk, the hooded skunk, the spotted skunk, the most active and alert of the group, and the relatively scarce hog-nosed skunk. The matter of subspecies need not concern us here.

Taken as a group, they are the most common and best-known members of the weasel family. Their ranges are best broken down as follows:

Striped Skunk: Found in all of the original forty-eight states in a blanket, excepting only extreme southern Florida; all Canadian provinces except Yukon Territory; none in Alaska. One of the most common and widespread of North American mammals, they are found as far north as the southern shore of Hudson Bay and deep into Mexico.

Hooded Skunk: Far more widespread in Mexico than in the United States; found only in southwest Texas and in parts of southern Arizona and New Mexico.

Spotted Skunk: Our second most common and widespread skunk: all of Mexico and up the Pacific Coast to extreme southwest British Columbia. None on eastern seaboard except in Florida and in western North and South Carolina. Found across bottom of the United States, and, rarely, in Canada— just north of the border west of the Great Lakes and on the Pacific Coast.

Hog-nosed Skunk: Here again is a Mexican animal that has spread its range north of the border. Found in the southern half of Texas, southwestern Arizona, through most of New Mexico into southeastern Colorado. Nowhere common.

Courtesy U.S. Department of Interior, Fish & Wildlife Service

A striped skunk in Olympic National Park, Washington.

Skunks have a great many common names, but most of them are meant to be humorous rather than descriptive or definitive. All are variously known as polecat or wood-pussy; the spotted skunk is sometimes known as hydrophobia or phoby skunk, or phoby cat because of its history of being infected with rabies. It is also called civet in many areas. The hognose is often called rooter or badger skunk because of its habit of digging after food. In French-speaking Canada the skunk is *mouffette*. While we are on the subject of names, the striped and hooded skunks belong to the genus *Mephitis*. Translated from the Latin, *Mephitis* means "a noxious or pestilential exhalation from the ground."

Appearance and Distinguishing Characteristics

All skunks have at least this in common: they are rather small, glossy black animals with a more or less impressive tail and white markings. They can be most readily recognized by the nature of these markings, although there is great variety within each group. The descriptions provided below are generalized, and it must be remembered that the width of the marks, even their distribution and extent, are subject to endless individual themes. You might say that what follows is a chart presenting four idealized skunks. The real ideal skunk, as we shall be seeing, is one that is at least twenty feet away.

The Ideal Skunk

	LENGTH	WEIGHT	TAIL	GENERAL DESCRIPTION
Striped	20–28 in.	6–10 lb.	7–10 in.	Black body with narrow white stripe up middle of forehead. Broad white area on top of head and back of neck, which usually divides into a "V" at the shoulders and becomes 2 white lines which may continue to the base of the bushy tail. Tail *may* have white tip.
Hooded	26–31 in.	4–10 lb.	14–15 in.	LARGEST SKUNK TAIL—as long as body, elaborately plumed. Two chief body patterns: (1) whole back is white, including tail, or (2) back nearly all black with 2 white stripes on sides. Belly all black. Hair on scruff of neck forms ruff.
Spotted	13–23 in.	1–3 lb.	4–9 in.	SMALLEST, MOST SLENDER AND GRACEFUL SKUNK—most weasel-like. Black with white spot on forehead and under each ear. Four broken white stripes along neck, back and sides—"wildly" patterned. White tip on tail; silky fur; proportions of white and black vary greatly.
Hog-nosed	21–31 in.	5–10 lb.	7–12 in.	Piglike snout naked on top for about an inch. Entire back and tail are white—lower sides and belly black. A regular two-tone effect. Fur short and coarse when compared to that of other skunks.

From the tiny one- or two-pound spotted skunk to the big, fat ten-pound striped, hooded, or hog-nosed skunk, these animals truly carry forward the theme that a "rose by any other name . . ." Whereas even the amateur can quickly learn to tell one skunk from another by sight, by smell they are all very much the same!

Habits

When discussing these animals it is only right (and fully expected) to go first to that characteristic for which they are best known. Their stench (and their great talent for spreading it around) is an ever-present hazard to the nature observer, and although no one has ever died of it, a great many people have thought they were about to. As with seasickness, most victims regret the news that they will survive.

With keen muscular control, the skunk ejects his musk from twin jet nozzles located just inside the anal tract. Happily, they can be disarmed by any veterinarian, since once deprived of this noxious device, skunks make good pets. The musk itself is stinging, acrid, and yellowish. It clings like glue once it lands. It is very painful to the eyes on contact. The animal is generally loath to use this device, since it is his main line of defense. Only a badly injured skunk will discharge his full load. One fully in possession of his not inconsiderable faculties will give a series of short bursts, as the occasion demands. He can be accurate to fifteen feet; larger animals, more mature specimens, may be more accurate than younger ones.

When disturbed or threatened, a skunk will often stamp his front feet. His tail will snap up in warning, and then let the intruder beware! He *may* arch his back, he *may* go up on his front legs in a graceful handstand (spotted skunks often but not always do this before spraying), or he may just brace his legs. He can get you if you are behind him, and he can get you if he is facing you. Don't depend on being in a safe position. He can get you from just about any angle if you are close enough. It is not necessarily true that one being carried by his tail cannot spray you, so let the nature lover who wants to move in that close beware! Such a person stands in danger of losing his enthusiasm for wildlife.

If you are caught off guard and are sprayed, you will have a bad time of it. There are all sorts of things you can do for your clothing, but the best solution is a good fire. Burying them, soaking them in ammonia, all of these things will help salvage your clothes to some degree, but it is generally not worth the trouble. On rainy days, the smell comes back. Believe it or not, tomato juice is the best thing for the skin. Water won't touch the oily residue unless ammonia

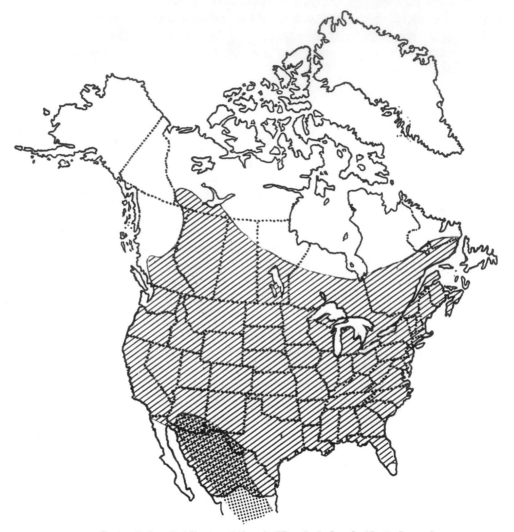

Striped skunk (diagonal lines). Hooded skunk (dotted area).

is added. Alternating baths in ammonia and tomato juice, followed by a good scrubbing with strong soap, is about all you can do. It is suggested that the treatment be administered in the open. Your bathroom will smell for months if you bring your victimized person indoors.

Most animals will not attack a skunk, although hungry predators occa-

Spotted skunk (diagonal lines). Hog-nosed skunk (dotted area).

sionally have a go at it when things are really bad. Great horned owls probably take more of them than any other natural enemy. Skunks find it so hard to believe that anything will really challenge their right of way that they fall victim to automobiles by the tens of thousands every year. Who has driven in the country and not smelled skunk?

These little animals are very adaptable. The striped variety is found just about everywhere, and it is all but impossible to describe its known range of habitat choices. From city parks to suburbs to wilderness areas, he is our most common weasel family member by a very large, odoriferous margin. The little spotted prefers brushy areas away from dense stands of timber and wide, open spaces. He will live in any desert area with a minimum of plant cover. The hooded skunk likes arid country. The hognose chooses wooded areas as well as open. He, like the others, will go up into mountainous country. The spotted has been found to 6,500 feet and the striped nearly as high.

Our skunks are truly omnivorous. Their diets vary greatly, more according to range than species. Most of them will eat any of the following: snakes, lizards, grasshoppers, crayfish, beetles, grubs, frogs, fish, snapping-turtle eggs, ground-nesting birds' eggs, insect larvae, small rodents, carrion, fruit, corn, prickly pears, truck-garden crops, and, on occasion, the fruit of the henhouse. Henhouse raids tend to be rare in most areas but can be rather costly if a local skunk gets the taste of this easy prey. They will take hens' eggs as well.

Most skunks tend to be rather slow fellows, seldom in a hurry. They all swim well if they have to and are far more active at night than in the day. Dusk is a good time to find them about. The relatively lithe little spotted is the most active. He is lighter and more supple. He alone of our skunks climbs trees. He is agile and alert, but all young skunks tend to be playful and energetic. Depending on the local conditions, spotted skunks are generally active in the winter. The striped may sleep part of the winter in the North but remains active all year in the South. No skunk is a true hibernator, although in the northern parts of their range some take very, very long winter naps. A warm spell in midwinter will mean skunk tracks in the snow, however.

Skunks twitter, growl, screech, churr, scold, coo, and whistle. They are territorial but tend to have small, compact home ranges. They migrate only when the range is overrun or when a traditional food source gives out.

Reproduction

Living conditions vary smartly from the Mexican border country to the southern Yukon Territory, and so do skunk breeding habits. As we did with their general description, we will give only generalized descriptions of their reproductive habits.

The striped and hooded skunks breed at about one year. They may be monogamous, or the male may breed with a number of females. The young are born after a gestation period of about sixty-three days in a dry, vegetation-

Courtesy U.S. Department of Interior, Fish & Wildlife Service

An Oregon spotted skunk busy at his meal.

lined den underground, in a hollow log, niche, cranny, or cave. Almost any sheltered, dark area will do. The litter size varies from one to seven, with five about average. The young weigh about an ounce and are born with their eyes closed. They nurse for six or seven weeks and probably live for eight or ten years. They are taught to hunt by their mother and are often seen walking single file behind her at dusk as they set off for an evening's education and feeding.

The gestation period of the spotted skunk is not known. She mates in late winter, and the young are born anytime from April to July. There may be a second litter later in the year, particularly in the southern parts of the range. The litter varies from two to six in size, with four or five usual. The young are nearly naked and weigh about one third of an ounce. They are furred at 21 days, have their eyes open at 32, get their teeth first at 36, and start on soft, solid food at 42. They are generally weaned by the time they are 56 days old and attain full growth at 104.

The hognose dens up in almost any safe rocky place or takes over another animal's hole. Gestation is reported at forty-two days, and the litter size varies from one to four. The mother, as with the other skunks, cares for the young.

Observation

It is all but impossible to start listing places to look for striped and spotted skunks. They are literally everywhere. Wherever you live, drive off in any direction and before going too many miles you will be in skunk country. Look to any farm, any thicket, any watercourse and skunks will not be too far off.

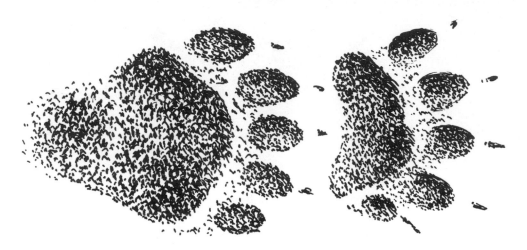

Striped skunk tracks.

Spotted skunk tracks.

If in doubt, drive around at night and use your nose. You will soon enough get the message.

The hooded and hog-nosed skunks are another story. The hooded is found in the Texas Big Bend region, particularly in Brewster, Presidio, and Jeff Davis counties. In parts of southern Arizona and New Mexico they may occasionally be found as well. Look to stream courses near rocky ledges or tangles of vegetation. The hooded skunk does not like being far from cover. Look at dusk and after dark.

The hognose is most common in the hill country of south-central Texas but does range, as has been pointed out, in some parts of Arizona, New Mexico, and southern Colorado. Look to partly timbered or brushy foothills. Look for "plowed" areas, where the hognoses have been at work overturning rocks and other debris looking for grubs. They are largely nocturnal and generally start their forays at dusk. If you want to see our largest skunk, the Gulf Coast hognose, look in Texas' Aransas, Brooks, Cameron, Kleberg, Nueces, and Webb counties.

In any skunk country a nighttime stroll with a flashlight is likely to turn up a skunk or a skunk family. Since they like carrion, they often work along country roads looking for carcasses. This contributes, of course, to their high mortality rate. Your night's stroll, then, needn't take you far off the road. In farm areas you will do as well along the shoulder of a tar road as you will do in most back fields. It is a good idea to proceed cautiously. You may get too close before you realize it—and truly, it is a dreadful mess when it happens. Half-blind and retching though you may be, few people will want to get close enough to offer sympathy. Skunk misery is the loneliest kind!

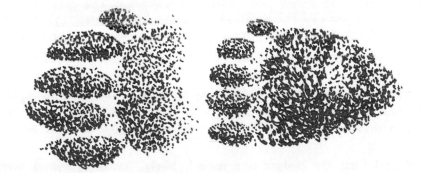

Hog-nosed skunk tracks.

27

The Down-to-Earth Weasel: The Badger

Names and Range

There is a group of rough and tough weasels in the United States and southern Canada known as badgers, or *blaireaux* to French-speaking Canadians. No longer pursued for their fur as they once were, they are quite common in parts of their range.

Badgers are found all over the western United States, from Mexico into Canada. In southern Canada they are found as far east as southwestern Ontario, in the United States as far east as central Ohio.

Appearance and Distinguishing Characteristics

Badgers average between twenty-two and thirty inches in length and weigh from thirteen to twenty-five pounds. Their unimpressive, short, bushy tail is seldom over six inches long, often much shorter. The general ground color can best be described as a mottled yellowish gray-brown. On their face they have very distinct markings: a white stripe runs from the nose over the top of the head; there are white cheeks, and a black slash in front of each ear. The feet are black, the belly and tail yellowish in most specimens.

A single hair from a badger's pelt may be gray at the base, blending to grayish white, then black, and ending in a silvery tip. His long, grizzled fur is still used in shaving and artists' brushes and occasionally to dress up other fur.

In general form the badger is a robust, burly, flattened weasel with a pointed, slightly upturned nose, pointed, widespread ears, and extremely long

A badger and his burrow, Lake Erie district.

front claws. He is most distinctive in appearance and cannot readily be confused with any other North American mammal.

Habits

The badger is a resident of relatively treeless country; dry, open spaces are his choice. He will range up into mountain country (at least thirteen thousand feet in California and ten thousand feet in Texas) but prefers the flatlands. He is a very adaptable fellow and can get along almost anywhere if forced to do so. He seems to be chiefly nocturnal in habit but is seen about during the day. Whether or not he comes out when the sun is up probably depends on how he did in his hunting the night before. He tends to be solitary except during the breeding and rearing season.

The badger can swim well and some say he is adept at climbing trees. Whether or not a badger can climb is somewhat of a moot question because it is a talent he will seldom use.

Some individuals are great wanderers and won't stay long in one place. Others are strictly territorial with limited home ranges. They thrive on small rodents and dig rapidly after those that have gone underground. They take rabbits, birds, eggs, snakes (including rattlesnakes), lizards, insects, snails, honey, bee larvae, and carrion.

A badger is one tough animal and has few natural enemies. Occasionally a bobcat or coyote will have a try, but they usually fail, and even a pack of dogs can be routed by one mature badger. He has many things going for him in a fight, not the least of which are powerful teeth, murderous front claws, and a powerful musk testifying to his kinship with the skunks. His loose skin makes him all but impossible to hold, and he can dig completely underground in a matter of seconds. He has great strength and a weasel's disposition and tenacity. He is built so low to the ground that it is all but impossible for a predator to get at his throat or belly without being bitten through and sliced open themselves. Few animals can best a badger!

Badgers variously growl, chatter, grunt, and hiss. They are so secure in their defenses that, like the skunk, they are seldom in a hurry. They amble about in their own good time and are generally left unmolested except by the young and foolish. In the North they sleep away part of the winter in deep underground chambers.

Like the skunk the badger is frequently victimized on the highway. He comes there to look for carrion and somehow can't get it through his head that someone or something would dare attack him. In stupid conceit he awaits his death. In a recent trip across Kansas I counted four dead badgers on less than twenty miles of highway.

Reproduction

Badgers den up underground with the actual chamber anywhere from five to thirty feet away from the entrance. The hole is slightly flattened to admit their oddly shaped body.

Photo by Wilford L. Miller

A badger and his prey, North Dakota.

They breed in the fall, but the actual development of the young doesn't start until February due to delayed implantation. After about six weeks of true gestation the one to five (usually two) kits are born. They are furred but blind. Their eyes open in four to six weeks, and they are weaned by midsummer, when about half grown. Both parents help care for the young, and the family disbands before fall arrives. In captivity badgers have lived thirteen years, and barring automobile encounters, they probably do as well in the wild.

Observation

Badgers are not hard to find. They are to be seen along highways at night, at dusk, and at dawn. They are to be found in flat open areas where rodents are available as food. The distinctive burrows they make will quickly tell you

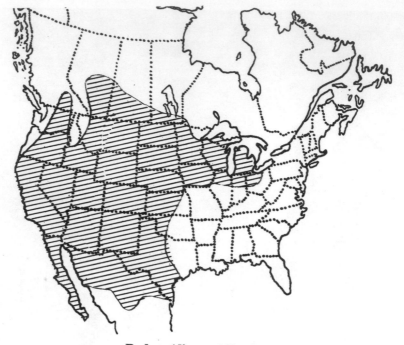

Badger (diagonal lines).

if they are in the area. (They can be baited with smelly fish; a can of sardines left open all day in the sun will reek enough at night to lure badgers from a fair distance).

Although you certainly don't have to go to parks and refuges to find your badger, here is an abbreviated list where they are regularly to be found. There are many, many more, of course:

Banff National Park   Southwestern Alberta
Desert Game Range   Southern Nevada
McNary National Wildlife Refuge   Southern Washington
Monte Vista Wildlife Refuge   South-central Colorado
National Elk Refuge   Western Wyoming
Prince Albert National Park   Central Saskatchewan
Quivira National Wildlife Refuge   Central Kansas

Red Rock Lakes National Wildlife Refuge	Southwestern Montana
Riding Mountain National Park	Southwestern Manitoba
Waterton Lakes National Park	Southwestern Alberta
Wichita Mountains Wildlife Refuge	Southwestern Oklahoma

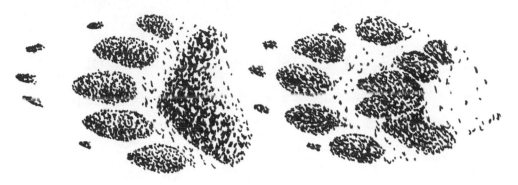

Badger tracks.

28

Our Seals, Walruses, and Sea Lions

A GROUP OF ANIMALS, worldwide in distribution, has adapted itself to a life spent almost totally in the sea. Known as the Pinnipedia, these animals have front and hind limbs developed into true flippers (not the flipperlike hind feet of the sea otter) and a body far better adapted to life in the sea than on land. All of the seals, sea lions, and walruses of the world belong to this group.

Names and Range

Of the thirty-one species of pinnipeds in the world, a large number reach the shores of the United States and Canada on at least rare occasions. It is extremely difficult to define the range of any of these animals accurately, since most are truly oceanic at one time or another and crop up at odd times in the most unlikely spots. Those that migrate often do so over vast distances and may come to shore during bad weather, or if harassed, at a place where they have seldom if ever been seen before. Some, like the harbor seal, remain on land much of the time while others, like the northern fur seal, will be at sea from six to eight months of the year.

In this one chapter it will serve our purposes best to construct one master chart containing information about range and distinguishing characteristics. Working from this chart, and using a good pair of binoculars, it shouldn't be too difficult to determine the identity of any pinniped you encounter at the seashore.

Master Chart—Pinnipeds of the United States and Canada

	SIZE	COLORATION AND CHARACTERISTICS	RANGE

The Eared Seals

(External ear showing; rear flippers can turn outward, adapted for travel on land.)

California Sea Lion	5–8 ft.	Brown to blackish. High forehead. Small pointed ears and large eyes. Honking bark.	Generally from Monterey Bay southward along coasts and islands of California. May be seen from British Columbia to Mexico well below Baja California. Fairly common.
Northern or Steller's Sea Lion	8–11 ft.	Yellowish brown. Low forehead. Larger and less noisy than California sea lion.	From along the Aleutian Island chain to the southern coast of Alaska, down the coasts of British Columbia, Washington and Oregon to about Santa Rosa Island off southern California.
Alaska Fur Seal	4–6 ft.	Blackish above to reddish underneath. Frequently gray on shoulders and neck. Face often brownish. Rare piebald specimens noted.	Breed in Pribilof Islands and other Bering Sea localities. Oceanic in winter and may be seen at sea as far south as California. Not on shores of United States except Alaska north of Aleutian Islands.
Guadalupe Fur Seal	4–6 ft.	Dark-brown, silvery grizzling on head and neck. Reddish snout. Pointed muzzle.	*Rare:* Possibly extinct in all but a very few areas. Breed on Guadalupe Island off Baja California. Rarely and sporadically off southern California (Piedras Blancas, 1938; San Nicolas, 1949). Rarely seen. *Total world population probably well under 500.*

Master Pinniped Chart (Continued)

	SIZE	COLORATION AND CHARACTERISTICS	RANGE

The Walruses

(Extremely large and heavy animals; two down-pointing tusks distinguish them from all other pinnipeds.)

Walrus (*East or Atlantic and West or Pacific*)	7–12 ft.	Dark-gray to brown. Prominent heavy whiskers. Puffy upper lip. Very heavy.	An Arctic animal; from northern coast of Alaska around Arctic Circle to coasts of Greenland, south to northern Hudson Bay. Rarely south of Bering Sea in west and Hudson Bay in east but record from Massachusetts. *Rarely seen south of true Arctic waters.*

Hair Seals

(No external ears visible; flippers less well adapted to life on land.)

Harbor Seal	4–6 ft.	Spotted; yellowish and brown; proportions of colors vary.	Four subspecies: very widespread East and West Coasts. From Arctic and Greenland down entire East Coast of Canada and United States to North Carolina (35 degrees north). In the west from Bering Sea and northern Alaska coast south to middle Baja California. At river mouths down both coasts.
Ribbon Seal	4–6 ft.	Brown with distinctive bands of yellow around neck, rump, and front flippers. No other seal so marked.	Movements not known. Most common in Bering Sea, Aleutians, and coasts of Alaska. Not known south of Alaska Peninsula.
Ringed Seal	4–5 ft.	Various yellowish and brownish tones. Dark streaks, blotches and spots on back, generally continuous.	All across Arctic; south to Bering Sea in west and Labrador in east. Found deep into Hudson Bay. (Three subspecies found on shores of Canada and Alaska.)

Master Pinniped Chart (Continued)

	SIZE	COLORATION AND CHARACTERISTICS	RANGE
Saddleback or Harp Seal	5–6 ft.	Unique: Grayish or yellowish with a dark-brown to black face and irregular band of same color on back and rump. Some dark smaller spots. Piebald.	In east only; North Atlantic and Arctic to Hudson Bay, and Gulf of St. Lawrence. Nowhere resident the whole year. Farthest south reported was Cape Henry, Virginia, but that extremely rare or unique.
Bearded Seal	7–11 ft.	Uniform gray to yellow tone. Prominent tufts of long, flattened bristles on both sides of muzzle.	Arctic; across northern coast of Canada; rarely if ever seen south of Bering Sea in west or Newfoundland in east.
Gray Seal	9–12 ft.	Dull gray—blotchy. Very large and plain.	Rare off North America, Labrador; extremely rare south as far as New Jersey (40 degrees north). Not likely to be seen except off eastern Newfoundland Island.
Hooded Seal	6–8 ft.	Slate-gray to blackish with lighter sides and streaked or spotted with white to yellowish white. (Young are all white.)	Far northern animal found in Canadian Arctic from Baffin Island to Labrador, Newfoundland, Gulf of St. Lawrence and rarely Hudson Strait. Migratory in small groups.
Northern Elephant Seal	8–18 ft.	Pale-brown and gray tones. Generally lighter underneath. Males have distinctive overhanging proboscis or snout.	To be found from islands off southern California southward. Regularly on or near San Miguel Island and San Nicolas Island, thence to Baja California. Total world population probably under 10,000.
West Indian Seal	6–7 ft.	Brown tinged with gray; sides paler with underparts yellow to yellowish white.	*May be extinct.* Extremely rare small seal from West Indies. Two sightings in Texas waters in past; Galveston and Point Isabel. Sighting extremely unlikely on coast of United States.

Photo by Victor B. Scheffer, courtesy U.S. Department of Interior, Fish & Wildlife Service

Approximately one ton of male Steller's sea lion on St. Paul Island, Alaska.

The best way, perhaps, to review the pinnipeds seen along the coasts of the United States and Canada is to make an imaginary trip from the high Arctic in the west down the coasts of Alaska, British Columbia, Washington, Oregon and California to Mexico. From there we will skip eastward to the Atlantic and start up the coast along the eastern seaboard to Canada and once again into the frozen vastnesses of the Arctic wasteland. In real life it would be an exhausting trip of many, many thousands of miles, but if we were lucky enough to see the fourteen species of pinnipeds involved, it would be more than worth it!

We will start our trip in the Arctic near the North Pole and work southward to the northern coast of Alaska. On the frozen ice we will see the bearded seal. There are probably no more than 75,000 to 150,000 bearded seals in the world, and they are all to be found around the edge of the Arctic ice. Of great importance to the Eskimos, he is hunted successfully on the ice and from open boats. He may be solitary or can be found in groups of up to fifty during the breeding season. He prefers shallow waters and on occasion will ascend a far northern river temporarily free of ice.

The much more common ringed seal also inhabits these icy waters. He still numbers in the many millions and has a great range. He is about half the size of the bearded seal and, as the chart points out, is much more interestingly marked. He is the most important seal in the economy of the Eskimos and is taken by the thousands each year. He is seldom seen away from the edge of the Arctic ice pack.

On the north coast of Alaska, and Canada's Northwest Territories, we will see the small harbor seal's spotted yellow-brown-gray coat. Whether he is yellow with brown-gray spots or brown-gray with yellow spots is open to question. There are well over half a million of these little animals in the world today, and we will see him again and again on our journey around North America. They have the habit of popping up just about anywhere, and often with fair regularity. They travel in small family bands and stay close to shore. If it is spring, we will see small white and woolly pups in company with the adults. If the young tire, the mothers will take them on their backs for a free ride.

In company with the bearded, ringed, and harbor seals north of Alaska will be found the great Pacific walrus. There is a great deal of discussion as to whether or not he is the same species as the Atlantic walrus, but for our purposes he is the same animal. He is massive, up to three thousand pounds in weight, and is truly the monarch of the polar seas. Diving to three hundred feet or more, he dredges up clams and other shellfish with his long tusks and crushes their shells with his flattened teeth. He may drift southward in the fall, staying with the edge of the ice, but by spring he is back into the Arctic Ocean. He can move fast in the water but has to beach himself on an ice floe or a barren shore to rest. It is said he can drown if he becomes exhausted far from ice or shore. The single young, born on the ice in spring, are four feet in length at birth and weigh a hundred pounds or more. One male will breed with many females, and vicious fights among the bulls occur at breeding time. The heavy tusks on a mature bull can be a yard long. A female with a calf is especially dangerous and will attack anything that threatens the calf's safety.

Around the top of Alaska, before we start down the coast, we may be fortunate enough to encounter a few stray specimens of the relatively rare ribbon seal. In all the world there aren't fifty thousand of these brightly marked little animals, and they are not found in large groups like so many of their cousins. If any Eskimos spot the ribbon before we do, all we will see is the skinned carcass before it is cut up for a feast. The fur is highly prized for its decorative qualities. The ribbon seal is also a favorite prey of the polar bear.

As we pass westward around Alaska and approach the Aleutian Islands, we will encounter the valuable Northern or Alaskan fur seal. There are probably well over two million of these animals left, and controlled hunting will keep this number nearly constant, although at one time it looked as if indiscriminate slaughter would push their kind to extinction. There are three herds of the Northern fur seal left in the world: one on a small island north of Japan, another in the Commander Islands east of the USSR, and a third in the Pribilof Islands. The last-named location in the Bering Sea is the home of the largest herd in the world.

Each summer 80 percent of the world's Northern fur seals congregate on St. Paul and St. George Islands (each about thirty-five square miles in area) 350 miles west of the Alaskan mainland and 250 miles north of the Aleutian chain. Early in May the great bulls (known as beachmasters) arrive and take up their stations. They are at least seven years old at this point and may be as much as twenty. A month or so later, the mature females arrive. Whereas the bulls waiting for them may weigh as much as six hundred pounds, these females will seldom weigh more than one hundred. The females arrive almost ready to deliver the pup from the previous year's breeding (gestation eleven to twelve months) and eventually end up in a harem that may number as many as a hundred cows; the average, though, is about forty-five. Younger, immature animals arrive later and haul up away from the harems. During this season the bulls are fiercely belligerent. The ten-to-twelve-pound pups are born between the middle of June and late July. In October and November the herds disperse over the vast reaches of the Pacific, the cows and immature animals traveling as far south as southern California. The breeding bulls remain near the Bering Sea until the next spring sends them back to their ancient breeding grounds.

South of the Alaska Peninsula, as we head east toward the Canadian mainland, we will encounter our first specimens of the ten-foot-long Northern or Steller's sea lion. There are, perhaps, as many as 150,000 of these animals

Courtesy U.S. Department of Interior, Fish & Wildlife Service

A bull walrus. He does not appear to be amused with the photographer's intrusion.

left in the world, and we may again encounter them as far south as Baja California, where they share ranges with the southern or California sea lion. Our best chances, though, will occur off southern Alaska and among the thousands of islands guarding the shore of British Columbia. This, the largest of the eared seals, is a belligerent animal and seldom seen in zoos. A male may weigh over a ton, and the true nature of their diet is little known. They apparently live on fish, squid, and a wide variety of marine life. These great sea lions breed throughout their range. In June and early July both sexes haul up on favorite wave-beaten rocks and small islands. The male holds a harem of ten to twenty females. A single pup is born to each female, and she is bred again before returning to the sea. The pup lives on its mother's milk for at

Courtesy U.S. Department of Interior, Fish & Wildlife Service

A young harbor seal with his first salmon. He didn't catch it—it was a gift from the photographer.

least three months before starting on the sea's bounty. The pups are taught to swim by their mother and are reluctant at first to so much as enter the water.

As we pass eastward along Alaska's south shore and turn southward along the coast of British Columbia, we will pass scatterings of harbor seals and more northern sea lions. On very rare occasions we may encounter a stray Arctic seal that somehow drifted down south of the Aleutian chain. Such sightings are extremely rare, however.

As we pass along the southern end of the British Columbian coast, offshore of Vancouver Island, and enter the waters of the State of Washington, we enter the northern limits of the popular California sea lion. He is the well-known "trained seal" of circus and television fame. More than a hundred thousand of these active seven-foot animals ply the waters from here south to central Mexico. They are a common sight all along this vast and varied coastline. These sea lions breed on offshore islands from Santa Barbara southward into Mexico during May and June. The long gestation period is just about a year in duration. As with all eared seals, just one pup is born to each cow in the big bull's harem. Shortly after the birth the animals breed again for the next year's crop. These fast and seemingly happy sea mammals live on squid, octopus, herring, rockfish, hake, and ratfish. They have voracious appetites and can be very short with each other. They are alert animals and make the best pets, perhaps, of all pinnipeds.

As we pass along the shores of California from the rocky north to the sandy south, we will see more and more California sea lion, fewer and fewer northern sea lion, and the ever-present harbor seals. At the junction of California and Mexico's Baja California we reach the extreme southern limit of the northern sea lion, reach the middle of the north and south range of the California sea lion, and encounter two strangers.

A few of the two- to five hundred Guadalupe fur seals left in the world occasionally reach the waters of southern California. These six-foot eared seals still may breed in extremely small numbers on Guadalupe Island off Lower California (in Mexican waters), and a few drift north. One was seen on California's San Nicolas Island in 1949 and again in 1951. Little is known of their private life.

On rare occasions the massive northern elephant seal wanders north far enough to enter the waters of California. There are fewer than ten thousand left in the world, and now that they are no longer being slaughtered for their blubber their tribe may increase. The twelve-to-eighteen-foot males are very distinctive with their great fleshy "trunks." Not a thing of beauty by any means, they are impressive. In winter some of them drift as far north as Vancouver Island. On the southern breeding grounds, on small islands off Mexico's coast (and a few off California's), the bulls gather a harem of ten to twelve females. They breed from December to March, and the gestation period is just under a year, about eleven and a half months. The males are more casual about their harems than most other seals.

We will find these elephant seals from here on southward, as well as California sea lions and an occasional Guadalupe fur seal. Few other pinnipeds frequent this coastline until southern South America is reached.

Going thousands of miles eastward we come to the West Indies, and here may live yet a few of the West Indian seal. On very, very rare occasions, one or two of these little animals have drifted north, to be seen along the Texas coastline. They prefer sandy beaches for hauling out and are generally very sluggish and indifferent to intruders. This fact led to their slaughter and near extinction. It appears that the young are born in December, although little data is available. We are very unlikely to be blessed with a sighting.

As we pass northward along the eastern seaboard of the United States, we start spotting harbor seals by the time we reach North Carolina's shore. We will see them from time to time until we again reach the Arctic wastes. East of the Canadian Maritime Provinces we start seeing the six-to-eight-foot slate-gray hooded seal. This is the extreme southern limit of his range, and his spottings will be very rare until we are much farther north. He is migratory and nomadic and is usually found in deep waters, except at breeding time, when they gather in the world of thick ice. The main concentrations occur from June to September. They haul out on the ice to give birth in late February.

Farther north, with the harbor seals still with us, we begin to encounter the handsomely marked harp or saddleback seals. The piebald adults are very distinctive, but the pups are pure white. About a dozen pounds at birth, the pup is nursed until a weight of sixty or seventy pounds is reached and is then abandoned. A few weeks of living off his fat is enough, and the pup soon flops off the ice (if he hasn't been eaten by a polar bear) and starts his life in the sea living on a diet of crustaceans and fish.

We are soon again in the world of the walrus, and our untrained eyes won't be able to tell the difference between these and the ones we saw in the North Pacific. We also are encountering the ringed seal again and soon enough the bearded. Only one new seal will be added to our roster, the nine-to-twelve-foot gray. He is very rare south of Labrador, and there probably aren't fifty thousand in the whole world. We shall be very fortunate to see even one. He is also known as the winter seal, since he increases his tribe in early winter, a strange time for pups to be born in so hostile a world.

All of the animals we have discussed in this chapter live on marine life of one kind or another. In a number of cases little is known of their diet. Many of these animals are hunted by large sharks and all are victimized by the killer whale. Man, however, is their greatest enemy.

In this chapter, which, by necessity, differed so much in format from the others in this book, we have taken an imaginary voyage thousands of miles in length. We cruised among islands, rounded peninsulas, and generally followed the two great coastlines that mark the east and west boundaries of mainland United States and Canada. We don't even know how many islands and islets we passed, but surely they number in the tens of thousands.

Among these islands, on the great sheets and fractured chips of floating ice we passed, and along the endlessly changing shoreline live fourteen species of extremely interesting mammals. No one reading this book will ever see all fourteen. A lifetime spent in such a pursuit could barely accomplish it. Still, there is a chance that the next trip to the seashore, the next visit to a continent's edge might turn up yet another species to mark off the lifetime checklist. In each coastal state that you visit a call on the local conservation office or even Coast Guard station may pay off with specific information about where local pinnipeds are known to gather. Letters written well in advance will tell you what is the best time of the year to visit these coasts.

Most of us will take greater interest in the landlocked species of mammal we normally think of as part of our fauna. The pinnipeds are not to be overlooked, however, for as they feed along our continental shelves they are truly a part of our own wildlife heritage. They are to be found where the ocean and the land meet in ever-changing patterns.

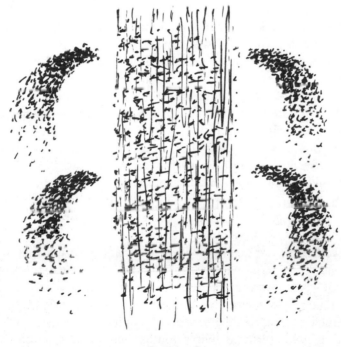

Seal tracks.

___ 29

Visitors from the Deep: The Whales

IN MANY WAYS, the most dramatic mammals properly identified with our continent are the great whales who sometimes visit our coastal waters. When their almost unbelievably great forms heave into sight from the deep realms of our bordering oceans they bring with them all the mystery of distant seas and lands, all the wonder of a life lived away from our view and knowing, and all the majesty of the greatest animals the world has ever known. They bring with them, too, a kind of insight into history, for in their brief moments within our sight they shed the missing illumination needed if we are to understand the wondrous and adventuresome days of the great whaling fleets and ships of sail. Who can understand those old mezzotints or the scrimshawed ivory who has not with his own eyes seen a mighty whale rise and blow?

It is an academic point whether or not a whale is properly considered a part of this continent's fauna. Actually, of course, they belong to no continent; they are part of the sea, wherein they were born and wherein they will die except in rare instances. Yet, a nature lover standing on a rocky cliff watching a hundred tons of whale curve gracefully from a black and wrinkled sea cannot but feel a certain kinship with this apparition, because this huge form is a mammal as much as a squirrel, bear, or porcupine is a mammal. It requires air to breathe, it gives birth to living young, and suckles its calves in their infancy.

In this chapter we will discuss briefly those whales that are known to approach our shores. Not all are regular visitors by any means, but all are to be seen by someone, somewhere almost every year. We will eliminate from this discussion those extremely rare forms only known to have come in sight of our shores a few times in the last century.

Courtesy U.S. Department of Interior, Fish & Wildlife Service

Only in tragic death, when they are inexplicably washed up on our beaches, do we get close to the mighty whales. In this case it is a sperm whale in Washington State.

When we speak of whales we will speak of the porpoises and dolphins as well. These active little marine mammals are also whales, only small ones. All together these animals—whales, porpoises and dolphins (not to be confused with a fish also known as a dolphin)—are called cetaceans. Elsewhere in the world some small cetaceans ascend rivers and have given up the sea completely to spend their lives in sweet water. We have no such animals in the United States and Canada. All our whales belong to the sea, and the sea, alone, knows all their secrets.

Not the least fascinating aspect of the cetaceans is the fact that they appear to be of extremely high intelligence. Their language is complex, and they definitely communicate with each other. Some scientists believe they are the most intelligent animals on this planet next to man, and some go beyond this in their estimates. Elaborate studies are now in progress to develop a language that may be used by man in communicating with some of the cetaceans. Many men believe they are intelligent enough to understand us once we unlock the secret codes they have developed for use in their life in the sea. This is an exciting idea indeed, especially when a new motive is revealed. It is believed that our ability to communicate with life on other planets (for such *must* exist) will grow from our ability to communicate with the most intelligent animal life on our own planet. Surely, such wonders, such thoughts are in keeping with the fascination of the whale itself and are reason enough to look to our seas on every occasion and hope that a great form will rise from below and share a moment of its life with us.

In most cases you will see a whale for only a few moments. In rare cases you will encounter a pack or, more properly, a pod of whales playing near the surface for many minutes, even hours; but your best look at a whale will come when a strange and unexplained tragedy strikes. From time to time, whales beach themselves. Each year, somewhere along our great and varied coastline, some whales come ashore to die. Literally, they suffocate. Even their massive muscle structure cannot keep heaving their great weight up to allow their lungs to fill. Inevitably, all stranded whales must tire and die. So adapted to the sea have they become that they cannot survive without a liquid medium to support their weight. The reasons for these strandings are not

Courtesy U.S. Department of Interior, Fish & Wildlife Service

The dramatic and the despised—killer whales, Monterey Bay, California.

known, although endless theories have been put forward. The suggestion that whales run aground to avoid attacks from the predacious killer whale seem untrue, for killer whales themselves are often victims of this strange behavior. Recent theories put forward suggest a contagious respiratory ailment as the cause. Perhaps, but no more than perhaps.

All cetaceans are immediately recognizable because they lack the fish's vertical tail. They have instead flattened flukes, which they pump up and down to drive themselves through the water.

Whales can be distinguished from other marine life and from each other when they rise to breathe. They exhale through one or two blowholes on the *top* of their head. Nature kindly allowed their nostrils to migrate when ancient forms returned to the sea. The spout, condensed vapors exhaled from their mighty lungs, often assumes characteristic forms that are useful, even critical, for identification.

These, then, are our whales—more accurately, those of the world's whales who sometimes come to call at the gateways of our land:

The Right Whale

This is one of the baleen whales. Instead of teeth he has vertical plates in his cavernous mouth to filter plankton from the sea. Together they are rather like a long, hairy, vertical venetian blind. At least 250 strips curtain the great upward-curving mouth of the right whale. This baleen was the "whalebone" of the last century. There are two right whales that can be seen from our shores, the Atlantic and the Pacific. The former grows to lengths ranging from about 35 to 55 feet. The Pacific form may be as long as 70 feet. Both forms are black and lack a dorsal fin. A warty protuberance is found on their snout. Their belly is smooth, and they have short, broad pectoral fins. When they blow, it comes out in twin jets forming a high "V" as much as sixteen feet high. (All baleen whales have twin blowholes, the toothed whales one.) They can remain submerged for fifteen to twenty minutes. Normally they make five or six shallow dives before sounding for the depths. The mother bears one young at a time and nurses it for a year or more. On the Atlantic side right whales may be found from the Arctic to South Carolina. In the Pacific they occur from the Aleutian Islands to southern California. The two forms represent different species. Hunted by man for over a thousand years, they are now rare and protected. The right whale is *baleine franche* to French Canadians.

The Bowhead Whale

The 50-to-65-foot bowhead is one third head. Nearly seven hundred baleen plates, some as long as twelve feet, line his massive jaws. He is generally dark or grayish brown in color and may float along with part of his back above water. There is no dorsal fin. There is a distinctive hump at the back of the head. Bowheads seldom leave the edge of the ice and are found only in the Arctic most of the year. They range across the top of the world and can be seen as far south as the Bering Sea in the West and to the St. Lawrence River in the East. They have been seen near the Pribilof Islands, but 250 miles north of the Aleutian Islands. Now very rare. (Called *baleine arctique* in French Canada.)

The Gray Whale

This 35-to-45-foot whale is regularly seen off our West Coast. Each spring they make a four-thousand-mile journey from their breeding grounds in the Lower California lagoons to their summer feeding grounds in the Arctic. They can be seen from San Diego's Point Loma spring and fall. They stick close to shore and enter shallow water to bear their sixteen-foot calves. Gestation is estimated to be one year. They are a blotched grayish black in color and are quite slender. Their spout comes in quick succession, seldom achieving heights of more than ten feet. The gray has two to four longitudinal folds on his chin. There is no dorsal fin but a slight hump on the back. Once nearly hunted to extinction, they are now protected and on the increase. Regularly seen.

    CAUTION: Do not approach a gray whale in a small boat. They are considered to be short-tempered and have been said to attack and smash boats that got too close. This reputed practice earned them the name of devilfish. (*Baleine grise.*)

The Common Finback Whale

This 50-to-70-ton giant may grow up to eighty feet long. He is gray on top and white underneath. He is an extremely fast, streamlined animal with many longitudinal folds on the throat. The baleen is splotched purple and white. The spout is columnar and may be as high as twenty feet. It is generally accompanied by a loud whistling sound. There is a small dorsal fin just in front of the tail. When the finback sounds, he may assume an almost vertical position before disappearing, bringing his flukes out of the water. They have been known to play around ships. In the Atlantic they are found from Iceland to the Gulf of Mexico and throughout the Caribbean. In the Pacific they are seen from high in the Bering Sea to the coasts of Mexico's Baja California. This is probably the most common of our large whales. (*Rorqual commun.*)

Closely related to the finback are: (1) the sei whale (also known as pollack whale or Rudolphi's rorqual), found from Labrador to Florida and from the Bering Sea to Baja California; length 50 feet, rarely reported; (2) the little piked or minke whale, found from Iceland to New Jersey, from the Bering Sea to Baja California; length twenty to thirty feet, and the dorsal fin has a distinctive curved tip; prefers coastal waters.

The Blue Whale

This mammoth creature is often called the sulfur-bottom because of a characteristic yellowish film of microscopic algae that forms on his underside. Weighing as much as thirty-five elephants (140 tons or more), this is the largest animal that ever lived on this planet. The calf is as much as twenty-six feet long at birth and requires two hundred pounds of its mother's milk every day! The record length for this animal stands at 113 feet, but 70 is about average. He is the most valuable whale in the world and is still hunted in the Antarctic, but almost nowhere else. He is a baleen whale and feeds his incredible hulk on small marine animals, tiny shrimp known as krill. Once seen

Blue whale (75–100 feet).

anywhere along our seaboards from Iceland to the Canal Zone and from the Bering Sea to the shores of South America, he is today a rarity and sighting him a thrill beyond compare. He is bluish gray above and yellow to white underneath. There are many long furrows on the chin and belly and the dorsal fin is small, situated far back on the body. The spout is vertical and may be twenty feet high. (*Rorqual gris* or *baleine bleue.*)

The Humpback Whale

One of the most exciting sights on land or sea is the great leap of this squat, chunky whale of fifty feet. For reasons unknown this mighty animal periodically leaps from the sea and lands back with a shock that seems likely to push the sea upon the land. This monster-size frolic *may* be part of a monumental courtship ritual. The humpback has a knobby head and also knobs on the leading edge of his extremely long pectoral flippers. The trailing edges of the flippers are crenulated, or scalloped. The color is black with white mottling below. The spout is frequent and rapid and forms an expanding column twenty feet high. At times, the humpback will inexplicably stand on his head and beat the water to a froth with his mighty flukes. Seen on occasion from Iceland to Trinidad and from the Bering Sea to Panama, the sight is a thrilling one but no longer very common. The young are fifteen feet long at birth and weigh a dainty one and a half tons. French-speaking Canadians know this animal as *baleine à bosse* or *mégaptère.*

Humpback whale (40–50 feet).

The Sperm Whale

This is the largest of the toothed whales and one of the most important forms of wildlife in the history of the United States, for he was once the prize catch of the whaling ship. Empires were built on the oil and other raw materials his mighty body provides. He is also known as *cachalot, cachalot à la grosse tête* (French Canadian) and *Pottfisch* (German). The bull sperm can reach sixty or more feet, but that is exceptional, and specimens today seldom exceed forty-five to fifty feet. He has a very narrow lower jaw and a massive, blunt, square head that constitutes about one third of his total length. Only the lower jaw has teeth (about twenty-two to the side), and they fit into sockets in the upper jaw. Food consists mainly of squid and some of these are large and taken at

Sperm whale (40–60 feet).

great depths, apparently after a herculean battle. Few sperms are taken without sucker scars on their heads. The sperm is a dark grayish blue above and lighter below. There is no dorsal fin but a pronounced hump on the back, with a series of little humps behind it. The spout is single, prolonged, and characteristically *points forward*. This is a social animal that travels in pods of fifteen or more. Bulls will be found in polar seas during their respective summers, returning to their cows and calves in tropic seas during the winter. Calves are thirteen or more feet at birth. Known on our coasts from Iceland to the Gulf of Mexico, from the Bering Sea to Gulf of Panama. Sightings scarce.

The Pygmy Sperm Whale

This is one of the smallest of the true whales. Lengths seldom exceed a dozen feet, although the young are disproportionately large, up to five feet at birth.

There is a small, low back fin, and coloration runs black above and gray below. The head is about one sixth of the total length, the snout is blunt and protruding, the jaw narrow. Like the mighty sperm, this pygmy eats squid. Range is universal, and they are apt to show up just about anywhere. On our coasts they have been seen from Halifax Harbor to the Florida Keys, from southern British Columbia to Mexico. Rarely reported. (*Cachalot pygmé.*)

The Beluga or White Whale

This is one of our smaller whales and one of the handsomest. While young the color is a dull gray but at maturity (four or five years) the color changes to a velvety white. Lengths seldom exceed twelve feet, and there is no dorsal fin. The startling white color and small size make this animal immediately recognizable. They usually travel in pods that may number sixty, eighty, or more. Essentially creatures of the Arctic seas, they have ranged south as far as Cape Cod, and even New Jersey on at least one occasion. The range is generally given as Hudson Bay, Labrador, to Gulf of St. Lawrence, and across the top of the world. A related animal apparently ranges into the Bering Sea from the West. Common enough in the Arctic, the beautiful white whale (no relation to Moby Dick, who was an albino sperm) must be considered extremely rare elsewhere. He is *marsouin blanc* to French-speaking Canadians.

The Narwhal

Unicorns don't exist, we know today, but the strange tusk of this odd little whale "proved" to Europeans of the Middle Ages that they did. The nine-foot, clockwise-spiraling tusk growing from the male narwhal's left upper jaw distinguishes him from all other cetaceans. Lengths run to twelve feet, and the back is mottled gray, the belly mottled grayish white. They are rarely if ever seen far south of the Arctic ice fields. Range is given as Labrador to northern Hudson Bay, to Alaska coasts. A strange little sea mammal seen only by those who travel far, they are often seen in company with white whales.

In addition to the true whales we have discussed so far, there are eight or so other whales known as the beaked whales, which reach our shores from time to time. These are the beaked whales, and they may be sighted on the coasts indicated:

	LENGTH	MARKINGS AND CHARACTERISTICS	RANGE
Baird's Beaked Whale	35–42 ft.	Black with whitish area on lower belly. Snout into true beak. Small dorsal fin.	*Rare.* Bering Sea to Monterey Bay, California.
Sowerby's Whale	16 ft.	Snout elongated, black or dark gray above, pale on sides and underneath. Dorsal fin far back.	*Rare and little known.* Sighted off Nantucket Island.
Blainville Whale	12 ft.	Little known but strange lower jaw formation thickening toward rear.	*Rarely seen.* Recorded at Massachusetts and New Jersey. Also Nova Scotia.
Gervais' Whale	22 ft.	Dark slate-gray with lighter sides and white or whitish belly. True beak. Short, narrow pectoral fins.	Long Island to Atlantic City and even Florida Keys. Sightings rare.
True's Beaked Whale	15–17 ft.	Slate-black back; sides yellow-purple flecked with black. True beak.	Cape Breton Island, Nova Scotia to North Carolina. Not common but less rare than several others discussed.
Cuvier's Beaked Whale *(Goosebeak)*	18–28 ft.	Variable; gray to black with occasional white markings. Sides sometimes brownish. Social and active.	Rhode Island to Georgia, Alaska to San Diego. May turn up anywhere. Fairly common.
Bottle-nosed Whale	20–30 ft.	Black to light brown above, whitish about head. Well-developed beak. Dorsal fin white in old males, it is reported.	St. Lawrence River south past New England at least. Not rare.

Less dramatic than the whales, perhaps, but generally of a more "loving" image are the approximately twenty-five species of porpoises and dolphins that reach our coastal waters. Actually nothing more than small whales, the porpoises and dolphins, with one or two notable exceptions, have a good public image. They gambol and play, they are "bright and cheerful," and are said to "come to help those in distress" in their watery realm. All human qualities aside, these animals are apparently very intelligent in terms of the animal life that they represent and, strangely, many species, or perhaps just individuals, seem to have an affinity for human beings. Ancient legends about dolphins and children becoming friends were relegated to fancy until just a few years ago, when very real friendships, very well documented and photographed cases of wild cetaceans' taking up with children at public beaches, were made known. I do not know of any such affiliations along our own beach fronts, but the whole matter is one of endless fascination and promises wondrous revelations when research into the intelligence of the whole family has progressed farther. As you stand on the beach or the deck of a boat and watch dolphins or porpoises gambol about in their graceful arching leaps, you may be justified in asking yourself, "I wonder what they are *thinking?*" There are few, if any, other cases in the animal kingdom that warrant the use of that word.

The words "dolphin" and "porpoise" are used interchangeably in many parts of the world. Few people can distinguish between them, and we will try here to make some apt distinctions as it applies to common names. (Once again, dolphin must be understood to be the mammal of that common name, not the fish.)

The Killer Whale

There are two, the Atlantic and the Pacific, and together they have had more nonsense conjured up around them than almost any other animal you can name. They are large (the males grow to an estimated thirty-one-foot maximum, females about half that) and they *are* dolphins. They are distinctly marked with white flashes on their sides and head, otherwise being shiny black. Quickest identification is made by their dorsal fins. They are extremely long—six feet or more—and put the shark's "ominous fin" to shame. The odd legend about killer whales slitting whales open with this fin is just so much poppycock. The fin is so soft that it frequently flops over like a cocker spaniel's ear! Much has been written about whether or not this great predator of the high seas is a man-eater. People have been claiming it for donkeys' years, but no one seems to know the name of a victim. They do, however, hunt in regular packs and do prey on larger whales, other small cetaceans, sea otters, and pinnipeds. They are cosmopolitan and may pop up just about anywhere

Atlantic killer whale (15–30 feet).

from South America to Long Island Sound to Hudson Bay, with a like distribution in the West. Both the Pacific and Atlantic species are commonly known as orca; to the French Canadians he is *orque* or *epaulard*.

Not too far removed from the killer whales are the grampus (nine to thirteen feet, blunt-nosed, with a streaked gray to blackish body, sighted at Cape Cod, off New Jersey, and off Monterey, California); and the false killer whale (thirteen to eighteen feet, black and unmarked, slender, *small* dorsal fin, blunt snout, rounded head, seen off North Carolina, Florida, in the Caribbean, and off Baja California); but neither is as dramatic or so surrounded by myth and invective.

The Blackfish or Pilot Whale

Billed in marine shows as a true whale, this fourteen-to-twenty-eight-foot animal is actually a large dolphin. He is uniformly black and has a large, recurved dorsal fin set well forward on the body. He has long flippers and a high, rounded forehead. He is often seen traveling in large schools and is gentle in captivity, and apparently extremely intelligent. He is also known as the caaing whale, and as *globicephale* or *epaulard à tête ronde* to French-speaking citizens of Canada. He apparently feeds at night, largely on quids. The Atlantic species ranges from Quebec to Virginia, the Pacific species from Alaska to southern California, and the fifteen-to-twenty-foot short-finned blackfish from New Jersey to the Gulf of Mexico, Louisiana, and Texas.

The Common Dolphin

This handsomely marked "baby whale" is often encountered by ocean voyagers as he gambols with his pod-mates at the bow of a ship. He is handsomely marked: back and flippers are a glossy black, flanks distinctly yellowish, and belly white. He wears eye-rings that are connected by two white lines across the rear end of his six-inch beak. Generally between six and nine feet long, he normally travels in very large pods. His distribution ranges up and down our two main coastlines, although the Pacific and Atlantic versions of this exciting and common animal are considered separate species.

The other dolphins include:

Bottle-nosed dolphin (or *cowfish*). Atlantic species from Maine to Texas, Pacific species all along Pacific Coast. Nine-to-twelve-foot lengths recorded; grayish coloration with lighter belly in both and small (three-inch) beak. The lower jaw is slightly longer in both.

Rough-toothed dolphin. Florida and California. Eight feet, well-developed back fin, beak elongated and narrow and set off from forehead by groove.

Spotted dolphin. North Carolina to Texas. Five-to-seven-foot lengths, grayish black with numerous small white spots on back. Long beak and medium-sized dorsal fin.

Common dolphin (6½–8½ feet).

There are about another seven species of dolphins, but they are difficult to distinguish for anyone who has not made a study of the group.

The true porpoises are generally smaller relatives of the dolphins. Their

Atlantic harbor porpoise (4–6 feet).

snouts are less pronounced, and they are seen along our coasts in less variety. The most often reported is the common or harbor porpoise, a four-to-six foot animal that is extremely active as it travels about close to shore in large pods or schools. Also known as the puffer or puffing pig for the sounds he makes when he blows, he has a triangular back fin, a black back and flippers, and pale sides to white underparts. The Atlantic species is found regularly from Greenland to New Jersey, the very similar Pacific form from the Bering Sea all the way south to Mexican waters. Both species live mainly on fish and squid, and both grow to a maximum weight of 100 to 120 pounds. Confusion may be avoided by remembering that the distinctly different bottle-nosed dolphin is also known as the common porpoise in some areas. Its three-inch beak is enough to separate the two species at a glance. The true common porpoise is a porpoise, and not a beaked dolphin.

Our Pacific Coast waters (from the Aleutians to southern California) also play host to the attractive Dall's porpoise. This five-to-six-foot beauty has a black back that shades to gray on the neat little triangular back fin. The white belly extends upward on the sides behind the front flippers. He often plays around ships plying the Inside Passage to Alaska and is much more common in the northern part of his range. His markings make him readily distinguishable from the harbor porpoise.

In these few pages we have reviewed some of the more common cetaceans that are seen from the shores of the United States and Canada. We have talked of the great baleen whales, the largest animals ever to live on this planet; we have talked of the much more varied and numerous toothed whales that range from the mighty sperm down through the smaller beaked whales, porpoises, dolphins, and strange little white whales and narwhals. This group,

The popular bottle-nosed dolphin, most beloved of the whales.

the great mammals that have completely relinquished their historic claim to solid land, includes the most valuable individual animals on earth. The dollar value of a blue whale far, far exceeds that of any other creature. Their oil is still used in the manufacture of literally dozens of products consumed or used by man. Their very tasty meat is important to millions of protein-starved people. In our hemisphere, the whale is of economic importance only to the residents of the Far North, the Eskimos, who still rate a stranded whale the event of the year. To the rest of us, the whale is a curiosity, a brief connection between our own lives and those of earlier Americans whose empires and fame were built on the backs of these mighty leviathans. The whale is still the most dramatic mammal on earth, and we are endlessly intrigued by those chance spottings that can so enrich a seaside visit. What man is so sophisti-

Photo by John A. Castle

This is what we generally see of our great whales. In this case it is a finback off Cape Cod getting ready to sound.

cated that he would not turn his head and strain for a better view at the words, "There's a whale!"

Statistics, particularly the kind with an endless stream of zeros stringing off the right end, tend to be rather meaningless in terms of our own experiences, but perhaps there is some value in pointing out that it would take twelve million shrew moles from a coastal forest in Oregon to equal the weight of one really large blue whale. Yet, both animals breathe in essentially the same way, breed in the same general fashion, and produce living young over which the mother is similarly solicitous. As different in appearance as a snake is from a bird, yet both are truly mammals without reserve or qualification. No other group of animals has such a range, has such dramatically different forms within it. Perhaps that is why, or at least one reason why, the mammals are, always have been, and surely always will be of such endless interest and fascination for our kind. Another reason is that our own bodily processes, our own structure and functions make us related with both the shrew mole and the blue whale. Whatever our sophistication, whatever the form and bizarre size of other mammals, a mammal is a mammal, and our kinship within this ever-fascinating group is forever established and eternally unaffected by the clever usages of our sciences. If a whale is difficult to reconcile with our own kind, he is all the more interesting for it.

30

The Unlikely Mermaid: The Manatee

Names and Range

Manatee or sea cow, by either name this strange member of the very limited group of mammals known as the Sirenia is now one of America's rarest mammals. It formerly ranged from Beaufort, North Carolina, down and around all of Florida and westward to Texas. Hunting greatly reduced the numbers of these inoffensive and defenseless creatures, and today they are protected and may even increase. Seldom seen north of Miami, they concentrate on the southern tip of Florida and range sparsely westward to some parts of coastal Texas.

Appearance and Distinguishing Characteristics

More closely akin to the elephant than to the whale, the manatee is unique in appearance in our hemisphere. He is a dull grayish, large, robust, aquatic mammal with a rounded body and a small head. He has a squarish snout with very thick lips. The upper lip overhangs the lower; it is centrally divided and covered with stiff bristles. Each half of the upper lip, which is prehensile, moves independently. The manatee's eyes are small, and he has no external ears except very small holes. His forelimbs have evolved into flippers, and his body ends in a broad, horizontally flattened, rounded fluke. Sparsely distributed over his graceless hulk are individual short, bristlelike hairs. Males and females run about the same size and are the same color. Maximum length is usually given as eight to twelve feet, although a fifteen-plus-foot male is on record. Weights probably run from five- to twelve hundred pounds.

[249]

Habits

The manatee is an inhabitant of coastal estuaries and lagoons, sheltered, shallow marine bays, and sluggish rivers. In all cases he prefers turbid water and will travel far upriver to gain a murky, quiet site, there to pursue his inoffensive ways. He is shy, can't stand cold (he will migrate to get away from it) and has no voice, as far as we know. He will be seen alone or with a few others of his kind. He appears to be active (but not very much so) at all hours, lying at the bottom of mucky pools, resting quietly and surfacing perhaps four times an hour for air. He may be able to remain submerged for more than fifteen minutes, but there doesn't seem to be much reliable information on the subject. He lives on aquatic vegetation and shore plants that hang over the water. Stories about him coming out on land to browse seem without foundation, and one look at his body would seem to relegate such stories to the world of fancy. He is particularly keen on water hyacinths and performs a real service in clearing canals and boat channels of this plant pest. There appears to be a short northward migration along the Atlantic coast of Florida and the Gulf coast of Texas during warm weather.

Reproduction

Manatees are said to breed first between their third and fourth years. Gestation is thought to be 152 days, but that is not known for certain. One calf (rarely twins, it is reported) is born underwater and is immediately brought to the surface by the mother. Within twelve hours after birth the mother has trained it to submerge on its own and generally function like a true manatee. The calf looks very much like the adult, except that it is pinkish and, of course, much smaller. About three feet long at birth, they weigh about forty pounds. They may stay with the mother for as long as two years, during which time mother and calf may be seen swimming along together with their flippers joined. Some reports have the mother rising partially out of the water, clasping her suckling infant to her breasts with her flippers. Related species live in the West Indies and South America (also known as manatee) and in the Indian Ocean (dugong).

Observation

Compared to some animals, your search for the manatee will be restricted to a small area—that is, on the map. Actually, there are tens of thousands of miles of lagoons, island shores, and rivers for you to search in. Some are said to gather seasonally around the Miami Avenue Bridge. The coastal fringes of

American manatee.

Everglades National Park have a fairly large and well-protected population, and some have been seen in the following Texas areas: Cow Bayou near Sabine Lake, Capano Bay, Laguna Madre, and around the mouth of the Rio Grande.

Your first clue will be a movement in turbid water. If the disturbance moves in a specific direction, it is being caused by the up-and-down movement of the spatula tail of the manatee as it moves along the bottom. Follow quietly, and within fifteen minutes you should see the face partially emerge and hear the animal breathe. If it is cold, you may not see your manatee, for he will probably have moved off to warmer climes. If there is a sudden cold snap, you may see your manatee dead. If the water temperature drops too fast or reaches forty-six degrees, he is in extreme peril. Look in sheltered areas with plenty of aquatic vegetation, particularly water hyacinths; look for murky water, quiet water, shallow water. Some day you may be lucky enough to cross this very rare animal off your checklist. It will be a red-letter day.

31

Our Second-Largest Rodent: The Porcupine

As we glance over the bewildering array of rodent life that graces our natural scene, it becomes immediately obvious that nothing like a comprehensive description is possible in anything but a major scientific work. Many of these creatures have no common name and are known only by scientific nomenclature.

Obviously, all we can do in the chapters that follow is present the groupings of rodents and give some generalized characteristics. The reader should be aware of the fact that he is reading generalized statements and be inspired, perhaps, to look farther for more precise information about these fetching little animals.

Prey to all our meat-eating mammals, to many of our more impressive birds, and to a large number of our snakes, the rodents are a vital link in the food chain that supports much of our wildlife. Without rodents our land would be barren, for our wolves, coyotes, foxes, mountain lions, lynx, bobcats, weasels, hawks, owls, and many other forms would perish in most, if not all, areas. The pressure that would be put on our hoofed animals by the predators to compensate for the loss would upset their balance as well. Rodents can truly be said to be vital to the whole wildlife scene on this continent. Every one of our predators relies on rodents for at least part of the year, or for part of its diet all year round.

Names and Range

The porcupine, porky, or quill-pig, is one of North America's more interesting mammals. He is sometimes referred to as a hedgehog, but that is a misnomer. The true hedgehog of the Old World is not a rodent but an insecti-

Porcupine (dotted area).

vore. Our large and deliberate porcupine is found throughout all of Canada except for the extreme North, and in most of Alaska. In the original forty-eight states he is found in the Northeast as far south as northern Virginia. Most of the western half of the country has a population except the western coastal zones. To French-speaking Canadians, the porcupine is *porc-épic*.

Appearance and Distinguishing Characteristics

There isn't much likelihood of anyone's confusing a porcupine with any other animal. If you are looking at an animal with true quills on this continent, you are looking at a porcupine. He is a flat-footed, deliberate, robust, short-legged, clumsy rodent. He is generally blackish in color, but mature

Photo by Wilford L. Miller

Mother and young in Colorado.

specimens develop lighter tips on scattered hairs. Western porcupines are generally lighter in color than the so-called eastern or Canadian species.

This fascinating, unhurried creature is not really very pretty. He has a small head, short ears, and beady eyes. His muzzle is blunt, and his very important tail short and muscular. His actual fur is long, soft, and woolly. He has four toes on each front foot and five on each rear. All his toes are equipped with strong, curved claws.

The chief distinguishing characteristic of the porcupine is the quill. There are about thirty thousand distributed on the animal from the crown of his head to the tip of his tail. They are yellowish white with dark tips and are very hard and stiff. Sharp at the tip, they are covered with scales that act as tenacious barbs once they are imbedded in someone else's flesh. There are no quills on the animal's underside. Porcupines may weigh anywhere from ten to forty pounds and may be from twenty-five to forty inches long, although the latter figure is an extreme.

Habits

Clumsy though he may be, the porcupine climbs and swims well. His quills are hollow and doubtlessly provide buoyancy in the water. He spends a good part of his time aloft, often on surprisingly thin branches. He is largely nocturnal in habit but can from time to time be seen about during daylight. He is active all winter, even in the northern parts of his range.

The porcupine is a woodland animal. He prefers areas with conifers and poplars (aspens) but finds many other kinds of forest cover to his liking as well. (They are even found in some desert areas.) He is dull, rather surly, and not gregarious except during mating time and when dens are scarce, at which time he will share his shelter with others of his kind.

Categorically, the porcupine does not shoot his quills, nor does he attack any other animal. He doesn't have to, for nature has provided him with a superb defense. So smug behind this defensive screen is he that he is the easiest of all wild animals to approach, with the possible exception of the skunk. When threatened, the porcupine puts his unguarded snout between his forelegs, arches his back, and spins around to keep his rump toward the enemy. He seems to know that his undersides are vulnerable, and he instinctively drops his center of gravity when attacked so that he is hard to turn over. His defensive posture is accompanied with much clicking of teeth and warning grumbling sounds. If the enemy doesn't take heed, the porcupine slaps out

Porcupine, Ontario's Bruce Peninsula country.

with his tail. His quills are very loosely anchored to his skin, and when they touch a target, they go in by the dozens.

Domestic animals are often victimized by the porcupine's defenses. Most wild animals give him plenty of room to pass by unmolested. The fisher, though, regularly preys on the quilled one and has learned how to turn him over without being slapped full of barbed spears. Some porcupines are undoubtedly taken by wolves, bobcats, mountain lions, and other predators, but only when the pickings are lean. Predators hit in the face may die of starvation when they find it impossible to eat.

In some areas, porcupines have become a nuisance by destroying valuable timber. In winter they live largely on bark, and when trees are girdled they die. At various times of the year porcupines eat the bark, buds, and foliage of a number of trees. The bark and small twigs of cottonwoods are preferred, but willows, aspens, hemlocks, jack pines, elms, basswood, sugar maples, fruit trees, spruce, and birch are all part of the feast. Orchard fruit, truck-garden crops, particularly corn—all are eaten. The average porcupine will have a home range of a little more than five acres. Some individuals become great wanderers, however, and may be found far from home territory. When certain crops are in season, porcupines gather from far and near to raid the field. Whole cornfields can be ravished when the ears are in milk.

These strange, lumbering creatures have an absolute passion for salt. Any tools left around will be attacked and the handles gnawed off. This is evidently caused by the attraction of the salt residue from perspiration. Soap similarly attracts their attention. The two great gnawing teeth in the front of the jaw keep growing as long as the animal lives, and constant activity is needed to keep them worn down so that the animal can close his mouth and bring his rear grinding teeth to play on food before it is swallowed.

Reproduction

Porcupines breed in late fall or early winter. One or rarely two young are born 209 to 217 days later, April to June. The breeding itself is accompanied by an elaborate courtship ritual. If you hear a male uttering squeaky falsetto notes, he is looking for a mate. If you hear a female squalling, she is announcing her availability. When the two noisy creatures come together there will be a lot of nose-rubbing to confirm the arrangement. At birth, the young are larger than a bear cub. Their eyes are open, they are as much as ten inches long and can weigh up to twenty ounces. Within a half hour their quills harden, and they are ready to defend themselves. They start on some solid food after about two weeks but may continue to nurse for four or five months. At least one captive specimen lived ten years, but that certainly is unusual. Under natural conditions, five or six years is probably tops.

Observation

Look for your porcupine where the named species of trees grow. Although some may be found in brushy areas, most seek out their livelihood in real woodlands. They can be easily approached at night with a flashlight and seldom make much of an effort to escape. Any effort that is made will be vertical. They may climb to escape notice.

Porcupines make their dens in crevices under a ledge, in any rock debris, in hollow trees or logs, or under stumps or root systems. Trees with the bark chewed near the ground, or way up at the top, are sure indications that a porcupine isn't too far off.

If you live or are camping in porcupine country, there are two sure ways to attract them. Buy a salt lick at a farm-supply store and set it out, or soak logs or stumps with very soapy water. Sit up at night and sooner or later you will see your porcupine. In the summer months you may be lucky and see a mother with young. No porcupine can long resist a salt lick. Be careful about attracting porcupines into a campsite. They are no fun to stumble over in the middle of the night! Also, it is a very good idea to keep your pets locked up or chained if porcupines are around. Pets seldom know enough to let them alone and the results can run up a handsome bill at the veterinarian as he sets about what is to him a very common surgical procedure. It is, by the way, unnecessarily cruel to subject a pet dog to the torture of having quills removed without anesthesia.

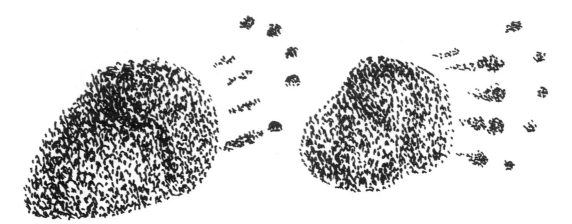

Porcupine tracks.

32

King of North American Rodents: The Beaver

VAST AREAS of North America were explored because of the beaver. This, the largest of our rodents, lured wave after wave of explorers, traders, and trappers into the American and Canadian wilderness. For scores and scores of years, his fur was the most important single commodity over hundreds of thousands of square miles. The American Indian, in his eagerness to trade beaver pelts for white man's oddments, sacrificed his hold on his private Garden of Eden. Just as the whaling fleets built empires in Salem, Boston, and New Bedford, so beaver pelts built empires that reached back to Europe. Some of the greatest real-estate holdings ever known on this continent were built with the profits made from selling beaver pelts in London, Paris, and Rome. Few wild animals ever meant as much to a nation as the beaver once meant to both the United States and Canada.

Names and Range

Castor to French Canadians, he is a beaver to all English-speaking peoples, and he has close relatives in Europe. Originally the beaver ranged over most of North America from Alaska and Labrador down to the Rio Grande, but the pursuit of his pelt became so intense that he vanished over much of this great area. Now protected and his worth now understood, he is on the way back in many areas. So valuable is he to the natural order of things, as we shall see, that he is transplanted with great care and treated as the royalty he is.

Beaver (diagonal lines).

Appearance and Distinguishing Characteristics

The beaver is, as we have said, the largest rodent found in the United States and Canada. He may be anywhere from thirty-four to forty-three inches long and can weigh as much as sixty-eight pounds, although mature specimens start at about thirty pounds. He is robust, high-rumped, short-eared, and has five toes on all four feet. His hind feet are fully webbed. His tail is quite remarkable; it is broad, flat, and scaly, and can measure as much as sixteen inches by four and a half. His fur, that great trade item that led hundreds to their fortune or death, is truly beautiful. Long, hard guard hairs of chestnut brown stand out from a luxuriously soft underfur notable for its reddish tinge. His underparts are lighter and his head brighter in tone. His great gnawing teeth, by the way, are a shocking shade of orange, and they grow as long as the animal lives. Constant gnawing is needed to keep them at a "workable" length. The two characteristics that keep him from being confused with other aquatic rodents are his great size and his broad, flat tail.

Habits

The beaver is active at all hours. He is never far from water and prefers wooded regions to all others. His food consists of the bark, twigs, and even the wood of deciduous trees, with a marked emphasis on poplars, cottonwoods, and willows. He also consumes quantities of aquatic plants and various grasses.

Large as he is, the beaver still has enemies. Bears, wolves, fishers, lynx, and wolverines all refuse to observe the man-made injunction against killing the beaver. An unfortunate number must perish every year.

A word or two concerning the beaver's tail is in order. He *does* use it as a rudder in the water, he *does* slap the water with it, very loudly indeed, to warn other beavers of impending danger, and he *does* use it as a kind of fifth leg when he rears up on land. As to whether or not he uses it as a trailer and carries mud with it, much has been written. Some claim to have witnessed the event, others claim it is pure nonsense. Pick your own expert and come to your own conclusion seems to be the rule.

It is a well-known fact that beavers are the master mechanical engineers of the animal kingdom. They construct dams of incredible strength that hold back vast amounts of water. They do this, very simply, to create an environment that they can live in. In the middle of the artificial lakes they create they build their elaborate domed houses of twigs, mud, and logs. The entrance and exit plunge holes are all below the waterline, discouraging predators from a direct assault. They store the tender branches they require throughout the winter underwater as well. The floor of their house is above the waterline, snug, dry, and warm the year round. The marvels that are the beaver house and the beaver dam have been often described at length. The strength,

Courtesy Canadian Audubon Society

Beaver felling a tree in Saskatchewan's Prince Albert National Park.

determination, and skill required to accomplish these major structures constitute one of the most amazing episodes in the life stories of American wildlife. But how are these engineering feats important to anybody or anything other than a beaver?

Canadian naturalist Bruce Wright calls the beaver "a key to wildlife abundance." In his *Wildlife Sketches—Near and Far* he charts the story of beaver activity as it plays its role in the natural environment of a northern woodland. Young beavers separate from their family some time after they are a year or even two years old and seek a life of their own. Finding an area where tender young poplars grow, they start the immediate construction of a dam across a stream. Upstream from the dam they begin the construction of a house. As the artificial pond fills up, they anchor a large raft of tender young poplars in the deepest water against their winter needs.

As fall approaches, a moose family finds the new pond and settles down in the area for the winter. The poplars and balsam firs at the pond's edge constitute a preferred winter diet for the species. As the pond grows in size, sediments falling from the trees overhead and debris carried down by the stream settle to the bottom, forming a rich and fertile muck. Pond weeds and water lilies find their way in and grow in wild profusion except where the industrious beavers clear them away from their main working area. "Now," in the words of Mr. Wright, "we have a trout pond of an acre in extent where we had nothing but a swift brook a few years ago—and the local farm boy, as well as the visiting sportsmen, are duly appreciative."

As the years go by, the beavers exhaust the supply of poplars in the immediate vicinity of their pond and they abandon the area to build a new

Courtesy Province of Ontario, Department of Lands & Forests

Beaver dam discovered fifty feet from Trans-Canada Highway near Nipigon, Ontario.

dam farther downstream. The water lilies and pond weeds now run wild, and the moose family that showed up before the winter set in returns to feed in the summer richness of the beaver pond. The area now provides both summer and winter range to these great animals. In an endless parade, other wildlife move in to take advantage of the profits of the beaver's industry. Black ducks, wood ducks, and goldeneye arrive to raise their broods. As the abandoned dam begins to leak, the water level drops. A sedge meadow appears, and white-tailed deer move in as the moose move out. As coarse saw grass takes over, the woodcock moves in. Eventually the dam gives way completely, and the fringe of alders move in and deposit their leaf mold. A whole history of forest succession and a thrilling wildlife panorama grow directly from the dam building of the young beavers in Mr. Wright's fascinating analysis. Again, in his words: "Summer moose range and woodcock breeding range in eastern Canada seem to be a function of beaver abundance." Truly, this is one of the most amazing tales from the vast store of our rich natural heritage.

It should be noted that the beaver means more to man than a new trout pond. Beavers are now trapped and moved into new areas where their efforts are required to help retain melting snow and spring floods. The beaver is today assigned to areas where man's industry is not up to the task. The beaver does it better and faster, or at least a lot cheaper.

It should be noted that all beavers are not true geniuses. Some misjudge and are killed by trees they themselves fell. Others pick bad locations for dams and have to start over at new points on the stream's course. Generally, however, they do pretty well at their complex chores.

Reproduction

Beavers are believed to mate first at two years. In keeping with his industrious ways, the beaver is monogamous and generally mates for life. The litter of two to six (average four) is born from late March to May, from a January or February breeding. The young weigh about a pound each and arrive fully furred and with their eyes wide open. Soon they are nibbling on tender bark and swimming with their parents. They are playful but must start learning the ways of the beaver before the end of their first year or at least early in their second. After that, the family pond is too small to hold them, and they must be on their way to change the landscape in the next valley. It is on their trek from home pond to new area that they are most vulnerable to attack by the predators that favor their flesh. Without man joining in the hunt, however,

Courtesy Province of Ontario, Department of Lands & Forests

Adult beaver and poplar cuttings.

enough survive to carry on the ancient beaver tradition of creating their own best of all possible worlds.

Observation

It is easy enough to know when you are in beaver country. The neatly constructed dams (some have been found as much as a half mile long!) and the turret-shaped houses (as much as eight feet tall and some more than thirty feet across) are the sure signs. You may note smaller dams in the area, too. These are constructed to create waterways to facilitate the floating of newly cut trees to the main body of water for use in construction or storage as food. The other beaver signs are the pointed tree stumps and nipped-off pond-side rushes and reeds. The beaver's efforts so dominate an area once his industry is turned loose that you can hardly fail to recognize the signs all around you. Approach quietly, use binoculars, watch intently, and you will see one of the great miracles of animal behavior. If you are careless in your approach you will hear a great swacking sound echo through the trees and see a mighty spray of water—then all will be quiet. Having closed their nostrils and ears, having lowered waterproof but transparent membranes over their eyes, the beavers will have submerged and disappeared into their snug home via the carefully constructed plunge holes that provide them with safe and easy access.

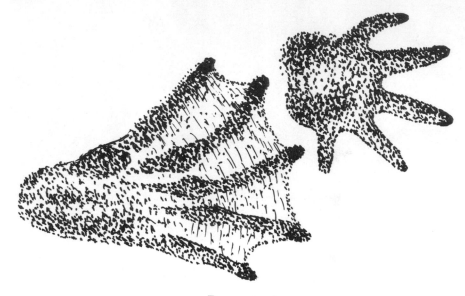

Beaver tracks.

Some of the areas where beavers may be found are:

Algonquin Provincial Park	Ontario
Banff National Park	Alberta
Bear River Migratory Bird Refuge	Utah
Bosque del Apache National Wildlife Refuge	New Mexico
Cape Breton Highlands National Park	Nova Scotia
Carlos Avery Wildlife Management Area	Minnesota
Carolina Sandhills National Wildlife Refuge	South Carolina
Erie National Wildlife Refuge	Pennsylvania
Fort Niobrara National Wildlife Refuge	Nebraska

Courtesy Province of Ontario, Department of Lands & Forests

Beaver home in Algonquin Provincial Park.

Fundy National Park	New Brunswick
Glacier National Park	Montana
Havasu Lake National Wildlife Refuge	Arizona–California
Imperial Wildlife Refuge	Arizona–California
Jasper National Park	Alberta
Kenai National Moose Range	Alaska
Kirwin National Wildlife Refuge	Kansas
Kootenay National Park	British Columbia
Malheur National Wildlife Refuge	Oregon
Moosehorn National Wildlife Refuge	Maine
Mount McKinley National Park	Alaska
National Bison Range	Montana
National Elk Refuge	Wyoming
Necedah National Wildlife Refuge	Wisconsin
Olympic National Park	Washington
Piedmont Wildlife Refuge	Georgia
Prince Albert National Park	Saskatchewan
Red Lake Wildlife Management Area	Minnesota

Red Rock Lakes National Wildlife Refuge	Montana
Rice Lake National Wildlife Refuge	Minnesota
Salt Plains National Wildlife Refuge	Oklahoma
Santa Ana National Wildlife Refuge	Texas
Seney National Wildlife Refuge	Michigan
Tamarac National Wildlife Refuge	Minnesota
Terra Nova National Park	Newfoundland
Waterton Lakes National Park	Alberta
Wichita Mountains Wildlife Refuge	Oklahoma
Yoho National Park	British Columbia

There are hundreds of other areas as well, and new areas are being added each year. A check with the state conservation office of the area of interest will produce more precise information to help you in locating and observing one of the world's most interesting mammals.

33

Something New Has Been Added:
The Nutria

EARLY IN THE 1930's, a Mr. E. A. McIlhenny brought a small selection of large South American rodents to Louisiana as an experiment. The *coypus,* or nutria, as they are now known, have a good practical fur, and they are good eating. Before the experiment had progressed very far, a hurricane roared in from the Gulf, and twenty of the stout little animals dug their way to freedom during the excitement. Small numbers of other nutria were brought in from time to time, and today we must consider this rodent a part of our wildlife scene. He has become established and soon will be known in many parts of the country where at present he is still a stranger.

Names and Range

Although the nutria has many relatives in South America, just the one species has become established here. As they spread their way across this continent, which they shall surely do, new popular names will crop up. Many of them will undoubtedly include the word *rat* and refer to the animal's semiaquatic nature. For the moment they are known as nutria. They are most common in the marshes of Louisiana and Oregon, but they are spreading rapidly. In the central states they have already been seen as far north as the Canadian border. It is safe to say that in the decades that lie ahead, the nutria will spread to all of the original forty-eight states and all the provinces of Canada adjoining the United States.

Appearance and Distinguishing Characteristics

The nutria looks somewhat like an overgrown guinea pig with a tail. He has a solid, heavy body with a short neck and a wide head that narrows toward the eyes and mouth. He has small eyes, small, round ears, and his hind feet are webbed. His top fur is red-brown to brownish in color, while the soft underfur is often a distinct bluish gray. His twelve-to-seventeen-inch tail is scantily haired and round. His overall length can be from thirty-four to forty-two inches; weights generally run from fifteen to eighteen pounds.

As this immigrant spreads to new areas, he will be confused most often with the muskrat, the subject of our next chapter. It should be noted that confusion can best be avoided by observing two points: (1) The nutria is very much the larger of the two animals and (2) his tail is distinctly round, while the muskrat's is flattened vertically. They really are two very different animals.

Habits

The nutria is semiaquatic and will seldom be found far from water. He can remain submerged for at least seven minutes, so if you think you see a specimen and he suddenly disappears, stick around awhile; he may be back. He is a strong swimmer, with only his hind legs doing the work. Essentially a twilight animal, he will be most active as dusk settles across his swampland home. He uses established trails on land and has very sensitive hearing and touch. His eyesight is dull, and he probably can't do much more than detect movement. He is a vicious fighter and even very large dogs are in trouble when they attack an adult specimen.

The nutria dines on a variety of plants, mainly on their stems. So far he has taken a liking to sugar cane, rice, various aquatic plants, corn, cabbage, lettuce, peas, and other garden crops. As he wends his way across this land, his appetite will find new taste thrills.

Reproduction

The polygamous nutria is sexually mature at eight months and has at least two litters a year. The young may be born in any month and number from two to thirteen; they appear after a gestation period of 127 to 132 days. They are born well furred, with their eyes open, and take to water within twenty-four hours after birth. Weaning occurs in seven or eight weeks, and their life span probably doesn't exceed four years. (The female's nipples, it should

Courtesy U.S. Department of Interior, Fish & Wildlife Service

An adult Louisiana nutria in his natural marshland habitat.

be noted, are along her back and not her belly.) The young are born, and the adults spend their days, in tunnels at the water's edge or on floating islands of vegetation. The nutria is very adept at weaving grass nests and often does so on those spongy masses of plant life so often seen in our southern marshes.

Observation

The nutria offers a unique opportunity to amateur nature observers. He is an exotic form only recently arrived. Science has no fixed boundaries for his range, and nobody knows for sure how well he is going to do or to what extent natural enemies from our own native fauna will control him. In the years ahead this visitor—he must now be considered permanent—will be spreading to new areas. When he will show up in Maine and Massachusetts, on the Florida Keys and in Nevada is not known, but show up he will. Amateur observers have an opportunity to be of real service to science. When you spot a nutria and are sure it isn't a muskrat or a beaver, report it to your wildlife agencies. They are trying to keep a tab on this newcomer.

Look to wet bottomlands; look in swamps, marshes, and along lake and pond edges where the vegetation is thick. Look at dusk, look after dark. Watch for his form as it progresses across open water leads mostly submerged. You will see little more than his nose and his V-shaped wake. You will be seeing not only "The Man Who Came to Dinner," but a valuable furbearer who is already important to the economy of segments of our population. It is not yet clear whether or not the value of his fur and flesh will outweigh the negative aspects of his fondness for garden crops. It remains to be seen, too, what his presence will do to the balance of nature in the areas he is invading. He *may* bring about an increase in the populations of some predators and he *may* drive some less aggressive competing forms to the verge of extinction.

34

Common Swamp-Dweller:
The Muskrat

Names and Range

Known also as marsh rabbit and marsh hare (they are sold for human consumption under those names), the muskrat (*rat musqué* to French Canadians) is one of our most widespread rodents. Our muskrat ranges throughout almost all of the United States and Canada except the extreme northern parts of Alaska, Quebec, and Newfoundland, and some pockets in several states where he is missing. Florida alone of our mainland states is without any muskrats at all. As we shall see, there is a local replacement on hand to fill the ecological niche.

Appearance and Distinguishing Characteristics

The average muskrat runs from eighteen to twenty-five inches in length (eight to eleven inches of that is tail) and weighs from two to five pounds. He is a stocky little animal with a broad head and short legs. His eyes are small, and his ears are barely visible above his fur, although they are of good size. His underfur is dense and waterproof and his guard hairs long and coarse. On his back he is generally a blackish brown shade, blending to yellowish or reddish tones on his sides to a silvery belly. His throat usually carries a white flash. He has four clawed toes on each front foot, five on each hind. His hind feet are partially webbed at the base of the toes. His almost universally applied common name comes from his distinctly musky and not altogether pleasant odor.

The muskrat—note the quality of his fur.

For purposes of identification the muskrat's tail is most important. It is long, naked, black, scaly, and *vertically* flattened. Its shape keeps its owner from being confused with various water rats with their round tails and with the beaver with his great paddlelike tail. Remember: *tail vertically flattened— muskrat!*

Habits

The pugnacious muskrat, a fighter among his own kind, is a swamp animal. He prefers still or slowly running water with vegetation both in the water and along the margins or banks. He is mainly nocturnal but is active in daytime during spring and early summer. He can swim backward as well as forward, at two or three miles an hour, using his hind legs for propulsion while his forefeet are tucked up under or against his chin. He can stay submerged for as long as seventeen minutes, it has been recorded. He may migrate for short distances during the spring and autumn, but if his home range becomes overpopulated and faces a "feed-out," he may travel twenty miles or more. It is only during these treks made at an ambling gait or by slow hops that he can be found far from water.

Despite his substantial size, the muskrat has his enemies. Snakes, owls, hawks, various weasels, and any number of other predators enjoy his sub-

Muskrat (dotted area).

stance, and his numbers are kept under natural control in this way in any
relatively undisturbed environment. He himself is an insatiable eater, his diet
being dictated by the vegetation available at the moment. He eats mostly
the roots and stems of a wide variety of plants, including cattails, bulrushes,
lotuses, corn, clover, bluegrass, wild celery, muskgrass, and many garden

plants. Although few people seem to realize it, the muskrat, although a rodent, eats a quantity of animal foods. He will eat clams, snails, crayfish, fish, frogs, reptiles, young birds, and carrion, including other muskrats. He does not hibernate but does eat some hibernating animals he digs up. He can be quite destructive to some agricultural enterprises.

Although a cooperative and diligent worker, the muskrat is a quarreler. He variously squeals, squawks, snarls, moans, and chatters his teeth. He is something of an architect and—although nowhere near the master builder that his large cousin the beaver is—does create some pretty impressive structures. He builds conical houses two or three feet above the water line, usually of marsh vegetation cleverly woven into a watertight unit. The essential purpose of the house is to provide his family with a dry nest of constant temperature. When he doesn't build a house above the surface he burrows and makes the same cozy nest below ground. He creates plunge holes to aid in escape and deep underground runs to confound his enemies. He digs impressive canals to connect feeding areas and often conjures up floating feeding stations, again of marsh vegetation. Although he seldom stores food against the winter and is often left hungry for his shortsightedness, the muskrat is a busy, industrious member of the complex swamp community.

Reproduction

The muskrat gestation period is brief, twenty-two to thirty days. A litter may consist of anywhere from one to eleven young and may appear at any time of the year. Actually, in different parts of his range, certain months are favored. Litters appear in rapid succession, the breeding taking place immediately after birth. Little wonder there are so many muskrats!

At birth the four-inch, three-quarter-of-an-ounce muskrat is blind, naked, and helpless. At the end of the first week the fur appears and is markedly duller than that of the adults. The eyes open in fifteen days, and at about that time the swimming lessons start. Their weaning is completed before the animal is four weeks old, and full growth is achieved by six months. The life span is relatively short—a four-year-old muskrat is a real old-timer. The average is probably considerably less than two years, largely due to predation.

In Florida, the muskrat's niche is filled by animals known as Florida water rats or round-tailed muskrats. They are found in all of Florida as well as in southeastern Georgia. They have rich brown fur and are, in appearance, small editions of the muskrat. They generally run about thirteen inches in length,

Courtesy Province of Ontario, Department of Lands & Forests

A muskrat house in Ontario's Lake St. Clair.

five inches of that being tail. Here again, we must call attention to that naked tail. In the Florida water rat, as in the nutria, the tail is round and distinctly different from the muskrat's vertically flattened appendage. Much of what has been said about the muskrat's life and habits apply to these small rodents as well.

Observation

It really isn't necessary to list parks and refuges where the muskrat may be found. They exist in almost every national park in the United States and Canada—perhaps all—and in a vast number of game refuges and preserves as well. They also are found in just about all of our vast wetlands. This writer has found them without difficulty from Louisiana to New York, from Maine to California. They are in wilderness areas, in suburbs, and within city limits. Anywhere there is relatively still water and a good growth of edible vegetation, there are apt to be muskrats. Unless it is late spring or early summer, you will do best at dusk or just after dark. Look along the banks where water weeds grow and watch for the telltale V-shaped wake in open leads between stands of water plants. Watch for the conical houses, look for established runs along the banks and the distinct plunge holes. In most areas, you will have very little trouble finding your muskrat. The muskrat will be one of the first mammals of good size that you will cross off your lifetime checklist. He has been first for millions of Americans and Canadians down through the years.

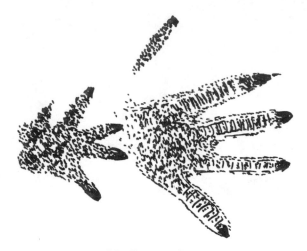

Muskrat tracks.

35

The Challenge: The Voles

THERE COMES A POINT at which nature smiles benignly at anyone who attempts to simplify the record of her accomplishments. Such presumptuousness must come acropper! The voles represent such an impasse in our efforts, for any adequate record of their range, habits, and diversity would exceed the length of this book.

Names and Range

Known as voles or meadow mice, this group of animals has within it a number of species, each different from all of the others. We can do no more than give a generalized picture of this extremely important group of mammals here.

The voles are blessed with many dozens of common names. Some include reference to range, others to habitat, and still others to physical features; Pennsylvania meadow mouse, forest meadow mouse, and gray meadow mouse are examples of all three.

It would be far easier to list the places where the meadow mice are not than to list where they are. From the far northern tundra to deep, shaded forests, to open plains, from burning deserts to southern swamps they blanket our continent. From high mountain summits to coastal areas where the sea has conquered the land they live their brief and hectic lives. Every state, every province has not a few but often many species. Any attempt to break these ranges down would involve us in a county-by-county census, and any attempt to break the species down by descriptions would involve us in details of skull structure impossible for the layman and fine distinction in coloration that would require dozens of specimens for comparison. It is quite an impossible situation in a book of this size.

Appearance and Distinguishing Characteristics

The voles generally are small, stocky, robust rodents with large heads, short legs, and *short, furred tails.* They have small, beady, black eyes and furred ears, which are hidden for the most part in their fur. Characteristically, the forefoot has four clawed toes and a very small clawed thumb; the hind foot has five clawed toes. Lengths are not often over five or six inches, but there are some larger and some very much smaller species. The coat is generally glossy, often coarse, and sometimes grizzled. There are many dozens of color combinations, and even with endless drawings and color charts it is a bewildering affair.

The voles can be distinguished from other small micelike rodents (and from other mice) by the *short, furred tail.* That one-to-three-inch tail is shorter in proportion to the overall length of the animal than in other mice and rats; the fact that it is at least lightly furred is a distinct departure from the

New York Zoological Society Photo

The little pine vole, or northern mole pine mouse. These are not animals for the amateur to attempt to identify in the field!

characteristically naked "rat" tail of so many other rodents. Another point of distinction is that the hind legs are *not* elongated. As we shall see, they are in some other forms.

So, if you are looking at a stocky little mouse with ears you can barely see, with a tail that is both short and furred, and with "normal"-sized legs, you are looking at one of our bewildering array of meadow mice or voles.

Habits

The vole is a neat, clean little creature that spends much of his time grooming his fur and maintaining his living quarters. Depending on the species and range, he may nest above ground or in an excavation at various depths below the surface. Above ground he will construct his covered home of coarse, heavy grasses and line it with softer vegetation. He may make it in clumps of weeds or under piles of debris and will generally have several entrances to facilitate escape from his seemingly endless list of natural enemies.

A sure sign that you are in meadow-mouse country is the appearance of his intricate maze of runs. These well-defined runways are both on top and under the surface. Holes about two inches in diameter connect the two networks. On the surface the two-inch-wide runways appear as paths where the vegetation has been neatly clipped off close to the ground and packed down as a kind of natural, spongy pavement. The maze is endless and often leads to common feeding grounds where several ranges cross and connect. The range of an individual animal seldom exceeds one fifteenth of an acre. In forested areas, these mazes occur under the carpet of leaves and other forest debris. In rocky areas they are not as easy to detect but will be found to be little mats of clipped grass and weeds between the boulders. The voles are not deterred by water and can swim well both on and below the surface.

Some voles hibernate, others do not. It is strictly a matter of range. In the more temperate areas, they move about on or under the snow except during the very worst of weather, when they take long naps. Many species appear to be on a kind of four-hour schedule. They feed and move about for the first two hours, and sleep for the second two. This goes on around the clock. Other species are almost exclusively nocturnal, others diurnal. The variations and combinations are endless, as they vary even within a range by season and local peculiarities.

The vole is a hungry little animal—all of the time. He consumes a surprising quantity of foodstuffs every twenty-four hours and would not be long in starving to death. His choice of foods, of course, is a book in itself. It all depends on where you are—or rather, where he is. He likes the tender stems, leaves, roots, tubers, flowers, seeds, and fruits of grasses, sedges, and many other plants. He enjoys most fruits and berries and will not turn his nose up at certain animal foods. Insects, snails, crayfish, and other mice all play their parts in his diet, as does the tender inner bark of trees, shrubs, and vines.

A thrifty little fellow, the vole stores food against thin seasons in underground chambers or in such aboveground treasure chests as hollow stumps and logs. A single cache will contain as much as two gallons of roots, tubers, and seeds.

Small though he is, the vole is not without a temper. Some species are more feisty than others, but most can put up quite a show when challenged. They variously squeak, squeal, growl, and chatter. When really upset they stamp their hind feet.

The voles of our two countries are of extraordinary importance to our natural scene. For countless species of predatory animals they are the link between the world of plant food and the world of flesh. Almost all of our predatory animals prey on the vole. Snakes, owls, hawks, eagles, all of our wild felines and canines, all of our weasels, even some turtles, frogs, and fishes take him when they can. The disappearance of the voles would mean utter catastrophe to our natural balance. Fortunately, as we shall see, his reproductive potential enables him to withstand the assault.

Reproduction

The vole is just about our most prolific mammal. Depending on range, he breeds all year round. In some areas this reaches a peak in spring and fall. Gestation is a brief twenty-one days, and a female can be pregnant and nursing at the same time. Litter size varies from one to seven, with three to five being average. Females can breed by the time they are twenty-five days old and may bear young within forty-five days of their own birth. This explosive reproductive rate is, of course, nature's way of feeding her predatory species.

Newborn voles are pink and hairless when they appear; they weigh but one tenth of an ounce and have their eyes closed. Under the careful solicitation of their mother they grow rapidly. Their first fuzzy fur appears on the fifth day, teeth on the sixth or seventh, and their eyes open on the eighth. They are weaned in their second or third week and achieve full growth in less than three months. Long before that they will have already added to the local vole population.

Considering the speed with which they must work, female voles are very careful mothers. They quickly move their brood away from a disturbed nest and constantly clean both their young and their bedding. There is a kind of frantic quality to the whole business of reproduction. With half the world looking to eat them, they seem to know that they must reproduce as rapidly as possible before their short, hectic lives are ended between the crunching teeth or in the beak of some predator. Their fecundity is one of the wonders of the natural world.

Observation

No matter where you live, a meadow mouse is not far away. Observing them is largely a matter of patience and eyesight. They are small, however, and extremely shy for obvious reasons. Their whole diminutive being is keyed to escape, and they will use all of their skill and all available natural cover to avoid you. It is an interesting kind of challenge.

Aside from lying on your stomach and waiting, there is another way of getting to know your local vole population. This book does not advocate the disturbance of our natural scene, but if you are to get to know these small mammals a trap may be necessary. The kind of trap that kills or injures animals is certainly not suggested, but there are traps that catch small

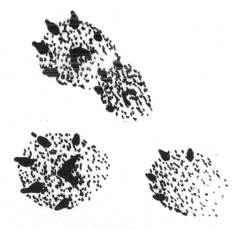

Vole tracks.

mammals unharmed and offer an opportunity for examining them close up before releasing them. These traps are inexpensive to buy and even fun to build.

A WORD OF CAUTION: Be sure to put a good supply of food in the trap if there is any chance you will be unable to get back to it within twenty-four hours. To set a trap that is barren of foodstuffs and leave it for several days is to condemn some harmless little creature to starvation.

Voles, when taken in these harmless box traps, can be kept in a captive colony. They are particularly rewarding, since they reproduce so rapidly and so surely. Excessive handling, however, may result in their death and will expose the captor to a fair bite. Remember, too, they can and do burrow. Unless precautions are taken, your colony of voles may disappear overnight, leaving a neat little pile of earth behind to taunt you. A very large metal or heavy wooden tray covered with fine screening and provided with a mat of sod with live grass is ideal. Given vegetable debris and left alone, they will soon enough build their nests and bear their young, giving you a chance to study their ways. Be sure to provide enough food for your colony and ample cover. Garden crops will serve one purpose, grass the other.

36

The Restricted Ones: Our Aplodontia

Names and Range

In a narrow band along our Pacific Northwest coast there exists a unique little rodent found nowhere else in the world. Belonging to a family unto himself, he is correctly called aplodontia, but he is more commonly known as mountain beaver (although he is far removed from the true beavers). Sometimes (and just as incorrectly) he is called groundhog or woodchuck, but he is no closer to those animals than he is to the dam-builder. A number of Indian names are also used by locals, and these include *showtl, sewellel,* and *squallah.* In a few areas he is called mountain boomer.

Aplodontia exist in pockets in southwest British Columbia, western Oregon and Washington, and in a few isolated areas in California. Even in these areas he is little known, for he does not seek or welcome the company of man.

Appearance and Distinguishing Characteristics

He runs from thirteen to eighteen inches in length, and in weight he runs from two to three pounds. He is robust, has a short neck, and a heavy, blunt head. His eyes and ears are both small, and his overall appearance is rather "square" and solid. His tail, a distinguishing characteristic, is seldom as much as an inch and a half long and is generally not visible at all.

The upper parts of the aplodontia are a uniform buff to cinnamon, with a few black hairs scattered along the spine. He has a white spot at the base of each ear and grayish to tan underparts. All in all, he is rather a respectable-looking rodent.

The wonderful face of the little-known and seldom seen aplodontia. Note the size of the front claws.

Habits

Although the names mountain beaver and mountain boomer would seem to put the aplodontia at high altitudes, such is not necessarily the case. Although he may be found up to nine thousand feet, this solid little creature seems to prefer lower areas, where damp glens may be found. He is strictly a creature of moist situations, and he doesn't mind at all if his burrow is flooded by overflowing streams. He just swims about underground, as he does on the surface. He creates elaborate underground labyrinths, burrowing endlessly into the moist soil near streams and in deep, damp pockets of forests where ferns grow. For these reasons he is seldom seen and little known. To add to the problems of the observer, he is almost strictly nocturnal. Not a hibernator in any part of his range, the aplodontia burrows around under snow as readily as he does underground. He is a hardy little animal and quite a fighter. His powerful digging claws and sharp gnawing teeth make him something of a problem to have in hand until he calms down.

Our aplodontia survive on green vegetation only. The foliage, tender, young branches and blossoms of a variety of plants, shrubs, and small trees, and ferns are included in his diet. He cuts and stacks his food neatly outside his den entrance, allowing it to cure in the sun for a day or two before taking it below for storage. He is a thrifty, quiet, unobtrusive little animal that unfortunately falls prey to a number of flesh-eaters. Various eagles, owls, and hawks favor his flesh, as do some felines and canines. Weasels probably take a share as well, but the aplodontia appears to be holding his own at least for the present.

Reproduction

Very little is known about the reproductive habits of this elusive little rodent. Birth takes place in a carefully lined chamber off to one side of the main underground burrow. There the temperature is constant, and dangers from predation are few. Most litters appear in June and number from two to five young. They are weaned in two or three months, it is reported, and separate from their mother soon after that to start on their own underground construction projects.

Observation

Few people get to see the aplodontia unless they really put in time and effort. That's what makes him such an intriguing project. His name crossed off your checklist indicates either a bit of very good luck or real dedication on your part.

In coastal Oregon and Washington look to deep glens beneath tall timber. Look for very moist areas where the ferns grow tall. Look at night or at least at dusk and move about very quietly. They are preyed upon by so many creatures that they are very sensitive to sound and movement. At dusk, watch out for your long shadows. If an aplodontia sees them he will dive into the nearest burrow entrance and be gone for good. To him your shadow will look like that of a large predatory bird about to descend on him, and he is well keyed to that danger.

Here are a few specific places to look:

(1) The west slope of Mount Hood in Clackamas County, Oregon.

(2) The Chilliwack-Sumas region on western side of the Cascade Mountains, southwestern British Columbia.

(3) The north bend and mouth of Kalama River, Washington.

(4) Paradise Creek, south side of Mount Rainier, Pierce County, Washington.

(5) The Trinity Mountain region of northwestern California, southwest as far as Rio Dell, Eel River, Humboldt County.

(6) Newport, mouth of Yaquina Bay, Lincoln County, Oregon.

(7) Weitchpec, Humboldt County, California.

(8) Point Arena, Mendocino County, California.

(9) Point Reyes, Marin County, California.

Aplodontia tracks.

37

The Seldom Seen: The Phenacomys

SINCE IT IS the avowed purpose of this book to at least mention every mammal group found in the United States and Canada, we must pause here and acknowledge the presence of a small, rare group that *is impossible to identify in the field*. Knowledge of their existence, however, may prove valuable, since specimens are rare even in museum collections and any information obtained about them is important. Perhaps you will be the one to add one more little fact to our poor store of phenacomys knowledge.

Names and Range

Since the ranges of the several phenacomys generally coincide with that of the spruce tree, they are often called spruce mice. They are also known as lemming mice, and two arboreal species as tree mice. They are found across Canada in grassy areas within the colder forested regions. They occur in small pockets on high mountaintops in the western United States. Few people have seen them, and fewer people yet have realized what they were seeing when the rare occurrence took place.

Appearance and Distinguishing Characteristics

These volelike little creatures are extremely elusive. No amount of descriptive rhetoric here will help you make a positive identification. The phenacomys can only be distinguished from the voles by scientific examination of the cranium and teeth. It is an impossible task for the average layman, at least in the field.

Habits

Some species inhabit grassy parks on mountaintops, others, strips of forest along grassy glades at high altitude, yet others, areas along small streams in humid forests, and a last group, trees in coniferous forests. The arboreal groups build their nests in trees, the others on the ground, very much like the voles. The ground-nesting groups make strangely large nests of needles and twigs of various firs as well as of grass. These nests may be four to ten inches deep and as much as a foot in diameter. The motivation for such a grandiose structure is not known.

The phenacomys do not hibernate. They are active all year and feed on seeds, stems, and the soft parts of a number of plants. Two species, at least, dine on the needles of the spruce and a few other conifers. Not much is known about their natural enemies, but at least one species of jay is known to tear their nests apart to get at the young.

Reproduction

Very little is known. It is assumed that more than one litter is born to a female each year. Reportedly a litter may contain from four to nine young, with three or five being average. The young are born with their eyes closed and little or no fur. They weigh about one ninth of an ounce. The fur starts to appear on the fourth day, and the eyes open in nineteen. They are apparently independent at the end of their first month.

Observation

The study of the phenacomys is an important project but not a very practical one for the amateur. If anyone is really interested in picking a group of mammals where his observations can materially add to science, then this is a group to consider. It would be impossible here to give much concrete advice beyond the suggestion that a visit to a mammalogist at a museum within the states named may bring forward some good, reliable local information. Specialists within those states undoubtedly are keenly interested in any data that can be found, even from amateurs, and if you appear sincere in your interest, they will probably help. For the general reader, for the amateur student, it is suggested, however, that the phenacomys may prove to be too difficult and too unrewarding a project until many others have been accomplished.

If you are the very determined type, here are a few leads:

(1) North and northwest of Kamloops, British Columbia, at an altitude of five thousand feet or more.

(2) Pass Creek Pass and Blue Mountains in southeastern Washington.

(3) In mountains north of Snake River in Idaho.

(4) Blue and Cascade Mountains in Oregon.

(5) Mount Shasta in northern California.

(6) Wasatch and Uinta Mountains in Utah.

(7) St. Mary Lake, Glacier County, Montana.

(8) Kimsquit River, Cornice Creek, near head of Dean Inlet, British Columbia.

(9) Tuolumne Meadows, Yosemite National Park, California.

(10) Fort Chimo, Ungava District, Quebec.

(11) Rigolet, Hamilton Inlet, Labrador.

(12) Swanson Creek, Riding Mountain National Park, Manitoba.

(13) Redwoods, near Arcata, Humboldt Bay, California.

(14) Marshfield, Coos County, Oregon.

(15) Tillamook, Tillamook County, Oregon.

Phenacomys tracks.

38

A Little More Confusion:
The Lemmings and Bog Lemmings*

SO FAR we have discussed two groups of short-tailed mouselike creatures that are difficult to distinguish from each other. Before coming to the true mice a few chapters hence, we must add one more group to the voles and phenacomys. There is a third mouselike, short-tailed group—the lemmings.

Names and Range

The lemmings of the United States and Canada can be easily divided into three distinct groups. The bog lemmings (also known as lemming mice, or *campagnol lemming* to French Canadians) are broken down into southern and northern forms.

The collared or varying lemmings are found only in the extreme North. They range barely south of the Northwest Territories of Canada into the northern corner of Ontario. They, obviously, are the least often observed.

The common lemmings range throughout all of Alaska and northwestern Canada to the polar regions. They are only slightly less remote than the collared lemmings.

Appearance and Distinguishing Characteristics

In general, the lemmings are thickset, blunt, little mousy creatures that are superficially rather like voles. They have short ears, very short tails, large heads, short legs, and small eyes. Their pelage is coarse and often quite thick.

* The bog lemmings are animals quite distinct from the true lemmings but are lumped together here in the interest of having a book of readable length.

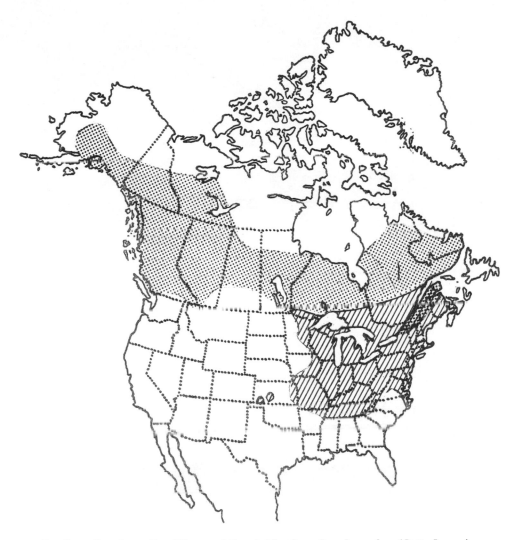

Southern bog lemming (diagonal lines). Northern bog lemming (dotted area).

The bog lemmings generally run about five inches in length. Less than an inch of that is unimpressive tail. The collared or varying lemmings run to six and a half inches and have a very small, almost indistinguishable, tail. The collared lemmings turn white in winter. In the true lemmings the claws become greatly enlarged on the forefeet as the long winter sets in. The common lemmings run to seven inches in length and are more or less the

Collared lemming (dotted areas).

giants of the group. Their tail runs slightly over an inch in length. Their fur is dense and long.

It is a fairly simple matter to tell one group of lemmings from another: Look at a map. Their ranges are generally well separated and their habitats, as

Brown lemming (dotted areas).

described below, will also help. As to how to tell a lemming from a vole or from a phenacomys on the basis of a quick look in the field, there is no simple way. Long and careful study is a prerequisite if real skill and accuracy are to be acquired.

Habits

The bog lemming is what his name suggests, a denizen of wet bogs and meadows with a thick mat of ground vegetation. He can be found actively feeding there both day and night. The collared forms are strictly tundra animals. Far in the North they play a vital role feeding all carnivores with their vast and ever-blossoming populations. Hawks, owls, eagles, bears (black, grizzly, and polar), and the various foxes, wolves, and weasels all feed on the lemmings.

The common lemmings are also tundra animals but, unlike their varying cousins, they do range south of the timberline. They are slightly larger in size but may be easily confused with their more northern kin in areas where the ranges overlap.

All lemmings burrow, either underground or in sphagnum moss or other vegetation cover. Depending on where they live, they eat a variety of grasses, seeds, bulbs, mosses, lichens, fungi, and even insects. In short, they eat whatever is available. They are colonial and their settlements blanket vast areas in the Far North. The range of an individual animal probably doesn't exceed an area much over a hundred feet in diameter. They carve endless

Courtesy Department of Mines and Resources, Bureau of Northwest Territories & Yukon

Back's lemming, photographed near Bowman Bay, Foxe Basin, Northwest Territories.

runways out of their environment and are constantly scurrying about eating and trying not to be eaten.

A strange phenomenon involves the northern forms. There occurs a periodic population explosion that leads to vast migrations ending in the suicide of thousands of individual animals. In various places, at various periods down through the years, these upswellings have occurred at regular intervals. Quite inexplicably, whole populations suddenly become excessively nervous, terribly hyperactive. Suddenly, the exodus begins. Out of every clump of grass, from every meadow, valley, and hillside, lemmings pour forth in an endless parade. Predatory birds and mammals in the area go fairly mad as they swoop down on the abundant supply of available food. Thousands are consumed on the march. Whatever the obstacles, the march leads eventually to the sea. Gulls join the marauding bands of predators as the animals push to the edge of the sea and plunge in. Their little forms can be seen for miles bobbing up and down amid the fractured floating ice as they swim to their doom. The number that perish on such a mass migration can only be guessed at, but it must be immense.

What has happened is simple to understand in the overall but not at all understood in the specifics. Nature must keep a great store of lemmings available for her predatory species. They are essential. This great store exceeds itself cyclically, perhaps due to availability of food, and must thin itself out before a range is permanently damaged by overfeeding. As we shall see, the fecundity of the lemming compensates for the losses that result from predation and natural attrition, for some lemmings always stay behind and within a few weeks have the population on the upswing again. What is confusing, thrilling even and a little frightening is the mechanism by which nature starts the migration and through which she selects who will stay behind, survive, and continue the species. What tells an individual lemming that he must leave to be eaten as he marches exposed across barren land or to be drowned as he plunges into the freezing sea? What signals are used by nature once she makes her choice? How little we really know!

Reproduction

Lemmings all handily construct globular nests from six to eight inches in diameter. They generally have from two to four entrances and are located above ground in summer, below in winter.

The actual period of breeding depends on species and range. In the South it occurs all year round with peak periods discernible in spring and fall. A litter of from one to seven (three to five is average) is born after twenty-one to twenty-three days. The female mates again immediately and may often be found to be pregnant and nursing at the same time. The young are naked and blind at birth, weighing little more than one tenth of an ounce. Their hair begins to appear on the fifth day, their eyes open on the twelfth, and they breed after a few more weeks, long before they achieve maximum size.

Observation

Common lemmings and collared lemmings are not at all hard to find, if you happen to be in the Far North. Just watch the bears, wolves, various weasels, owls, and foxes, and you will see them hunting the furry creatures in the summer grasses. In the winter you will see them digging their living larder from under the snow.

Since most of us do not get to spend much time in the Arctic, or even in the Far North of Canada and Alaska, we will have most of our experiences with the southern forms, the bog lemmings. A check with the Mammalogy Department of a local museum will tell you if fertile fields are close by. A trip into the bogs and damp meadows of the promising areas, preferably with the guidance of an experienced hand, will sooner or later uncover a colonized area. Without help, however, you will have some difficulty in knowing whether you have come upon a bog lemming or one of the dozens of voles that inhabit the same general range. It is a tricky business for the amateur but endlessly fun in the same way all puzzles and problems are fun. The reward, the very personal reward of accomplishment is great. Small box traps, the

Lemming tracks.

kind that do not injure the animals, will enable you to examine the local population with care and precision and will greatly increase your chances for making identification. A fleeting glance as your quarry disappears into a maze of vegetation or down a hole to a subterranean runway will provide little chance at all for recognition.

39

The Mound Builders:
The Pocket Gophers

Names and Range

Our various pocket gophers with their many individual ranges cover most of central and western North America. Some are found in the Southeast, but most are found from just south of the Great Lakes westward. In Canada they are found in the four western provinces adjacent to the United States.

Appearance and Distinguishing Characteristics

In general the pocket gophers are small to medium-sized rodents of stocky build. Running from six and a half to fourteen inches in length, they have broad heads, stout necks, and a solid, substantial look about them. Weights run from seven to eleven ounces on the average. Their one-and-a-half-to-three-inch tails are either entirely naked or very scantily haired. In all species the ears and eyes are small and well adapted to their subterranean existence. Their front claws are curved and enormously enlarged for the task of endless digging to which they are assigned.

Pocket gophers are mostly brown—some shade of the many browns, that is—but colors can range from almost white to nearly black. They vary in color and markings (which are not pronounced but consist rather of shadings) not only from species to species but from individual to individual.

If it is difficult to impossible for the amateur observer to tell one pocket gopher from another, but it is simple to tell them as a group from all other

One of the *Thomomys* pocket gophers, photographed near Fallon, Nevada.

animals. All pocket gophers have *external, fur-lined, reversible cheek pouches* or pockets. (These openings are not readily apparent unless the animal has stuffed his pouches with food.) Slits on either side of the mouth open into these pouches, which extend back to the neck. Another distinguishing characteristic is the peculiar nature of the large, yellow incisor or gnawing teeth. They are always visible, as the lips close behind them. In brief, if you are looking at a stocky little rodent up to a foot in length with great yellow teeth showing even when his mouth is closed, with cheek pouches, with great curved claws on his front feet and with a short, naked tail, you are looking at one of our many pocket gophers.

Habits

All pocket gophers are, of course, burrowers and as such are seldom seen above ground. They churn away in their endless tunnel building about a foot below the surface. A single animal may construct a complex covering an entire acre. The main tunnel may be five hundred feet long with innumerable short laterals and storage chambers. The main chamber, the den, may be as much as six feet down, although two or three feet is more usual. They prefer slightly moist but well-drained sand and loam that is easy to work.

At the end of each of their lateral tunnels there will be a characteristic mound. It will be from eighteen to twenty-four inches in diameter and may be six inches high. It is *fan-shaped* and has the actual hole at the narrow end. That hole, however, is almost always plugged, since the little burrowers prefer a "closed system." Earth is pushed up from below to plug the hole and is removed only occasionally to let sun and air in. The mound and plug are so distinct that once seen will always serve to identify the animal that made them. These animated little bulldozers are very important to the conditioning of the soil in many areas. It has been estimated that in an area where the pocket gopher is common, the soil is completely worked and turned every two years.

Pocket gophers eat tubers and roots encountered in their underground excavations but do occasionally come up and take surface vegetation. Grasses, legumes, various small fruits and grains are utilized, and even an occasional mouse or dead pocket gopher. They eat about one half their own weight each day. On the surface the animal seldom moves more than two or three feet from a hole and is very nervous and alert. They cut their forage into

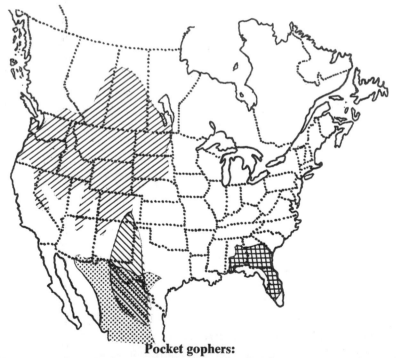

Pocket gophers:
Pygmy (dotted area). Mexican (diagonal lines). Southeastern (checkered area).
Northern (diagonal lines).

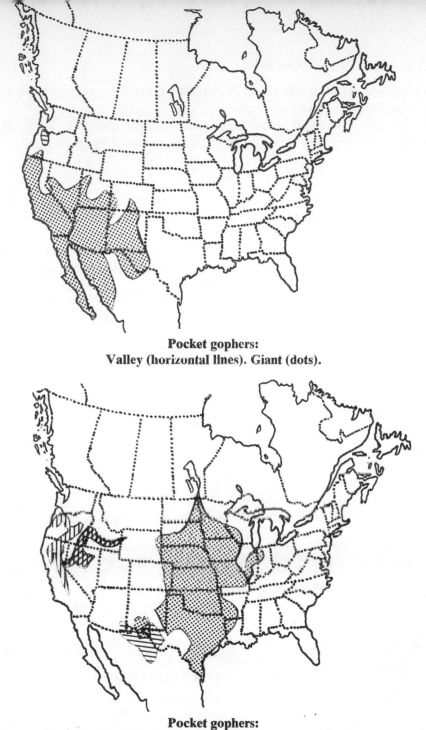

Pocket gophers:
Valley (horizontal lines). Giant (dots).

Pocket gophers:
Bailey (horizontal lines). Plains (dotted area). Sierra (vertical lines). Townsend (crosshatched area).

small sections and stuff the pieces into their pouches for transporting below for storage in special chambers.

Active day and night, these little creatures are generally quiet. When trapped and handled they variously squeal, squeak, and grind their teeth.

Reproduction

Litters of from three to five pocket gophers are born from March to May in deep underground chambers that have been lined carefully with vegetation. It is believed by some experts that the gestation period is about four weeks and that only one litter is born to a female each year. The young are about two inches long and weigh about a fifth of an ounce at birth. They are naked and toothless but only for a short time. Weaning takes place in about six weeks and almost immediately after that the young are off on their own. Except during mating and the rearing of the young, pocket gophers are solitary animals.

Observation

It is not easy to get to see a pocket gopher. It is no trick at all to see their mounds, but the animal itself is quite another story. Look to alfalfa, clover, and hay-crop fields. Look to pastures, along roadways and railroad right-of-

Courtesy National Parks Bureau, Ottawa, Canada

A gopher in Banff National Park, Alberta.

ways, anywhere where the soil is loose and partially sandy. Most pocket gophers will only come up on the surface to feed at dusk, at night, and on overcast days. Males are frequently active in early spring looking for mates, and that entails some surface travel.

The pocket gophers are preyed upon by so many animals—birds, mammals, snakes—that they are shy and alert. A good pair of binoculars is almost a necessity. If you attempt to approach a "surfaced" specimen, move very slowly and quietly. Their eyesight is not good, and they probably won't notice anything but your movement. They will be quick to sense your presence, however, unless you walk lightly. They are very sensitive to vibrations. Almost any farmer within their range can tell you where to find them.

Pocket gopher tracks.

40

The Whistlers:
The Woodchucks and Marmots

BEGINNING WITH THIS CHAPTER, and in the five chapters that follow, we will discuss the squirrel family. It is a large and complex group of rodents. The family is of particular interest to amateur observers because all its members (except the flying squirrels) are diurnal, and although they are often very shy and alert, they offer some of the best opportunities for prolonged observation in nature. For millions of people, members of the squirrel family have provided the first opportunity to really watch a wild animal about its natural ways. For that reason alone they are worthy of our notice and protection.

Names and Range

In this first chapter on the squirrel family we will discuss the ever-fascinating marmots or chucks. The burrowing species of the East are commonly called woodchucks. The mountainous species of the West and Northwest are variously known as marmots, rock-chucks, and whistlers.

Appearance and Distinguishing Characteristics

The woodchucks and marmots reveal their very close kinship in their appearance. They are nothing more than different species of the same animal adapted somewhat to their quite different environments.

Generally, the marmots and chucks run from eighteen to twenty-seven inches in length. They are the largest members of the squirrel family and weigh from five to fifteen pounds. Anywhere from four to nine inches of their

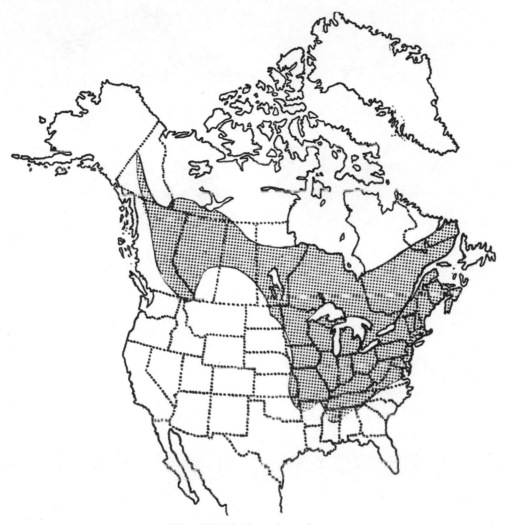

Woodchuck (dotted area).

length is well-furred, slightly flattened tail. All members of this family, by the way, have a well-furred tail. It is one distinguishing characteristic.

The chucks, flatland and mountain varieties, are compact, heavy-bodied, and short-legged. Although they can hit ten miles an hour in a dash for safety and can both climb and swim fairly well, they are best described as clumsy.

Hoary marmot (dotted area). Yellow-bellied marmot (diagonal lines).

They have small ears, moderate-size eyes, and small *internal* cheek pouches. They have long digging claws on their front feet.

Coloration and markings vary tremendously. Albino and melano specimens are not uncommon. The woodchucks or flatland marmots are yellowish to blackish brown-gray. Their belly tends to be lighter in color and less densely furred. They have a frosted overall look and generally have dark-brown to black feet. They seldom display any white markings except perhaps under the nose.

The marmots, the mountain folk of the group, have markedly different coloration. Many have white between the eyes and buffy patches on the sides of the neck. In the yellow-bellied marmot (he *has* a yellow belly) the feet are lighter, never black. In the more northern hoary marmot the feet are always black and the head and shoulders boldly marked with black and white. The hoary, it should be noted, is the largest single animal in the squirrel family. He can be as much as thirty-one inches in length and can weigh an impressive fifteen pounds or more.

Habits

All of the chucks or marmots hibernate. The length of their sleep depends on the length and severity of the winter in the range occupied. In northern Alaska the deep winter sleep runs from September to April! This is not a case of an animal taking a winter nap like a bear. It is true hibernation. The body temperature drops, the rates of heartbeat and respiration slow down to a marked degree. The animal can be dug up and handled without its waking, at least not for several hours, until its body processes work their way back up to normal.

Since the chucks are abroad during the daylight hours they provide a wonderful opportunity for observation. And although they are all solitary and fight among themselves in defense of a burrow, where you find one, you will find others close by.

The woodchucks prefer forested and brushy areas near open clearings. In farming areas they favor ravines, creek banks, and fence rows. They can often be seen on the grassy islands separating lanes of superhighways. This is certainly the case in New York, Ohio, Pennsylvania, and many other areas visited by the author. They construct complicated burrow systems often as much as forty feet long and up to four or five feet deep. There will be a front and a back door and often a number of well-hidden side doors as well. The home range of an individual animal may be a quarter to half a mile in diameter. These very clean little animals often have several dens. Those in open areas are summer residences and those deep in the brush are winter homes for hibernation and little else. The mounds found outside the foot-wide entrances may be four to five feet across. They serve as sunning and observa-

Photo by Wilford L. Miller

A woodchuck out of season.

tion platforms and as toilets, since the chuck is most fastidious about his home.

All chucks love to sun themselves, and they can be found luxuriating on a warm day on one of their mounds or on rocks or logs not too far removed from cover and safety. They have many enemies, although they are such good fighters that the young are usually the victims. They spend most of the summer getting ready for the winter. By fall they are rolling with fat.

The diet of the woodchuck consists of leaves, flowers, and stems of a variety of plants. Grasses, clover, alfalfa, wild herbs, garden crops, apples, papaws, and even some bark are all favored. Very little animal food is consumed, perhaps less than 1 percent of their diet being so constituted.

The diet of the mountainous members, the marmots, is similarly comprised. The differences are dictated by availability. The choice herbage of the mountain meadow provides essentially the same kind of diet as the lowland farm meadow, although the scientific names of the plants may be different. The home of the marmot may be a regular chuck burrow in an alpine meadow, or may be a nest under a ledge or deep in the jumble of a rock slide. Their life story is not really very different from that of the woodchuck. Both

Photo by Wilford L. Miller

Hoary marmots in Glacier National Park.

Photo by Wilford L. Miller

The yellow-bellied marmot in Yellowstone National Park.

animals whistle when excited, or grind their teeth, although the marmots are more talkative. The shrill warning whistle of the hoary marmot is loudest of all and may be heard a good mile away. When danger threatens in the form of a bobcat, eagle, or coyote, the marmot gives his shrill excitement open vent before plunging below to safety. Animals all around are alerted as the warning is repeated by marmot after marmot and the rock walls echo the message, sending it careening down the canyons. Marmots, like the wood-chucks, like to sun themselves and can be seen on open rock ledges enjoying their midday siesta. The woodchucks, more than the marmots, perhaps, serve a very important function. They provide living quarters to a great variety of animals. Weasels, foxes, coyotes, and a host of other creatures enlarge and enjoy abandoned woodchuck burrows.

Reproduction

The marmots and chucks breed at about one year. They mate from March to April, one male joining with several females. Two to six young are born in April or May, 31 to 32 days later. There is only one litter a year. The young are naked and blind, about four inches long, and weigh not more than an ounce and a half. The life expectancy is given as five to six years.

Observation

Since woodchucks are considered good sport (for reasons very difficult to fathom) most sporting-goods stores can tell you where to look. Actually, unless they have been hunted out of a particular area, they are very easy to find. A drive in the country will usually reveal some along the road or at least in meadows that can be seen from the car. Here are a few hints on timing: In early spring they will be abroad from dusk into night, the males looking for mates. In April and May they are out of their burrows anytime during the day, but particularly in the early morning and late afternoon. June through September will find them very active from just about an hour before sunset to dusk. On nice, warm days, look for a sunning platform.

It takes a bit more doing to find a marmot, so here are a few concrete suggestions that can help in the task:

(1) Northern Sierra Nevada in California from eastern Siskiyou and Modoc counties south to vicinity of Lake Tahoe.

(2) Interior valleys and foothills of southern British Columbia south of Williams Lake in Fraser River Valley. Eastern Washington, but west of

Courtesy Canadian Audubon Society

The golden marmot.

Cascades in vicinity of Bellingham Bay; south of Kootenai County in western Idaho.

(3) Higher ranges of White Mountains in Mono and Inyo counties, California.

(4) Jefferson, Nye County, Nevada.

(5) Kane, Washington, Iron, Beaver, Sevier, and Wayne counties in southern Utah.

(6) Flathead Lake, Montana; Wasatch and Uinta Mountains of northeastern Utah.

(7) Grand and San Juan counties, southeastern Utah; Wet Mountains and Greenhorn Range in Custer, Pueblo, and Huerfano counties, Colorado.

(8) Alaska and Yukon, from Portland Canal north on coast to Bristol

Bay; interior to Endicott Range and mountains lying west of Fort Good Hope, Mackenzie.

(9) Teslin Lake and Laird River south to Barkerville, British Columbia.

(10) From Chilcotin Plateau between middle Fraser River and Coast Mountains, west to upper Bella Coola Valley, British Columbia.

There are hundreds of other areas, of course, but these are a few potentially rewarding leads for travelers and residents in these areas.

HINT: In approaching a marmot, watch your shadow. If it falls on or near him, he will vanish. He is too alert to the danger of large, predatory birds to miss anything as threatening as the shadow of a man.

Woodchuck tracks.

____41

The Chatterers: The Tree Squirrels

Names and Range

There is a remarkable variety of tree squirrels to be found in the United States and Canada. Some major groups are easily recognized through differences in coloration and by a knowledge of their ranges.

The ubiquitous eastern gray squirrel dwells over the entire eastern half of the United States from the Atlantic Ocean to an almost straight line running north and south through central Texas to eastern North Dakota. He is found in southern Canada as well.

The western gray squirrel is found only in Washington, Oregon, and California and can therefore hardly be confused with his eastern cousin.

The eastern fox squirrel can easily be confused with the gray, however, and it takes some practice to tell them apart. The fox lives over the eastern half of the United States—from south of Pennsylvania into the Great Lakes region, and westward to the Dakotas.

The wonderfully colorful tassel-eared squirrel can be found only in New Mexico, Arizona, Colorado, and southeastern Utah. He is readily recognizable, as we shall see.

The red squirrel has a vast range. He is found all over Canada far to the north; his range in the United States includes New England, the Great Lakes region, and the Montana, Wyoming, and Idaho region. In the East he ranges south to Georgia.

The chickaree or Douglas squirrel is the western counterpart of the red squirrel and can be found in British Columbia, Oregon, Washington, and

Red squirrel (dotted area). Chickaree (diagonal lines).

California. He would be difficult to tell from a red squirrel if their ranges overlapped.

There are, of course, many more with highly restricted ranges. For the average observer, though, more interested in watching wild animals about

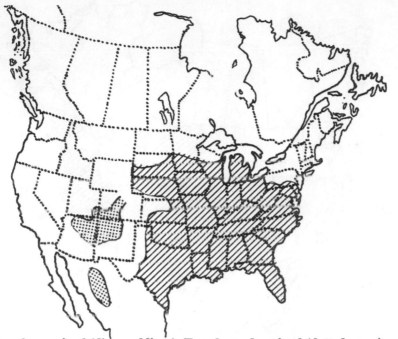

Eastern fox squirrel (diagonal lines). Tassel-eared squirrel (dotted areas).

their private ways than in the finer distinctions of subspecific identification, this list will do.

Appearance and Distinguishing Characteristics

A squirrel is movement, he is a shadow on a tree trunk, a moving branch, a flicker in the sun. He is nervous, yet he can be very trusting. He is noisy, very noisy indeed, and often scolds an intruder for walking under his tree. His scolding is a warning to other wildlife and more than one nonsquirrel has been saved from danger by the squirrels' chattery ways.

Somewhat more specifically, a squirrel is a smallish, highly active rodent with a bushy tail often nearly as long as his head and body. He is a powerful climber (head up going up, head down coming down), a great leaper, a hopper, runner, and darter. He has large, beautiful, liquid dark eyes with a decidedly oriental cast. His fur is short except on his exaggerated tail and occasionally on the tips of his alert ears. He has dexterous "hands" and the powerful hind legs of a jumper.

Western gray squirrel (dotted areas). Eastern gray squirrel (diagonal lines).

Speaking of the squirrels we mentioned earlier in this chapter, these abbreviated descriptions may help in quick identification:

The eastern gray squirrel runs from fifteen to twenty inches, from seven to ten of which is bushy tail. He has many color phases, including black (which is not uncommon) but he is usually some shade of gray. He is washed with a fulvous tone in summer, and his tail is usually bordered with white-tipped hairs. These hairs are a good distinguishing characteristic.

The western gray is larger, often twenty-two to twenty-four inches long, including a ten-to-twelve-inch tail. His white belly distinguishes him, although otherwise he looks very much like the eastern gray.

The eastern fox squirrel is generally a rusty yellowish gray with a pale yellow to orangy belly. He may have some black on his head, with a few white markings on his ears and nose. Flitting overhead from branch to branch, it is easy to confuse him with the gray. He is the larger of the two, however, and can be anywhere from nineteen to thirty inches long. His tail is from nine to fourteen inches. He can weigh up to three pounds, twice as much as a gray. He is about as closely related to a fox, by the way, as you are.

Courtesy Province of Ontario, Department of Lands & Forests

The very common and ever-delightful gray squirrel is the first contact with wildlife other than birds for millions of Americans.

The tassel-eared will not be confused with any other squirrel. Not a large animal (eighteen to twenty-two inches, eight or nine inches tail), he is very attractive, being the most colorful, perhaps, of all North American squirrels. He has tufts on the tips of his ears that give him a particularly alert and often quizzical look. His sides are gray and his back fulvous. His belly may be either white or black. North of the Grand Canyon his tail will be all white; south of that great scenic feature his tail will be white underneath and along the edges.

The red squirrel, technically slightly removed from those we have already described, is a handsome little animal as well. He has a kind of yellowish-reddish color with a white belly. He is grayer in winter and grows ear tufts for the cold season. In the summer, when he's at his prettiest, he develops black

Courtesy Province of Ontario, Department of Lands & Forests

The eastern gray squirrel in a black coat, a relatively rare melano.

side markings. He may be from eleven to fourteen inches long with a four-to-six-inch tail.

The chickaree is a reddish olive-brown little animal seldom more than thirteen inches long. His tail runs to half a foot and may carry some of the rusty reddish color he sports on his belly. All in all, he is quite an attractive fellow.

Habits

Squirrels generally molt twice a year. In most areas the months of April through June and September through November will see the local squirrel citizenry doff their old coats and don their new. Some species, in some areas, may molt only once.

Above all, squirrels are active. They are packed with enough energy to satisfy any breakfast-food manufacturer and they expend this vital force on

Photo by Wilford L. Miller

The pine squirrel, or chickaree, is one of the handsomest of the tribe. This bright-eyed specimen makes his home in Yellowstone National Park.

the many delights of living. One squirrel will consume as much as a hundred pounds of food a year and will spend much of his time gathering this impressive hoard. His food consists of many tree products (in Missouri, one species is known to utilize seventy-six different local foods!) including nuts, fruits, berries, buds, seeds, twigs, and flowers. He loves corn. In general, diet depends upon local availabilities and is very seasonal.

Squirrels are noisy, to the last one they are noisy. Their vocabulary is surprisingly elaborate, and with a little experience you can learn to understand what they are "talking" about. They variously grunt, purr, chatter, and even growl. When excited or angry they make a loud *chert-chert-chert* noise that serves as a warning to others; when contented they have a peculiar *quack-quaaa-quack-quack-quaaa* call that unmistakably says that all is right with the

The handsome red squirrel, a welcome sight on any woodland walk.

world. The red squirrel particularly is a noisy fellow with his endless ratchet-like chatter.

None of our tree squirrels hibernate, although bad weather keeps them indoors for several days at a time. They dislike cold, snow, rain, or high winds. They are busiest during the fall, gathering nuts, which they store, as every child knows, against the winter. Strangely, they do not store all of their nuts in their nest or even near it. As much as a hundred feet from their nest tree they may bury nuts in shallow depressions which they cover with leaves. These buried treasures are not necessarily for personal use. With their keen sense of smell they locate caches of other squirrels and eat what they find. This does not seem to lead to any particular social disorder. Many of the buried nuts lie uncollected until sun and rain combine and a new tree sprouts. The squirrels are the Johnny Appleseeds of the animal kingdom.

The squirrel's tail is a remarkable piece of equipment. In his endless sallies through the treetops he uses it as a balance; when he drops down suddenly (as much as fifteen feet from a high branch to a low) he adjusts it and uses it as a kind of parachute. It serves as a sunshade in the summer and a blanket in the winter. It is sensitive to touch and to air currents and may have some kind of warning function that keeps the little animal from being unexpectedly wafted out of a tree by a tricky gust.

These little arboreal bundles of energy are most active just after dawn and in the late afternoon. They love to sleep and sun themselves on high branches during the day, but they often come to earth to forage in the shade. They both hop and walk on the ground and can leap five feet or more if startled. They can travel overland at fifteen miles an hour. If frightened while aloft, they will lie along a branch and freeze until the coast is clear or until they are startled into moving off. Occasionally a squirrel will come out on a moonlit night, but they are generally diurnal.

Squirrels den alone, but when the weather turns really cold a number will curl up together for warmth. Though they prefer hollow trees for their dens, they will readily construct leaf nests if none are available. An individual range will extend for some two hundred yards around a single nest tree, but this is seasonal. As different crops mature they will shift ranges, moving over a five-square-mile area in the course of a year. If things go wrong in their neighborhood, whole populations will move off to a new area.

Reproduction

Habits vary somewhat from species to species and from area to area, but speaking of the eastern gray squirrel at least, females bear two litters a year. Males can breed anytime, but not so females. They can mate from ten to fourteen days twice a year (December–January and May through July). Gestation is about forty-five days, so litters are born from February to March and from July to September. Average litter size is two or three, but from one to six may be born. The young are hairless, weigh half an ounce, and have their eyes and ears closed. Within three weeks their hair and teeth begin to appear and the ears open. In four or five weeks the eyes open, and after six or seven the young start to leave the nest. They are half grown at eight, and weaned after about ten weeks. Young born in the spring generally spend the summer with their mother. Young born in the fall may on occasion winter with her.

Many predators pursue the squirrel, and it is extremely doubtful that half those born ever see their first birthday. While they live, however, they are a delight to the eye and ear.

Observation

Squirrels are nearly everywhere, and it is difficult to make any hard and fast generalizations. Your chances will be good, however, if you look to these timber areas for the types mentioned:

Eastern gray squirrel—Look to the eastern hardwoods and growths of pine *near* hardwoods. Look to hickory, pecan, oak, walnut, elm, and mulberry. Look to almost any nut or shade tree.

Western gray squirrel—Look to almost any living oak or pine tree within their range.

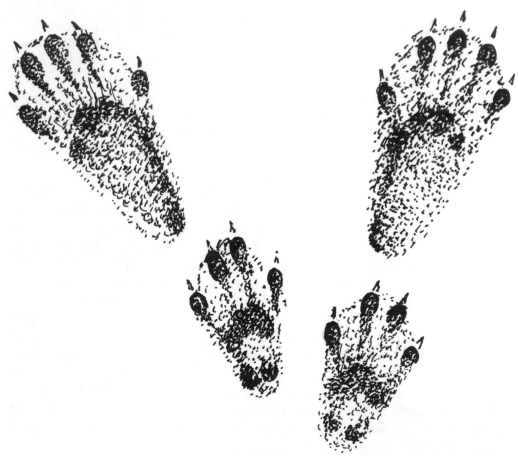

Gray squirrel tracks.

Eastern fox squirrel—Look to well-foliated nut trees. They may on occasion enter a stand of pine, but the nut trees are their favorites.

Tassel-eared squirrel—Watch the conifer forests of the southern Rocky Mountain states.

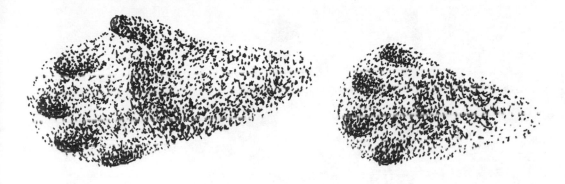

Tassel-eared squirrel tracks.

Red squirrel—The evergreen forest is his favorite home. He may sometimes be found in deciduous forests, however.

Chickaree—Like the red, he likes the evergreens best.

In looking for squirrels, remember that they are most active between five and seven in the morning and from five to six in the afternoon. They will often be found on the ground during these hours but may appear there at any time if the weather is right.

Look around under nut trees. Gnawed nut shells and other food debris will tell you if the tree is regularly inhabited. As nervous and alert as they are, the squirrels will see you before you see them. It is wisest to enter an area quietly, get comfortable, and wait for the little creatures to accept you. If you are not threatening or overly aggressive in your curiosity, you will soon enough become part of the scenery. As anyone who has spent any time wandering around city parks can tell you, squirrels become very tame and will eat from your hand once they get to know you. Although they can bite like fury, they can and do make delightful pets. They are best left uncaged, however, and allowed to come to you when they want to. There is something essentially tragic about confining so active an animal behind bars or glass. A wild squirrel that comes to you of his own free will is far more enchanting than any slave held in bondage.

IMPORTANT: Squirrels follow the crops. Find out which trees are bearing nuts, fruit, seeds, and berries, and look there first.

Courtesy Nebraska Game Commission

A woodland and thicket dweller, the fox squirrel.

42

Night Gliders: The Flying Squirrels

Names and Range

There is a southern flying squirrel and a northern form. It will be noted from the maps that the ranges of the two general forms overlap, and anyone lucky enough to see a flying squirrel in the wild probably won't be able to tell one from the other. That requires close examination.

Appearance and Distinguishing Characteristics

Flying squirrels are quite distinct in their appearance and are not apt to be confused with any other animal. They are obviously squirrels. They are not impressive in size, being about a foot long, with a three- to five-inch tail. They have a short, perky, upturned nose, prominent ears, and very large appealing black eyes. When caught in a bright light, those black eyes shine a brilliant ruby red from the reflection against cells enlarged for seeing in the dark.

The tail of this gliding sprite is flat, broad, and has a rounded tip. Uniquely, they have broad folds of skin on their sides that extend from their wrists back to their ankles. The flap encloses a slender cartilaginous spur that is attached to the wrist. This mechanism fills with air like a parachute when the animal launches itself from a tree and enables it to execute a rather well-controlled glide.

The fur of the flying squirrel is soft and silky. It is most variable in color and can run from a nondescript, drab gray-brown to a flamboyant pinkish cinnamon on top, with pinkish buff tones on the side, to a white belly. The underfur is usually slate in color, the head grayish, and the ears light brown. The hind feet are generally brown with white toes. There often is a narrow

A flying squirrel in Ontario ready to launch himself from a dead tree.

black ring around the eyes. In the summer months the animal is somewhat darker than in the winter.

If you should happen to be holding a flying squirrel in your hands, here is how you can tell whether he is a northerner or a southerner: Blow on his belly. If the hairs are white to the base, you have the southern form, while if they have white tips only and are lead-colored at the base, you have a northerner. You might have a little difficulty in executing this test, as a wild flying squirrel flits for a brief second through the beam of your flashlight thirty feet overhead.

Habits

Flying squirrels are almost never out during the daylight hours and rarely come to ground. For these reasons you are going to be somewhat slow in marking them off your checklist.

A beautiful specimen of the flying squirrel in an uncommon daytime appearance.

These little wood creatures are most abundant in the forests of the colder zones. They prefer forested regions where there is a good water supply close by. Their high-pitched voices, their musical chirping and occasional angry squeals are never heard far from a good stand of timber. They are more nearly completely arboreal than any other member of the squirrel family and cannot, of course, fly. They *glide* from tree to tree, branch to branch, and only rarely from tree to ground. When they land they correct the angle of glide until their head is tilted upward. Their feet are well padded to stand the shock of repeated landings.

They generally nest between twenty and thirty feet above the ground, usually in a hole made by a woodpecker. They line their nests with fur and bits of soft vegetation. They rarely so much as stick their nose outside that hole until the sun is well below the horizon. It is quite possible to have a

Northern flying squirrel (dotted areas). Southern flying squirrel (diagonal lines).

family live in your back yard for years and never know that they are there. They are poor swimmers and never enter the water willingly.

The diet of the flying squirrel is rather what you would expect it to be— nuts, seeds, blossoms, berries, buds, bark, grain, insects, some small quantity of meat when it is available, corn, and mushrooms. Like their larger cousins, they store food and sometimes bury it on the ground under leaves and other forest debris. The flying squirrel itself figures in the diet of martens, owls, tree-climbing snakes, and whatever ground predators can catch him.

Reproduction

Although there is some variation depending on range, flying squirrels mate twice a year. The joining occurs in February and March, and again in May through July. The young are born after a forty-day gestation period in March and April and in July through September. The litter can consist of from one to six young, but three or four is usual. The newborn are naked and pink and have their eyes and ears closed. They weigh about one ninth of an ounce. Mothers are very courageous in defense of their young despite their small size even at full growth.

Observation

You won't have any trouble putting yourself near flying squirrels, but you may find it something of a problem to see them. They will not cooperate by coming out when the sun is up and often stay so high up that even with exceptional night vision you won't be able to spot them. There are a few things you can do, though, to increase your chances.

Look for oak and hickory trees, particularly tall specimens at which woodpeckers have had a go. If you suspect the tree of housing flying squirrels (look for their food debris on the ground), you may have a chance by

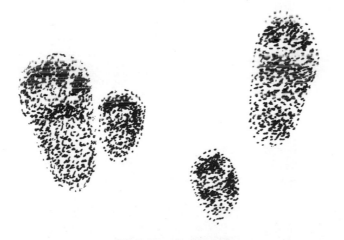

Flying squirrel tracks.

engaging in a very rude practice. Take a stout stick and soundly rap the trunk of the tree. If they are at home they *may* come out to see what fool it was who shattered their sleep. But you should not do this between March and mid-September lest you disturb a mother with young. She may feel compelled to move her family to a new nest. Flying squirrels like their privacy.

These little wood nymphs are attracted to bird feeding stations and show a marked fondness for peanut butter. A pale red light will not disturb them, since they are color blind, but one hung over a bird feeder may reveal this small and extremely attractive night caller to your more sophisticated eyes. Sit quietly, though, and don't make any noise. Special red-sensitive film will enable you to photograph them on these occasions.

43

The Exquisite Ones: The Chipmunks

Names and Range

Dozens and perhaps hundreds of common names have been applied to chipmunks in one place or another (including many derivatives from Indian names), but they are largely historical. Today, most members of this group are known as chipmunks with a defining adjective or two tacked on the front referring to either a range characteristic or a color variation. We can best divide them into two very general groupings.

The western chipmunks are the most varied. This group of animals has adapted into virtually every environment west of the Great Lakes. They are found from Lake Huron west to the Pacific Ocean. Most of the many varieties are found from the Rocky Mountains westward. They range far to the north, well into Yukon Territory.

The eastern chipmunks cover eastern North America and are found in the South to Louisiana, but not in the Southeast.

Appearance and Distinguishing Characteristics

The differences between many of the chipmunks are very subtle, between others they are quite marked. On a recent trip I had an opportunity to observe a desert variety in the Badlands of South Dakota and another variety in the Rocky Mountains only a few days later. The difference was literally night and day. The desert variety was pale, so pale the stripes barely showed at a distance of ten feet. The variety observed in the Rocky Mountains was brilliantly marked, and his stripes were clearly discernible as soon as the animal was spotted.

Photo by Wilford L. Miller

A streak, a flurry, a speck of life on the move—the blurred image of a rufous-tailed chipmunk on the go.

Chipmunks are almost textbook reflections of the color tones of their environment. They have adapted themselves to dozens of environments and have changed their color gradations to match. Yet, all have essentially the same markings.

Basically, the chipmunk is a small, terrestrial squirrel with a well-haired but not squirrel-bushy tail that is slightly flattened. The ears are narrow, erect, and alert; they are covered with short hairs. The head is rounded, and there are matched cheek pouches.

The western forms are smaller and more slender than the eastern varieties and have narrower stripes. They lack the bright-colored reddish rump and hips of their eastern cousins. In all chipmunks there are five dark- and four light-colored longitudinal stripes from the shoulder to the base of the tail. The dark stripes are more or less black, and the light are whitish or buffy. In many varieties the sides are grizzled, and there is a whitish patch back of the ears and sometimes a whitish stripe above and below the eyes. The belly is a slate-white. The western form runs from twelve to thirteen and a half inches in length, three and a half to four inches of which is flicking tail.

The eastern chipmunks are a little larger, twelve and a half to fourteen inches plus. The stripes are broader, and the rump and hips are often diffused with a brightish pink. They are generally grizzled overall, with a rusty red to reddish-brown tone. All chipmunks are brighter in the summer months than in any other season.

Habits

One word describes these little flickertails—*alert*. They are constantly tuned to their surroundings, forever sampling its sensations and loudly commenting on them. Bright and cheerful, they hop about chipping and chirping, often scolding, constantly working their tail, so providing punctuation marks to their comments.

Although they are completely terrestrial, chipmunks can climb. On occasion they seek food above the ground and will take to a tree if danger catches them away from a burrow or ground cover. They can and do swim well. They have many enemies and are constantly on guard. As tense as they seem to be, they can be quite nervy and will come surprisingly close to scold or, perhaps, just to watch. In time they can learn to be very tolerant of a man and even eat from his hands. One false move, however, sends them all scampering like so many very guilty thieves.

Chipmunks prefer timber borderland to deep forests but will be found in virtually every environment. In deserts, on the plains, in swamp areas, in the mountains the chipmunks have altered their ways just enough to fill a niche and make a living. Their diet consists of seeds, nuts, various fruit, some insect and animal food such as birds' eggs, and whatever other treasures their chosen environment has to offer.

These little creatures are not social and engage in noisy battles in defense of home burrow or food cache. They nest underground with their main entrance near the foot of a stump or beside a rock or log. The tunnel may be twenty or thirty feet long, traveling along just ten inches or so below the surface. The lined nesting chamber will usually be two and a half to three feet down. There are side chambers, escape hatches, and the usual niceties of the

The handsome little yellow-bellied chipmunk, representative of a numerous tribe.

burrowing rodent home. In good country a home range will cover two fifths of an acre. In country where the pickings are poor, the range may be two or even three acres in extent.

Chipmunks are true hibernators. The length of the hibernation period varies according to range, being longest and most complete as you approach the extreme eastern and extreme northern parts of the animal's range. In the West, and in the South, some do not hibernate at all.

Reproduction

One or two litters appear each year, depending on range. The farther south you go, the longer the breeding season is, and the more likelihood of a second litter. Where there are two litters, they appear in April and May and in July and August, after a thirty-one-day gestation period. Litter size can vary from one to eight, with four or five being average. The young, weighing one tenth of an ounce each, are blind and hairless. Their striped coats appear in eight days, and their eyes open after a month. By five or six weeks the little flickertails are out of the nest ready to be weaned.

Observation

Look in lightly treed areas near forests. Look along stream banks, in city parks, near stone walls, log piles, rocky ridges, rubbish heaps, and old buildings. Look in areas where a shy, alert little animal can feel secure with cover at hand.

You will seldom see chipmunks out in the open. They are almost always near some vertical object, some place where they can seek cover by running into or ducking under.

If you tempt a chipmunk into the open with a choice morsel of food, notice how his steps become more hesitant, how his body hugs the ground. This uneasiness will increase with each step he takes away from cover. The deeper into cover *you* go, the closer to his burrow you get, the nervier he will become. Standing close to his burrow entrance he will stand up and scold you as if he were ten feet tall. He is a fresh little animal and all the more fun to watch because of it.

You will have no difficulties in your search for chipmunks. The problem is to have the patience to observe them properly, to get to know and understand them. The first time a completely wild chipmunk announces to the world that you are to be trusted by coming up and accepting food from your fingers, you

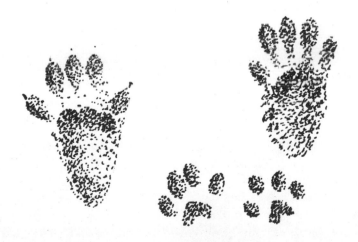

Chipmunk tracks.

will know that your time has been well spent. They are, by the way, often attracted to bird feeding stations and are great fun to watch. There is much to be said for watching them through a window as they feed at your sill-mounted station only inches away. To gain maximum benefit, cover your window with a sheet of one-way plastic now available from scientific supply houses. Inches away you can really enjoy this really very funny little animal without him being disturbed by your presence.

44

The Sociable Ones: The Prairie Dogs

AT THE TURN OF THE CENTURY one Vernon Bailey reported a prairie dog town on the high plains of Texas. It extended for a hundred miles in one direction, for two hundred and fifty miles in the other. It was estimated that the settlement contained four hundred million animals! No such prairie dog towns are left in the world. More are gone than remain, and the opportunities for studying these delightful little plains dwellers are rapidly disappearing.

Names and Range

All of our prairie dogs are to be found in the western United States, ranging only incidentally into southern Canada east of the Rocky Mountains. Actually, opportunities to see them in most areas are few and far between.

There are dozens of names for the prairie dog, but most of them are either semihumorous local applications or strictly historical. Almost everyone knows them as prairie dogs, with an occasional use of the major commonly observed distinguishing characteristics; there is the black-tailed prairie dog (an animal of the short-grass prairies), and the white-tailed prairie dog (an animal of the upland meadows).

Appearance and Distinguishing Characteristics

The *petit chiens* ("little dogs"—who are not *chiens* at all!) are chunky, robust, terrestrial squirrels with broad, rounded heads. They have an abbreviated, well-haired tail and short legs. They are grizzled, fat, and have blunt noses. The two main types, although immediately recognizable, are not really very different.

Photo by Wilford L. Miller

An enchanting close-up of a prairie dog made in southwest North Dakota.

The lowland black-tailed prairie dog is from fourteen to seventeen inches long, including a three-to-four-inch tail. He weighs from two to three pounds. His color is a yellowish tone with dark pink-cinnamon nuances. His ears may be darker, and his belly runs from pale buff to whitish. *The terminal one third of his tail is black.*

The upland white-tailed prairie dog is essentially the same animal, only somewhat smaller. He is twelve to fourteen inches long, with a tail that seldom reaches two and a half inches. He weighs from one and a half to two and a half pounds. *The terminal one third of his tail is white.* Both animals have a whitish or buffy patch on the sides of their nose, on their upper lips, and around their eyes in the form of a ring. Actually, of course, the animals are different, but only those distinctions mentioned, size and tail color, will be readily apparent in the field. As for basic fur color, there will be as much variation between individuals in one group as between the two groups.

Habits

Prairie dogs are, of course, burrowers. In a prairie dog town the bare mounds that mark the entrance holes will be from twenty-five to seventy-five feet apart and from one to two feet high. There will be a well-constructed and frequently reinforced dike against flooding from sudden rains. The entrance holes themselves are funnel-shaped and from three to four inches in diameter. They lead down a steeply slanting corridor that may plunge fifteen or sixteen feet into the earth before leveling off for another fifteen to twenty feet. There are side chambers for storage, for nesting, and for escape should the tunnel be invaded by a rattlesnake, ferret or badger, or should it be flooded.

Many animals feed on the prairie dog. Hawks, owls, eagles, ravens, coyotes, badgers, ferrets, and snakes all have a go at the nearest prairie dog town when hunger strikes. The strictly terrestrial little burrower has only one defense that works, a quick disappearing act. Actually, they are good little fighters and can hold one of the smaller, less determined predators off for a while. But time has proved that a plunge below is a better insurance policy than a show of bravado.

When a predator approaches a town, the first animal to see him gives a sharp warning call, bobs up and down in excitement, calls again, and then plunges below. Other sentinels farther from the danger zone take up the watch, and as the hungry enemy moves among them, the call, and the bobbing and disappearing sentinels, mark his course. He seldom catches a prairie dog unaware, for there are always sentinels on duty in the well-developed social order of these towns. A soaring bird of prey moving in from on high need do no more than cast a shadow before all prairie dogs in sight plunge for safety. They variously chirp, whistle, and bark to express their moods and attitudes. Their barking gave them the name *dog;* they are, of course no more a dog than an elephant.

The various native plants of the Great Plains make up the prairie dog's diet. All kinds of grasses, roots, and blossoms are eaten and occasionally some garden crops. Very little animal food is included on the menu.

Prairie dogs have a short hibernation period that entirely depends on the

A prairie dog town in Roosevelt Park, North Dakota.

part of the range and the severity of the season. As it occurs, though, it is true hibernation.

Reproduction

One litter is born to the prairie dog female each year. Breeding occurs from March to May, and birth evidently can take place from May on. Actually, although these animals have been observed by scientists for a very long time, little about their breeding habits is known.

Litter size is recorded as one to eight, with four or five being usual. The young are blind and hairless, and their eyes don't open for 33 to 37 days. At about six weeks they begin to appear aboveground and are ready to be weaned. They almost certainly separate from the mother by early fall at the latest.

Observation

Look for your prairie dogs in early morning or late afternoon. They sleep during the midday high sun and do not come out at night. Look for them where the grass is short. They will not settle an area where the vegetation is high because they cannot tolerate any situation where there is cover for an enemy. They don't like surprises and can best avoid them by living where they can only be approached across open space.

There are a few "wild" prairie dog towns around and several protected ones. Some are to be found near Lubbock, Texas, in the Wichita Mountains Wildlife Reserve in southwestern Oklahoma (visited and thoroughly enjoyed by the author), at the Kirwin Wildlife Refuge in Kansas, and near Devils Tower National Monument in eastern Wyoming. A letter to the conservation department of the state of interest will bring some specific suggestions.

If a farmer has to shoot a favorite horse or a valuable steer because it stepped into a prairie dog hole and broke its leg, I can understand his emotions. A little varmint, "a good-for-nothing rodent," after all, is hardly worth preserving at the cost of thousands of dollars' worth of livestock. It is

Photo by Wilford L. Miller

A family group; the black-tailed prairie dog.

understandable that ranchers want prairie dogs off their land and are willing to spend hard-earned money on poisoned grain, traps, gas, and ammunition to rid themselves of the pests.

On the other hand, there must be some places in this vast land that can be set aside for these delightful little animals so that they may survive. Perhaps Texas can't accommodate towns of four hundred million animals, but the Great Plains states should do more than they are presently doing to save them. They provide food for many of our most attractive predators (who wouldn't be as attracted to livestock if their natural prey weren't disappearing) and they offer a wonderful observation project for amateurs and professionals alike. If future generations cannot offer their children an opportunity to see these prairie dog towns, they will not be able to communicate to them the great treasures of our wonderland continent as it once was. The often featureless plains can ill afford to lose this unique attraction. Hopefully, more space will be set aside so our prairie dogs will survive to delight and amuse us. It would be sad indeed if they didn't.

Prairie dog tracks.

45

In Great Variety: The Ground Squirrels

Names and Range

There is an interesting group of small rodents in our two countries known collectively as ground squirrels. There are hundreds of common names for these animals, including antelope squirrel, rock squirrel, and, quite inaccurately, gopher or gopher squirrel. Our discussion of the group in this chapter will perforce be generalized.

The ground squirrels are essentially animals of the western half of this continent although some, like the very widespread thirteen-lined ground squirrel, range eastward to the central Great Lakes region. Other forms, like the Arctic ground squirrel, range far to the north, all the way to the northernmost coast of Alaska. Basically, the ground squirrels are found in every northern and central state west of Lake Huron, in all southwestern states, and in all western Canadian provinces from Manitoba on.

Appearance and Distinguishing Characteristics

The ground squirrels are small, slender, terrestrial squirrels. They have large eyes, small ears set low on their head, cheek pouches, and a sleek overall look. Their color variations are seemingly endless, running from a nondescript dull smoke-gray without differentiation to mottled, speckled, grizzled, or striped. The striped varieties can be readily distinguished from the chipmunks, since they don't have the consistent and reliable stripe formula of their smaller cousins: five dark, four light.

In size these animals are equally variable. Depending on species, they run from seven to twenty-one inches overall when full grown. The difference can

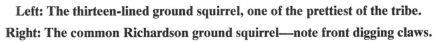

Left: The thirteen-lined ground squirrel, one of the prettiest of the tribe.

Right: The common Richardson ground squirrel—note front digging claws.

be a result of either body or tail length. The body of the small prairie-dwelling thirteen-lined ground squirrel can be as short as four and a half inches, while the Arctic ground squirrel can be fourteen inches without tail. The tail of the Townsend ground squirrel rarely exceeds two inches and is usually not more than an inch and a third; the rock squirrel of the arid Southwest, on the other hand, can have a ten-inch tail. Unfortunately, we can't assign a generalized body-to-tail ratio. Some species have tails less than a fifth of their body length, while others will have tails equal to body and head.

For all the confusion, largely in telling one from another, ground squirrels can be quickly differentiated from their rodent cousins. They are smaller than marmots, they are altogether different from pocket gophers, as a review of that chapter will reveal, and they don't have the chipmunk's regular formula markings. They are active, bright, and altogether attractive little creatures.

Habits

Like all other terrestrial squirrels, the rock squirrels are burrowers. They construct complex underground networks, one animal creating several each year. The burrow typically has several entrances, with no mounds showing. They carefully carry excavated dirt away in their cheek pouches. During the day, several entrances to a burrow will be open. At night all are plugged with grass or sod. The two-inch opening leads into a tunnel that can drop from half a foot to four feet almost straight down. The tunnel then turns at right angles

Photo by Wilford L. Miller

The handsome golden-mantled ground squirrel, photographed in Montana.

Courtesy Canadian Audubon Society

The alert Columbian ground squirrel near his burrow entrance.

and can meander twenty feet or more in several directions. There is an underground drainage system, there are storage chambers, a lined nesting chamber, and escape hatches. It is a major undertaking.

Many creatures prey upon the ground squirrels. Depending on range, wolves, coyotes, bears, foxes, skunks, weasels, minks, badgers, domestic cats and dogs, hawks, owls, snakes, and whatever wild felines are in the area—all dine on them with as much regularity as individual skills will allow. As a result, these little animals are very alert and quite shy. They are never out when the sun isn't up; nine in the morning to late afternoon is when they are to be found. They even stay below on very cloudy days.

The ground squirrels are all true hibernators. When they curl up in the fall in their carefully lined underground nesting chamber, it is for a really deep sleep! Their body temperature drops from a high of 106 degrees to a near-freezing 37. The heartbeat slows down from a high of 350 beats a minute to a low of five. The rate of respiration drops from fifty breaths a minute to four. During this sleep the little animal can lose as much as one third to one half its body weight.

These little terrestrial sprites consume an amazing amount of animal food. Some species may depend on these sources for as much as 50 percent of their diet. They eat insects, earthworms, lizards, eggs, young birds, mice, and carrion, as well as seeds, nuts, roots, foliage, grasses, legumes, bulbs, and, unfortunately, garden crops. The collecting and hunting range of an individual animal is usually about an acre and a half in extent. They are solitary in their ways but somewhat colonial in that they build their burrows close to others of their kind. They are, however, openly hostile to a visitor on their home range. Although it is incidental to their regular way of life, the ground squirrels can climb with a fair amount of skill.

These trilling, whistling little squirrels are attractive to watch and fun to study. They are curious little creatures and are characteristically seen sitting up not far from a burrow entrance with their forefeet held tightly against their body and their tails stretched straight out back as a brace. They are rigid little figures as they crane for a better view of the passing parade. On an open prairie they look like so many tenpins.

Reproduction

Ground squirrels generally breed shortly after coming out of their deep winter sleep. Gestation is a brief twenty-seven to twenty-eight days, so most litters appear by mid-May. Litter size is large, one to fourteen being recorded, with the average between eight and ten. The young are blind, toothless, and completely helpless, weighing no more than a tenth of an ounce. The fur appears on the twelfth day, the teeth on the twentieth; the eyes open within twenty-three to twenty-six days after birth, and they are out of the nest and ready to be weaned by the sixth week.

Observation

Look only when the sun is bright and the season is warm. When the frosts start, the world is done with the ground squirrel for another year. Look in open spaces, for although there are exceptions among this group, these are animals of open areas. Like the prairie dogs, most ground squirrels prefer a good view of the surrounding territory and will prefer a hole in the ground to a tree any day of the week.

A check with a local museum will reveal the nature of indigenous species. You may be in an area where the rocky jumbles of slightly higher ground will pay off better than open bottom lands. In farm country local agrarians can usually give reliable advice, since they often spend hours each week attempting to clear these little rodents from their land. It is bad enough that they make holes all over the place and steal corn and other crops intended for market, but when they steal newly hatched chicks as well, well, that's a *varmint* in any farmer's book.

Ground squirrel tracks.

46

The Unwanted: The Old World
Rats and Mice

As THE READER may have detected by now, I am on the side of wildlife. I am a staunch conservationist; I am for the preservation of native species at all costs. There comes a time, however, when even the most energetic of animal lovers must part ways with the animal kingdom. Such a separation often occurs when the Old World rats and mice are discussed.

Asia has given us three unwanted gifts that have remained to plague us in a thousand different ways. The so-called Norway rat, the black rat, and the house mouse are all natives of Asia that came to our shores via Europe. It is believed that the house mouse arrived here first around the time of our Revolutionary War. It promptly spread across both the United States and Canada. The black rat arrived in Central and South America in 1554. It is known to have come ashore at Jamestown in 1609 and promptly began its march across the continent from there. The Norway rat is not an original native of Norway at all but is called that because its first scientific description came from that country. It, too, came to Europe from Asia, beginning to arrive in North America in 1775. It is much more aggressive than the black rat and rapidly gained in the competition between the two species. Believe it or not, *the most successful predator of the black rat is the Norway rat.*

No matter how much you like animals, there is *nothing* good to be said for any one of these three. They are dangerous, destructive, expensive creatures, a menace to man and animal alike. In order of villainy they rate: Norway rat, house mouse, black rat. The extinction of any one of the three, although

Courtesy U.S. Department of Interior, Fish & Wildlife Service

This photo illustrates two characteristics of the Norway rat that contribute to its destructive qualities: fecundity and filth.

almost certain never to come about, would be a great joy to all mankind. It should be pointed out that all three were once simply wild animals in balance with the environment. They were adaptable, however, and grasped the opportunity to coexist with, and become parasites on, man.

It is estimated by the United States Government that in this country alone there are fifty million rats on farms, thirty million in towns, and twenty million in cities. *Each one of these rats costs the American people ten dollars per year; a hundred million rats cost a billion dollars annually.*

Rats destroy human food by the millions of bushels. "They attack it in the field, on the farm, in the elevator, mill, processing plant, store, and home, and in transit." That is a quote from the United States Department of the Interior. What they don't eat they contaminate. Each rat drops from 25 to 150 pellets a day. A rat voids 10 to 20 cubic centimeters of urine each day. Every rat sheds some of its five hundred thousand hairs each day. Much of this is directly on food intended for human consumption. A survey of cereal storage facilities in one state alone revealed that 43 percent of all stored grains were contaminated by rats; 59 percent by mice. In one section of the country only 3 percent of the corn reaching market was free from rat and mouse filth. One state chemist found rat hairs in thirteen of forty-three different brands of *canned* food. In one single incident 1,800,000 pounds of sugar were ruined by rat urine.

Every night of the year hundreds of baby chicks are killed by rats. Broilers and adult hens are often killed as well. Baby pigs, lambs, and calves are injured, and many must be destroyed.

Rats carry fleas and lice, mites and ticks. Their parasites spread plague and typhus fever to man. Rats themselves carry amebiasis, infectious jaundice, food poisoning, and tapeworm infections which they spread to man. Each year hundreds of children are bitten, some seriously injured, some, at least, killed. Our pets and livestock contract many serious diseases from rats. These include contagious abortion, distemper, equine influenza, mange, mastitis, paratyphoid, pseudorabies, rabies, swine erysipelas, tracheitus, trichinosis, and tuberculosis.

Rats and mice destroy property by their endless gnawing and burrowing. They cost us millions on that score alone. Every year human beings die in fires caused by rats and mice gnawing the insulation off electrical wiring. Hundreds

Photo by Wilford L. Miller

The house mouse may be humorous as the little creature that frightens ladies or runs from cats in animated cartoons, but there is nothing funny in the actual damage he does.

of valuable items used by man ranging from carpeting to harnesses, from press rollers to factory drive belts, from soap to fire hoses to flower bulbs to books and tapestries are all destroyed by rats and mice each year.

What do the rat and the mouse give us in return? Exactly one thing: domesticated strains including the popular white that are useful in laboratory research. What a dreadful price we pay!

Not only is man victimized by rats and mice, but wildlife is as well. In area after area, on islands and continents, one after the other, as the rat followed man around the world, wildlife was destroyed. Ground-nesting birds were the first victims in each new area. The young of other mammal species were attacked and killed while still too small to protect themselves. Natural balances were upset forever by the competition of these aggressive exotics.

Who are the villains?

The Norway or brown rat is a medium-sized rodent that requires little description. He is a uniform grayish brown, somewhat paler on the underparts. He has a long, scaly, scantily haired tail. He is usually from twelve to eighteen inches long and weighs about ten ounces. He is omnivorous and will eat literally anything he can ingest. He is particularly fond of dumps, feed stacks, barns, and any area where sanitation tends to be substandard.

The black rat (which is gray-black) has larger, broader ears. He is more slender than the Norway rat and has a thinner, finer-scaled tail. His tail is longer than his head and body combined.

The house mouse is distinguishable from our native mice by his scantily haired tail and by the yellowish tinge to his underparts. He is usually six or seven inches long and weighs from half an ounce to an ounce. He has protruding black eyes.

A major problem in dealing with these unwanted guests is their rate of reproduction. The rats breed at three months of age. Gestation is a brief twenty-one days, and litters run from one to *twenty-two* in size. A female rat can easily deliver twelve litters a year. The house mouse female delivers from one to thirteen young in eighteen days. She matures at six weeks and breeds continually from then on. She may have thirteen or more litters a year, delivering over one hundred young. In some areas the house mouse population can run thousands to the acre!

It is extremely doubtful that man can ever win the endless war he must wage against rats and mice. As long as man lives, he will have to fight them in every way possible. He will spend more on rats and mice than he will spend on many of his most important enterprises. What could our schools be like if we had that extra billion dollars per year? Our hospitals? Our juvenile guidance facilities? We don't have that extra money, however, because a few rats and a few mice came to our shores two hundred years ago and continue to arrive even now in every port city along our coasts. It is a continuous immigration.

Rat and mouse populations reflect food availability. The best weapon against these destructive creatures is starvation. Information obtainable from conservation agencies and from city, state, and federal governments tell how to protect your own property and how to help your community in concerted action. In the interest of our own health and welfare and in the interest of the health and well-being of our domestic stock and our wildlife, all efforts should be extended in the war against these most harmful of all the vertebrate animals. Remember, all of the other backboned animals in the world combined (amphibians, reptiles, fishes, birds, and mammals) don't cause man a small fraction of the misery and expense the Norway rat alone causes every day of the year, every year of our lives.

47

Three Native Rats:
Rice, Cotton, and Wood

THE UNDESIRABLE EXOTICS we have already discussed, the Norway and black rats, are not the only animals properly identified as rats that we have on this continent. There are four other kinds, three of which we will discuss in this chapter. None of them is as destructive or objectionable as those unwanted imports from Asia.

Names and Range

The rice rats of the United States are found along the eastern seaboard from New Jersey to Florida and thence to the West through all of the Gulf states to eastern Texas. In the northern part of their range they are found inland from the Atlantic as far west as southern Illinois.

We have an interesting little animal known as the cotton rat that is to be found all across the southern United States from Florida to extreme southern California.

A much larger group is the genus *Neotoma,* known collectively as the wood, pack, or trade rats, and their ranges are large and varied.

The most successful of the three types is the wood or pack rat. He ranges far to the north in Canada and is found from the Florida Keys to New York, from desert to mountain, from plains to swamp. Although nocturnal, he is one little animal you are apt to encounter if you spend much time in wild places.

Appearance and Distinguishing Characteristics

The first and most important problem is to determine how we can tell a rice rat from a wood rat, and a wood rat from a cotton rat. Also, how do we tell all three from the Norway and black rats? It is not quite as difficult as it may seem. Although they are generally the same in size and structure, it is sometimes possible to distinguish between them in the field with a little attention to detail.

The rice rat is a slender animal between nine and twelve and a half inches long. He is a grayish or sometimes a fulvous brown with a distinctly light-gray or fulvous belly. He has a long, scaly tail not unlike the Norway and black rats, but *it is paler below*. His feet are whitish, and this, with his lighter belly, can help make a distinction of sorts.* For purposes of identification it is important to note that his fur is *short, coarse,* and *not grizzled*. His tail is shorter than a black rat's. He can be distinguished from the cotton rat, as we

Courtesy U.S. Department of Interior, Fish & Wildlife Service

The not very prepossessing rice rat, Oryzomys.

* This is not a totally dependable point of distinction since the Norway rat is quite a different animal away from civilization. He, too, can have a bicolor tail and paler feet.

Courtesy Colorado Game & Fish Department

A bushy-tailed wood rat from Colorado. An active and attractive native species.

shall be seeing, because he is smaller, less robust, and because the cotton rat has long, grizzled fur. He is not likely to be confused with the wood rat, who has a hairy, not a scaly tail, although the wood rat's tail is sometimes sparsely haired. The wood rat, too, is a larger animal. To round him out, the rice rat has small, well-haired ears and short, unimpressive whiskers. He is definitely a rat in appearance.

The cotton rat, too, is a relatively small animal, but he is more robust than his cousin the rice rat. His length can run from eight to fifteen inches, including a three-to-seven-inch tail. That tail, by the way, is sparsely haired. Although you won't be able to see them, he has very small, internal cheek pouches. You will be able to distinguish the cotton rat because he is smaller than the Norway rat, has a shorter tail and longer, more grizzled, fur. He can usually be distinguished from the rice rat because he is more robust and has a generally shorter tail and longer, more grizzled fur. He is smaller than the wood rat, has coarser fur, and has a scaly, not a bushy or even sparsely haired tail.

The wood rat is about the same size as the Norway rat, but he can have a *hairy, even bushy, tail.* That alone can set him apart from all other rats in the United States and Canada. To help in identification, he has somewhat larger ears than the other rats, and his feet and belly are often white.

In brief, if the rat you see has (a) a bushy tail, he is likely to be a wood rat; (b) a robust body, a short, scaly tail and coarse, grizzled fur, he is likely to be a cotton rat; (c) a body and tail like a Norway rat except a more slender build and a tail that is light on the underside, you may have a rice rat. By no means are these characteristics anything approaching 100 percent reliable. It is, at very best, a tough job distinguishing between our native and imported rats. It can be an interesting project, however. (All of our native rats, like our imports, range through the gray-browns in general body color.)

Habits

In nature, a successful species is one that can adapt to different situations without being so adversely affected that it dies out. Different climates, different habitats, and different foods all can cause a species to vanish if it is not successful at adapting itself. The rats, as we know, are extremely success-

Rice rat (dotted area).

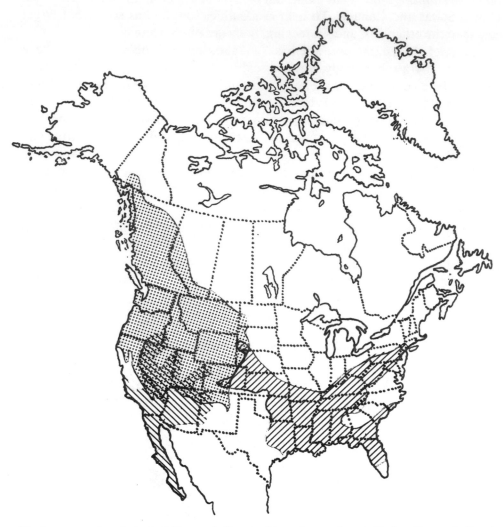

Eastern wood rat (⁄ ⁄ diagonal lines). Desert wood rat (＼＼ diagonal lines). Bushytail wood rat (dotted area).

ful. It is a moot point whether or not our native species are as successful as the imports, but they are successful enough and have adapted to a wide variety of living environments on this continent.

Of the three, the rice rat is probably the least adaptable. He will rarely be

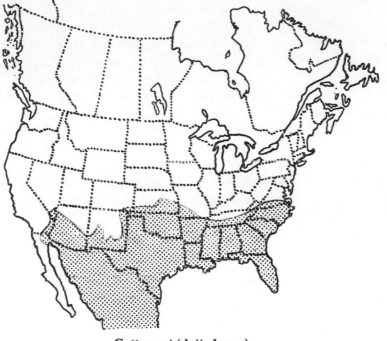

Cotton rat (dotted area).

found far from moist situations. He prefers grasses and sedges bordering swampland and lives off a variety of grasses, sedges, foliage, and seeds. He eats some animal food but not much. An occasional snail, amphibian, or insect will be taken, but the amount is inconsequential. He is strictly nocturnal

Rice rat tracks.

and will rarely be found abroad during daylight. He is shy and retiring but can put up a fight if cornered. He occasionally proves to be a problem to farmers, but he is nowhere near the villain our imports are. The rice rats do not hibernate. They swim well, underwater as well as on top. They fight among themselves, and the victor is likely to kill and eat the vanquished.

The cotton rat prefers dense grassy fields and overgrown roadsides where the weeds are thick. He will also set up residence in the waste borders of cultivated land. Although more active at night, he will on occasion be found abroad when the sun is high and is *the* rat you are most apt to see disappearing into roadside weed growth as you drive along a country road in the southern half of the United States. If you stop your car and follow his trail, you will find that he creates well-defined runways in the grass. His home range is small, seldom over an acre and a quarter in extent.

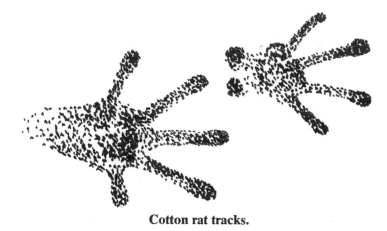

Cotton rat tracks.

The cotton rat is characteristically pugnacious and excitable. He is active the year round and is very quarrelsome with his own kind. He is a strong swimmer and won't hesitate to take to water. He eats a variety of stems, leaves, roots, seeds, and dotes on alfalfa, cotton, and truck crops. He will take insects, birds' eggs, and carrion as available. Much more so than the rice rat, cotton rats are destructive to farm crops and second only to the exotics on the farmer's "get rid of 'em" list.

The wood rats are the most adaptable of all. In mountainous terrain they live in rock cliffs and on small, sheltered ledges. Piles of sticks and rubbish give away their nest sites. On the plains they construct houses two to four feet in diameter at the base, and as many feet high, of sticks and cactus. Their houses are found in clumps of brush or cactus. On the West Coast they often nest in oak and other trees. The range of an individual animal seldom exceeds an area one hundred feet in radius from the nest site. The wood rats are pugnacious with their own kind but are otherwise shy and retiring. They do not hibernate, although they will stay hidden when the weather is really bad. They are nocturnal all through the year and will usually not be abroad when the sun is high unless their nest is disturbed. They are all excellent climbers and jumpers and swim without hesitation. One of the best places to see pack rats in daytime is in caves and abandoned mine tunnels where they are usually without any fear of men and will come over and sniff at your shoes.

Wood rats are not large eaters. They are vegetarians in general but will take animal food—insects, small snails, and even a dead bird. They normally eat a variety of buds, leaves, stems, bark, roots, fruit, fungi, and other forest offerings. They are not destructive to man's enterprises and are probably just about the nicest rats in the world although they often den in outbuildings and cabin attics.

The wood rats get their other names (pack or trade rats) from their perfectly amazing passion for useless debris. They cannot resist shiny, oddly shaped, or otherwise mysteriously enticing objects. Just what a wood rat needs a button, empty cartridge case, or jackknife for may puzzle some. They use these treasures, of course, as building materials for their nests. The story has it that the wood rat will not steal anything from you unless he has something to trade for it. This is not true, although the end result is about the same; for your nice Swiss army knife left carelessly on your camp cot you will get a small stone or twig. What really happens is that the wood rat is seldom found without a treasure tightly clamped between his teeth. He is almost always heading home with some woodland goody, and if he spots something even more enticing he will drop what he has and take the more attractive item. More than one camper has traded his wristwatch for an empty cartridge case without having a say in the deal. Some valuable personal items have been lost to these little woodland thieves, and nests in regularly used camping areas have given up an amazing assortment of jewelry, coins, and other small but expensive utensils.

Reproduction

The prolific rice rat can breed at seven weeks, before full growth, and can produce as many as six or seven litters a year. The spherical nest, twelve to eighteen inches in diameter, is carefully woven of shredded, dry leaves and is either on the ground or suspended from vegetation. The choice of nesting site depends on how damp the ground is. The first breeding of the year takes place as early as February, and the young, after a gestation period of twenty-five days, begin to appear in March or April. Litter size runs from one to seven very small, helpless creatures.

The cotton rats build small nests of dry grass under rocks or logs and sometimes underground in short, shallow burrows. They will occasionally take over the burrow of a more skilled underground worker and be found in deeper chambers. They breed all year round and have a twenty-seven-day gestation period. Litter size is large, anywhere from one to twelve having been recorded, although five to seven is usual. The young are very precocious and have their eyes open after eighteen hours. They are weaned in ten days, but the process may start after only five. They are prolific and active.

The wood rats, because of their great range, have varying breeding habits. In the North they have as few as two or three litters a year. In the South they breed all year long. Gestation is believed to be thirty-nine days, although this is not certain. Litter size runs from one to six, with two or three being average. It takes fifteen to twenty days for the little wood rats to open their eyes, and they are not weaned until they are four weeks old. They are nowhere near as fast in development as their cousins, the cotton rats.

Observation

Since our native rats are fed upon by everything from muskrats and cottonmouth water moccasins to timber wolves and grizzly bears, they are shy and retiring. They are highly sensitive to sound and will disappear at the slightest sign of intrusion on their limited home range. They are difficult to see, difficult to observe.

You are bound to see some wild rats sooner or later. In the daytime it is likely to be a cotton rat anywhere in the South. The farther north you go, the more likely it is to be a wood rat, and by the time you reach the Canadian border, it can be nothing else. Their tracks (difficult to distinguish by anyone but an expert) may be all you see unless you discover one of their distinctive nests.

Since these animals are shy, small, and either entirely or largely nocturnal, depending on species, you must do one of two things to get to examine them. Either you must choose an area and become so familiar with every inch of it and know every track, trail, crevice, and nesting site that nothing escapes your notice, or you must resort to harmless box traps. These humane devices will enable you to examine the local "little people" each morning before releasing them unharmed to go back to their private lives. If you do want to get to know the rodent fauna of a given area, you really must use these traps. If you are careful not to leave them too long, and if they are properly set, you can learn a great deal, see animals you would never otherwise get to view, and do no harm at all in the course of the project. You must remember that you are dealing with very bright, adaptable little creatures whose every wish and movement is keyed to escape. Their great overpowering desire is not to be seen. When you start listing all their enemies it is little wonder.

A WORD OF CAUTION: If you do catch any of these rodents, be careful in handling them. They are frightened, of course, and will bite at the first opportunity. While being nipped by a wood rat is not the same as being opened up by an angry grizzly bear, the bite can be deep, and an infection can result. The proverbial kid glove won't do at all; rats are to be handled by people wearing good, heavy leather or canvas gauntlets!

48

Delicate Beauty:
White-footed or Deer Mice

Names and Range

From the Gulf of Mexico to Hudson Bay, from north-central Alaska to northern Labrador, in all of the original forty-eight states, in Alaska, in every province of Canada, the delicate beauty of the white-footed mouse is to be found. There are many hundreds of common names for these little creatures, and since one name refers to one species in one place and another species in a different area, the problem approaches the hopeless. For our purposes, all but the few we can call pygmy mice will be known as white-footed mice.

Appearance and Distinguishing Characteristics

The pygmy mice are native to the southern parts of Texas, New Mexico, and Arizona only. They are, of course, common in much of Mexico. They are the smallest of our mice and generally run from three and a quarter to four and a half inches in length, including a one-and-a-quarter-to-two-inch tail. They are dark brown to blackish in color, always paler underneath. They look very much like the young of our imported and unwanted Asian house mouse but can be distinguished by the fact that their tail is lighter on the underside and is covered with short hairs, as opposed to being naked.

The white-footed mice all have the characteristic white feet. They usually have white bellies as well, and their backs range from one end of the brown

The nest of a white-footed mouse built on top of that of a wood thrush.

tone scale to the other; they are often washed with a fulvous or pale-yellow tint. Lengths in these mice generally run from seven to eight inches, with the tail accounting for half of that. There are internal cheek pouches that will not be seen in the field, and the alert little ears are scantily furred. The most common of the lot is the deermouse found throughout all of Canada except the extreme North—to the shores of Hudson Bay, to northern Labrador and central Alaska, and throughout all of the United States except the Southeast. He runs in body color from pale grayish buff to deep reddish brown. His tail is always sharply bicolor—dark above, light below.

Habits

The white-footed mice are not only nocturnal, they generally won't move around even on bright moonlit nights. For them, the dark world is the only safe one. They dwell in a vast variety of habitats that range from woods and forests to prairies and tundra. The arid Southwest is perfectly suitable to their needs, as are rocky slopes and even old buildings. They are adaptable and prolific. In moist areas they will even forage in water up to half an inch deep. (They can swim well for at least short distances.) Most are ground-dwellers, a few are arboreal and nest in trees. Despite the northern latitudes to which they have spread, none of them hibernate. They are active under and on top of the snow.

Photo by Henry B. Kane, courtesy Canadian Audubon Society

The meek and the beautiful, the white-footed mouse.

The size of the home range of the individual mouse depends on how rich the pickings are. Usually one half to one and a half acres will do, but in some areas, at least at certain times of the year, five to ten acres are required to provide the necessary food. They have a powerful and little understood homing instinct and will find their way back to their nest even if captured and released a few miles away. They are very clean about themselves, frequently washing and grooming, but they are extremely careless about their nests—so careless are they that they must often abandon a nest and construct another every few weeks. Even they can't stand their own housekeeping habits.

The range of nesting sites is great. One animal may have several underground nests in cavities near roots of trees or shrubs, under logs or boards, or in the tunnel of another animal. Sometimes the nests are placed aboveground in hollow fence posts, stumps, or logs. An old squirrel or bird nest will be taken over and a dome woven of leaves, stems, grass roots, sedges, bark, feathers, and fur will be added for security. The domes are generally spherical, with a single side entrance that is closed from the inside when the animal retires.

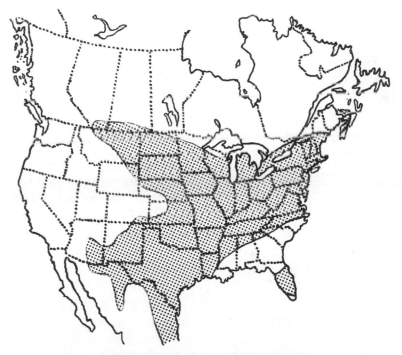

White-footed mouse (dotted areas).

The white-footed mouse is not a quiet animal and has many things to say to and about the world around him. He has various high-pitched squeaks, trills, and chitters for a variety of occasions, but he is most dramatic when he buzzes. His shrill buzz can last for five to ten seconds and can be heard up to fifty feet away. When really excited he drums his forefeet in a wild fury.

The food of the white-footed mice is as varied as the extent of their range and habitat choices would indicate. Insects, nuts, wild seeds, domestic grains, fruit, fruit pits, some leafy vegetation, fungi, snails, worms, spiders, centipedes, millipedes, eggs, young birds, and dead mice all contribute to their diet. They store food against lean seasons.

The animals that eat the white-footed mice are as varied as the food the little animal himself eats. He is a very important link in the chain that connects the meat-eaters to the world of vegetable matter. Snakes, lizards, all wild canines and cats (including the domestic varieties), bears, all the weasels, other rodents, many birds, almost every animal that will even on occasion eat meat hunts the white-footed mouse, and he is therefore always on guard. He survives as an individual by his wits (but usually doesn't get to see old age, however witty he may be) and as a species because of his fecundity.

The population of white-footed mice in a given area runs in cycles. In the long-term cycle, the population will hit a peak every three or five years. On the short term, there are peak months. In Missouri, for example, the peak months are March to June. The lowest months are July through October. When white-footed mice are scarce, other animals suffer as the predators look elsewhere to meet their needs. Appetite is not cyclic.

Reproduction

These little animals breed regularly in spring, summer, and fall. If a winter is mild, breeding occurs then as well. Females come into heat every fifth day for about twenty-six hours. The periods of heat resume within twenty-four to forty-eight hours after a litter is delivered. Gestation is 21 to 23 days. Litter size varies from one to nine, with three or four being usual. A healthy female in an area where the food supply is good can deliver ten or eleven litters a year. The young weigh about one fifteenth of an ounce and are blind, toothless, and naked. The teeth appear in six days, the eyes open in two weeks, weaning is accomplished in three weeks, and maturity is achieved in five weeks or so, depending on season of birth. Young born in the early spring can themselves breed before the first day of summer. And so, prey as the predators might, there will always be more white-footed mice to carry on.

Observation

These small and extremely attractive mice are everywhere to be found where there is suitable food and cover. To see them is a matter of patience. They are most active in the early evening and just before dawn, but are not easy to see in the dark. They will scoot for cover at the first sign of movement or noise. It is possible to see them move about if you are very, very quiet and take up your watching station before the sun sets. Don't move, however, or you will never see your mouse.

These small mice, like most others, can be lured into the open and into harmless box traps with a bait consisting of peanut butter, molasses, and table salt. They find this mixture impossible to resist. Trapping them is about the only way you will get a close look at them unless you uncover one of their nests. They are handsome little additions to our wildlife scene.

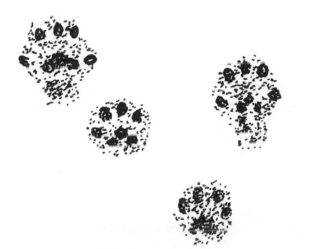

White-footed mouse tracks.

___ 49

Four Other Native Mice: Grasshopper, Harvest, Pocket, and Jumping

Names and Range

Though it may not seem possible, there are yet five other kinds of mice to be found in North America. We will discuss four of the five in this chapter: the grasshopper mice, the harvest mice, the pocket mice, and the delightful little animals known as jumping mice. These animals have so many common names in the various parts of their widespread ranges that it is extremely doubtful that it would even be possible to catalog and properly assign them. If it is possible, it wouldn't be practical here.

The grasshopper mice are western animals all. The harvest mice are more widespread and are found across the continent from coast to coast. All of the pocket mice are western animals, like the grasshopper mice. They are to be found in specialized ranges throughout the western United States, Mexico, and extreme southern Canada in the west and central provinces.

We can define three species of jumping mice. There is a western, a meadow, and a woodland species. The accompanying maps provide a generalized picture of their ranges. We must understand, however, how very broad these range descriptions are. We are dealing here with animals some of whose representatives will live across an area the size of several European countries, while a close cousin will live in a single valley or on a single island and nowhere else in the world. Even when scientifically defined, ranges are approximations and assumptions more than anything else. The best we can do, here, certainly, is give a general impression of where the animal in question is to be found.

Appearance and Distinguishing Characteristics

It is no small task to distinguish between the various wild mice of our two countries. To be able to do so with any kind of certainty testifies to an interest and a determination well beyond the average. Even so, there are some guidelines—a little fuzzy, at times, perhaps—but guidelines nonetheless for distinguishing at least between the major groups.

The sturdy little five-to-eight-inch grasshopper mouse is generally colored to match his prairie and arid-country environment. He runs from gray to pinkish-gray to cinnamon above, white underneath. His fur is short, rather like that of the white-footed mouse, but the one-to-two-and-three-quarter-inch tail is thick, short, tapering, and sharply bicolored: dark above, white or gray below. *The tail is white-tipped.*

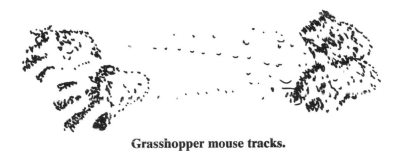

Grasshopper mouse tracks.

The four-to-seven-inch harvest mouse is not as easy to identify. His two-and-a-fifth-to-three-inch tail will tell you little, and his small brownish body is similarly unrevealing to the casual eye. You will have to examine his front

Harvest mouse tracks.

gnawing teeth and note lengthwise grooves to be sure, and this you are not apt to do. He can be brown, gray, or fulvous, with a belly that ranges from dark gray to white. His ears are large, but he still looks rather like a house mouse. He has no cheek pouches, but you are not apt to note that, either. All in all, the harvest mouse is a small, dull, seldom seen little animal.

The pocket mouse has small, *externally opening* fur-lined cheek pouches, a characteristic unique among our mice. His front feet are weak, his hind feet strong and well developed. His tail is at least as long as his head and body combined, often longer; he is from eight to ten inches long overall. His color may be pale yellowish to dark, dark gray, but he is often white or whitish on the belly. His fur is very soft, and one group, on the West Coast, has distinctly spiny hairs on the rump. The pocket mice in general resemble the kangaroo mice, which we will discuss in the next chapter. They can be distinguished, however, by the fact that the tail of the pocket mouse is *not* swollen in the middle like that of the kangaroo mouse. Without that characteristic to go by, confusion is likely.

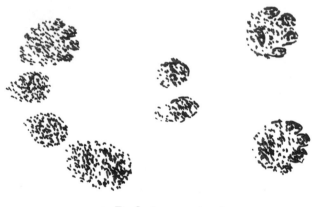

Pocket mouse tracks.

The jumping mice are handsome little creatures. They are small to medium-sized (eight to ten and a half inches overall) and have very long, scaly tails. That tail can be anywhere from four to seven inches long and is a characteristic to note for identification purposes. They have no cheek pouches, internal or external, and have very well-developed hind legs. They

Jumping mouse tracks.

tend to be a yellowish or orangy tone on their sides, darker above, and white on the belly. *Their small ears are edged with white or buff.* To identify a jumping mouse look for (*a*) that very long tail, (*b*) powerful hind legs, and (*c*) a white edging to the short ears.

Remember, in trying to identify these wild native mice we will be to some degree confounded by the individual variation. A mouse just doesn't read the guide books and doesn't know what he is supposed to look like. He is perfectly happy turning out a dull gray as long as the tone helps him hide from his enemy, even if you are looking in his neighborhood for a mouse with distinct sky-blue-pink fur because that's what the book says to expect. Be ready for individuality. It is quite noticeable among our mice.

Habits

A successful animal is, of course, one that has adapted his habits, his way of life, to match his environment. Only an animal that has succeeded in doing so will survive to maintain the blood of his kind. For this reason it is difficult to make too many generalizations about our mice. They live in every kind of

Courtesy U.S. Department of Interior, Fish & Wildlife Service

One of the active pocket mice (*Perognathus*), near Voltage, Oregon.

habitat, eat all kinds of food, have all kinds of enemies. As a result they have adapted and readapted until the possible combinations of behavioral traits exceed our powers of description, much less the size of this book.

In general, the grasshopper mice are nocturnal creatures of the prairie and desert country. They are nonhibernating burrowers with a great many enemies and are shy and alert. Unlike any other native rodent, the diet of this small creature is largely animal food, chiefly insects. They eat grasshoppers, crickets, scorpions, beetles, larvae, some other mice, and some seeds and greens.

The harvest mice generally prefer dense, low vegetation. They eat a variety of seeds, grains, fruits, and greens; about a third of their own weight is consumed each day. Their ranges are small, one half to one and a half acres generally. They and their grass nests will generally be found in open grassy areas. They do not hibernate and are active night and day. They alternately sleep and eat around the clock. They have many enemies and are a significant element in the diet of many predators in their range lands.

The arid to semiarid country pocket mice are strictly nocturnal. They are

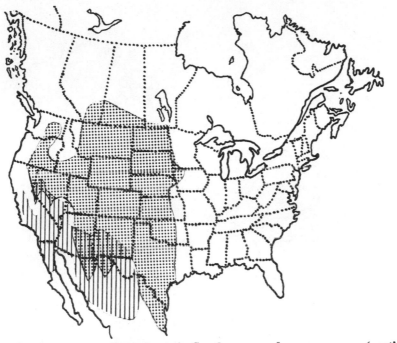

Northern grasshopper mouse (dotted area). Southern grasshopper mouse (vertical lines).

social animals that burrow to shallow depths to build their nests. These beautiful little animals do not hibernate but will be active even with snow on the ground. They eat a variety of seeds, mainly, and are themselves victim to a variety of appetites. They are never found in dense forests or woods, preferring rather open plains and deserts with a minimum of cover.

The very wary and nervous jumping mice prefer damp meadows and open forests as well as open grassy areas. They eat a variety of grass seeds, fruits, roots, and some animal matter. They consume a weight equivalent to one half their own body every twenty-four hours. They move around a great deal and generally prefer moist areas to dry ones. They are active nights and on cloudy days. They climb well and can swim underwater for at least a full minute. The jumping mice all hibernate, some for as long as seven months. They confound their many enemies by hopping in a zigzag fashion, taking anywhere from one-to-six-foot hops. They can jump ten feet or more, but can walk and run as

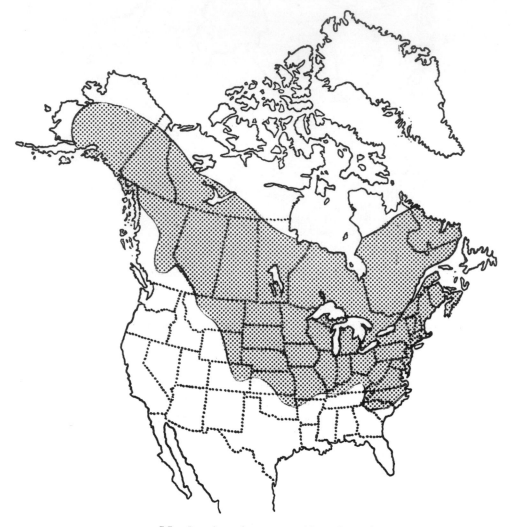

Meadow jumping mouse (dotted area).

well. Trying to catch one is rather like trying to toss a net over an animated, very eccentric spring. The summer nest of the jumping mouse is woven of grass and leaves and is spherical or oval in shape. It may be found on the ground, in shrubs, or suspended from vegetation; or it may be from three to

Western jumping mouse (diagonal lines). Woodland mouse (dotted area).

six inches underground. The winter nest is always underground and has no opening. The mice weave themselves in for their very long and very deep sleep.

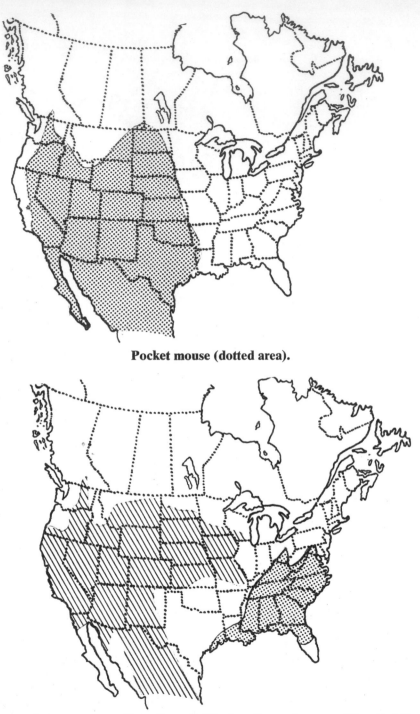

Pocket mouse (dotted area).

Eastern harvest mouse (dotted area). Western harvest mouse (diagonal lines).

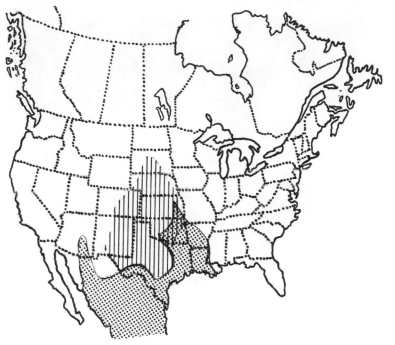

Fulvous harvest mouse (dotted area). Plains mouse (vertical lines).

Reproduction

The harvest mice reportedly breed all year round, but this activity reaches a crescendo from spring to fall. Gestation is a short twenty-three days, and litter size varies from one to seven, with three or four being usual. The young weigh about one twenty-fifth of an ounce. Their eyes and ears open in eight to ten days, and after three or four weeks in the care of the mother they are on their own. Very shortly after that they are ready to breed themselves. A mouse born early in the spring can be a grandparent before the first snow falls.

The pocket mice breed for a longer season in the southern parts of their range. From one to seven is reported litter size, although four or five is probably nearer to average. It takes more than twenty of their young to weigh one ounce. They are weaned within the month of their birth and are quickly seeking mates of their own.

The jumping mice start to breed as soon as they come out of hibernation. The young continue to arrive until the end of August. The gestation period is

Courtesy U.S. Department of Interior, Fish & Wildlife Service

One of the jumping mice from the Olympic Forest, Oregon. Note the length of the back legs.

seldom longer than eighteen days, and as many as three litters will be born to a female in one summer season. Litter size runs from one to nine, with five or six being normal. The young weigh less than a thirtieth of an ounce but are ready for weaning within four weeks. Growth is rapid and sexual maturity quickly reached.

Observation

The problems of finding and observing our native mice are the same as with any other small mammal. A visit to a local museum is in order, preferably to include a talk with a mammalogist. He can give you lots of tips as to where fertile fields lie. From then on it is up to your powers of observation, your patience, and your skill with a trap. Try the bait prescribed for other small rodents—a mixture of peanut butter, molasses, and salt—and see what you have when the traps snap shut. If you know where some mice runs are, you may want to just sit and wait without disrupting their busy little lives by a few hours in captivity. Remember, as we have cautioned before: Don't set traps unless you intend to return to them in a matter of hours. The rate of metabolism is so high in these smaller mammals that they will die of starvation very quickly.

50

The Last of Our Rodents:
The Kangaroo Rats and Mice

Names and Range

There is a group of highly active little rodents known as kangaroo rats, which is restricted to the western part of the United States and only incidentally to the southwest of Canada. And there are even smaller rodents, also restricted to the western half of the United States, which are known as kangaroo mice or pygmy kangaroo rats. (By no stretch of the imagination are any of these animals related to the kangaroos.)

Appearance and Distinguishing Characteristics

The robust, silky kangaroo rats are amazingly constant in coloration. Any differences that can be noted will have to do with shading; it is a difference of degree, not kind. The belly is always white, while the upper parts run from pale yellow to dark brownish. The very long tail is usually dark above and below, with white stripes running down the sides. The facial markings are usually white and black, although they may be very pale in some species. Most have a white band across the thighs.

The kangaroo rats have extremely long hind legs, small front feet and legs. The terminal one fifth of the tail carries a crest of long hairs. The average size is eight to fifteen inches, four and three quarters to nine inches of that being tail. They are extremely good-looking animals, quite possibly the most handsome rodents on this entire continent.

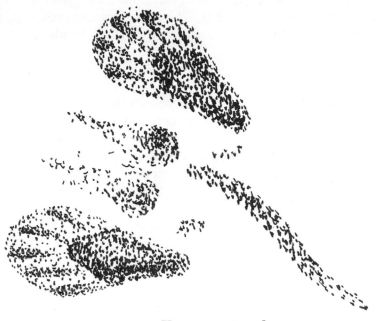

Kangaroo rat tracks.

The kangaroo mice (we prefer that to pygmy kangaroo rats) are small, brownish or blackish little rodents with, like their larger cousins, disproportionately powerful hind legs. They run from five to eight inches in length, including a two-and-a-half-to-four-inch tail. That tail is quite distinctive and can be used in telling a large kangaroo mouse from a small kangaroo rat. In the mouse there is no tuft of hair at the end of the tail, which is thickened in

Kangaroo mouse tracks.

the center. The hair base is characteristically lead-colored or whitish, and the tip of the tail is blackish in one group (the so-called dark kangaroo mice) and not in the other (the pale kangaroo mice). They are attractive enough as spry little animals usually are, but they are nowhere near as handsome as the rats.

Habits

The kangaroo rats and mice have many enemies. In the arid to semiarid conditions favored by the rats, reptiles abound. Rattlesnakes from western Texas to California favor the kangaroo rat as a main course. Weasels, skunks, felines, canines, and birds of prey all take a heavy toll.

The kangaroo rats themselves eat little animal food, subsisting for the most part on seeds and grains and some leafy foliage. The kangaroo mice live almost entirely on seeds and grains. The latter group favors sandy soils for burrowing, and although relatively rare and seldom seen, they are colonial. Where you find one kangaroo mouse, you will find many. They can honey-comb and completely undermine a burrowing site.

The burrowing kangaroo rats are gentle and clean. Many but not all are social animals and make very good pets. They are much more commonly encountered than the mice. They are capable of spectacular six-foot leaps if startled and can bound about like a bouncing rubber ball. Their burrows are large, clean cut, and not concealed. You can't, after all, conceal a hole in the ground from a hungry rattlesnake. These spry little creatures are nocturnal and do not hibernate.

Reproduction

Surprisingly little is known about the reproduction of either animal. The rats and mice start breeding sometime in February and have two or more litters per year. The average litter of the rats is believed to contain from three to five young, that of the mice from two to five. Both animals bear their young in underground chambers and nurse them there until ready to be weaned. A kangaroo mouse or rat encountered on the surface is usually an animal about to be turned loose by its mother, however small it may seem. The gestation period is probably under twenty-five days for both animals.

Observation

As well adapted to arid conditions as both animals may be, they are not abroad when the sun is up. Even their highly modified bodily processes could

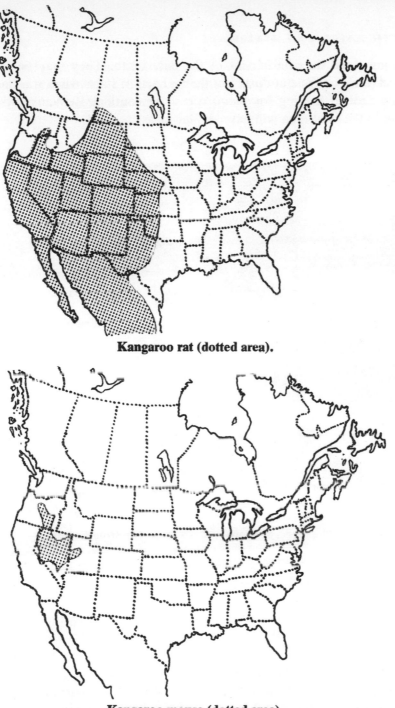

Kangaroo rat (dotted area).

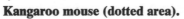

Kangaroo mouse (dotted area).

not long stand the punishment of the desert sun. They may be seen about around dawn and just at dusk, but the real action starts when it is dark. When poking around looking for them, use some caution. Remember that rattle-snakes in the same area will have similar ideas.

Courtesy U.S. Department of Interior, Fish & Wildlife Service

Merriam's kangaroo rat—a specimen from Colorado.

If you are in kangaroo-rat and kangaroo-mouse country you will know it by the tracks that cross and crisscross the area from one clump of vegetation to another. If you enter a kangaroo-mouse colony you will know it because you are likely to crash through the honeycombed ground to a depth of a few inches.

When you have established the regular trails and tracks used by these little animals, set your box traps using cage-bird seed or processed cereals as bait. It will not be too long after sundown before your traps will be sprung. In the morning you will have a chance to examine your catch before turning it loose. It is cruel to carry these little animals too far from their home range before setting them free in desert country. They may die of the heat before reaching suitable cover. You may want to entertain the idea of keeping a few of the rats for pets. They are delightful and settle down very quickly.

_____ 51

The Hay-Makers: The Pikas

IN THIS CHAPTER and the two that follow we will discuss animals commonly thought of as rodents. Actually, the pikas, hares, jackrabbits, and rabbits are not rodents at all but are properly known as lagomorphs. All in all, they are an enchanting group of animals. (They have two pairs of upper incisors instead of the rodents' one pair.)

Names and Range

The pikas are variously known as rock rabbits, calling hares, whistling hares, little chief hares, and, inaccurately, coneys. The local common names are virtually endless in number.

The main concentration of our pikas is found in two Canadian provinces, British Columbia and Alberta, and in ten of our western states. There is a pocket of very closely related animals in Alaska and the Yukon Territory.

Appearance and Distinguishing Characteristics

The pikas are essentially rat-size rabbits without powerful hind legs. All four of their legs are about the same size. Their coloration is protective: grayish, buffy, or brownish above, somewhat lighter below. Their fur is soft and very dense, and they have short, broad, rounded ears, usually rimmed with white. They have bright shoe-button eyes and a prominent nose. There is no visible tail, and their body and head length runs from six and a quarter to eight and a half inches. Their weight runs from four to seven ounces. It is not easy to confuse these animals with any others because, as we shall see, just about the only other small mammal that shares their choice of habitat is the

Pika (dotted area).

marmot, which is very much larger and has a distinguishing short, bushy tail.
(The nocturnal pack rat also has a bushy tail but is not apt to be confused
with the marmot.) Remember, on the rock slides of high mountains: tail
—marmot; no tail—pika.

Habits

The strictly diurnal, nonhibernating pika lives in mountainous rock slides and in areas just adjacent to the timberline. Although essentially terrestrial, he will climb into the lower branches of aspens, elders, and chokeberries to nip off tender twigs and leaves. In the alpine meadows he favors, usually between eight and twelve thousand feet above sea level, he harvests over thirty kinds of vegetable matter. Leaves, flowers, stems, nettles, chokeberries, currants, aspen, goldenrod, fireweed, and many more are included in his diet. He cuts and carries his harvest to an area just in front of his den, where he spreads it for drying. After it is cured, he carries it below for storage. One little five-ounce pika may store up to fifty pounds of fodder against the severe mountain winter. The small piles of fresh hay in a rocky area are sure signs of a pika residence. The piles are always close to the entrance because everything is carried below when it rains and not brought up to finish curing until the sun is high and bright again.

With his short hind legs, the pika is not a hopper like his rabbit and hare cousins; he is a scurrier. The soles of his feet are densely furred and effectively nonskid; he can jump from one rock to another without slipping. If attacked by an enemy too far from his den to gain effective cover, the pika will scurry about at great speed and may be helped out by neighbors. Observers report having seen several pikas materialize quite suddenly when one was being pursued. They all scurried about crossing and recrossing each other's trail until the pursuer was so thoroughly confused that he gave up. It is nice to think of these little animals helping each other even to the point of risking their own hides, but such is probably not the case. It is doubtful that such altruism exists among these little creatures. It is probably a case where these alert, nervous little animals are excited beyond containing themselves at the sight of an enemy and scamper and scurry as a matter of nervous reflex. Perhaps, though, we should let the illusion stand. The enemies that can cause such a flurry of excitement are martens, weasels, bears, coyotes, eagles, and hawks.

The pika is a noisy little bundle of energy and his peculiar short squeaks and bleats are very distinctive. They have been likened to the noise made by a rusty hinge and have a ventriloquistic effect that can be quite confounding. As you make your way across a mountain meadow, the *ka-ack ka-ack* that seems to drift across to you from far away may in fact be issuing from an animal almost underfoot.

Photo by Wilford L. Miller

A comic-strip character come to life—a pika in Glacier National Park.

Pikas usually settle a suitable area at a density of about six to an acre. They can be seen, with a good pair of binoculars, sunning themselves on rocks during the midday heat. Their coats, you will note, blend very well with the rocks on which they rest. When their sleep is over, they sit up and set about washing themselves from stem to stern, looking for all the world like so many little tailless cats with uncatlike ears.

Reproduction

Very little is known about the reproductive habits of the pika. It would be a very good project for the advanced amateur to undertake. They appear to breed between May and September and probably don't have more than one litter per year. Litter size varies from three to four, and the young, born in nests under the rocks, weigh about a third of an ounce. They are apparently weaned quite early.

Observation

Pikas are not easily crossed off your lifetime checklist and are therefore very desirable observation projects. It will take a little doing on your part, but it will be worth it.

Photo by Wilford L. Miller   Photo by Wilford L. Miller

Left: Protective coloration illustrated—a pika among the rocks in Montana.

Right: A pika's cuttings curing in the sun.

Locate a pika colony and make note of the piles of hay. These will tell you where the den entrances are. Return on a day when rain is predicted for the afternoon, following a sunny morning, and get to your observation platform before the clouds roll over. As the weather deteriorates, you will see some very busy little pikas making trip after trip to get their curing hay below before it is drenched. It is suggested that you bring some foul-weather gear along, for a rainstorm at twelve thousand feet on an exposed rock slide can be nasty. Don't try to negotiate the slippery rocks in the rain. Sit it out.

If you want to try to catch your pikas at work in the alpine meadows near their homes, get there before sunup. They work their fields in the very early morning and in the late afternoon. As any self-respecting pika can tell you, the warm, sunny hours are for sleeping.

In pursuit of the pika you will have a good chance of success in the following areas:

Waterton Lakes National Park	Alberta
Jasper National Park	Alberta
Yoho National Park	British Columbia
Kootenay National Park	British Columbia

Banff National Park	Alberta
National Elk Refuge	Wyoming
Yellowstone National Park	Wyoming
Glacier National Park	Montana

One of the very nicest things about pursuing the elusive pika is that you get to see some of the most beautiful country on earth in the process.

Pika tracks.

52

Nature's Athletes:
The Hares and Jackrabbits

A LOGICAL FIRST QUESTION, the one most often asked when the hares and rabbits are discussed, concerns the differences between the two related but distinctly different groups of animals. What is the difference between a rabbit and a hare, between a rabbit and a jackrabbit?

The jackrabbits and hares of the United States and Canada belong together in one genus, *Lepus*. The rabbits of this continent belong to another genus, *Sylvilagus*. Essentially, the hares have longer ears and larger hind legs and feet in relation to body size than the rabbits. They are larger animals overall, with lankier bodies. The young of hares are born well furred, with their eyes open, and are ready to run about in a matter of hours. The rabbits, on the other hand, give birth to naked, blind, helpless young. These few distinctions are about all that will be apparent in the field. The others—and a good many more exist—belong to the scientist and the dissecting table.

Names and Range

The hares as represented in the United States and Canada vary greatly in appearance and in range characteristics. A complete breakdown would be hardly more revealing for our needs than a general grouping of major forms.

The Arctic hare is an animal of northeastern and north-central Canada found far up into the polar regions, across to the island of Greenland. He has many local names, some of which have been adapted from Indian and Eskimo

Arctic hare (dotted areas). Tundra hare (vertical lines). White-tailed jackrabbit (diagonal lines).

dialects. To the English-speaking world he is Arctic hare, to French-speaking Canadians, *lièvre arctique d'Amérique.*

The tundra hare is a western version of the Arctic hare and is found in northern and western Alaska.

Snowshoe hare (diagonal lines).

The white-tailed jackrabbit is found throughout southern British Columbia, Alberta, Saskatchewan, and Manitoba into Wisconsin and west to Washington, and south to New Mexico.

The varying or snowshoe hare has a vast range. He is found all across Canada far to the north, in the northern United States, and south to New Mexico.

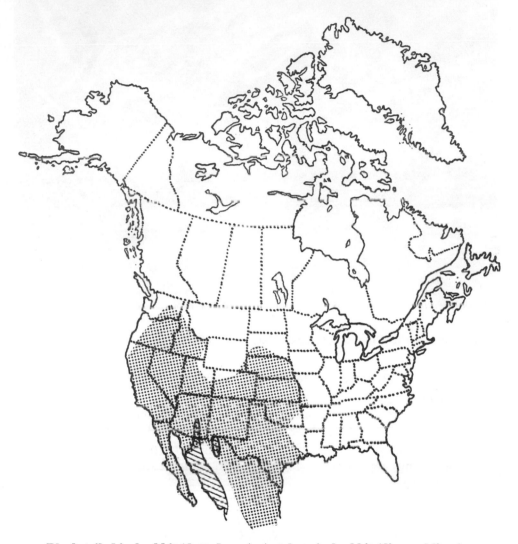

Black-tailed jackrabbit (dotted area). Antelope jackrabbit (diagonal lines).

The so-called European hare is not a native at all but an introduced species that has become well established. His expanding population is currently centered in the Great Lakes region on both the Canadian and American sides of the border. He does not seem to make a distinction. He has been here since the early 1900's.

The giant antelope jackrabbit ranges into southern Arizona only inci-

Photo by Wilford L. Miller

The young of the white-tailed jackrabbit, as appealing as a little animal can be.

dentally. His real home is Mexico. He may very well be moving north, however, and his range may expand in the years ahead.

The widespread black-tailed jackrabbit is an animal of the West and Southwest. He is found from Washington far south into Mexico.

There are many others, of course, and some subgroups as well, but these major groupings represent the limits of field identification potential for the amateur observer.

Appearance and Distinguishing Characteristics

In general, hares and jackrabbits appear to be large, lanky rabbits with extremely long ears, long and powerful hind legs, soft fur, and very short, cottony tails. They have large eyes, and their upper lip is divided. The soles of their feet are densely furred.

The Arctic hare is a seventeen-to-twenty-four-inch animal weighing from six to twelve pounds. His ears are from three and three quarters to four and a half inches long and are shorter in relation to the animal's overall size than those of the southern jackrabbits. His color characteristics vary. In some parts of his range he is all white the year round, while in other parts he turns gray or brown in summer. The tail is always white, and where and when the fur is white, it is white to the base.

The very large tundra hare averages between twenty and twenty-four inches in length with a weight of nine or ten pounds. As hares go his ears are also rather unimpressive, up to four and a half inches long. He is always brown in summer, white in winter, again with hair white to the base and with a permanently white little tail.

The white-tailed jackrabbit looks more like a typical hare. Although his length seldom exceeds eighteen to twenty-two inches, his ears are at least five or six inches long, and he weighs a modest five to eight pounds. Here we have the typical rangy jackrabbit with his antenna ears. He is a brownish gray in summer and white or very pale gray in winter. Once again, the tail, above and below, is always white.

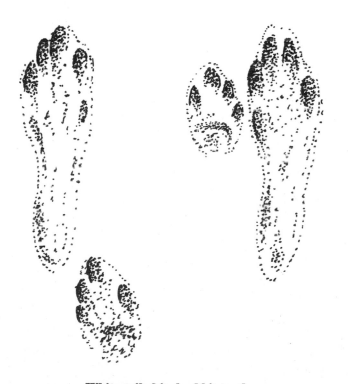

White-tailed jackrabbit tracks.

The varying or snowshoe hare is a little animal, seldom over eighteen inches long and often only thirteen or so. He weighs from two to four pounds and has three-and-a-half-to-four-inch ears. He is white in winter, dark brown in summer. His fur is white at the tips only, yellowish below. He has exceedingly large feet.

The European hare is a very large animal, often twenty-five to twenty-seven inches long. He has five-inch ears and is brownish gray all year long. His large size sets him apart from other animals in his limited range.

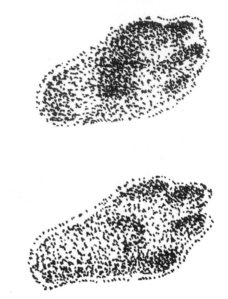

European hare tracks.

The antelope jackrabbit runs from nineteen to twenty-one inches in length, with huge seven- or eight-inch ears, and a very small head. Those ears, it must be noted, *do not* have black markings. His grayish body tones are modified on the sides and hips with a whitish cast.

The black-tailed jackrabbit can be distinguished from the antelope by his six-to-seven-inch ears; *they are black-tipped*. His tail has a black streak on top. This three-to-seven-pound, seventeen-to-twenty-one-inch animal is a grayish-brown color.

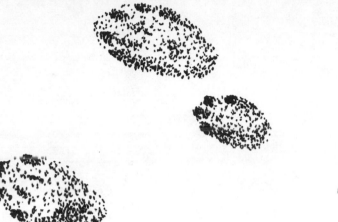

Black-tailed jackrabbit tracks.

Habits

All hares and jackrabbits are animals with many enemies. Although large and very fast, they are preyed upon by a variety of predatory mammals, reptiles, and birds. The young fall prey most often, and it is extremely doubtful that two out of every hundred see five years of life.

Nature has given them a number of devices to help them in the matter of survival. They have acute hearing and a very keen sense of smell. They are extremely sensitive to motion and are quick to react if a branch or blade of grass moves in an unaccustomed way. And due to the peculiar shape, size, and location of their eyes, they can see in front, to the side, and behind at the same time.

Not only are the hares and jackrabbits capable of detecting danger, they have the means of escape. They have a springy, easy, bounding gait, and readily take five-to-ten-foot jumps. If startled, they can leap from fifteen to twenty feet and hit thirty to thirty-five miles an hour. Since danger is often below, and since they can confound enemies by putting obstacles in the way,

Photo by Wilford L. Miller

The white-tailed jackrabbit in his autumn coat, a North Dakota specimen.

they go from two to five and a half feet up while they are making their prodigious strides forward. Any animal who can go nearly six feet up and twenty feet away in one step is hard to catch.

Individual hares may have a range of one or two square miles, but the population is often so dense that it is difficult to envision any range structure at all. Four hundred animals per square mile is not at all unusual, and six times that many have been reported. I once drove through an area in Oklahoma in an effort to do a count along the road and get an estimate of the local jackrabbit population. It was entirely hopeless. Never were there fewer than six or eight animals within the range of my headlights. At times there were at least two dozen. After a few minutes of counting I was quite dizzy and had to content myself with just enjoying the wonderful spectacle of fecund nature at her bouncy best. Driving along that road one got the impression that some invisible force stood off in the dark, hurling jackrabbits into our path by the hundreds. As a matter of fact, there was such a force, and this demonstration of her power to distribute and maintain the spark of life was overpowering.

Hares and jackrabbits normally feed at dusk, in the early hours of the evening, and just before dawn. The amount they eat is simply amazing. It has been estimated that 30 jackrabbits eat as much as a large sheep, 128 jackrabbits as much as a cow. The food varies tremendously, of course, as does the range. Grasses and many domestic crops (cabbage, alfalfa, clover, and soybeans, to mention a few), sagebrush, and cactus all figure in the summer diet. In the winter, dried grass, twigs, bark, and roots are all consumed. Strangely, rabbits and hares do not do a very thorough job of digesting their food the first time and often eat their own droppings newly enriched with bacterial growth from the first passage. It has been suggested that their droppings are rich in vitamins not to be found in the original food.

The hares and jackrabbits are far-flung creatures with many individualistic traits and behavioral patterns. The Barren Ground, truly Arctic, Arctic hare is obviously exposed to different forces than the common black-tailed jackrabbit of the grasslands and open areas of the American West. The open-country European hare lives a different life from that of the snowshoe hare with his love of the forests and swamps of the colder regions of this continent. Similarly, the white-tailed jackrabbit from the northern plains and western mountains lives a distinctly different life.

All these animals have their own enemies, their own foods, and their own methods of dealing with both. Nevertheless, there are a number of common denominators that make a hare a hare wherever he may be. He is active, alert, fast, and nervous. He is a great eater and a great burner of energy. He breeds rapidly to maintain his species against all comers and, all in all, he is a tough little creature. Whether he is eating, breeding, running, fighting, or jumping, he does so rapidly and readily.

Courtesy Commonwealth of Massachusetts, Division of Fisheries and Game

The varying hare, shy with good reason, winter as well as summer.

Reproduction

Since the variations in breeding habits are relatively slight, we will let the common black-tailed jackrabbit speak for the whole genus in this regard.

Courtship is a wild affair. The buck, as the male is called, engages in a furious "dance" with the doe, involving great leaps and bounds. They run at each other, leap over each other, and generally act in a very revealing way.

In the South, breeding goes on all year long. In the North, it is a spring and summer affair. Gestation is forty-one to forty-seven days, and litter size varies from one to eight, with two to four being average. The young, or leverets, weigh from two to six ounces and are five and a half to eight inches long. As we pointed out at the beginning of the chapter, they are furred, have their eyes open, and are capable of moving around a few hours after birth. Within a month they are on their own, and their mother is gravid again.

Normally, hares and jackrabbits scratch out a shallow form in which to rest during the day. It is an unimproved hole in the ground. When a female approaches the hour of birth, she takes more pains with her form and carefully lines it with the softest vegetation she can find. That is the extent of her nest building.

Observation

There is no great trick to the observation of our hares and rabbits beyond putting yourself where they are. In desert country, and when there is snow on the ground, you will know soon enough if they are around; their tracks will be everywhere. In areas where they abound, you will think they rained down from the skies above. The one question you will ask yourself is, Where do they go during the day? It never ceases to amaze an observer that an area that is alive with them at night seems absolutely devoid of life during the day. They are, of course, snugged down into their shallow forms awaiting dusk, the time of eating and breeding.

53

The Meek: The Rabbits

Names and Range

For the purposes of a generalized introduction to the rabbits of the United States and Canada we will rather arbitrarily break them down into groups and give eight of these as examples:

The eastern cottontail has a large range covering a variety of habitats. He is found from New England to the Dakotas, and south into Mexico. In Canada he is found in the southern parts of the eastern provinces only.

The mountain cottontail is an animal of the western part of this continent. He ranges from northern New Mexico and Arizona west and to the southern parts of the western Canadian provinces.

The New England cottontail centers his range in the New England states but may be found south as far as Georgia.

The desert cottontail is a western animal with a range that extends from the Southwest north to Montana and west to the Pacific Ocean.

The brush rabbit is found in coastal Oregon and California, and in Mexico's Baja California.

The marsh rabbit is an animal of the Southeast ranging through parts at least of Florida, Alabama, Georgia, North and South Carolina.

The swamp rabbit is found in the deep South from eastern Texas to eastern Alabama. He can be seen as far north as southern Illinois.

The diminutive pygmy rabbit is found in seven states only: Montana, Idaho, Utah, Nevada, California, Oregon, and Washington.

It can be argued, of course, that these aren't the best divisions and this or that rabbit should be included instead of rabbit A, B, or C. We should

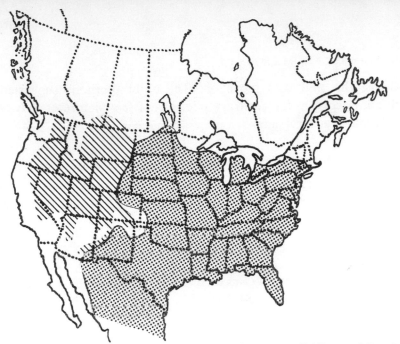

Eastern cottontail (dotted area). Mountain cottontail (diagonal lines).

Swamp rabbit (vertical lines). New England cottontail (crosshatched area). Pygmy rabbit (∕∕ diagonal lines). Marsh rabbit (∖∖ diagonal lines). Desert cottontail (dotted area).

acknowledge this and then move on. The eight divisions suggested here, although admittedly on the arbitrary side, give a fair picture of *Sylvilagus* in the United States and Canada.

Appearance and Distinguishing Characteristics

All of our rabbits are reddish, grayish, or brownish in color, or some combination thereof. They range in size from the tiny pygmy rabbit often no more than eight and a half inches long to the large seventeen-inch cottontails of the Northeast. The following table gives some important measurements:

	Overall Length (*in inches*)	Length of Ears (*in inches*)	Weight (*in pounds*)
Eastern cottontail	14–17	2½–3	2–4
Mountain cottontail	12–14	2½–2⅗	1½–3
New England cottontail	16–17	2¼–2½	3–4
Desert cottontail	12–15	3–4	1⅖–2¾
Brush rabbit	11–13	2–2⅗	1¼–1⅘
Marsh rabbit	14–16	2½–3	2½–3½
Swamp rabbit	14–17	3½–4	3½–6
Pygmy rabbit	8½–11	2¼–2½	½–1

Identification can sometimes be made in the field by attention to details of color. The eastern cottontail has the distinctive white cottony tail and is a grayish brown in color. The yellow-washed gray mountain cottontail resembles him closely but is the only cottontail over most of his range. The New England cottontail is reddish in summer, but is sprinkled with white, giving him a reddish-gray appearance in winter. He has a dark patch between his ears that sets him apart.

The desert cottontail, as might be expected, is pale grayish lightly washed with a faint yellow. The brush rabbit, also quite predictably, is distinctly brown and is set apart as well by his small size. The marsh rabbit can be distinguished by his dark-brown and very coarse coat. His feet are reddish brown on top, even darker below. His tail is a dirty white on the underside only.

The swamp rabbit is a rich brown gray with coarse fur. *His hind feet are rusty above*. The tiny pygmy rabbit is slate gray with a slightly pinkish tinge.

A cottontail nest—short-lived peace.

All rabbits have a split upper lip; they have ears, hind legs, and feet smaller in proportion to body size than the hares and jackrabbits.

In all honesty, it is no easy task to tell the rabbits apart when they are spotted in the field scooting for cover. It is an interesting challenge, however, and since rabbits are so common, so often seen, the reader may be inspired to accept the challenge and consult a more advanced text that emphasizes identification.

Habits

Once again we are dealing with a fairly large group of animals with a wide variety of habitat preferences. Although they are adaptable, each group of rabbits has an ideal situation:

Eastern cottontail	Heavy brush patches—always near cover although may wander into open
Mountain cottontail	Mountainous areas—seldom below pines
New England cottontail	Open forests—mountainous preferred
Desert cottontail	Valleys and arid Southwest
Brush rabbit	Heavy brush cover
Marsh rabbit	Wet areas with dense cover—near water
Swamp rabbit	Wet areas near streams
Pygmy rabbit	Dense sagebrush

The very common eastern cottontail, particularly, is highly adaptable and will live in all types of cover, although he prefers open brushy or forest areas. He delights in border areas, fence rows, hedge fences, thickets, dense high grass, weedy growth, and brush piles. Like all rabbits he scratches a form or slight depression near cover. In winter he holes up in the underground dens of other animals. He follows regular paths through the brush, weeds, and grass.

The range of an individual animal will cover one to five acres if the pickings are good. In a poor area ranges may extend over ten or even fifteen acres and often overlap.

The food choices of the rabbits are seemingly without end. They consume great quantities of leaves, stems, flowers, sedges, and herbs. Among their favorites are goldenrod, bluegrass, timothy, chickweed, red clover, sorrel, alfalfa, soybeans, wheat, rye, and truck crops. Of the woody foods they prefer dwarf sumac, staghorn, white oak, dogwood, black oak, and sassafras. In times of extreme hunger they will eat some animal food: moth pupae, snails, and even carrion. Like the hares they eat their own droppings to get the nourishment missed the first time through.

The rabbits do not hibernate, and they seldom hole up even in bad weather. When the temperature drops below twelve degrees, however, they do hide for short periods.

Normally rabbits hop along slowly, stopping often to sit up on their hind legs and scan the area for potential danger. When frightened they run in a zigzag course and then freeze. To escape notice a rabbit is capable of remaining perfectly still for fifteen minutes or more. They are very high-

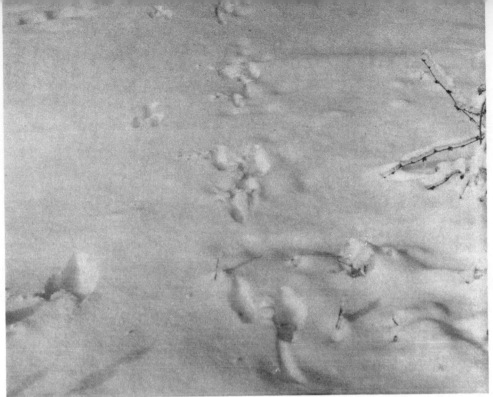

Distinctive tracks in the snow—a winter scene found over much of North America.

Cottontail tracks.

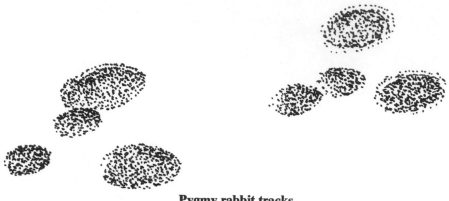

Pygmy rabbit tracks.

strung and can die of shock if handled or caged. They swim well when they
have to but don't seem to seek out opportunities to prove it.

Reproduction

Rabbits, like hares, engage in a wild and woolly courtship with very
athletic displays. They generally breed between March and September and
have a 26–30 day gestation period. Litter size can run from one to nine, with
four or five being the usual count. A healthy doe can deliver an average of
sixteen young in four litters a year. She may have as many as six litters in
some areas. The newborn are four to five inches long and weigh about an
ounce. Their eyes open in six to eight days, and they are weaned in twenty.
They are kept well hidden in a carefully lined nest in a shallow depression.
They have so many enemies that they seldom see their second birthday. Most
never reach maturity.

Observation

Here again there is no trick to it at all. Rabbits are everywhere, and a
walk through the right kind of countryside will seldom fail to turn up a
specimen or two. Their main feeding hours are the three to four hours after
sunrise and late afternoon to an hour after sunset. Actually, you are apt to
find a rabbit abroad almost any hour of the day or night, but the best times are
early morning and late afternoon to early evening.

Photo by Wilford L. Miller

The cottontail, winter or summer, is a valuable food link in the balance of nature. Few specimens live to die of old age.

Rabbits offer a particularly good chance for observation because they don't run very far before stopping and waiting for you to make the next move. If a rabbit scoots out from underfoot while you are walking across a meadow, just stop and watch him. Before he has gone very far he will stop to study you. That is the time to use your binoculars and your camera. A telephoto lens will help.

54

Smallest of the Big Game:
The Peccary

THE HOOFED MAMMALS of the world are divided into two major groupings. Those with an odd number of toes (horses, donkeys, zebras, tapirs, rhinoceroses) are known as the Perissodactyla, and those with an even number of toes (pigs, hippopotamuses, camels, llamas, deer, elk, moose, caribou, giraffes, antelopes, cattle, buffalo, bison, gazelles, sheep, goats, and many more) are known as Artiodactyla. There are no *wild native* odd-toed animals left on this continent. Once there were many, but they died out before man arrived, or at least during the earliest days of his occupancy. One odd-toed animal, the tapir, is found in South America, but his range doesn't even approach our southernmost boundaries. This chapter and those that follow, then, concern the ten groups of Artiodactyla or even-toed animals still found, often in great numbers, in our two countries.

Names and Range

The one wild *native* piglike animal found in the United States is the collared peccary. He has many other names including tayassu, javelina, and musk hog. He ranges from Mexico into southwestern Texas, southeastern Arizona, and southern New Mexico. He is found nowhere else in this country.

Before going on to discuss our peccary we should note that there are wild pigs in parts of Georgia, North Carolina, Tennessee, Texas, New Hampshire, and on some islands off southern California. Nowhere do these animals overlap the range of the peccary and in no way can they be considered as part

Fast and tough—America's native wild pig, the collared peccary or javelina.

of our native fauna. These are feral animals, domestic animals that have gone back to the wild whence their ancestors came. These wild pigs do not resemble the peccary at all; as a matter of fact they hardly resemble the domestic stock from which they came. They are frequently several times as large as the peccary and can be quite aggressive, even very dangerous, animals. If their presence is noted, they should be avoided if you are on foot and not well armed. (Some wild pigs or boars from other parts of the world have also been released in the United States and have a limited range.)

Appearance and Distinguishing Characteristics

The collared peccary averages about thirty-six inches in length, between twenty and twenty-four inches in height at the shoulder. A good-sized animal will weigh between forty and sixty pounds. The basic colors are grizzled black and grayish. There is a dark dorsal stripe in most specimens, and almost always a lighter area over the front of the shoulders. The fur is very coarse. The young are reddish to yellowish brown in color. In the adult there is a mane that extends from the crown of the head to the rump. It is most obvious when the animal is excited.

This rather blunt and aggressive animal has a short but distinctly piglike snout, fairly large ears, almost no tail, and daggerlike canines or tusks. He has four toes on each front foot, quite in keeping with his being an even-toed animal, but somehow his rear end went astray. He has only three toes on each hind foot. Otherwise he is quite piglike.

Habits

The peccary is an animal of the brushy semidesert areas of the three states mentioned. He prefers to live where the prickly pear grows but is found in almost any dense thicket in the area. Chaparral or scrub oak suits him very well. He likes rocky canyons for the cover they offer.

The diet of the peccary consists of cacti (particularly the prickly pear), mesquite, various beans, nuts, and roots, sotol, lechuguilla, a number of other succulents, mast, fruit, insects, and snakes. Like the domestic pig, the peccary is apparently able to tolerate the bite of a rattlesnake that would at least hospitalize even a healthy man weighing three or four times as much.

The peccary is usually observed as part of a band—usually consisting of about six animals, though it may be as small as three in number, or as large as twenty-five or more. The band has a limited home range and will stay within it for long periods of time. Peccaries are most active during the early morning hours and in the late afternoon. During the fierce heat of the midday sun, they bed down in dense brush. They den in hollow logs or in hollows in the ground. It is never a very elaborate affair.

The peccary makes a good pet only when he is quite young. As he grows older he becomes more and more testy and is a particular hazard for strangers. A mature animal cannot be trusted.

Despite his size, his strength, and his very formidable tusks, the peccary has enemies. The jaguar, cougar, bobcat, and wolf all take a toll, but not a very large one. Although he has poor eyesight, the peccary has exceptionally keen hearing and a sense of smell that would put a bloodhound on his guard. Peccaries are quick to sense danger and will usually retreat. However, if their young are endangered, a band of peccaries can become a very dangerous mob of excitable animals. Even the largest predators will back away from a showdown with half a dozen grunting, squealing boars and sows. When really stirred up, there is little they won't take on.

Although you will probably put to flight any peccaries that become aware of your presence, it would be unwise to surprise a band in close quarters. If you should inadvertently put yourself between a band and an escape route, you could be badly hurt in the ensuing panic. Be careful on foot, and even on horseback.

These wild pigs have a powerful musk gland on the top of the rump. The odor is almost always apparent, and if there is any excitement at all it becomes very strong. You may very well smell your first peccary before you see him.

Reproduction

The peccary is a polygamous animal that knows no breeding season. The boar will take one of his harem any month of the year, and three and a half months later one to five one-pound piglets will be born. It is suggested that average litter size is two. The young can follow their mother about after a few days and join the band immediately after that. They normally stay close to their mother and she can be very aggressive in their defense.

Observation

The peccary is considered to be big game, and as such his presence and numbers are matters of public knowledge. Inquiries made in sporting-goods stores and of conservation officers will usually result in fairly accurate information about the whereabouts of local bands. Don't hunt them up during the heat of the day because the best you can hope to do is stumble upon them by accident and cause a panic. They will soon outrun you, and you will have a grand view of a lot of grizzled-gray rumps disappearing into a draw. Pick high ground before the sun is up and use your binoculars. Move slowly down into gulleys and look for tracks, wallows, and signs of the animals having taken dust baths. Move slowly, very quietly, and if the wind starts blowing from behind in the direction you believe the animals have gone, go home and try again another day. Do as the pig does and constantly sniff the air if you think you are getting close. They are detectable by their musky smell. If you miss out in the early morning, try again for an hour or two before sundown. The use of an experienced guide will help your chances of success immeasurably.

There are three refuges with a fairly stable peccary population. You can do very well in:

Aransas National Wildlife Refuge, on the Blackjack Peninsula of Texas' Gulf Coast.

Laguna Atascosa Wildlife Refuge, on the Texas coast near Port Isabel.

Cabeza Prieta Game Range, in Yuma and Pima Counties, Arizona.

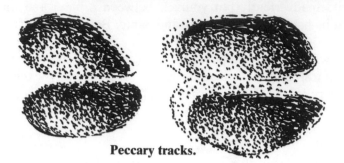

Peccary tracks.

55

Monarch of the West: The Wapiti

Names and Range

The United States and Canada are blessed by the presence of the majestic wapiti. Commonly known as elk, these animals are among the most impressive on our continent. To many they are the very symbol of American wildlife. The name elk properly belongs to the European moose, but its use is so widespread in our two countries as a name for the wapiti that there is little chance of correcting this slight error. There is no point, really, in pursuing the matter, so *elk* it is.

The elk were formerly found over much of the continent and are believed to have reached the Atlantic seaboard. They have been hunted out over most of their range and are today limited to the West. Their range is indicated on the accompanying map.

Appearance and Distinguishing Characteristics

A mature elk can weigh anywhere from five hundred to eleven hundred pounds, will stand 4½–5 feet at the shoulder, and will be 7½–9½ feet long. An elk in his prime is a magnificent animal.

The ground color of the elk is usually some shade of reddish brown, with legs and underparts dark chocolate to black. The neck is usually a deep chestnut brown, and males have a pronounced mane. There is a yellowish white rump patch and a five-to-seven-inch white tail. The coat is much heavier in winter than at other seasons and can have a shaggy look by the time spring comes around. The small tule elk is paler than the other races, and his markings are much more subtle.

[421]

Wapiti (dotted areas).

The elk belong to a family of animals known as the Cervidae; the group also includes our deer, moose, and caribou. One of the characteristics of the group is that they shed their antlers every year. The huge spreading antlers of the majestic elk start to grow in March and early April. They are covered with velvet and are quite soft throughout the summer, but when fall arrives they are hard and sharp. The antlers consist of a main *beam* with branching *tines*. There is a special vocabulary that goes with these great trophies. In the normal bull, the main beam sweeps upward, outward, and backward. Ideally there will be six tines to the antler when the bull is in his prime. The lowest tines project out over the brow and are known, logically, as *brow tines*. The second set are known as the *bay* or *bez tines*. The first and second together are variously called *dog-killers, lifters,* or *war tines*. The somewhat shorter third tine is called the *tray* or *trez tine*. The fourth, largest, and deadliest tine is the *royal,* or *dagger-point,* tine. The two points forming the antler's divided tip are the *sur-royals*.

Bull elks are classed according to their antlers. A bull with a total of twelve tines or *points* is known as a *royal stag*. A fourteen-point bull is a *Wilson* or *imperial stag*. The antlers may be up to six feet long, with a spread of forty-seven inches.

Habits

The elk is an animal of semiopen forests that summers in the mountains and winters in the valleys. He migrates in search of new feeding grounds. The animals have a strong social instinct and will be found in herds containing as many as a hundred animals. They feed on grasses, leaves, twigs, evergreen and deciduous bark, and foliage. They will enter farmlands when things are bad and take hay destined for domestic stock.

These great animals have excellent eyesight, a good sense of smell, and very keen hearing. Their sharp senses serve to protect them against a variety of predators. Bears, cougars, wolves, coyotes, all try but not too many succeed. Although some young fall victim, a bull elk can readily hold off more than his weight in bobcats. (That's an exaggeration for emphasis, of course!) With his sharp front hooves and his great spread of antlers and powerful neck muscles—and with half a ton of bulk behind these— a bull elk is nothing to fool with, be it man, wolf, cat, or bear.

An elk can easily cover the ground at 28 or 29 miles an hour. In bursts, it is reported, he can hit from 35 to 45 miles an hour. A seven-foot fence is hardly reckoned an obstacle. He is also a powerful swimmer.

The bugling of the elk is thought by many to be the most thrilling sound in all of nature. It starts low, rises sharply to a clear bugle tone, then flats out to a combination grunt and bray. It can be heard for miles and generally announces the onset of the breeding season or rut. Let other bulls beware, for that bugling is a challenge that can lead to a duel to the death.

Part of a wapiti herd in Alberta's Buffalo National Park. Photo taken near Wainwright.

Reproduction

The polygamous elk comes into rut in September and October. Great battles are fought by herd males in defense of harems that can contain thirty or more cows. In order for a bull to take a harem away from another bull he has to all but kill him. Great wounds are inflicted as the six-foot antlers are wielded in deadly earnest.

The gestation period is about eight and a half months long, and one or rarely two young appear in May or June. At birth the calves weigh from thirty

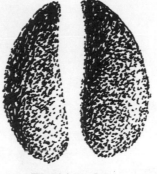

Wapiti tracks.

to forty pounds and are up to three feet long. They walk within a matter of hours and can run when they are a week old. At that time they also eat their first greens, but their weaning is not completed until winter has settled over the land. Maturity is not reached for four years.

Observation

There are controlled herds of elk in many national parks and game refuges. Among these are:

Banff National Park	Alberta
Desert Game Range (introduced herd)	Nevada
Fort Niobrara Wildlife Refuge	Nebraska
Fort Peck Game Range	Montana
Glacier National Park	Montana
Jasper National Park	Alberta
Kootenay National Park	British Columbia
National Bison Range	Montana
National Elk Refuge	Wyoming
Olympic National Park	Washington
Prince Albert National Park	Saskatchewan
Riding Mountain National Park	Manitoba
Sullys Hill National Game Preserve	North Dakota
Waterton Lakes National Park	Alberta
Wichita Mountains Wildlife Refuge	Oklahoma
Yellowstone National Park	Wyoming-Montana-Idaho
Yoho National Park	British Columbia

Photo by Wilford L. Miller

A lone wapiti bull with an impressive spread of antlers challenges the photographer in Yellowstone National Park.

There is an introduced herd of some 300 animals in the Guadalupe Mountains in Texas.

Hint: If you are in Riding Mountain National Park look to the plains and woodlands in the vicinity of Lake Audy for a large herd.

The California Department of Fish and Game estimates that there are some 2,830 animals in the wild in that state, of three races. They give the following population and area advice.

Area	County	Race	Estimated Population
Bear Valley	Del Norte	Roosevelt	40
Prairie Creek State Park	Humboldt	Roosevelt	40
Big Lagoon, Gold Beach, Orick	Humboldt	Roosevelt	1,000
Scattered areas	Humboldt	Roosevelt	920
Squaw Creek	Shasta	Rocky Mountain	200
Santa Lucia	Monterey	Rocky Mountain	100
Santa Rosa Island	Santa Barbara	Rocky Mountain	150
Cache Creek	Lake–Colusa	Tule	80
Owens Valley	Inyo	Tule	300

56

Our Most Common Big-Game Animal: The Deer

THE DEER of the United States and Canada are of particular interest to most observers. They are the most common large-game animal in our two countries and the animal most readily seen. Very often a deer is the only hoofed animal recorded by an observer on his checklist until he has traveled far and spent a good deal of time in the field.

Names and Range

All of our smaller deer, namely the white-tailed and closely related mule deer (in the strict scientific meaning of the word our elk, moose, and caribou are deer, too) belong to a single genus and are closely related.

The white-tailed deer range from Canada to extreme southern Central America. There is probably no state today that doesn't have at least some white-tailed deer hiding behind a thin screen of wooded land beside a meadow somewhere within its boundaries.

The mule deer (including the black-tailed) range from Mexico to the southern Yukon. This represents a solid blanket covering all of the United States and Canada south of the Northwest Territories and east to Manitoba and eastern Colorado.

Appearance and Distinguishing Characteristics

If you saw a whitetail one day and a mule deer another, you might have a little trouble in recognizing very many distinct differences. Side by side, however, the two animals would reveal many—be they variations on one theme.

White-tailed deer (dotted areas).

In size, there isn't too much difference: both animals run from three to three and a half feet at the shoulder, both run from 55 to 75 inches in length. The whitetail shows a spread in weight of 50 to 350 pounds, the mule from 125 to 475 pounds. Any deer over 250 pounds, however, is unusually large and will be seldom encountered. Both animals have the same basic color

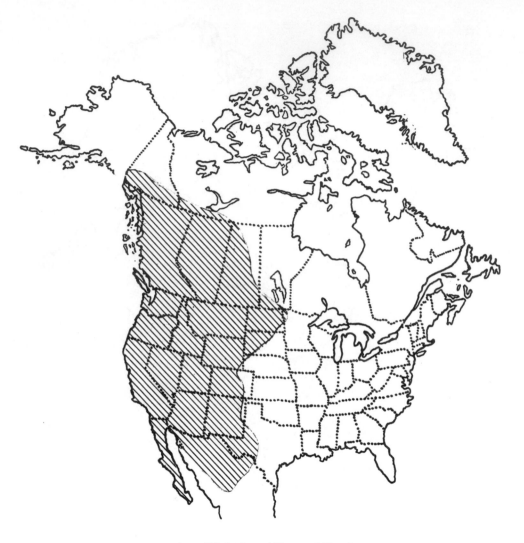

Mule deer (diagonal lines).

combinations. They are some shade of reddish brown in summer, some shade of blue-gray in winter. There are many variations within these colors, but the differences are as great within a group as between the two groups and are therefore totally unreliable.

Handsome white-tailed buck in Ontario's Algonquin Provincial Park.

There are some reliable characteristics, however. The ears of the mule deer are one fourth longer than those of the whitetail, hence the name. The mule deer has relatively large feet, those of the whitetail are quite small and dainty. The tail of the whitetail is larger than that of any other deer in North America. It is *always* reddish brown on top, always *white* underneath. The tail of the mule deer, on the other hand, is subject to great variation in color pattern. In most mule deer, the tail is white underneath and brown on top except for a black tip. In the black-tailed deer (considered one of the mules) the tail is black on top from tip to base. Since there is some interbreeding, it is believed, there are gradations in the amount of actual black that shows. However, the black tip or the black streak immediately identifies one of the mule deer from the whitetails. Both animals generally have a white, or at least whitish, rump patch.

All in all, the white-tailed deer is the more graceful animal, at least in appearance. He has a long, slender neck, a narrow face, and beautiful, baleful eyes. He is dainty in appearance. The mule deer tends to have a rather thickset body and stocky legs. Still a graceful animal by any standards, he is the chunkier of the two. In both groups there are marked *individual* differences. Like people, deer come short and fat, tall and thin, awkward, gawky, and graceful.

When all else fails, the antlers will tell all. Note the differences between the two types:

The antlers of the *whitetail* are *low* and *compact*. The main beams rise from the back of the head behind the eyes and curve upward, outward, and

White-tailed deer tracks.

forward, then curve inward over the face. There are a series of short, *un-branched* tines or points that extend *upward* from the beam. The record length stands at 31⅜ inches total length for the main beam, with *eight points to the side*. These antlers are shed between December and February. They start growing again in April or May.

The antlers of the *mule* are *high* and *branched*. They project upward and forward. They do not have the regular tines of the whitetail, but the main beam of each is evenly divided at the first fork. Each branch then divides again. There are usually *four points to the side*. They, too, are shed from December on.

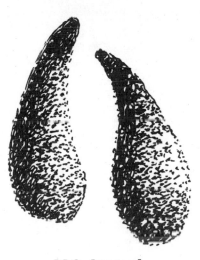

Mule deer tracks.

Habits

The swift and graceful deer display a characteristic of most really fast animals the world over: they are *unguligrade*—they walk on their toes. They can hit speeds of thirty-five miles an hour when in a real hurry, and can maintain twenty-five miles an hour for several miles without stopping. They have been known to take jumps of twenty-nine feet, can reach a height of eight feet, and can easily and gracefully take a whole series of twenty-foot bounds without apparent effort. They are excellent swimmers, showing not only speed in the water but remarkable endurance.

White-tailed buck, central North Dakota.

Although not asocial, since they are often seen close together where the browsing is good, our deer are not really herd animals. Males and females are together during the breeding season, and does are often seen with their fawns, but, for the most part, our deer lead fairly solitary lives. The whitetail will often establish a home range of a square mile or so. The mule is less likely to do so, being more of a wanderer, and will often drift to higher altitudes during the summer—eight thousand feet is not at all unusual. The whitetail, at least, displays a social adaptation in his tail. He uses it as a flag, as a signaling device to warn other deer of danger. When he snaps that tail upright, displaying its white underside, you can expect all deer within sight to move off as quickly as possible. When a whitetail wants to sneak away, he keeps his tail clamped down against his rump.

All three senses are very sharp in all of our deer. They need their senses because they are the most preyed upon of all of our large animals. Bobcat, lynx, wolves, coyotes, dogs, bears, mountain lions, jaguars, even wolverines, all of these prey on our deer. In the West, the golden eagle is said to prey on fawns. In almost every state, the domestic dog is the most serious predator, however.

When alerted to danger, the usually mute deer will make a loud, whistling snort before taking off, quite literally, over the nearest clump of vegetation. At times he will turn and fight with sharp hooves powerfully driven. When in rut, a buck is a dangerous adversary for most predators to tackle.

Nature, in her unfathomable wisdom, provided the deer as a key prey animal for our large predators. Swift, alert, even aggressive at certain times of the year, a healthy deer can usually take care of himself long enough to become a parent and continue a strong blood line. With man's decimation of his natural predators, the deer has fallen victim to his own fecundity and weaknesses. Weak, old, and sickly animals, the specimens destined to be eaten in any natural situation, are not killed off and live to breed and produce young reflecting, often accentuating, their own weaknesses. They overbrowse their range, producing starvation conditions that further the trend toward a weakened strain. Man continues this mayhem by hunting, since he quite naturally looks for the best buck with the best antlers. He thereby kills off

Courtesy Province of Ontario, Department of Lands & Forests

White-tailed fawn at Port Arthur, Ontario. Instinctively it will wait in complete silence for the return of its mother.

prime bucks displaying the largest size and best condition. These are the very animals needed to strengthen the strain. The result of all this is far too many deer in a great many areas and thousands dead from starvation every year. The best thing that could happen to the deer in this country would be a resurgence of wolf and mountain lion population and a moratorium on hunting by man for a decade or two. In this way our deer population would stabilize itself, with the weak falling prey and the strong surviving. Neither is likely to happen. Man, nature's great meddler, can no more stop killing every wolf and mountain lion he meets than he can stop selecting prime bucks with big antlers when he hunts. It is a sad, destructive trend that is not likely to be reversed.

One special point is most important in the discussion of our deer. When we come to reproduction a few paragraphs hence, you will note that fawns are left unattended by the does. They are sometimes found by well-meaning hikers and brought home as pets. Does are sometimes killed on highways, or shot by daring sportsmen, and fawns are found nearby. While it is true that there is no more appealing animal in all of nature than a baby deer, *they should not be taken home as pets*. If you have no reason to believe the baby is motherless, leave him alone. If you handle him and leave your terrible man-smell on his coat, his mother may abandon him to starvation. If you *know* the animal to be an orphan, take him to a zoo or a game ranger. That little wide-eyed fawn who drinks so beautifully from a baby's bottle may grow up to be a real killer. When he reaches maturity and enters his periodic rut, he is as dangerous as an animal can be. All his killer instincts will rise, and he may put you, a family member, or a friend in the hospital, or even in the grave. More people are seriously injured by pet deer in this country every year than have been hurt by wolves or our wild felines in the last century. However good your intentions, you are not doing the deer or yourself any good by bringing him home. Should you be strong enough in purpose and will to release your pet after you have raised him, you are doing him no good at all. He will have lost his absolutely essential fear of man and will be the easiest prey possible for the next man who comes along with a gun. If he survives the hunters, he may come close to human habitation and there cause trouble when he goes into rut. *Deer do not make satisfactory pets.*

Deer are browsers and eat a great variety of vegetable matter. They love sunlit woodland glades and sheltered meadows for the sense of security they provide and for the browse available there. They eat fresh green leaves, shrub twigs, lower branches of trees, and many kinds of grasses. Among their

Photo by Wilford L. Miller

Mule deer in Yellowstone National Park.

favorite foods are blackberry vines, raspberry canes, greenbrier, witch hazel, elderberry, maples, oaks, sassafras, dogwood, wild rose, water lilies, sedges, aspens, ash, chokeberry, currant, grape, mushrooms, mistletoe, algae, and ferns. In the fall they eat nuts, fruits, seeds, acorns, and apples. In winter they will feed on evergreen needles, sprouts of various spruces, balsam, white pine, dead and dry grass and leaves, and several mosses. It is this ability to live off so many different plant substances and thrive that has enabled our deer to spread so far and last so well.

Reproduction

The rut starts in September and runs through February; it reaches its height in November. During this period, the buck is dangerous, even vicious. Does mate at eighteen months, sometimes earlier. Bucks mate first sometime after they are a year and a half, often not until they are two and a half. Fierce battles are fought between bucks, and cases are known where two contenders came together so violently that their antlers became interlocked. In such cases, both animals eventually die of starvation.

Gestation lasts about two hundred days, and anywhere from one to four young appear from April through June. The first birth delivered by a doe is usually single; after that multiple births are common, with twins being the norm. The fawn weighs about six pounds and is bay-red with white spots. He must nurse within the first hour and is expected to stand within the first twelve. He has no odor and instinctively knows how to lie perfectly still for long periods of time. Right after his birth his mother licks him all over and thus comes to know him from all other fawns in the area. During his early weeks of life he will see his mother only at mealtime. Otherwise he is alone and unattended, albeit well hidden. For hours on end he will lie still in a clump of bushes or in deep grass or weeds. Predators can pass within a few feet of him, but neither sound nor scent will give him away. At the end of his first month his spots will begin to fade. By September they will be gone. He is weaned sometime between his third and fourth month. If he is not killed, or doesn't starve to death, he might live to be twenty, although that is certainly an extreme age. Normal life span runs from ten to fifteen years, it is believed.

Observation

How many times have you driven down a road or highway, seen signs cautioning you that you were in a deer-crossing area, and wondered why you never saw any deer? Almost every observer has had that experience sometime during his career. The secret is *time of day*. If you drive that same road at sunup, or for an hour or two before and after, and if indeed you are in a deer-crossing area, you will be likely to see your deer. Try the same area just about sunset; you are apt to have luck then as well. Deer feed in the open in the very early morning and in the late afternoon and early evening; it is then that you see them.

With one notable exception, little specific advice is needed to help you find your deer. If you don't seem to be having any luck, check with local hunters, farmers, and conservationists. Station yourself near good browse, near good cover. Deer are extremely fond of apples and can be tempted into an observation area from the woods in which they hide by spreading some around. Salt licks obtained from a farm-supply store will serve the same purpose. It is, by the way, not only the worst kind of bad sportsmanship to use either device to lure them into rifle range, it is illegal. Similarly, "jacking" deer with bright lights is against the law.

They are the smallest deer in the United States and Canada and quite possibly the rarest.

No large animal in the United States and Canada will offer you so many opportunities for observation as our deer. An automobile trip in almost any region on this continent will turn them up at roadside. I have seen them in the arid Southwest, I have seen them within a hundred feet of the south rim of the Grand Canyon in the dead of winter, in Maine, California, Florida, Kansas, in northern Ontario, in perhaps thirty states and a good many Canadian provinces. I maintain a salt lick and a supply of timothy hay on the grounds of my Easthampton, Long Island, home for the regular visitors we have there. A sighting never fails to be an exciting experience. A large wild animal is a stimulating vision even for the most urbane citizen. Long may that white flag wave.

57

The Majestic One: The Moose

Names and Range

In general, the moose of North America range from Alaska to Labrador; they are found in all Canadian provinces and in between sixteen and twenty of the original forty-eight states. Actually, hunting has so reduced their numbers that you will be hard put to find any at all in much of the area embraced by those states. In many areas they are strictly protected. With their population so depressed, it is a shame and a wonder that any hunting is allowed at all.

If you referred to a "moose" when talking to a European, you would probably draw a blank look. The closely related animals found across northern Europe are known there as "elk."

Appearance and Distinguishing Characteristics

To begin our description, we can cite three distinctions held by our moose: (1) he is the largest antlered animal in the world; (2) he is the tallest mammal in all of the Americas; and (3) he runs a close second to the bison for the title of heaviest herbivorous land animal in the New World. Obviously, the moose is a large creature.

A large moose can stand from five to six and a half feet or more at the shoulder, can be up to ten and a half feet long, and may weigh as much as eighteen hundred pounds, although the average weight normally runs between seven hundred and thirteen hundred pounds. Quite aside from his great size, he is a very distinctive-looking animal. He has a great overhanging snout, a kind of pendulous muzzle, and from his throat there hangs a pendant "bell"; it

[441]

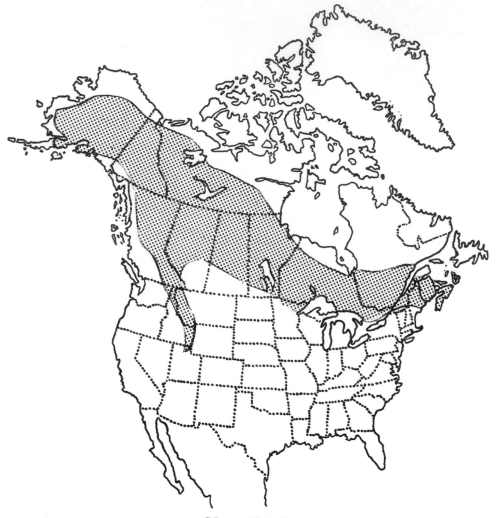

Moose (dotted area).

may be up to a yard long in a prime bull. He is most ungainly looking with his thick, bulging neck, short, inconspicuous tail, small rump, large donkeylike ears, and coarse, brittle fur. His color runs from blackish brown to very nearly black, with brownish-gray legs. Quite literally, he is so ugly he is handsome.

Courtesy Canadian Audubon Society

Lakeside view at dusk.

He rather looks like the offspring of a confused mule and some wanton, prehistoric deer. At best he is confusing-looking.

Most distinctive are his massive antlers. They extend outward from the sides of the head above and in front of the ears. The heavy beam divides into two main branches, both of which are palmated. The smaller branch reaches forward and outward, the larger one (actually a continuation of the main beam) sweeps backward, where it spreads into a great, flattened palm with many points. These antlers can be nearly forty-eight inches from tip to tip and can weigh up to eighty-five or ninety pounds. They are shed between late fall and early January. As a member of the deer family, the moose must grow new ones each year.

Habits

The moose is not a herd animal. Only during the breeding season do adults come together. In an area where the browsing is particularly good, several may congregate for a short time, but in no sense of the word is this herd behavior. They barely tolerate each other as long as it isn't time to breed.

The powerful moose has extremely poor eyesight but compensates for this shortcoming with a keen sense of smell and very sensitive hearing. If the wind is blowing from the animal toward you, you should be careful when approaching on foot. It is possible to surprise them, and when they are startled they can do surprising things. Eyesight is not affected by wind, but both hearing and smell are. For this reason, the moose can be quite touchy about the sudden appearance of anything as threatening as a man. They are not vicious, except during rut, but they are far too large an animal to take for granted.

That great ungainly-looking creature is anything but slow. He can cover ground at amazing speeds and in the water can do better than any man. He

Courtesy Province of Ontario, Department of Lands & Forests

Prepared for a long swim. Note the turbulence, indicating strength and speed of the animal in the water.

can paddle at a steady six miles an hour for long distances and won't shy away from even a fifteen-mile swim. Reportedly he can remain submerged for three or four minutes.

His ability in the water is no mere accident. The moose, although not aquatic in the real sense of the word, is water-oriented. He thrives in dense forests bordering on shallow lakes. He is most often seen in or near water, where he browses on underwater plants. His food covers a wide variety of woodland substances: twigs, leaves, bark of deciduous and evergreen trees, water lilies, and the roots of many aquatic plants. He will stand on his hind legs and push a tree as thick as three inches over to get at tender leaves and shoots. The much publicized "moose yard" is nothing more than a network of trails in the snow in a winter browse area.

As big as he is, the moose has some enemies besides man. Grizzly bears, cougars, and timber wolves sometimes have a go at moosesteak, but they don't often succeed. A large and particularly determined pack of wolves can make a kill, as can a large mountain lion that manages to drop onto a moose's neck from a tree or ledge, but usually an adult moose can hold his own. That great lumbering hulk of an animal may look silly as he trods along on the tips of his toes, but don't try him. He likes his peace and quiet, and the virtuous dignity of being one of the largest land animals in the world.

Reproduction

The bull moose does not maintain a harem. He comes together with a single cow and remains near her for about ten days. He then abandons her and seeks another. Beginning in September, this goes on for as long as the rut lasts—for four to eight weeks, depending on the animal. During that time violent battles break out between males. A quarter to half an acre of woodland can be torn up by the infuriated bulls as they try to maul each other. During this period they are vicious, suspicious, extremely dangerous animals and will attack anything that annoys them. Occasionally battling bulls lock antlers and die of starvation.

Gestation lasts a full eight months, and the twenty-five-to-thirty-five-pound youngsters number from one to three. Colored like their mother, they do not display the spots of other young deer. They are on their feet and nursing within the first hour, but spend their first two weeks in seclusion. When they are about a month old, and until they are nearly a full year, they remain very close to their mother wherever she goes. They grow extremely fast and gain pounds each day.

Just before she gives birth, the female seeks a quiet, secluded spot. Frequently she selects a peninsula or island on some backwoods lake. When she has her young with her, she is second in temper only to a rutting bull. *Do not approach a female moose with young nearby. You are apt to draw a very determined charge.*

Photo by Wilford L. Miller

A favorite summer-moose pose.

Observation

The sighting of an adult moose in the wild is still one of the richest experiences available to the amateur observer on this continent. Down through the years the opportunities to have this experience have been steadily reduced. In all of the United States, or at least in the original forty-eight states, there probably are no more than 12,000 wild moose left. When you note that there are perhaps 150,000 moose in Canada, it is easy to see that the better part of the animal's range today lies in that country.

When you see your moose, remember you are looking at an animal descended from giant forms who once trod this land with antlers large enough for several men to sit in. The great monarch of the woods is a link with Europe, and a link with the past.

When you look for your moose, look in the early morning hours or the late afternoon and at dusk. Don't bother looking too far from water because your chances will be slight.

Courtesy Province of Ontario, Department of Lands & Forests

Moose tracks in the snow.

There are a number of parks and refuges that proudly list the moose among their fauna. You will have a chance of success in the following preserves:

Agassiz Wildlife Refuge	Minnesota
Banff National Park	Alberta
Cape Breton Highlands National Park	Nova Scotia
Fundy National Park	New Brunswick
Glacier National Park	Montana
Jasper National Park	Alberta
Kenai National Moose Range	Alaska
Kootenay National Park	British Columbia
Moosehorn National Wildlife Refuge	Maine

Mt. McKinley National Park	Alaska
National Elk Refuge	Wyoming
Prince Albert National Park	Saskatchewan
Red Rock Lakes National Wildlife Refuge	Montana
Riding Mountain National Park	Manitoba
Seney National Wildlife Refuge	Michigan
Terra Nova National Park	Newfoundland
Waterton Lakes National Park	Alberta
Yellowstone National Park	Wyoming
Yoho National Park	British Columbia

Moose tracks.

58

The Important One: The Caribou

THE CARIBOU are the only wild terrestrial mammals left in our two countries still supporting human beings in large numbers. The Eskimos depend on the caribou for meat, skins, and other products derived from their sizable carcasses. Once, all men on this continent except the few agricultural peoples and some extremely primitive "gatherers" depended on the vast store of hoofed animals for their food and clothing, often their housing. Moose, bison, elk, deer, pronghorns—these were animals in awe-inspiring numbers that supported dozens, perhaps hundreds of tribes. Of these only the caribou remains of true economic significance. The hunting of the rest is called sport.

Names and Range

There are four races of caribou still to be found in our northlands. The Barren Ground caribou ranges across the top of the world, from Alaska to Labrador. The large woodland caribou lives in the evergreen forest belt of Canada, mainly in the West but to some degree still in the East. The mountain caribou enjoys a similar habitat but is found in lower latitudes along the mountain chains that bring Arctic conditions southward. The small Greenland caribou is found only on that vast island.

Caribou were once found in all or most of our northern border states. Today, only Minnesota can boast any at all, and that population is very limited. The northern reaches of all Canadian provinces except the southern maritimes still have caribou, although not in the numbers formerly known.

[449]

Appearance and Distinguishing Characteristics

The caribou is a moderately large deer with a broad, well-haired muzzle, long, loose, brittle fur, a pronounced mane, and a short, inconsequential tail. Body and head lengths run from fifty to ninety inches, shoulder heights from forty to sixty inches, and weights from two hundred to seven hundred pounds.

In the summer the caribou is dark brown; during the winter months his thick coat assumes a grayish-brown tone. At all times of the year, the neck, belly, feet, rump patch, and tail range from pale gray to yellowish white. The Barren Ground caribou is a smaller and paler animal, the woodland caribou a darker, heavier one. The mountain caribou, now very rare, is the largest and darkest of all. In the summer months his coat approaches black but never quite gets there.

The antlers of all the caribou follow a basic pattern, although there are distinct differences between the species. The main beam literally sweeps backward, upward, and outward and ends in a very flattened palm. Usually only one antler or the other has a forward-projecting brow tine. Occasionally it is seen on both antlers. The second or bez tine is also palmated to some degree in most specimens. The antlers of the Barren Ground caribou tend to be long and relatively simple, while those of the woodland caribou are heavier, less rangy. The caribou is the only deer where the antler is seen in both sexes. The females shed theirs at fawning time, May and June.

Habits

The high-stepping caribou is a swift animal. He can hit thirty-two miles an hour if pressed and will readily take to water. He will undertake very long swims without hesitation. He is strictly a herd animal and is seldom seen alone.

The migration of the caribou has been described many times and remains one of the most thrilling sights of our wildlife scene. The woodland caribou migrates only short distances and in relatively small groups. His is a trek from summer to winter feeding grounds. Although the Barren Ground caribou migrates for the same reason, it is a more awe-inspiring sight. From the open tundra, where they have spent the summer luxuriating in the brief but explosive plant growth, the caribou depart in August. With their noses pointed to the south and the sheltered woodlands, the animals congregate on ancient routes. From all directions they drift, feeding as they go. As the herd builds, the tempo increases. From as far away as the eye can see, even when airborne,

The woodland caribou—a male and a female browsing.

the great bulls, the cows still with young tagging after them, come together like a giant living river with endless tributaries. These routes are known to wolves and bears as well, and the flanks of these great migrating herds are worried by the powerful predators until the weak and sickly are weeded out. Through mountain passes, across lakes and rivers already starting to freeze, the mass of animals moves. Then one day, there are no more. Where once there were tens of thousands, none remain. A few scattered bones picked at by ravens and foxes are all that mark the route. Not until another spring will these barren lands witness these vast herds.

Caribou live on twigs, leaves, shrubs, grass, lichen, moss, flowers, almost any plant matter available to them. Quite naturally, the rich Arctic summer meadow offers a greater variety than the poor winter woodlands, but somehow they survive the worst and continue their race.

The wolf, the wolverine, the lynx, and the bears all prey on the caribou herds. The wolverine and lynx take some young, and the wolves and bears take adults, but only the wolf is a really serious predator. There has been an endless stream of reports and studies, of opinions and guesses as to how

Courtesy U.S. Department of Interior, Fish & Wildlife Service

A new-born caribou calf near Nelchina, Alaska.

serious this predation is. Many believe, as does this author, that the wolf does more good than harm. A single wolf is hard put to kill a healthy caribou. Almost any healthy caribou can outrun a wolf. It is the sick, the old, the feeble that fall prey. This thinning, this removal of "deadwood" can only increase the strength of the strain. Killing off the wolf, as advocated by so many, will not save the caribou herds, it will temporarily increase their numbers, overstrain the winter browse, and eventually condemn a weakened strain to slow death. The caribou and the wolf are perfectly capable of working out a natural balance good for both if they are left alone. They did very well before man showed up with his rifles, his traps, and his poisoned bait and attempted to reorganize things as he thought they should be. Nature, the wolf, the caribou—none of them asked for this help. Man the meddler can help best by leaving things alone. Those taken by the Eskimos each year for their very important needs do not weaken the herds either. The Eskimos must recognize the need for economy, however, and not take the high-powered rifle he now has as license to kill more than he needs. Unless he does, and unless man in general leaves the wolf, the great thinner, alone, the caribou may soon be in very serious trouble. There will be no excuse this time. We have seen what we can do when we are at our destructive worst. Hopefully, man has learned his lesson.

Reproduction

By early September the caribou bulls are looking at each other with a suspicious eye. Their necks are beginning to thicken, and their tempers shorten. Then the fights start. The winners take harems of about twelve cows, and the losers drift off to either challenge another bull, or to remain unmated for the year.

The gestation period for the caribou runs between eight and nine months. In June the eight-to-nine-pound calves appear. The Barren Ground caribou normally delivers a single offspring, the woodland may have twins. They are ready to nurse within minutes of their birth and ready to follow after their mother in hours. They are weaned by September.

Observation

It is not an easy task to get to see your caribou. It is an accomplishment to dream of, however, and when you do put that check mark on your lifetime list, you can feel proud at how far you have come since ticking off the gray squirrel and the cottontail rabbit.

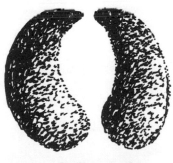

Caribou tracks.

Herds of caribou can still be found in the following protected areas:

Arctic National Wildlife Range (Barren Ground)   Alaska
Izembek National Wildlife Range (Grant's)   Alaska
Jasper National Park (Mountain)   Alberta
Mt. McKinley National Park (Barren Ground)   Alaska
Prince Albert National Park (Woodland)   Saskatchewan
Superior National Forest (Woodland)   Minnesota

59

The Nonconformist: The Pronghorn

Names and Range

The totally unique pronghorn is known as antelope from one end of his range to the other. He is no more an antelope than he is a giraffe, billy goat, or deer, with all of whom he shares some characteristics. In plain fact, the pronghorn is closely related to no other living animal. *He is distinctly not an antelope*. He is a bizarre remnant of an ancient family of bizarre animals.

Today, as he did hundreds and thousands of years ago, the pronghorn ranges through southern Canadian, western American, and Mexican prairie and wasteland areas. His numbers are much reduced, but he is still there. He prefers flat, open areas, where he can see his enemies before or as soon as they see him. Low, rolling ground suits him, too, for over the rises he can swiftly disappear.

Appearance and Distinguishing Characteristics

The graceful, slender pronghorn averages between four and four and a half feet in length, from 32 to 40 inches at the shoulder, and weighs from 100 to 125 pounds. He has long, thick hair that enables him to withstand biting cold winds. He has very large eyes and a white or buff five-inch tail. Basic body color runs from light tan to deep red-brown. The rump, sides of the head, and two stripes on the throat are white. The underparts of the body are white to yellowish. The tip of the nose and usually a patch under each eye are blackish brown. He is a very handsome animal.

The horn of the pronghorn (it is *not* an antler) is a hollow sheath over a bony core. It arises from his skull directly above the eyes and has one forward-

Photo by Wilford L. Miller

Big-eyed pronghorn kid. Note the size of its ever-alert ears.

pointing tine or prong about halfway up its average ten-inch length. The tip curves back. There are small, vestigial horns on the females. Before trying to put the pronghorn into some perspective with the rest of the animal kingdom, we should differentiate between horns and antlers. Antlers, found only in members of the deer family, are of a bony substance and grow up from the skull. They are shed every year. Horns, on the other hand, are of a horny substance and grow over a bony core arising out of the skull. Normally, they are not shed.

Now we must cast all that aside because there exists on this planet a creature known as the pronghorn. He has horns, not antlers, but he alone in this world sheds them as if they were antlers. (It is only the horny sheath, not the bony core, that is shed.) He is the only animal in the world with branched horns. The females have horns like most of the sheep and goats, who don't shed them, and all pronghorns have a gall bladder, also like sheep and goats. However, like the giraffe, the pronghorn does not have dewclaws. He is not closely related to the antelope, which is an Old World animal. Well, however confusing he may be, that is our pronghorn, and lucky we are to have him. He is a beautiful animal to behold and truly a unique feature on the face of this earth.

Habits

There are about 160,000 pronghorns left in the United States. It is estimated that there once were between forty and fifty million. Our weather didn't cause his demise because his tolerance is phenomenal. He can stand a temperature range of nearly 180 degrees. He can survive in heat of 130 degrees in the sun to 40 or more below zero in blizzards roaring down across the northern plains from the Arctic. Predators didn't cause the decline in his numbers because few can catch him. He is far and away the fastest land animal in North America, hitting bursts of seventy miles an hour. Sixty miles an hour is quite normal, and he can maintain forty miles for two, three, even four miles without slowing up. He takes fourteen-foot leaps and reportedly can leap as far as twenty-six feet or more. He is a good swimmer, although he is less fond of water than most of our other hoofed animals. Very few predators can get anywhere near him.

All that speed would be valueless if the pronghorn didn't have two other characteristics. He needs a high-strung, nervous disposition (which he has) and extremely sharp senses. Only an animal alert to danger and capable of detecting it can take advantage of the means of escape. Sharp senses he has to an admirable degree. His hearing and smell are acute, but they don't begin to match his eyesight. Try approaching a pronghorn from three or even four miles and he will detect your movement as abnormal and be gone. He is all but impossible to approach on open flat land. To make matters worse, he has two means of telegraphing his findings and can easily scatter every pronghorn in the area. When alerted to danger, he contracts the muscles in his rump and causes the white hairs there to flash. It is a signal other pronghorns can pick up two or more miles away. On top of that, in his excitement he exudes a musky odor from his scent glands that can be smelled by another animal grazing a full mile away. That odor and those flashing white hairs are relayed across the flat land until every pronghorn for miles is alerted. The odds are against the observer.

Man and man alone has caused the pronghorn's demise over much of his former range. Agriculture and hunting combined to reduce the herds to a fraction of their former size. It is a sad commentary but one often to be made. Here is an animal like no other, an animal that once gone will take with him not only a species but a family. If man doesn't let up, this creature, like so

Typical pronghorn, Yellowstone National Park.

many before him, will be gone from our land. We cannot afford to lose his special kind of beauty.

The pronghorn lives on a number of vegetable substances. Grasses, shrubs, bushes, weeds, all of these serve him well. Among his favorites are sagebrush, greasewood, juniper, chicory, onion, dandelion, and many, many more.

The sociable, herd-oriented pronghorn, up on the tips of his toes, migrates with the seasons. It is an up-and-down migration. He fears areas with deep snow. Only deep snow can trap him, harness his speed, and make him available to his enemies. He avoids it with deeply rooted, instinctive dread.

Reproduction

The bulls come into their rut in September. There are some fights, a great deal of sparring, but nothing very serious. Rarely is there an injury of consequence. The normal harem gathered by a successful buck is three or four strong. A particularly aggressive animal can gather eight or even ten does, but this is unusual. Gestation is eight months long, and the young appear in May and June. The first birth for a doe is usually single. In subsequent years she will have twins. The four-to-five-pound fawn is sixteen inches tall and is just about all legs, eyes, and ears. Within twenty-four hours after birth he will hit sprints of twenty-five miles an hour. He must, for he is most often preyed upon. His is a life of speed, and the sooner he gets to it, the better.

Observation

Item 1 for the observer of our pronghorn is a very good pair of binoculars. They are an essential. The second order of business is up-to-date information obtained locally. Seek out a game ranger, a conservation officer who knows the area. He will know where the local herds are feeding. You can spend all day in one draw while a fair-sized herd feeds in an adjoining one.

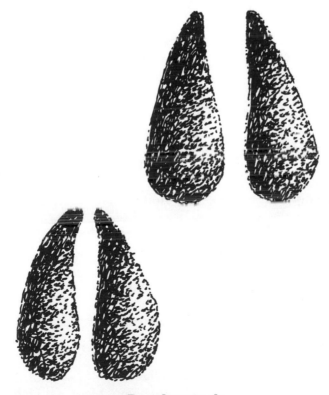

Pronghorn tracks.

There is no substitute for an expert's advice. I also recommend the hiring of a guide. He will know where to look and how to approach. The chances are you will need a vehicle other than the sedan or station wagon you are apt to be driving. The guide will have a jeep. Alone, or with a guide, keep down off the horizon. Move slowly, try to stay near any cover available (there usually isn't too much), and be careful with your camera and binoculars. Sun flashing off the lens will set every pronghorn in the area off like coiled springs.

There are still a number of areas where herds of pronghorns are normally to be found. Among these are:

Bamforth National Wildlife Refuge	Wyoming
Bowdoin National Wildlife Refuge	Montana
Cabeza Prieta Game Range	Arizona
Camas National Wildlife Refuge	Idaho
Charles Sheldon Antelope Range	Nevada–Oregon
Crescent Lake National Wildlife Refuge	Nebraska
Custer State Park	South Dakota
Desert Game Range	Nevada
Fort Peck Wildlife Refuge	Montana
Hart Mountain National Antelope Refuge	Oregon
Hutton Lake National Wildlife Refuge	Wyoming
Lower Klamath National Wildlife Refuge	California–Oregon
Malheur National Wildlife Refuge	Oregon
National Bison Range	Montana
Organ Pipe Cactus National Monument	Arizona
Pathfinder National Wildlife Refuge	Wyoming
Red Rock Lakes National Wildlife Refuge	Montana
Sheldon National Antelope Refuge	Nevada
Tule Lake National Wildlife Refuge	California
Valentine National Wildlife Refuge	Nebraska
Wichita Mountains National Wildlife Refuge	Oklahoma
Yellowstone National Park	Wyoming–Montana–Idaho

60

A Symbol for All: The Mighty Bison

NO ONE KNOWS for certain how many bison once roamed across our two countries. Some well-educated guesses put the herds at 100,000,000; others at between 60- and 75,000,000. However large the number might have been, it was impressive. By 1830 gunpowder reached the West in quantity, and the number of bison dropped to an estimated 40,000,000. As early as 1833, records reveal, over 100,000 buffalo robes were being taken out of one region alone each year. The number continued to mount, and the herds began to diminish. Still, though, they were vast—so vast that in 1871 Maj. Richard Dodge reported a herd from Kansas which ". . . was about five days passing a given point, or not less than fifty miles deep." From a high rock he could see ten miles across but couldn't see the far edge of the herd. A solid mass of animals covering five hundred square miles, at least.

But, in the same year Major Dodge made his report, in 1871, something else started. It was the great slaughter. Many whites wanted the bison exterminated. This great, shaggy animal was the backbone of the Plains Indians' economy. Without them they would have to choose between total dependence on the goodwill of the white man and starvation. Other white men thought that the bison and the growing herds of beef cattle couldn't coexist. Still other men saw the commercial interest in bison robes, bison tongues, and dried bison meat. Yet others, and truly they must have been mad, went wild in an orgy of destruction. With the railroads available to make travel easy, dudes from the East and nobility from Europe flocked to the Plains, where dozens of the great beasts could be slain in a day without any real exertion. It was an incredible display of man at his bloodiest, destructive worst.

Photo by Wilford L. Miller

Typical winter scene: deep-snow foraging.

By 1926, there were 4,376 bison left in the United States, 11,957 in Canada. The herds were gone, an era was past, and conservationists had forever a symbol to hold before the eyes of guilty man.

Actually, the Plains bison was in large part saved from extinction by two Indians, so the story goes. In the early 1870's, one Walking Coyote captured a few calves and held them apart from the slaughter. They eventually came into the possession of Michelo Pablo. Many of today's herds are descended from those few animals. At least that's the oft-told story.

Names and Range

Just as the pronghorn antelope is not an antelope, and the elk of North America is not an elk, the famous buffalo is not a buffalo. All true buffalo are native to Africa and Asia. The early French *voyageurs* saw in the bison something of the oxen of Europe. They called them *les bœufs*. This name easily became *buffle* to uneducated English-speaking frontiersmen, then *buffelo,* and finally *buffalo*. The fact that there existed elsewhere a great horned animal with that name strengthened the habit, and buffalo it is to this day. However, the buffalo is a distinct animal found elsewhere; our bison is quite a different creature.

There once were four races of bison in North America. The Great Plains bison, the typical bison of our childhood picture books, still exists in herds descended from Walking Coyote's calves. The wood bison of northern Canada still exists; the only truly *wild* bison herd on our continent is the herd of wood bison near Slave River in northern Alberta. The pale mountain bison of Colorado is now extinct, as is the eastern bison of Maryland, Pennsylvania, and Virginia. Neither existed in large enough numbers to withstand the insane slaughter that was unleashed on this continent by the gentle settlers who came here to build a better world.

The former range of the bison is of little concern to us now. The herds are gone, and all that remain, except the one herd on the Slave River, are for all intents and purposes captive animals. We will note the location of some of these herds in the "Observation" section of this chapter.

Appearance and Distinguishing Characteristics

The bison is the largest wild animal on this continent. He outweighs even the moose. He can be up to twelve feet long and six feet at the shoulder. A bull normally weighs about a ton, but three-thousand-pound specimens have been recorded. He has high-humped shoulders, a massive head, and a muscular neck. His head and neck are set low on the shoulders to accentuate the hunched appearance. He has surprisingly narrow hindquarters. The forequarters, neck, and head are wrapped in a shaggy mane that descends to the knees and extends back to just behind the shoulders. The rest of his body and his hind legs are covered with short hair. His eyes are set low on his head, and he has short, stout horns that curve upward and outward from the *sides* of his head. These horns are found in both sexes and are not shed. They can be as much as two feet long. There is a short tail with long hairs at the tip and a black beard hanging from the chin. In prime coat, the bison is dark chocolate-brown to blackish; he is darkest on his head and shoulders. He pales during the winter, and by the time of the spring molt he is yellowish brown.

The wood bison of the North is a larger animal, with his head placed higher on his shoulders. It is reported that the whites of his eyes don't show as they do in the Plains bison. The extinct eastern bison was a more blackish animal and had a much smaller hump.

Habits

In our guilt over the destruction of the wondrous herds that once were, we are apt to adopt a somewhat patronizing attitude toward the bison and think of him as a "poor little animal." Such is hardly the case, and a bull bison today, totally unaware that his kind has been victimized, is as disagreeable as

Photo by Wilford L. Miller

Bison herd on the Little Missouri River, North Dakota.

his ancestors were. A bison is a nasty fellow. He is nervous, testy, and easily tempted into a charge or a fight. Care should be used in approaching them on foot.

The bison are among the most gregarious animals on earth. Where there is one, there will be many. Seldom are they seen alone. They have very poor eyesight, which must contribute to their short tempers, but good hearing and an extremely keen sense of smell.

They are grazing animals and live almost exclusively on grasses. In winter, they will take whatever vegetable matter they can get. They normally have summer and winter ranges, but, of course, their naturally nomadic leanings are severely restricted today. Most herds are helped through the winter by food offerings from man.

Cow and calf, Prince Albert National Park, Saskatchewan.

The bison are victimized by a variety of biting insects and wallow in mud or dust to rid themselves of the pests. They are good swimmers and readily take to water. Somehow, though, they never learned that ice can be a hazard. Historically, during migrations, whole herds would move out onto a frozen lake or river until their combined weight caused the ice to give way. Thousands were drowned every year.

When moving from place to place, unless grazing along the way, the bison travels at about five miles an hour. An unfamiliar sound or a threatening smell will set the herd off at speeds up to thirty-two miles an hour in a peculiar bouncy, stiff-legged gait. When angry, the bison issues a shrill whistle. During rut the males have a deep and intimidating roar.

Reproduction

Bison bulls have their rut during June and July. During this time they are very short-tempered, and long, violent battles break out. These are particularly tenacious, and two bulls may keep it up for hours, even days, occasionally taking time out to catch their breath before starting in again. The winning bull takes a harem of up to twenty cows. The gestation period is nine and a half months long, and one and occasionally two calves appear from April through June. In two or three days the calves are running around after their mother and start on grass before they are very many weeks old. By the time they reach their first year they are weaned. Bulls take eight years to achieve maximum size. Twenty years is a normal life span, but forty-year-old specimens have been reported.

Observation

There is no trick to seeing bison today. You need only go to where they are maintained and look. It is like looking back a century or more when you watch these great, shaggy beasts quietly graze their way across a meadow. What must it have been to watch millions of these animals at once? What must a great stampede have been like?

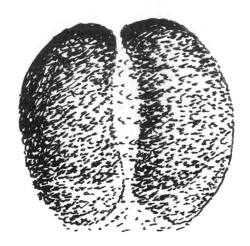

Bison tracks.

There are many places today where herds are maintained and are available for viewing. There is a small herd in a fenced area just outside of Denver, Colorado, and two herds are in Alaska, one in the Big Delta Region southeast of Fairbanks and another in the Copper River Valley. As was noted earlier in this chapter, the only truly wild herd is south of Slave River in northern Alberta. Herds are maintained as well in the following parks and refuges:

Custer State Park	South Dakota
Fort Niobrara Wildlife Refuge	Nebraska
National Bison Range	Montana
Prince Albert National Park	Saskatchewan
Riding Mountain National Park	Manitoba
Sullys Hill National Game Preserve	North Dakota
Theodore Roosevelt National Memorial Park	North Dakota
Waterton Lakes National Park	Alberta
Wichita Mountains Wildlife Refuge	Oklahoma
Wind Cave National Park	South Dakota
Yellowstone National Park	Wyoming–Montana–Idaho

___ 61

The Remote "Sheep-Cow":
The Musk-Ox

Names and Range

Far to the north there lives an animal who has characteristics in common with the sheep and with the cattle. He is neither, although his Latin name (*Ovibos*) indicates he is both. His closest living relative on this continent is *probably* the bison.

The musk-ox ranges today on the Arctic mainland of Canada, on some Arctic islands, and over northern Greenland. There are herds on the Canadian mainland in the Bathurst Inlet area, in the Thelon Game Sanctuary, and in the region between Wager Inlet and Boothia Peninsula. Islands known to maintain herds are Prince Patrick, Melville, Bathurst, Axel Heiberg, and Ellesmere. None of these areas are apt to be visited by the casual visitor. You must really want to see a musk-ox when you go and see one. He is strictly an Arctic animal.

Appearance and Distinguishing Characteristics

The sturdy, solid musk-ox once was more widespread than he is now. He became extinct in Europe and Asia during prehistoric time. He looks the same now as he did then, however.

His long, shaggy coat makes the musk-ox look bigger than he really is. His silky side hairs may be two or even three feet long on the neck and shoulders, giving him some of the longest hairs known in the animal kingdom. Actually

Musk-oxen in defense formation.

he seldom stands as much as five feet at the shoulder, rarely exceeds seven feet in length, and generally weighs under nine hundred pounds. He is a dark chocolate-brown but can be almost black. A black-faced race of musk-oxen is found from the southern Northwest Territories down into northern Manitoba, while a white-faced race is found farther to the north.

The musk-ox's tail is never more than four inches long and is usually not seen at all because of the long body hair. His head is short and broad. His horns, which are never shed, are massive. They arise close together on the top of the head between the eyes and sweep down in a graceful arc between the eyes and the ears, curling up in a wicked point at the end. They may be as much as twenty-eight or twenty-nine inches long and seven to ten inches wide at the base. They appear in both sexes.

Habits

The grazing musk-ox is strictly a herd animal. His herd may number three or four, or over a hundred. They graze along together on sedges, grasses, herbs, mosses, lichens, and willow. In winter they seek out slopes and ridges where the wind has blown the snow away. During a blizzard they seek gullies in which to hide. Their winter and summer ranges are seldom much more than fifteen miles apart.

The plucky musk-ox is fast on his feet despite his rather ungainly appearance. He swims well, runs well, and doesn't back away from a scrap. He is usually silent but when overexcited does give various angry snorts and grunts.

The only predator capable of giving the musk-ox a bad time is the wolf. Grizzly and polar bears may occasionally have a go at a lone animal, but it is a minor factor in the life of the musk-ox. When a pack of wolves attempts to worry a herd of these game creatures, they find themselves facing a solid wall of shoulder and horn. Instinctively, the musk-oxen form a circle when danger threatens, with the big bulls and occasionally some cows standing shoulder to shoulder facing outward. Calves are herded into the middle of the ring. This herd-defense formation, when combined with the musk-ox's sharp, heavy horns, nimble feet, and powerful bodies, makes the animal a very unattractive adversary. Only lone animals are likely to fall victim and probably not until they have claimed some wolf lives in return for their own.

Reproduction

The battles of the bulls during July and August are violent and relentless. More than one bull dies each year in attempting to assemble a harem. The gestation period is variously given as eight and nine months, and births are reported in April and May. The young stand about eighteen inches at the shoulder, are about twenty inches long, and weigh in the vicinity of twenty pounds. They are weaned in four months, just as the first snow begins to fall on their Arctic range. Their life span, it is believed, is fifteen years.

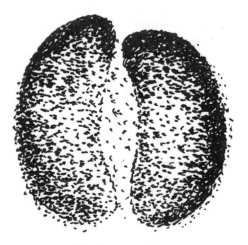

Musk-ox tracks.

Observation

Very simply, if you want to see a herd of musk-oxen, arrange for private air transportation, a guide, and allow for several weeks away from home. It is a long, arduous, and generally expensive proposition and one that you can look forward to as a climax to an observation career. Some attempts have been made to maintain small herds in the United States with the idea that their resistance to cold weather makes them an ideal beef stock animal for northern climes. So far little progress has been made in their domestication. They continue to be intractable, and there is a high mortality rate among the calves. It is possible that musk-ox steaks will one day be served in restaurants, and we may one day see descendants of these wild animals grazing on local farm pastures. For the moment, however, the sight of the wild musk-ox is an experience reserved for the hardy and determined.

62

The Magnificent Bighorns: The Sheep

Names and Range

The Dall or Alaskan white sheep is found in Alaska, the Yukon Territory, and British Columbia. The distinctly different-looking Stone or black sheep is a subspecies.

The American bighorn sheep starts his range about two hundred miles south of the southernmost point in the Dall sheep range. He is found from British Columbia to Mexico. The races of bighorn are usually given as follows: Rocky Mountain bighorn, Black Hills bighorn, desert bighorn, lava-bed or rimrock bighorn, Sierra Nevada bighorn, Nelson bighorn, Arizona or Mexican bighorn, Texas bighorn, and Gaillard's bighorn. Several other races are not found north of the Mexican border and are omitted here.

Appearance and Distinguishing Characteristics

The Dall sheep of Alaska and northwestern Canada are snow white. The subspecies commonly known as the Stone sheep is gray-blue to black in color. There are intergrades between the two, and all shadings imaginable between the extremes of white and black are found. The Dall sheep and their relatives are generally slightly smaller than the distinctive American bighorns. Both species have coarse, straight hair about two and a half inches long; they are all unguligrade and have nonskid, shock-absorbing pads on their feet.

The American bighorn is from 54 to 70 inches long, from 38 to 42 inches at the shoulder, and weighs about 185 pounds. Males have been taken up to 300 pounds. Both species are characterized by small ears and heavy bodies.

Bighorn (dotted areas). Dall (diagonal lines).

The American bighorns run through a whole spectrum of colors from several shades of grayish brown in the North to pale buff in the southern deserts.

The horns of the Dall and bighorn sheep have been a magnet that have drawn hunters to the high mountain slopes for years. High-powered rifles with their telescopic sights have taken their toll, and all subspecies are in need of

Photo by Wilford L. Miller

Fast on his feet, our native sheep, the bighorn. His powerful hindquarters give him the thrust he needs to move fast and hit hard.

constant protection. The horns are long and form a kind of loose corkscrew. They consist of a horny sheath over a solid bony core, and are never shed. The record length for a bighorn is 49½ inches along the curve. The tip-to-tip spread was 24½ inches. Any horn over 40 inches long is the exception, however.

Habits

The wild sheep of this continent are creatures of the high mountains. They can travel areas forbidding to most other animals, not to mention man, and

Photo by Wilford L. Miller

The bighorn in Yellowstone National Park, feeding on the lower slopes.

can move at startling speeds in areas where a footing seems impossible to find. They jump from rock to rock, as much as seventeen feet, with a fall of thousands of feet the reward for misjudgment. They will travel this way at thirty-five miles an hour. It is reported that they will jump down from heights of fifty feet and not be bothered by the impact. Their eyesight is phenomenal, and they are said to be able to see up to five miles. Their senses of smell and hearing are also very acute.

All of our wild sheep are dainty feeders. They select the greenest, most tender grasses, sedges, clover, twigs, fruits, and flowers. In winter they are somewhat less selective. They are sociable animals, but the sexes herd apart except during the breeding season. The ewes and kids are under the watchful eye and control of a rugged old grandmother, frequently the antecedent of all the animals in the herd. She holds sway as long as she herself is capable of bearing young.

A number of predators like the flesh of the wild sheep, but seldom get to taste it. Wolves, coyotes, wolverines, lynx, bobcat, cougar, and bears are all potential threats. The sheep, however, are so nimble, so swift, such great leapers and climbers that most enemies are left in the lurch. If a sheep is cornered on a ledge or is otherwise forced to fight, he has his massive horns and his apparently shockproof skull. Few animals, including a large bear, can withstand the blow of an angry wild sheep coming in full tilt.

Reproduction

Brutal battles are fought by the males during the breeding season—December and January. Squaring off at twenty paces, they charge straight on and smash together with blows that would kill almost any other animal. Both animals shudder, retrace their steps, and go at it again. This goes on till one or the other goes off a cliff, or gives up. The sound of the crashing can be heard for miles.

The winning male collects his harem and goes off in fairly good temper until challenged again. After a five-to-six-month gestation period, the young are born in May and June. There are usually twins. The ewe and her lambs remain in seclusion for a few weeks after the birth. The young start on solids within a week of their birth but nurse well into the winter. The life span is probably ten to fourteen years.

Observation

In most areas you will need a guide to take you to your Dall, Stone, or bighorn sheep. You will need trained mountain horses to pack you in and

Courtesy Arizona Game & Fish Department

Three rangy desert bighorns survey the world from high ground in Arizona.

plenty of gear to make the nights livable in the high altitudes where you will be traveling. A powerful pair of binoculars is an absolute must, and if you plan to take pictures, a powerful telephoto lens is a requirement.

It is useful to know the sheep's feeding pattern. They usually have their first meal between ten and eleven in the morning. By noon they are lying up in some sheltered area contentedly chewing their cuds. Early in the afternoon they normally feed again and then take a second siesta. The main feeding period runs from late afternoon until dusk, and then they bed down for the night. They are very hard to spot while they are bedded down, and are apt to see you first and be gone. Inevitably, a great valley will intervene between your lookout post and the sheep you are lucky enough to see. Occasionally you will be fortunate enough to get above them and spot them feeding in an alpine meadow below. It is then that you will have your best and longest view. When they are moving over broken rock they are extremely difficult to keep in sight.

You will not be likely to see your bighorn or Dall sheep by accident. A check mark beside his name on your list will be a sign that you have worked long and hard at the business of seeing American wildlife. Here are some protected areas where sheep are found:

Arctic National Wildlife Range	Alaska
Banff National Park	Alberta
Cabeza Prieta Game Range	Arizona
Death Valley National Monument	California
Desert Game Range	Nevada
Fort Peck Wildlife Refuge	Montana
Glacier National Park	Montana
Hart Mountain National Antelope Refuge	Oregon
Havasu Lake Wildlife Refuge	Arizona
Imperial Wildlife Refuge	Arizona
Jasper National Park	Alberta
Joshua Tree National Monument	California
Kenai National Moose Range	Alaska
Kofa Game Range	Arizona
Kootenay National Park	British Columbia
Mt. McKinley National Park	Alaska
National Bison Range	Montana
National Elk Refuge	Wyoming
San Andres National Wildlife Refuge	New Mexico
Waterton Lakes National Park	Alberta
Yellowstone National Park	Wyoming–Montana–Idaho

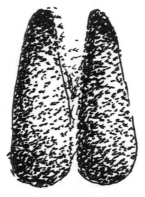

American bighorn tracks.

63

The Nimble: The Mountain Goat

Names and Range

The mountain goats in the United States and Canada are eagerly sought by men with rifles. Their numbers have been markedly reduced, and unless protection is extended, they may one day be seen only in parks and refuges. They are magnificent animals worthy of our most careful attention.

In general, the mountain goats range in the northwestern part of North America from Idaho and Montana and the Cascade Mountains of southern Washington north to Alaska. They range into the Arctic Zone and are found along jagged cliffs above the timberline.

Appearance and Distinguishing Characteristics

The mountain goat is a blunt, squarish-looking animal with a rather short body. (To confuse matters, he is not really a true goat but what is technically described as a goat-antelope.) He will be no more than 60 or 70 inches long, although up to 45 inches or more at the shoulder. He can weigh from 150 to 300 pounds. He has humped shoulders and a long, narrow head. There is a tuft of hair hanging from his chin.

The goat is always white mixed with a yellowish tint. His hooves and horns are polished black. The horns are small, slender, and backward curving, and they rise from the back of the head. They appear in both sexes and can be up to a foot long, although nine inches is closer to average. The spread from tip to tip can be ten inches.

The goat has a shaggy outercoat and a soft, woolly undercoat to protect him against the high winds and biting cold of his mountainous domain. His feet are of necessity equipped with cushioned, skidproof pads.

Mountain goat—*Oreamnos americanus* **(dotted area).**

Habits

The mountain goat is a gregarious creature and usually will be found in company with twenty or thirty of his kind. They have extraordinary keen eyesight and quickly spot any danger before it gets close enough to be of real

Photo by Wilford L. Miller

Mountain goat in Glacier National Park.

concern. This vision, of course, does not protect them against men with magnum rifles and ten-power scopes. Bears, both grizzly and black, cougar, lynx, wolf, and wolverine all like the flesh of this great mountaineer. Few ever have a chance to taste it. Goats are more sure-footed than any other native animal and will tackle ridges even the mountain sheep will shun. They take twelve-foot leaps, run at twenty miles an hour across the most forbidding heights, and swim very well when necessary. Even sheer, rocky faces, without any apparent footholds, offer enough for the goat. They will negotiate a cliff over a sheer drop of thousands of feet using ridges no more than an inch or two wide. Few predators care to follow an escaping animal that uses such a route.

Male goats tend to establish home ranges three or four miles square. They rest on high ridges where no other animals can reach them and move down to green slopes or alpine pastures to feed. They eat a variety of twigs, grass, flowers, and herbs.

Reproduction

The November rut finds some fighting among the males, but it is not a very serious affair when compared to similarly inspired behavior on the part of our other hoofed animals. The twelve-inch, six-to-seven-pound kids appear from April through June. Single births are the rule, twins the exception. The birth takes place in some very high, sheltered spot where predators cannot follow. Within minutes the kid is nursing. Within days he is following his mother on her incredible journey along impossible trails above the clouds. The goat is born and lives on top of the world.

Observation

Like the mountain sheep, the mountain goat is reserved for those who will travel far and endure much. They are not there for the asking. You will need an expert guide, specially trained horses, and plenty of equipment. Take a good sweater along; it gets chilly at night.

Mountain goats still exist and can be seen in the following areas by the determined observer:

Banff National Park	Alberta
Glacier National Park	Montana
Jasper National Park	Alberta
Kenai National Moose Range	Alaska
Kootenay National Park	British Columbia
Olympic National Park	Washington
Waterton Lakes National Park	Alberta
Yoho National Park	British Columbia

With our brief discussion of the rare and elusive mountain goat we have completed our survey of the mammals native to the United States and Canada. We have covered animals great and small, common and extremely rare. All of these animals have several things in common: they are all mammals; they give birth to living young and feed them with milk; and they are all part of our priceless wildlife heritage.

Man is never content to leave well enough alone, however, and must somehow always meddle with the world around him. One of the chores he has

Photo by Wilford L. Miller

Characteristic habitat of the mountain goat.

been performing of late is the transplanting of animals from one place to another. In our discussion we have seen what is happening with the nutria, and we have seen the great misfortune caused by the unintentional transplanting of Asian rats and mice.

In recent years, man has been moving larger forms of animal life around, sometimes with good results, sometimes with bad. Rabbits imported into Australia have become a plague, and deer imported into New Zealand are now classed as vermin and are being killed as quickly as possible because without natural controls they are eating off the sheep ranges.

In the years ahead it may be necessary for man to transplant some forms if endangered species are to survive. It can be a good thing to remove small herds of animals from a hostile home environment and establish them elsewhere. Indeed, such may be necessary if we are to have any large wildlife left at all. There are a number of exotics now in the United States, some in small numbers, some in large. We should not close our survey of the mammals of this continent without acknowledging their presence. A report published by the Texas Parks and Wildlife Department covering the status of exotics (called, there, *Texotics*) in 1963 will serve as a sample of what is going on in this country along these lines:

In 1963 there were 13,580 specimens of thirteen exotic hoofed species reported in Texas. Some of these were on ranches, some running wild. Six of them were deer, two sheep, four antelope, and one swine. The breakdown was as follows:

SPECIES	ORIGIN	COUNTIES INVOLVED	HEAD COUNT	BREEDING STOCK BEING SOLD
Axis deer	India–Ceylon	16	2,166	Yes
Sika or Japanese deer	Japan	11	634	Yes
Fallow deer	Mesopotamia	16	220	Yes
Sambar deer	India–Ceylon	2	38	
Barasingha deer	India	2	32	
Red deer	England	4	21	Yes
Barbary sheep (Aoudad)	Africa	26	1,588	Yes
Mouflon sheep	Corsica–Sardinia	18	1,846	Yes
Blackbuck antelope	India	21	3,693	Yes
Nilgai	India	3	3,334	
Eland	Africa	2	5	
Oryx (gemsbok)	Africa	1	3	
European wild boar	Europe	3 (?)	(?)	

It remains to be seen how these imports will affect our natural wildlife. Certainly, with as many hunters afield as there now are each year, the chances of these animals propagating to the point where they will become a nuisance are slight. It would be an altogether different thing, however, if anyone started to import predators. Then the trouble could begin.

Very often in the pages of this book I have taken "pot shots" at hunters and hunting. Perhaps that is not fair, for a man does, after all, have the right to seek his own recreation, to enjoy life as he sees fit within certain confines dictated by the best interests of the community. No one has yet defined hunting of legal game in the legal areas, in legal seasons as contrary to the good of the community, and we really shouldn't take it on ourselves to condemn what is legal and therefore presumably right. I myself hunted at one time. I still collect guns and can appreciate the enthusiasm of the gunner for his weapons, and of the outdoorsman seeking the thrill of the hunt. The fact that I have trained my rifles on tin cans and paper targets and instead turned my cameras toward wildlife does not mean that everyone should. I would like to make one last plea, however, to the inexperienced. A hunting license is not a license to slaughter and maim. It is a license to make specific kills as cleanly and swiftly as possible. Learn to use your weapons. Do not wound animals and leave them around to suffer lingering deaths. Do not exceed legal restrictions, for then you are overstepping the boundaries marking the good of the community. To the advanced sportsman, I would ask just this: Don't fill your quota of rare and vanishing game year after year. If you have your bighorn, your moose, your grizzly, or your goat, live with your memories. Remember, year after year, as you try to improve on the spread, the points, or the length of previous years, you are taking the best breeding males, you are reducing the chances of the species to propagate a healthy, durable line. If you must have one of everything, take *one* and leave it at that. And, just for the fun of it, try it with a camera one year. You might find that you like it better.

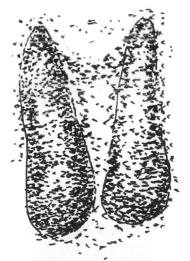

Mountain goat tracks.

Appendix

1. CLASSIFICATION

Taxonomy is the science of classification. It serves basically two purposes. It puts an animal or plant in its proper relationship with the animal or plant kingdom as a whole, and forever identifies it with a more or less permanent name equally understandable to a scientist in Japan, Borneo, Capetown, Paris, or Boston. However many common or popular names an animal or plant might have, or however many different animals or plants in the world may have the same common or "folk" name, a scientific name is constant and impossible to confuse. The world over, *Rangifer tarandus arcticus* is the Barren Ground caribou and *Lepus townsendii* is the white-tailed jackrabbit.

For permanent reference the following is the proper classification of the mammals of the United States and Canada as discussed in this book. In time, some changes almost certainly will be made, but the list as a whole is a constant.

The numbers in parentheses indicate the number of subspecies of that genus currently listed as occurring in the United States and Canada. Many of the genera, of course, have extensive representation from Mexico south, but are not so indicated here. To the right of the breakdown are English names for the groups of animals or of a representative species found within the genus.

The Mammals of the United States and Canada

KINGDOM	Animal	
SUBKINGDOM	Metazoa	
PHYLUM	Chordata	
SUBPHYLUM	Craniata	
CLASS	Mammalia	
SUBCLASS	Theria	
INFRACLASS	Metatheria	
SUPERORDER	Didelphia	
ORDER	Marsupialia	
SUBORDER	Polyprotodontia	
SUPERFAMILY	Didelphoidea	
FAMILY	Didelphiidae	
GENUS	*Didelphis* (3)	Opossums
INFRACLASS	Eutheria	
SUPERORDER	Monodelphia	
ORDER	Insectivora	
SUPERFAMILY	Soricoidea	
FAMILY	Soricidae	Shrews
SUBFAMILY	Soricinae	
GENERA	*Sorex* (83)	Shrews
	Microsorex (7)	Pygmy Shrews
	Notiosorex (1)	Desert Shrews
	Cryptotis (5)	Least Shrews
	Blarina (16)	Short-tailed Shrews
FAMILY	Talpidae	Moles
SUBFAMILY	Scalopinae	
GENERA	*Scalopus* (17)	Eastern Moles
	Parascalops (1)	Hairy-tailed Mole
	Scapanus (15)	Townsend Mole
	Neürotrichus (3)	Shrew Mole
SUBFAMILY	Condylurinae	
GENUS	*Condylura* (2)	Star-nosed Moles
ORDER	Chiroptera	Bats
SUBORDER	Microchiroptera	
SUPERFAMILY	Pyllostomatoidea	
FAMILY	Phyllostomatidae	
SUBFAMILY	Chilonycterinae	
GENUS	*Mormoops* (2)	Leafchin Bat
SUBFAMILY	Phyllostomatinae	
GENUS	*Macrotus* (1)	Leaf-nosed Bat

SUBFAMILY	Glossophaginae	
GENERA	*Choeronycteris* (1)	Hog-nosed Bat
	Leptonycteris (1)	Long-nosed Bat
FAMILY	Vespertilionidae	
SUBFAMILY	Vespertilioninae	
GENERA	*Myotis* (29)	Little Brown Bat
	Lasionycteris (1)	Silver-haired Bat
	Pipistrellus (7)	Pipistrels
	Eptesicus (4)	Big Brown Bat
	Lasiurus (4)	Hoary Bat
	Dasypterus (3)	Western Yellow Bat
	Nycticeius (2)	Evening Bat
	Euderma (1)	Spotted Bat
	Plecotus (*Corynorhinus*) (5)	Big-eared Bat
SUBFAMILY	Nyctophilinae	
	Antrozous (4)	Pallid Bat
FAMILY	Molossidae	
GENERA	*Tadarida* (5)	Free-tailed Bat
	Eumops (2)	Mastiff Bat
ORDER	Edentata	
SUBORDER	Xenarthra	
SUPERFAMILY	Dasypodoidea	
FAMILY	Dasypodidae	
SUBFAMILY	Dasypodinae	
GENUS	*Dasypus* (1)	Armadillos
ORDER	Lagomorpha	
FAMILY	Ochotonidae	
GENUS	*Ochotona* (32)	Pikas
FAMILY	Leporidae	
SUBFAMILY	Leporinae	
GENERA	*Lepus* (39)	Hares and Jackrabbits
	Sylvilagus (39)	Rabbits
ORDER	Rodentia	
SUBORDER	Sciuromorpha	
SUPERFAMILY	Aplodontoidea	
FAMILY	Aplodontiidae	
GENUS	*Aplodontia* (7)	Aplodontia

SUPERFAMILY	Sciuroidea	
FAMILY	Sciuridae	Squirrels
SUBFAMILY	Sciurinae	
GENERA	*Marmota* (22)	Woodchucks and Marmots
	Cynomys (6)	Prairie Dogs
	Citellus (76)	Ground Squirrels
	Tamias (10)	Eastern Chipmunks
	Eutamias (67)	Chipmunks
	Sciurus (29)	Squirrels
	Tamiasciurus (30)	Squirrels
SUBFAMILY	Pteromyinae	
GENUS	*Glaucomys* (30)	Flying Squirrels
SUPERFAMILY	Geomyoidea	
FAMILY	Geomyidae	
SUBFAMILY	Geomyinae	
GENERA	*Thomomys* (223)	Pocket Gophers
	Geomys (37)	
	Cratogeomys (5)	
FAMILY	Heteromyidae	
SUBFAMILY	Perognathinae	
GENUS	*Perognathus* (96)	Pocket Mice
SUBFAMILY	Dipodomyinae	
GENERA	*Dipodomys* (89)	Kangaroo Rats
	Microdipodops (15)	Kangaroo Mice
SUBFAMILY	Heteromyinae	
GENUS	*Liomys* (1)	Mexican Pocket Mouse
SUPERFAMILY	Castoroidea	
FAMILY	Castoridae	
GENUS	*Castor* (25)	Beaver
SUBORDER	Myomorpha	
SUPERFAMILY	Muroidea	
FAMILY	Cricetidae	
SUBFAMILY	Cricetinae	

	Oryzomys (5)	Rice Rats
GENERA	*Oryzomys* (5)	Rice Rats
	Reithrodontomys (24)	Harvest Mice
	Peromyscus (115)	White-footed Mice
	Baiomys (3)	Pygmy Mice
	Onychomys (22)	Grasshopper Mice
	Sigmodon (22)	Cotton Rats
	Neotoma (66)	Wood Rats

SUBFAMILY	Microtinae	
(TRIBE)	Lemmi	
GENERA	*Dicrostonyx* (8)	Collared Lemmings
	Synaptomys (15)	Bog Lemmings
	Lemmus (6)	Lemmings

(TRIBE)	Microtini	
GENERA	*Clethrionomys* (40)	Red-backed Mice
	Phenacomys (12)	Phenacomys
	Microtus (107)	Voles
	Pitymys (7)	Pine Mice
	Lagurus (5)	Vole
	Neofiber (3)	Florida Water Rat
	Ondatra (16)	Muskrats

FAMILY	Muridae	
SUBFAMILY	Murinae	
GENERA	*Rattus* (4)	Old World Rats
	Mus (2)	Old World Mice

SUPERFAMILY	Dipodoidea	
FAMILY	Zapodidae	
SUBFAMILY	Zapodinae	
GENERA	*Zapus* (33)	Jumping Mice
	Napaeozapus (7)	

SUBORDER	Hystricomorpha	
SUPERFAMILY	Erethizontoidea	
FAMILY	Erethizontidae	
SUBFAMILY	Erethizontinae	
GENUS	*Erethizon* (7)	Porcupines

SUPERFAMILY	Octodontoidea	
FAMILY	Capromyidae	
SUBFAMILY	Myocastorinae	
GENUS	*Myocastor* (1)	Nutria

ORDER	Cetacea	
SUBORDER	Odontoceti	
SUPERFAMILY	Physeteroidea	
FAMILY	Ziphiidae	
GENERA	*Berardius* (1)	Baird's Beaked Whale
	Mesoplodon (6)	Sowerby's Whale
	Ziphius (1)	Cuvier's Beaked Whale
	Hyperoodon (1)	Bottle-nosed Whale
FAMILY	Physeteridae	
GENUS	*Physeter* (1)	Sperm Whale
FAMILY	Kogiidae	
GENUS	*Kogia* (1)	Pygmy Sperm Whale
SUPERFAMILY	Delphinoidea	
FAMILY	Monodontidae	
SUBFAMILY	Delphinapterinae	
GENUS	*Delphinapterus* (2)	White Whale
SUBFAMILY	Monodontinae	
GENUS	*Monodon* (1)	Narwhal
FAMILY	Delphinidae	
SUBFAMILY	Delphininae	
GENERA	*Stenella* (3)	Spotted Dolphin
	Steno (1)	Rough-toothed Dolphin
	Delphinus (2)	Dolphin
	Tursiops (3)	Bottle-nosed Porpoise
	Lissodelphis (1)	Right-Whale Porpoise
	Lagenorhynchus (3)	White-sided Porpoise
	Grampus (2)	Killer Whale
	Grampidelphis (1)	Grampus
	Pseudorca (1)	False Killer Whale
	Globicephala (3)	Blackfish (Pilot Whale)
	Phocoena (2)	Harbor Porpoise
	Phocoenoides (1)	Dall's Porpoise
SUBORDER	Mysticeti	Baleen Whales
FAMILY	Eschrichtidae	
GENUS	*Eschrichtius* (1)	Gray Whale

FAMILY	Balaenopteridae	
SUBFAMILY	Balaenopterinae	
GENERA	*Balaenoptera* (3)	Finback Whale
	Sibbaldus (1)	Blue Whale
SUBFAMILY	Megapterinae	
GENUS	*Megaptera* (1)	Humpback Whale
FAMILY	Balaenidae	
GENERA	*Eubalaena* (1)	Right Whale
	Balaena (1)	Bowhead Whale
ORDER	Carnivora	
SUBORDER	Fissipedia	
SUPERFAMILY	Canoidea	
FAMILY	Canidae	
SUBFAMILY	Caninae	
GENERA	*Canis* (49)	Wolf and Coyote
	Alopex (5)	Arctic Foxes
	Vulpes (19)	Red Foxes
	Urocyon (13)	Gray Foxes
FAMILY	Ursidae	Bears
GENERA	*Euarctos* (15)	Black Bear
	Ursus (86)	Grizzly Bear
	Thalarctos (4)	Polar Bear
FAMILY	Procyonidae	
SUBFAMILY	Procyoninae	
GENERA	*Bassariscus* (7)	Ring-tailed Cat
	Procyon (25)	Raccoon
	Nasua (2)	Coatis
FAMILY	Mustelidae	
SUBFAMILY	Mustelinae	
GENERA	*Martes* (21)	Martens and Fishers
	Mustela (65)	Mink, Ferret, Weasels
SUBFAMILY	Guloninae	
GENUS	*Gulo* (5)	Wolverine
SUBFAMILY	Taxidiinae	
GENUS	*Taxidea* (13)	Badgers

SUBFAMILY	Mephitinae	
GENERA	*Spilogale* (11)	Spotted Skunk
	Mephitis (14)	Striped and Hooded Skunks
	Conepatus (6)	Hog-nosed Skunks
SUBFAMILY	Lutrinae	
GENUS	*Lutra* (25)	River Otter
SUBFAMILY	Enhydrinae	
GENUS	*Enhydra* (2)	Sea Otter
SUPERFAMILY	Feloidea	
FAMILY	Felidae	
GENERA	*Felis* (17)	Jaguar, Ocelot, Cougar, Jaguarundi
	Lynx (13)	Lynx and Bobcat
ORDER	Pinnipedia	
FAMILY	Otariidae	Eared Seals
SUBFAMILY	Arctocephalinae	
GENERA	*Callorhinus* (1)	Northern Fur Seal
	Arctocephalus (1)	Southern Fur Seal
SUPERFAMILY	Otariinae	
GENERA	*Eumetopias* (1)	Northern Sea Lion
	Zalophus (1)	California Sea Lion
FAMILY	Odobenidae	
GENUS	*Odobenus* (2)	Walruses
FAMILY	Phocidae	Hair Seals
SUBFAMILY	Phocinae	
GENERA	*Phoca* (9)	Harbor Seals
	Erignathus (2)	Bearded Seals
	Halichoerus (1)	Gray Seals
SUBFAMILY	Monachinae	
GENUS	*Monachus* (1)	West Indian Seal
SUBFAMILY	Cystophorinae	
GENERA	*Cystophora* (1)	Hooded Seals
	Mirounga (1)	Elephant Seals

ORDER	Sirenia	Sea Cows
FAMILY	Trichechidae	
GENUS	*Trichechus* (1)	Manatee
ORDER	Artiodactyla	Even-toed Ungulates
SUBORDER	Suiformes	
SUPERFAMILY	Suoidea	
FAMILY	Tayassuidae	
GENUS	*Pecari* (2)	Peccaries
SUBORDER	Ruminantia	
SUPERFAMILY	Cervoidea	
FAMILY	Cervidae	
SUBFAMILY	Cervinae	
GENUS	*Cervus* (6)	Wapiti (Elk)
SUBFAMILY	Odocoileinae	
GENERA	*Odocoileus* (24)	Deer
	Alces (4)	Moose
	Rangifer (14)	Caribou
SUPERFAMILY	Bovoidea	
FAMILY	Antilocapridae	
GENUS	*Antilocapra* (4)	Pronghorn
FAMILY	Bovidae	
SUBFAMILY	Bovinae	
GENUS	*Bison* (2)	Bison
SUBFAMILY	Caprinae	
GENERA	*Oreamnos* (4)	Mountain Goat
	Ovibos (3)	Musk-Oxen
	Ovis (12)	Mountain Sheep

2. LIFETIME CHECKLIST

A Word About This List:

It may look formidable now, but you will be surprised how quickly it begins to fill in. Quite naturally, if you take ten nature observers, give them a fixed period of time, and then check their lists, you will find: (1) certain animals are checked on all lists (raccoon, white-tailed deer, gray squirrel, etc.); (2) certain patterns of specialized interest will be reflected (weasels, rodents, hoofed animals, etc.); and (3) certain animals will be checked on few or no lists (musk-ox, black-footed ferret, sperm whale, elephant seal, etc.). Some sections of this list will be slow in filling in (whales, weasels, felines), and others will go fast. The trick is to keep at it. Be very careful that you are sure of proper identification before making an entry. There is room on the list for the gray squirrel, and there is room for the fox squirrel, but there is no room for an animal called "it-was-one-or-the-other." Remember, a questionable entry fools no one but the person who makes it.

As you start on this list, you cannot know how much of it will be checked off after one year, after two, or even ten. The only thing you can be sure of is that there is little chance of your ever completing it. You would have to spend a lifetime in the field to even come close. However, every check mark you do make will represent hours of fun, of beauty, and of abiding interest in the fabulous world around us. Each check mark should stand for a special memory. Good luck!

SPECIES	LOCATION	DATE
Group: Marsupials		
_____Virginia Opossum	_____	_____
Group: Moles and Shrews		
_____Eastern mole	_____	_____
_____Western mole	_____	_____
_____Hairy-tailed mole	_____	_____
_____Star-nosed mole	_____	_____
_____Shrew mole	_____	_____
_____Masked shrew	_____	_____
_____Pygmy shrew	_____	_____
_____Desert shrew	_____	_____
_____Least shrew	_____	_____
_____Short-tailed shrew	_____	_____
_____Water shrew	_____	_____

SPECIES	LOCATION	DATE

Group: Bats

_____Leafchin bat
_____Leaf-nosed bat
_____Hog-nosed bat
_____Little brown bat
_____Western pipistrel
_____Eastern pipistrel
_____Big brown bat
_____Evening bat
_____Silver-haired bat
_____Hoary bat
_____Red bat
_____Western yellow bat
_____Eastern yellow bat
_____Spotted bat
_____Western big-eared bat
_____Eastern big-eared bat
_____Pallid bat
_____Florida free-tailed bat
_____Mexican free-tailed bat
_____Big free-tailed bat
_____Western mastiff bat
_____Eastern mastiff bat

Group: Armadillo

_____Armadillo

Group: Bears

_____Black bear
_____Grizzly bear
_____Big Brown bear
_____Polar bear

Group: Canines

_____Red fox
_____Kit fox
_____Gray fox
_____Arctic fox
_____Coyote
_____Gray wolf
_____Red wolf

SPECIES	LOCATION	DATE

Group: Felines

_____Jaguar

_____Ocelot

_____Margay

_____Jaguarundi

_____Mountain lion

_____Bobcat

_____Lynx

Group: Coons

_____Raccoon

_____Coatimundi

_____Ring-tailed cat

Group: Weasels

_____Marten

_____Fisher

_____Short-tailed weasel

_____Long-tailed weasel

_____Least weasel

_____Mink

_____Black-footed ferret

_____Wolverine

_____River Otter

_____Sea Otter

_____Spotted skunk

_____Striped skunk

_____Hooded skunk

_____Hog-nosed skunk

_____Badger

Group: Seals, Sea Lions, and Walruses

_____California sea lion

_____Northern sea lion

_____Alaska fur seal

_____Guadalupe fur seal

_____Walrus

_____Harbor seal

_____Ribbon seal

_____Ringed seal

_____Harp seal

SPECIES	LOCATION	DATE
____Bearded seal		
____Gray seal		
____Hooded seal		
____Northern elephant seal		
____West Indian seal		

Group: Whales

____Right whale		
____Bowhead whale		
____Gray whale		
____Finback whale		
____Blue whale		
____Humpback whale		
____Sperm whale		
____Pygmy sperm whale		
____White whale (Beluga)		
____Narwhal		
____Beaked whale		
____Bottle-nosed whale		
____Killer whale		
____Grampus		
____Blackfish (pilot whale)		
____Common dolphin		
____Bottle-nosed dolphin		
____Harbor porpoise		

Group: Sea Cows

____Manatee		

Group: Rodents

____Porcupine		
____Beaver		
____Nutria		
____Muskrat		
____Florida water rat		
____Red-backed vole		
____Meadow vole		
____Mountain vole		
____Long-tailed vole		
____Aplodontia		

SPECIES	LOCATION	DATE
_____Phenacomys		
_____Bog lemming		
_____Collared lemming		
_____Common lemming		
_____Northern pocket gopher		
_____Pygmy pocket gopher		
_____Giant pocket gopher		
_____Plains pocket gopher		
_____Woodchuck		
_____Yellow-bellied marmot		
_____Hoary marmot		
_____Eastern gray squirrel		
_____Western gray squirrel		
_____Eastern fox squirrel		
_____Tassel-eared squirrel		
_____Red squirrel		
_____Douglas squirrel		
_____Southern flying squirrel		
_____Northern flying squirrel		
_____Eastern chipmunk		
_____Least chipmunk		
_____Red-tailed chipmunk		
_____Black-tailed prairie dog		
_____White-tailed prairie dog		
_____Arctic ground squirrel		
_____Thirteen-lined ground squirrel		
_____Spotted ground squirrel		
_____Rock squirrel		
_____Antelope squirrel		
_____Norway rat		
_____Black rat		
_____House mouse		
_____Rice rat		
_____Cotton rat		
_____Eastern wood rat		
_____Southern plains wood rat		
_____Desert wood rat		
_____Bushy-tailed wood rat		
_____Pygmy mouse		
_____White-footed mouse		
_____Grasshopper mouse		
_____Harvest mouse		
_____Pocket mouse		

SPECIES	LOCATION	DATE
_____Jumping mouse		
_____Kangaroo rat		
_____Kangaroo mouse		

Group: Lagomorphs

SPECIES	LOCATION	DATE
_____Pika		
_____Arctic hare		
_____Tundra hare		
_____White-tailed jackrabbit		
_____Snowshoe hare		
_____European hare		
_____Antelope jackrabbit		
_____Black-tailed jackrabbit		
_____Eastern cottontail rabbit		
_____Mountain cottontail rabbit		
_____New England cottontail rabbit		
_____Desert cottontail rabbit		
_____Brush rabbit		
_____Marsh rabbit		
_____Swamp rabbit		
_____Pygmy rabbit		

Group: Hoofed Animals

SPECIES	LOCATION	DATE
_____Peccary		
_____Wild boar		
_____Elk (wapiti)		
_____White-tailed deer		
_____Mule deer		
_____Black-tailed deer		
_____Key deer		
_____Moose		
_____Woodland caribou		
_____Barren Ground caribou		
_____Pronghorn		
_____Plains bison		
_____Wood bison		
_____Musk-ox		
_____Dall sheep		
_____Stone sheep		
_____Bighorn sheep		
_____Mountain goat		

3. BREEDING HABITS OF NORTH AMERICAN MAMMALS

ANIMAL	GESTATION IN DAYS	LITTER SIZE*	LITTERS PER YEAR	DELIVERED MONTHS
Oppossum	12–13	5–16	1–2	March–April (*North*) January–February, May–June (*South*)
Mole	28–42	2–5	1	March–May
Shrew	21–22	3–10	1–2	March–September
Bat	50–60	1–4	1	May–July
Armadillo	120	4 or 8	1	February–April
Polar bear	266+	1–2	1	December–February
Black bear	215–225	1–5 (2)	1	January–February
Grizzly bear	266+	1–4 (2)	1	January–February
Brown bear	266+	1–4 (2)	1	January–February
Wolf	63	3–14 (6)	1	March–April
Coyote	60–63	3–19 (6)	1	April–June
Fox	50–53	1–10 (4–6)	1	March–April
Jaguar	93–110	2–4	1	April–May
Ocelot	80–100+?	2	1	September–November
Jaguarundi	?	3 ?	1–2 ?	?
Mountain lion	90–104	1–6 (2–3)	1	No known season
Lynx and bobcat	50–60	1–5 (2–3)	2 (1)	April–May
Raccoon	63	2–7 (4)	1	April–August
Coatimundi	77	4–6	?	Spring–summer
Ring-tailed cat	40–50 ?	1–5 (3)	1	May–June
Marten	220–265 (delayed implanta- tion)	1–5 (3–4)	1	March–April
Fisher	350 (delayed implanta- tion)	1–5 (3)	1	April
Least weasel	?	3–10	1 ?	No known season
Long-tailed weasel	205–337 (delayed implanta- tion)	4–9	1	April–May

* First set of numbers indicates extreme litter sizes reported or suspected; set of numbers in parentheses indicates known or presumed average litter size.

Animal	Gestation in Days	Litter Size	Litters per Year	Months Delivered
Short-tailed weasel	220–340 (delayed implantation)	4–13	1	April–May
Mink	39–76	4–8	1	March–April
Black-footed ferret	?	3–6	1 ?	June–July
Wolverine	60	1–5	1	May–July
River otter	300–365 ?	1–5 (2–4)	1	January–May
Sea otter	240–270	2 (1)	1	April–July
Skunks	63	1–7 (4–5)	1–2	April–July
Badger	42 (true gestation)	1–5 (2)	1 ?	April–May
Seals and sea lions (most)	330–365	1	1	June–July
Manatee	152 ?	2 (1)	1	?
Porcupine	209–217	2 (1)	1	April–June
Beaver	50–60 ?	2–6 (4)	1	March–May
Nutria	127–132	2–13	2	No known season
Muskrat	22–30	1–11	Many	No known season
Voles	21	1–7 (3–5)	Many	No known season
Aplodontia	?	2–5	?	?
Phenacomys	?	4–9 (3–5)	?	?
Lemmings	21–23	1–7 (3–5)	Many	No known season
Pocket gopher	28–31	3–5	1	March–May
Woodchucks and marmot	31–32	2–6	1	April–May
Tree squirrel	45	1–6 (2–3)	2	February–March, July–August
Flying squirrel	40	1–6 (3–4)	2	March–April, July–September
Chipmunks	31	1–8 (4–5)	1–2	April–May, July–August
Prairie dogs	30 ?	1–8 (4–5)	1	May–September
Ground squirrel	27–28	1–14 (8–10)	1	May
Old World rat	21	1–22	12	No season
House mouse	18	1–13	13+	No season
Rice rat	25	1–7 (2–5)	6–7	No season
Cotton rat	27	1–12 (5–7)	Many	No season
Wood rat	39 ?	1–6 (2–3)	Many	No season
White-footed mouse	21–23	1–9 (3–4)	10–11	No season
Harvest mouse	23	1–7 (3–4)	Many	No season

Animal	Gestation in Days	Litter Size	Litters per Year	Months Delivered
Pocket mouse	23 ?	1–7 (4–5)	Many	No known season
Jumping mouse	18	1–9 (5–6)	3 ?	December–August
Kangaroo rat	25 ?	3–5	2 or more	From March on
Kangaroo mouse	25 ?	2–5	2 or more	From March on
Pika	?	3–4	1	?
Hares and jackrabbits	41–47	1–8 (2–4)	1–4	No season but mostly summer
Rabbits	26–30	1–9 (4–5)	6	April–October
Peccary	105 ?	1–5 (2)	?	No known season
Elk	255 ?	1–2	1	May–June
Deer	200 ?	1–4 (1–2)	1	April–June
Moose	240	1–3 (1–2)	1	From April on
Caribou	240–270	1–2 (1)	1	From May on
Pronghorn	240	1–2	1	May–June
Bison	285	2 (1)	1	April–June
Musk-ox	240–270	1–2 (1)	1	April–May
Mountain sheep	150–180	1–2	1	May–June
Mountain goat	150	1–2	1	April–June

In referring to the chart above keep in mind the latitude that exists. There are differences not only from species to species, even from subspecies to subspecies, but from individual to individual, from area to area, and even from year to year as the severity of seasons vary. Some of the figures included are questionable and are usually followed by a question mark. A lot of field work is needed before any chart like this can be considered definitive. Even when such definitive information is available, the final chart will have footnotes that will exceed the chart itself in size.

4. GIVEN THE TIME OF DAY

This is a list of highly generalized information about the time of day to look for certain animals. By no means is it definitive because animals vary their habits from season to season, from area to area. An animal abroad in daylight in a wilderness area may become nocturnal if man moves in and starts to build. Habits change during the breeding season, and the available food supply also has its effects. If an animal can feed itself during the daylight hours, it may den up during the night. If pickings are bad, the feeding may extend around the clock. However, even this generalized information can be helpful; basically it tells you what you can expect to find when you are afield at different hours. Where a ruling is very strict, that is, where an animal is rigid in its pattern, an asterisk will follow its name.

Nocturnal Animals

Bats (almost all*)	Ring-tailed cat	Lemmings
Armadillo	Marten	Pocket gopher
Shrew	Fisher	Flying squirrels*
Bears	Short-tailed weasel	Rice rat
Mole	Long-tailed weasel	Cotton rat
Wolf	Least weasel	Wood rat
Coyote	Mink	White-footed mouse
Fox	Black-footed ferret	Grasshopper mouse
Jaguar	River otter	Harvest mouse
Ocelot	Skunks	Pocket mouse
Margay	Badger	Jumping mouse
Jaguarundi	Porcupine	Kangaroo rat
Mountain lion	Beaver	Kangaroo mouse
Lynx	Nutria	Hares
Bobcat	Muskrat	Jackrabbits
Raccoon	Voles	Rabbits
Coatimundi	Aplodontia	

Dusk and Dawn Animals

Bats	Raccoon	Harvest mouse
Shrews	Coatimundi	Kangaroo rat
Armadillo	Black-footed ferret	Kangaroo mouse
Bears	River otter	Hares
Fox	Sea otter	Jackrabbits
Mole	Skunks	Rabbits
Wolf	Badger	Peccary
Coyote	Porcupine	Deer
Fox	Beaver	Moose

Jaguar
Ocelot
Margay
Jaguarundi
Mountain lion
Lynx
Bobcat

Nutria
Muskrat
Voles
Aplodontia
Lemming
Pocket gopher
Prairie dog

Caribou
Elk
Pronghorn
Bison
Musk-ox

Diurnal Animals

Shrews
Moles
Armadillo
Bears
Wolves
Coyotes
Foxes
Coatimundi
Marten
Mink
Black-footed ferret
Sea otter

River otter
Beaver
Muskrat (seasonal)
Voles
Lemmings
Pocket gopher
Woodchucks
Marmot
Tree squirrel
Chipmunk
Ground squirrel
Cotton rat

Harvest mouse
Jumping mouse (cloudy days)
Pikas
Mountain sheep*
Mountain goat*
Elk
Moose
Pronghorn
Bison
Musk-ox
Deer

Once again it must be stressed that this is generalized information and if considered as such can be useful on your trips afield. Proximity to built-up areas can have a marked effect on almost any animal, and you should be ready for surprises.

5. THE HABITS OF SOME ANIMALS

As we have pointed out so often, animals vary their habits from place to place, from time to time. It is useful to note certain basic habit patterns, however, and use them as a rough reference point. The following are lists of animals that either hibernate or take long winter sleeps, of animals that are at least in part arboreal, and of animals that at least on occasion burrow. It should be noted that many animals have a vast north-and-south spread in their range and may sleep part of the winter away in the North but not in the South. Some animals, like the marmot, will sometimes burrow and sometimes den up in a cave or rock slide. Other animals are aboreal part of the time, or in part of their range. Here, again, then, is some highly generalized information. Since very specific information is to be found in the text of this book, it has been decided to keep these lists generalized rather than have endless footnotes.

True Hibernators (H) and Winter Sleepers (WS)

Bats (H)	Badger (WS)	Chipmunks (H)
Bears (WS)	Voles (H and WS)	Prairie dogs (H)
Raccoons (WS)	Woodchucks (H)	Ground squirrels (H)
Skunks (WS)	Marmots (H)	Jumping mouse (H)

Burrowers

Moles	Marmots	Kangaroo rat
Shrews	Chipmunks	Kangaroo mice
Armadillo	Prairie dogs	Pikas (rarely)
Badger	Ground squirrels	Wolves
Aplodontia	Grasshopper mice	Foxes
Lemmings	Pocket mice	Coyotes
Pocket gophers	Jumping mice	
Woodchucks	Harvest mice	

Arboreal (at least in part or on occasion)

Opossum	White-footed mice	Margay
Coatimundi	Voles (some)	Jaguarundi
Gray fox	Porcupines	Mountain lion
Marten	Bats (nesting only)	Lynx
Fisher	Bears (*young* only)	Bobcat
Phenacomys	Jaguar	Raccoons
Tree squirrels	Ocelot	Coatimundi
Flying squirrels	Wolverine	Ring-tailed cat
Chickarees		

6. HABITAT TYPES

It is useful to know, at least in a general way, the kinds of animals that may be encountered in a given type of land area. These classifications are so broad and vary so much from north to south and from east to west that only the most generalized kind of statement can be made. In that context, only, then, there follows below a series of groupings that can be instructive as you travel around. Remember, a habitat type can change completely in a matter of yards or even feet. Swamp and high ground may be only inches apart, forest and meadow may have no transition zone. In trying to determine what kind of animal you are likely to encounter in a given area, take the entire region into consideration. Very often an animal will penetrate a habitat zone only secondary to its normal life pattern.

Coastal Regions

Opossum	Mink	Nutria
Shrews	River otter	Muskrat
Moles	Sea otter	Voles
Bats	Skunks	Lemmings
Bears	Seals	Woodchucks
Coyote (West)	Sea lions	Tree squirrels
Foxes	Walruses	Flying squirrels
Mountain lion	Manatee	Chipmunks
Bobcat	Porcupine	Wood rat
Raccoons	House mouse	Rice rat
Ground squirrels	Cotton rat	Elk
Old World rats	Rabbits	Deer
White-footed mice	Moose	Musk-ox
Weasels	Beaver	

Farmlands and Meadows

Opossum	Mink	Pocket gophers
Shrews	Skunks	Woodchucks
Moles	Porcupine	Marmots (high)
Bats	Muskrat	Tree squirrels
Armadillo	Voles	Flying squirrels
Bears	Wood rat	Chipmunks
Coyotes	Rice rat	Ground squirrels
Foxes	Cotton rat	Old World rats
Wolves (rarely)	White-footed mice	House mouse
Bobcat	Jackrabbits	Harvest mice

Lynx
Raccoons
Weasels

Hares
Deer
Lemmings

Pocket mice
Rabbits
Badger

Swamps and Marshes

Opossum
Shrews
Moles
Bats
Bears
Coyotes
Foxes
Jaguarundi
Mountain lion
Bobcat
Raccoons

Weasels
Mink
Skunks
River otter
Porcupine
Nutria
Muskrat
Voles
Aplodontia
Lemmings
Chipmunks

Rice rat
Cotton rat
Wood rat
White-footed mice
Pocket mice
European hare
Swamp rabbit
Marsh rabbit
Moose
Tree squirrels
Deer

Plains and Prairies

Opossum
Shrews
Moles
Bats
Armadillo
Coyotes
Foxes
Weasels
Black-footed ferret
Raccoons

Skunks
Badger
Voles
Chipmunks
Prairie dogs
Wood rat
White-footed mice
Grasshopper mice
Pocket mice
Lemmings

Jackrabbits
Hares
Pronghorns
Bison
Deer
Pocket gophers
Ground squirrels
Rabbits

Suburban Areas

Opossum
Moles
Shrews
Bats
Coyotes
Foxes
Bobcat
Raccoons
Ring-tailed cat
Weasels
Mink

Skunks
Porcupine
Muskrat
Voles
Woodchucks
Tree squirrels
Flying squirrels
Chipmunks
Ground squirrels
Old World rats
House mouse

Rice rats
Cotton rats
White-footed mice
Pocket gopher
Lemmings
Ground squirrels
Rabbits
Hares
Deer

Mountainous Areas

Shrews	Ring-tailed cat	Hares
Bats	Weasels	Rabbits
Bears	Skunks	Elk
Coyotes	Voles	Deer
Foxes	Phenacomys	Moose
Wolves	Chipmunks	Caribou
Mountain lion	Wood rat	Mountain sheep
Bobcats	Pikas	Mountain goats
Lynx	Jackrabbits	Pocket gophers
Raccoons	Marmots	Tree squirrels
Porcupines	Wolverine	Ground squirrels

Alpine Meadows

Shrews	Lynx	Hares
Bats	Weasels	Rabbits
Bears	Skunks	Elk
Coyotes	Voles	Deer
Foxes	Phenacomys	Moose
Wolves	Chipmunks	Caribou
Mountain lion	Pikas	Mountain sheep
Bobcat	Jackrabbits	Mountain goat

Tundra

Shrews	Weasels	Chipmunks
Bats	Wolverine	White-footed mice
Bears	Skunks	Hares
Wolves	Voles	Caribou
Foxes	Lemmings	Musk-ox

Heavy Forests

Shrews	Marten	Flying squirrels
Moles	Fisher	White-footed mice
Bats	Weasels	Rabbits
Bears	Wolverine	Caribou
Foxes	Skunks	Raccoon
Wolves	Porcupine	Elk
Mountain lion	Voles	Deer
Lynx	Phenacomys	Moose
Bobcat	Tree Squirrels	

Semiarid Regions

Shrews
Moles
Bats
Armadillos
Bears
Coyotes
Foxes
Wolves
Jaguar
Ocelot

Margay
Jaguarundi
Mountain lion
Bobcat
Coatimundi
Ring-tailed cat
Raccoons
Weasels
Skunks
Voles

Chipmunks
White-footed mice
Wood rat
Kangaroo rat
Kangaroo mouse
Jackrabbits
Hares
Rabbits
Deer
Bighorn sheep

Deserts

Shrews
Bats
Coyotes
Foxes
Bobcat
Coatimundi
Skunks

Voles
Chipmunks
Grasshopper mouse
Pocket mouse
Wood rat
Kangaroo rats
Kangaroo mouse

Jackrabbits
Hares
Rabbits
Peccary
Bighorn sheep

Brush and Light Woods

Opossum
Shrews
Moles
Bats
Armadillo
Bears
Coyotes
Foxes
Wolves
Mountain lion
Bobcat
Ocelot
Margay
Jaguarundi
Coatimundi
Ring-tailed cat

Raccoons
Weasels
Skunks
Beaver
Muskrat
Voles
Woodchucks
Marmots
Wolverine
River otters
Badger
Lemmings
Pocket gophers
Tree squirrels
Flying squirrels
Chipmunks

Ground squirrels
Wood rat
Rice rat
Cotton rat
White-footed mice
Harvest mice
Jackrabbits
Hares
Rabbits
Peccary
Elk
Deer
Caribou
Moose
Bison

7. STATE AND PROVINCE CHECKLISTS

It can be very useful to have a checklist of the mammals of a given region at hand for ready reference. The most practical system seems to be by political subdivisions—states and provinces. These lists are not always easy to come by, and, indeed, it seems that there are many areas for which none has been prepared. To temporarily fill this need the following partial lists are offered. They vary in comprehensiveness and are in no instance complete to subspecific level. They are, however, complete enough to satisfy the needs of any but the professional observer.

UNITED STATES

Alabama

Virginia opossum
Eastern mole
Southeastern shrew
Least shrew
Short-tailed shrew
Little brown bat
Eastern yellow bat
Eastern pipistrel
Red bat
Silver-haired bat
Hoary bat
Eastern big-eared bat
Big brown bat
Black bear
Raccoon

Bobcat
Long-tailed weasel
Mink
Striped skunk
Spotted skunk
River otter
Gray fox
Red Fox
Eastern cottontail rabbit
Swamp rabbit
Marsh rabbit
White-tailed deer
Woodchuck
Eastern chipmunk
Eastern fox squirrel

Eastern gray squirrel
Southern flying squirrel
Southeastern pocket gopher
Harvest mouse
White-footed mouse
Cotton mouse
Cotton rat
Rice rat
Beaver
Wood rat
Southern bog lemming
Pine vole
Muskrat
Manatee (?)

Alaska

Masked shrew
Dusky shrew
Pygmy shrew
Little brown bat
Silver-haired bat
Polar bear
Big brown bear
Black bear
Grizzly bear
Lynx
Marten
Least weasel

Coyote
Gray wolf
Sea lion
Walrus
Bearded seal
Harbor seal
Ringed seal
Northern fur seal
Ribbon seal
Moose
Elk
Bison

Snowshoe hare
Tundra hare
Porcupine
Hoary marmot
Arctic ground squirrel
Chickaree
Northern flying squirrel
Deer mouse
Beaver
Northern bog lemming
Brown lemming
Collared lemming

Short-tailed weasel
Mink
Wolverine
River otter
Sea otter
Red fox
Arctic fox

Reindeer (domestic)
Black-tailed deer (mule)
Barren Ground caribou
Mountain goat
Musk-ox
Dall sheep
Pika

Meadow vole
Red-backed vole
Long-tailed vole
Muskrat
Jumping mouse

Arizona

Dwarf shrew
Desert shrew
Northern water shrew
Leaf-nosed bat
Hog-nosed bat
Cave bat
Spotted bat
Western pipistrel
Red bat
Silver-haired bat
Hoary bat
Western big-eared bat
Big brown bat
Western mastiff bat
Mexican free-tailed bat
Big free-tailed bat
Black bear
Ring-tailed cat
Raccoon
Coatimundi
Jaguar
Ocelot
Jaguarundi
Mountain lion
Bobcat
Long-tailed weasel
Mink
Striped skunk

Hooded skunk
Hog-nosed skunk
Spotted skunk
Badger
River otter
Gray fox
Red fox
Kit fox
Coyote
Gray wolf
Peccary
Mule deer
White-tailed deer
Pronghorn
Bighorn sheep
Wild burro (feral)
Porcupine
Black-tailed jackrabbit
Antelope jackrabbit
Mountain cottontail
Eastern cottontail
Desert cottontail
Golden-mantled squirrel
Antelope squirrel
Rock squirrel
Spotted ground squirrel
Thirteen-lined ground
  squirrel

Colorado chipmunk
Least chipmunk
Arizona gray squirrel
Tassel-eared squirrel
Spruce squirrel
Black-tailed prairie dog
White-tailed prairie dog
Pygmy pocket gopher
Northern pocket gopher
Desert pocket mouse
Silky pocket mouse
Long-tailed pocket mouse
Desert wood rat
Bushy-tailed wood rat
Kangaroo rat
Muskrat
Grasshopper mouse
Pygmy mouse
Harvest mouse
White-footed mouse
Deer mouse
Cactus mouse
Cotton rat
Beaver
Red-backed vole
Mountain vole
Long-tailed vole
Jumping mouse

Arkansas

Opossum
Nine-banded armadillo
Eastern mole
Least shrew
Short-tailed shrew

Long-tailed weasel
Mink
Striped skunk
Spotted skunk
River otter

Southern flying squirrel
Plains pocket gopher
Pocket mouse
Harvest mouse
White-footed mouse

Keen myotis bat
Little brown bat
Gray bat
Eastern pipistrel
Red bat
Silver-haired bat
Hoary bat
Eastern big-eared bat
Big brown bat
Florida free-tailed bat
Raccoon
Bobcat

Gray fox
Red fox
Coyote
Red wolf
White-tailed deer
Black-tailed jackrabbit
Eastern cottontail rabbit
Swamp rabbit
Woodchuck
Eastern chipmunk
Eastern fox squirrel
Eastern gray squirrel

Deer mouse
Cotton mouse
Cotton rat
Rice rat
Beaver
Wood rat
Southern bog lemming
Prairie vole
Pine vole
Muskrat
Meadow jumping mouse

California

Opossum
Pacific mole
Shrew mole
Trowbridge shrew
Merriam shrew
Pacific water shrew
Desert shrew
Northern water shrew
Leaf-nosed bat
Hog-nosed bat
Little brown bat
Cave myotis
Western yellow bat
Pallid bat
Spotted bat
Western pipistrel
Red bat
Silver-haired bat
Hoary bat
Western big-eared bat
Big brown bat
Western mastiff bat
Mexican free-tailed bat
Big free-tailed bat
Black bear
Ring-tailed cat
Raccoon
Mountain lion
Bobcat

Striped skunk
Spotted skunk
Wolverine
Badger
River otter
Sea otter
Gray fox
Red fox
Kit fox
Coyote
Elk
Mule deer
White-tailed deer
Pronghorn
Bighorn sheep
Pygmy rabbit
Pika
Porcupine
Snowshoe hare
White-tailed jackrabbit
Black-tailed jackrabbit
Brush rabbit
Mountain cottontail
Desert cottontail
Golden-mantled squirrel
White-tailed antelope squirrel
California ground squirrel
Yellow-bellied marmot

Western gray squirrel
Chickaree
Northern flying squirrel
Northern pocket gopher
Desert pocket mouse
Long-tailed pocket mouse
Spiny pocket mouse
Pacific kangaroo rat
Desert kangaroo rat
Kangaroo mouse
Grasshopper mouse
Western harvest mouse
Canyon mouse
Deer mouse
Brush mouse
Cotton rat
Beaver
Desert wood rat
Bushy-tailed wood rat
Pacific phenacomys
Mountain phenacomys
Tree phenacomys
California vole
Red-backed vole
Long-tailed vole
Muskrat
Aplodontia
Western jumping mouse
California sea lion

Fisher
Marten
Short-tailed weasel
Long-tailed weasel
Mink

Round-tailed ground squirrel
Colorado chipmunk
Yellow pine chipmunk
Least chipmunk

Northern sea lion
Alaska fur seal
Guadalupe fur seal
Harbor seal
Elephant seal

Colorado

Eastern mole
Dwarf shrew
Masked shrew
Dusky shrew
Vagrant shrew
Least shrew
Northern water shrew
Little brown bat
Long-eared bat
Spotted bat
Western pipistrel
Red bat
Silver-haired bat
Hoary bat
Western big-eared bat
Big brown bat
Mexican free-tailed bat
Big free-tailed bat
Black bear
Grizzly bear
Ring-tailed cat
Raccoon
Mountain lion
Bobcat
Lynx
Marten
Short-tailed weasel
Long-tailed weasel
Mink
Striped skunk
Hog-nosed skunk

Spotted skunk
Black-footed ferret
Badger
River otter
Gray fox
Red fox
Kit fox
Coyote
Gray wolf
Elk
Mule deer
White-tailed deer
Bison
Pronghorn
Bighorn sheep
Pika
Porcupine
Snowshoe hare
White-tailed jackrabbit
Black-tailed jackrabbit
Mountain cottontail rabbit
Eastern cottontail rabbit
Desert cottontail rabbit
Golden-mantled squirrel
White-tailed antelope squirrel
Yellow-bellied marmot
Spotted ground squirrel
Thirteen-lined ground squirrel
Colorado chipmunk

Least chipmunk
Tassel-eared squirrel
Spruce squirrel
Black-tailed prairie dog
White-tailed prairie dog
Plains pocket gopher
Northern pocket gopher
Silky pocket mouse
Plains pocket mouse
Kangaroo rat
Northern grasshopper mouse
Plains harvest mouse
White-footed mouse
Deer mouse
Rock mouse
Cotton rat
Beaver
Eastern wood rat
Desert wood rat
Bushy-tailed wood rat
Mountain phenacomys
Meadow vole
Red-backed vole
Mountain vole
Prairie vole
Long-tailed vole
Muskrat
Jumping mouse

Connecticut

Opossum
Hairy-tailed mole
Eastern mole

Raccoon
Bobcat
Short-tailed weasel

Woodchuck
Eastern chipmunk
Eastern gray squirrel

Star-nosed mole
Smoky shrew
Masked shrew
Least shrew
Short-tailed shrew
Keen myotis bat
Little brown bat
Eastern pipistrel
Red bat
Silver-haired bat
Hoary bat
Big brown bat

Long-tailed weasel
Mink
Striped skunk
River otter
Gray fox
Red fox
White-tailed deer
Porcupine
Eastern cottontail rabbit
New England cottontail rabbit
Southern bog lemming

Red squirrel
Southern flying squirrel
Northern flying squirrel
White-footed mouse
Beaver
Meadow vole
Red-backed vole
Muskrat
Jumping mouse

Delaware

Opossum
Eastern mole
Star-nosed mole
Masked shrew
Least shrew
Short-tailed shrew
Keen myotis bat
Little brown bat
Eastern pipistrel
Red bat
Silver-haired bat
Hoary bat

Big brown bat
Raccoon
Long-tailed weasel
Mink
Striped skunk
River otter
Gray fox
Red fox
White-tailed deer
Eastern cottontail
Woodchuck
Eastern chipmunk

Eastern fox squirrel
Eastern gray squirrel
Southern flying squirrel
White-footed mouse
Rice rat
Beaver
Southern bog lemming
Meadow vole
Pine vole
Muskrat
Jumping mouse

Florida

Opossum
Nine-banded armadillo
Eastern mole
Star-nosed mole
Least shrew
Short-tailed shrew
Mississippi myotis bat
Eastern yellow bat
Eastern pipistrel
Red bat
Hoary bat
Eastern big-eared bat
Big brown bat
Florida free-tailed bat

Eastern mastiff bat
Black bear
Raccoon
Mountain lion
Bobcat
Long-tailed weasel
Mink
Striped skunk
Spotted skunk
River otter
Gray fox
White-tailed deer
Key deer
Eastern cottontail

Marsh rabbit
Eastern fox squirrel
Eastern gray squirrel
Southern flying squirrel
Pocket gopher
Eastern harvest mouse
Cotton mouse
Cotton rat
Rice rat
Eastern wood rat
Pine vole
Florida water rat
Manatee

Georgia

Opossum
Eastern mole
Star-nosed mole
Florida mole
Least shrew
Short-tailed shrew
Keen myotis bat
Little brown bat
Mississippi myotis
Eastern yellow bat
Eastern pipistrel
Red bat
Silver-haired bat
Hoary bat
Eastern big-eared bat
Big brown bat
Florida free-tailed bat

Black bear
Raccoon
Bobcat
Long-tailed weasel
Mink
Striped skunk
Spotted skunk
River otter
Gray fox
Red fox
Mountain lion (?)
White-tailed deer
Eastern cottontail
Marsh rabbit
Woodchuck
Eastern chipmunk
Eastern fox squirrel

Eastern gray squirrel
Red squirrel
Southern flying squirrel
Pocket gopher
Eastern harvest mouse
White-footed mouse
Cotton mouse
Cotton rat
Rice rat
Beaver
Southern plains wood rat
Meadow vole
Red-backed vole
Muskrat
Florida water rat
Jumping mouse

Idaho

Opossum
Pacific mole
Masked shrew
Dusky shrew
Pygmy shrew
Northern water shrew
Little brown bat
Pallid bat
California myotis
Spotted bat
Western pipistrel
Silver-haired bat
Hoary bat
Western big-eared bat
Big brown bat
Big free-tailed bat
Black bear
Grizzly bear
Raccoon
Mountain lion
Bobcat
Lynx
Fisher
Marten

Spotted skunk
Badger
River otter
Red fox
Coyote
Moose
Elk
Mule deer
White-tailed deer
Mountain goat
Bison
Pronghorn
Bighorn sheep
Pygmy rabbit
Pika
Porcupine
Snowshoe hare
White-tailed jackrabbit
Black-tailed jackrabbit
Mountain cottontail
Golden-mantled squirrel
White-tailed antelope squir-
  rel
Hoary marmot

Cliff chipmunk
Yellow pine chipmunk
Least chipmunk
Red-tailed chipmunk
Chickaree
Red squirrel
Northern flying squirrel
Pocket gopher
Pocket mouse
Kangaroo rat
Northern grasshopper
  mouse
Harvest mouse
White-footed mouse
Deer mouse
Beaver
Desert wood rat
Bushy-tailed wood rat
Mountain phenacomys
Meadow vole
Red-backed vole
Mountain vole
Prairie vole
Long-tailed vole

Short-tailed weasel
Long-tailed weasel
Mink
Striped skunk

Gray squirrel
Ground squirrel
Woodchuck
Yellow-bellied marmot

Muskrat
Jumping mouse

Illinois

Opossum
Eastern mole
Star-nosed mole
Masked shrew
Pygmy shrew
Least shrew
Short-tailed shrew
Keen myotis bat
Little brown bat
Mississippi myotis
Eastern pipistrel
Red bat
Silver-haired bat
Hoary bat
Western big-eared bat
Big brown bat
Raccoon

Least weasel
Long-tailed weasel
Mink
Striped skunk
Spotted skunk
Badger
River otter
Gray fox
Red fox
Coyote
White-tailed deer
Eastern cottontail
Swamp rabbit
Woodchuck
Thirteen-lined ground squir-
rel
Eastern chipmunk

Eastern fox squirrel
Eastern gray squirrel
Red squirrel
Southern flying squirrel
Plains pocket gopher
White-footed mouse
Deer mouse
Cotton mouse
Beaver
Eastern wood rat
Southern bog lemming
Meadow vole
Prairie vole
Muskrat
Jumping mouse

Indiana

Opossum
Eastern mole
Star-nosed mole
Southeastern shrew
Masked shrew
Least shrew
Short-tailed shrew
Keen myotis bat
Little brown bat
Mississippi myotis
Eastern pipistrel
Red bat
Silver-haired bat
Hoary bat
Western big-eared bat
Big brown bat
Raccoon

Least weasel
Long-tailed weasel
Mink
Striped skunk
Spotted skunk
Badger
River otter
Gray fox
Red fox
Coyote
White-tailed deer
Eastern cottontail
Swamp rabbit
Woodchuck
Thirteen-lined ground squir-
rel
Eastern chipmunk

Eastern fox squirrel
Eastern gray squirrel
Red squirrel
Southern flying squirrel
Plains pocket gopher
Harvest mouse
White-footed mouse
Deer mouse
Rice rat
Beaver
Eastern wood rat
Southern bog lemming
Meadow vole
Prairie vole
Pine vole
Muskrat
Jumping mouse

Iowa

Opossum
Eastern mole
Masked shrew
Pygmy shrew
Least shrew
Short-tailed shrew
Keen myotis bat
Little brown bat
Eastern pipistrel
Red bat
Silver-haired bat
Hoary bat
Big brown bat
Big free-tailed bat
Raccoon
Least weasel
Short-tailed weasel

Long-tailed weasel
Mink
Striped skunk
Spotted skunk
Badger
River otter
Gray fox
Red fox
Coyote
White-tailed deer
White-tailed jackrabbit
Eastern cottontail
Woodchuck
Thirteen-lined ground squir-
  rel
Eastern chipmunk
Eastern fox squirrel

Eastern gray squirrel
Red squirrel
Southern flying squirrel
Plains pocket gopher
Northern grasshopper
  mouse
Harvest mouse
White-footed mouse
Deer mouse
Beaver
Southern bog lemming
Red-backed vole
Meadow vole
Prairie vole
Pine vole
Muskrat
Jumping mouse

Kansas

Opossum
Nine-banded armadillo
Eastern mole
Least shrew
Short-tailed shrew
Little brown bat
Eastern pipistrel
Red bat
Silver-haired bat
Hoary bat
Western big-eared bat
Big brown bat
Mexican free-tailed bat
Big free-tailed bat
Raccoon
Bobcat
Long-tailed weasel
Mink
Striped skunk
Spotted skunk

Black-footed ferret
Badger
River otter
Gray fox
Red fox
Kit fox
Coyote
White-tailed deer
Porcupine
White-tailed jackrabbit
Black-tailed jackrabbit
Eastern cottontail
Swamp rabbit
Woodchuck
Spotted ground squirrel
Thirteen-lined ground squir-
  rel
Eastern chipmunk
Eastern fox squirrel
Eastern gray squirrel

Black-tailed prairie dog
Southern flying squirrel
Plains pocket gopher
Silky pocket mouse
Plains pocket mouse
Kangaroo rat
Northern grasshopper
  mouse
Plains harvest mouse
White-footed mouse
Deer mouse
Cotton rat
Beaver
Eastern wood rat
Southern bog lemming
Prairie vole
Pine vole
Muskrat
Jumping mouse

Kentucky

Opossum
Hairy-tailed mole
Eastern mole

Big brown bat
Raccoon
Least weasel

Eastern fox squirrel
Eastern gray squirrel
Southern flying squirrel

Star-nosed mole
Smoky shrew
Long-tailed shrew
Masked shrew
Least shrew
Short-tailed shrew
Keen myotis bat
Little brown bat
Eastern pipistrel
Red bat
Silver-haired bat
Hoary bat
Western big-eared bat

Long-tailed weasel
Mink
Striped skunk
Spotted skunk
River otter
Gray fox
Red fox
White-tailed deer
Snowshoe hare
Eastern cottontail
Swamp rabbit
Woodchuck
Eastern chipmunk

Northern flying squirrel
Harvest mouse
White-footed mouse
Cotton mouse
Rice rat
Beaver
Eastern wood rat
Southern bog lemming
Meadow vole
Red-backed vole
Pine vole
Muskrat
Jumping mouse

Louisiana

Opossum
Nine-banded armadillo
Eastern mole
Least shrew
Short-tailed shrew
Eastern yellow bat
Seminole bat
Eastern pipistrel
Red bat
Hoary bat
Eastern big-eared bat
Big brown bat
Florida free-tailed bat
Black bear
Raccoon

Mountain lion (?)
Bobcat
Long-tailed weasel
Mink
Striped skunk
Spotted skunk
River otter
Gray fox
Red fox
Red wolf
White-tailed deer
Eastern cottontail
Swamp rabbit
Nutria
Eastern chipmunk

Eastern fox squirrel
Eastern gray squirrel
Southern flying squirrel
Plains pocket gopher
Pocket mouse
Eastern harvest mouse
White-footed mouse
Cotton mouse
Cotton rat
Beaver
Eastern wood rat
Prairie vole
Muskrat
Manatee (?)

Maine

Opossum
Hairy-tailed mole
Star-nosed mole
Smoky shrew
Masked shrew
Pygmy shrew
Short-tailed shrew
Northern water shrew
Keen myotis bat
Little brown bat
Eastern pipistrel
Red bat

Mountain lion (?)
Bobcat
Lynx
Fisher
Marten
Short-tailed weasel
Long-tailed weasel
Mink
Striped skunk
River otter
Gray fox
Red fox

Porcupine
Woodchuck
Eastern chipmunk
Eastern gray squirrel
Red squirrel
Northern flying squirrel
White-footed mouse
Deer mouse
Beaver
Southern bog lemming
Northern bog lemming
Meadow vole

Silver-haired bat
Hoary bat
Big brown bat
Black bear
Raccoon

White-tailed deer
Moose
Snowshoe hare
New England cottontail rabbit

Red-backed vole
Muskrat
Jumping mouse

Maryland

Opossum
Hairy-tailed mole
Eastern mole
Star-nosed mole
Smoky shrew
Masked shrew
Pygmy shrew
Least shrew
Short-tailed shrew
Northern water shrew
Little brown bat
Eastern pipistrel
Red bat
Silver-haired bat
Hoary bat

Big brown bat
Raccoon
Least weasel
Long-tailed weasel
Mink
Striped skunk
River otter
Gray fox
Red fox
White-tailed deer
Eastern cottontail
New England cottontail
Porcupine
Woodchuck
Eastern chipmunk

Eastern fox squirrel
Eastern gray squirrel
Red squirrel
Southern flying squirrel
Harvest mouse
White-footed mouse
Deer mouse
Rice rat
Beaver
Eastern wood rat
Southern bog lemming
Meadow vole
Red-backed vole
Muskrat
Jumping mouse

Massachusetts

Opossum
Hairy-tailed mole
Eastern mole
Star-nosed mole
Long-tailed shrew
Pygmy shrew
Least shrew
Short-tailed shrew
Northern water shrew
Little brown bat
Eastern pipistrel
Red bat
Silver-haired bat
Hoary bat
Big brown bat

Black bear
Raccoon
Bobcat
Short-tailed weasel
Long-tailed weasel
Mink
Striped skunk
River otter
Gray fox
Red fox
White-tailed deer
European hare
Snowshoe hare
New England cottontail
Porcupine

Woodchuck
Eastern chipmunk
Eastern gray squirrel
Red squirrel
Southern flying squirrel
Northern flying squirrel
White-footed mouse
Beaver
Southern bog lemming
Meadow vole
Red-backed vole
Pine vole
Muskrat
Jumping mouse

Michigan

Opossum
Hairy-tailed mole
Eastern mole

Short-tailed weasel
Long-tailed weasel
Mink

Thirteen-lined ground squirrel
Eastern chipmunk

Star-nosed mole
Masked shrew
Pygmy shrew
Least shrew
Short-tailed shrew
Northern water shrew
Little brown bat
Red bat
Silver-haired bat
Hoary bat
Big brown bat
Black bear
Raccoon
Bobcat
Least weasel

Striped skunk
Badger
River otter
Gray fox
Red fox
Coyote
Gray wolf
Moose
Elk
White-tailed deer
Snowshoe hare
European hare
Eastern cottontail
Porcupine
Woodchuck

Least chipmunk
Eastern fox squirrel
Red squirrel
Eastern gray squirrel
Southern flying squirrel
Northern flying squirrel
White-footed mouse
Beaver
Southern bog lemming
Meadow vole
Red-backed vole
Muskrat
Jumping mouse

Minnesota

Opossum
Eastern mole
Star-nosed mole
Pygmy shrew
Short-tailed shrew
Northern water shrew
Little brown bat
Red bat
Silver-haired bat
Hoary bat
Big brown bat
Black bear
Raccoon
Bobcat
Lynx
Marten
Least weasel
Short-tailed weasel
Long-tailed weasel
Mink

Striped skunk
Spotted skunk
Badger
River otter
Gray fox
Red fox
Coyote
Gray wolf
Moose
Elk
Mule deer
White-tailed deer
Snowshoe hare
White-tailed jackrabbit
European hare
Eastern cottontail
Porcupine
Woodchuck
Thirteen-lined ground squir-
   rel

Eastern chipmunk
Least chipmunk
Eastern fox squirrel
Eastern gray squirrel
Red squirrel
Southern flying squirrel
Northern flying squirrel
Plains pocket gopher
Northern pocket gopher
Grasshopper mouse
Harvest mouse
White-footed mouse
Beaver
Southern bog lemming
Northern bog lemming
Meadow vole
Red-backed vole
Muskrat
Jumping mouse

Mississippi

Opossum
Nine-banded armadillo
Eastern mole
Least shrew
Short-tailed shrew

Black bear
Raccoon
Bobcat
Long-tailed weasel
Mink

Eastern fox squirrel
Eastern gray squirrel
Southern flying squirrel
Harvest mouse
White-footed mouse

Little brown bat
Eastern yellow bat
Evening bat
Eastern pipistrel
Red bat
Silver-haired bat
Hoary bat
Eastern big-eared bat
Big brown bat
Florida free-tailed bat

Striped skunk
Spotted skunk
River otter
Gray fox
Red fox
Red wolf
White-tailed deer
Eastern cottontail
Swamp rabbit
Eastern chipmunk

Cotton mouse
Cotton rat
Rice rat
Beaver
Eastern wood rat
Southern bog lemming
Pine vole
Muskrat

Missouri

Opossum
Short-tailed shrew
Least shrew
Eastern mole
Little brown bat
Silver-haired bat
Eastern pipistrel
Big brown bat
Red bat
Hoary bat
Lump-nosed bat
Coyote
Red wolf
Red fox
Gray fox
Black bear
Raccoon

Long-tailed weasel
Mink
Badger
Spotted skunk
Striped skunk
River otter
Bobcat
White-tailed deer
Nutria (?)
White-tailed jackrabbit
Black-tailed jackrabbit
Eastern cottontail rabbit
Swamp rabbit
Woodchuck
Thirteen-lined ground squir-
    rel
Eastern chipmunk

Eastern gray squirrel
Eastern fox squirrel
Southern flying squirrel
Plains pocket gopher
Beaver
Rice rat
Harvest mouse
White-footed mouse
Cotton mouse
Cotton rat
Eastern wood rat
Southern bog lemming
Muskrat
Jumping mouse

Montana

Masked shrew
Vagrant shrew
Northern water shrew
Little brown bat
Long-eared myotis
Spotted bat
Red bat
Silver-haired bat
Hoary bat
Western big-eared bat
Big brown bat
Big free-tailed bat
Black bear

Black-footed ferret
Badger
River otter
Red fox
Kit fox
Coyote
Moose
Elk
Mule deer
White-tailed deer
Mountain goat
Bison
Pronghorn

Thirteen-lined ground squir-
    rel
Yellow pine chipmunk
Least chipmunk
Red-tailed chipmunk
Red squirrel
Black-tailed prairie dog
White-tailed prairie dog
Northern flying squirrel
Northern pocket gopher
Pocket mouse
Kangaroo rat
Grasshopper mouse

Grizzly bear
Raccoon
Mountain lion
Bobcat
Lynx
Fisher
Marten
Least weasel
Short-tailed weasel
Long-tailed weasel
Mink
Striped skunk

Bighorn sheep
Pika
Snowshoe hare
White-tailed jackrabbit
Mountain cottontail
Desert cottontail
Porcupine
Woodchuck
Yellow-bellied marmot
Hoary marmot
Columbian ground squirrel

Harvest mouse
White-footed mouse
Beaver
Bushy-tailed wood rat
Mountain phenacomys
Meadow vole
Red-backed vole
Mountain vole
Prairie vole
Muskrat
Jumping mouse

Nebraska

Opossum
Masked shrew
Short-tailed shrew
Least shrew
Eastern mole
Little brown bat
Long-eared myotis
Silver-haired bat
Eastern pipistrel
Big brown bat
Red bat
Hoary bat
Free-tailed bat
White-tailed jackrabbit
Black-tailed jackrabbit
Eastern cottontail
Desert cottontail
Woodchuck
Black-tailed prairie dog
Thirteen-lined ground squir-
    rel
Spotted ground squirrel

Eastern chipmunk
Least chipmunk
Eastern gray squirrel
Eastern fox squirrel
Southern flying squirrel
Northern pocket gopher
Plains pocket gopher
Plains pocket mouse
Silky pocket mouse
Kangaroo rat
Beaver
Harvest mouse
White-footed mouse
Grasshopper mouse
Eastern wood rat
Bushy-tailed wood rat
Southern bog lemming
Meadow vole
Prairie vole
Pine vole
Muskrat
Jumping mouse

Nutria
Porcupine
Coyote
Red fox
Swift fox
Gray fox
Raccoon
Least weasel
Long-tailed weasel
Mink
Black-footed ferret
Badger
Eastern spotted skunk
Striped skunk
Bobcat
Fallow deer (introduced)
Mule deer
White-tailed deer
Pronghorn
Bison

Nevada

California mole
Vagrant shrew
Desert shrew
Northern water shrew
Leaf-nosed bat
Little brown bat

Badger
River otter
Gray fox
Red fox
Kit fox
Coyote

Least chipmunk
Western gray squirrel
Chickaree
Northern flying squirrel
Northern pocket gopher
Desert pocket mouse

Pallid bat
Spotted bat
Western pipistrel
Red bat
Silver-haired bat
Hoary bat
Western big-eared bat
Big brown bat
Mexican free-tailed bat
Big free-tailed bat
Black bear
Ring-tailed cat
Raccoon
Mountain lion
Bobcat
Short-tailed weasel
Long-tailed weasel
Mink
Striped skunk
Spotted skunk

Mule deer
White-tailed deer
Pronghorn
Bighorn sheep
Pika
Pygmy rabbit
Snowshoe hare
White-tailed jackrabbit
Black-tailed jackrabbit
Mountain cottontail
Desert cottontail
Porcupine
White-tailed antelope squirrel
Yellow-bellied marmot
California ground squirrel
Round-tailed ground squirrel
Cliff chipmunk
Yellow pine chipmunk

Kangaroo rat
Desert kangaroo rat
Dark kangaroo mouse
Pale kangaroo mouse
Southern grasshopper mouse
Northern grasshopper mouse
Western harvest mouse
Piñon mouse
Cactus mouse
Cotton rat
Beaver
Desert wood rat
Bushy-tailed wood rat
Mountain vole
Long-tailed vole
Sagebrush vole
Muskrat
Aplodontia
Jumping mouse

New Hampshire

Opossum
Eastern mole
Star-nosed mole
Smoky shrew
Pygmy shrew
Short-tailed shrew
Northern water shrew
Little brown bat
Eastern pipistrel
Red bat
Silver-haired bat
Hoary bat
Big brown bat
Black bear
Raccoon
Bobcat

Lynx
Fisher
Marten
Short-tailed weasel
Long-tailed weasel
Mink
Striped skunk
River otter
Gray fox
Red fox
White-tailed deer
Snowshoe hare
European hare
New England cottontail
Porcupine
Woodchuck

Eastern chipmunk
Eastern gray squirrel
Red squirrel
Southern flying squirrel
Northern flying squirrel
White-footed mouse
Beaver
Southern bog lemming
Northern bog lemming
Meadow vole
Red-backed vole
Pine vole
Muskrat
Jumping mouse

New Jersey

Opossum
Eastern mole
Star-nosed mole
Least shrew

Long-tailed weasel
Mink
Striped skunk
River otter

Red squirrel
Southern flying squirrel
White-footed mouse
Rice rat

Short-tailed shrew
Little brown bat
Eastern pipistrel
Red bat
Silver-haired bat
Hoary bat
Big brown bat
Raccoon
Bobcat

Gray fox
Red fox
White-tailed deer
Eastern cottontail
New England cottontail
Porcupine
Woodchuck
Eastern chipmunk
Eastern gray squirrel

Beaver
Eastern wood rat
Southern bog lemming
Meadow vole
Red-backed vole
Muskrat
Jumping mouse

New Mexico

Nine-banded armadillo
Masked shrew
Vagrant shrew
Desert shrew
Northern water shrew
Hog-nosed bat
Little brown bat
Pallid bat
Spotted bat
Western pipistrel
Silver-haired bat
Hoary bat
Western big-eared bat
Big brown bat
Pocketed free-tailed bat
Western mastiff bat
Mexican free-tailed bat
Big free-tailed bat
Black bear
Ring-tailed cat
Raccoon
Coatimundi
Jaguar
Ocelot
Mountain lion
Bobcat
Marten
Short-tailed weasel
Long-tailed weasel
Mink
Striped skunk
Hooded skunk

Hog-nosed skunk
Spotted skunk
Black-footed ferret
Badger
River otter
Gray fox
Red fox
Kit fox
Coyote
Peccary
Mule deer
White-tailed deer
Bighorn sheep
Pronghorn
Pika
Snowshoe hare
White-tailed jackrabbit
Black-tailed jackrabbit
Eastern cottontail
Desert cottontail
Porcupine
White-tailed antelope squir-
rel
Yuma antelope squirrel
Rock squirrel
Yellow-bellied marmot
Spotted ground squirrel
Thirteen-lined ground squir-
rel
Colorado chipmunk
Cliff chipmunk
Gray-necked chipmunk

Least chipmunk
Apache fox squirrel
Tassel-eared squirrel
Spruce squirrel
Black-tailed prairie dog
White-tailed prairie dog
Plains pocket gopher
Pygmy pocket gopher
Northern pocket gopher
Desert pocket mouse
Silky pocket mouse
Kangaroo rat
Southern plains wood rat
Desert wood rat
White-throated wood rat
Bushy-tailed wood rat
Mountain phenacomys
Grasshopper mouse
Western harvest mouse
White-footed mouse
Cactus mouse
Brush mouse
Least cotton rat
Yellow-nosed cotton rat
Beaver
Meadow vole
Red-backed vole
Mountain vole
Muskrat
Jumping mouse

New York

Opossum	Bobcat	Woodchuck
Hairy-tailed mole	Lynx	Eastern chipmunk
Eastern mole	Fisher	Eastern gray squirrel
Star-nosed mole	Marten	Red squirrel
Smoky shrew	Short-tailed weasel	Southern flying squirrel
Long-tailed shrew	Long-tailed weasel	Northern flying squirrel
Pygmy shrew	Mink	White-footed mouse
Least shrew	Striped skunk	Beaver
Short-tailed shrew	River otter	Eastern wood rat
Northern water shrew	Gray fox	Southern bog lemming
Little brown bat	Red fox	Northern bog lemming
Eastern pipistrel	Coyote	Meadow vole
Red bat	White-tailed deer	Red-backed vole
Silver-haired bat	Snowshoe hare	Pine vole
Hoary bat	European hare	Muskrat
Big brown bat	Eastern cottontail	Jumping mouse
Black bear	New England cottontail	
Raccoon	Porcupine	

North Carolina

Opossum	Bobcat	Southern flying squirrel
Hairy-tailed mole	Least weasel	Northern flying squirrel
Eastern mole	Short-tailed weasel	Harvest mouse
Star-nosed mole	Mink	White-footed mouse
Smoky shrew	Striped skunk	Golden mouse
Pygmy shrew	Spotted skunk	Cotton mouse
Least shrew	River otter	Cotton rat
Short-tailed shrew	Red fox	Rice rat
Little brown bat	Gray fox	Beaver
Eastern pipistrel	White-tailed deer	Southern plains wood rat
Red bat	Eastern cottontail	Southern bog lemming
Silver-haired bat	Marsh rabbit	Meadow vole
Hoary bat	Woodchuck	Red-backed vole
Eastern big-eared bat	Eastern chipmunk	Muskrat
Big brown bat	Eastern fox squirrel	Jumping mouse
Black bear	Eastern gray squirrel	
Raccoon	Red squirrel	

North Dakota

Masked shrew	Wolverine	Beaver
Pygmy shrew	Lynx	Gray chipmunk
Short-tailed shrew	Mountain lion	Little northern chipmunk
Northern water shrew	Bobcat	Pale chipmunk

Little brown bat
Red bat
Silver-haired bat
Hoary bat
Big brown bat
Black bear
Grizzly bear
Badger
Black-footed ferret
Fisher
Marten
Mink
Striped skunk
Spotted skunk
Least weasel
Long-tailed weasel

Short-tailed weasel
Gray fox
Kit fox
Red fox
Coyote
Gray wolf
Raccoon
Pronghorn
Bison
Woodland caribou
Mule deer
White-tailed deer
Elk
Moose
Mountain sheep
Cottontail

Varying hare
Porcupine
Black-tailed prairie dog
Woodchuck
Fox squirrel
Gray squirrel
Red squirrel
Thirteen-lined ground squirrel
Muskrat
Pocket gopher
Bushy-tailed wood rat
Grasshopper mouse
White-footed mouse
Harvest mouse
Red-backed vole

Ohio

Opossum
Hairy-tailed mole
Eastern mole
Star-nosed mole
Smoky shrew
Pygmy shrew
Least shrew
Short-tailed shrew
Little brown bat
Eastern pipistrel
Red bat
Silver-haired bat
Hoary bat
Western big-eared bat
Big brown bat
Black bear

Raccoon
Least weasel
Short-tailed weasel
Long-tailed weasel
Mink
Striped skunk
Badger
River otter
Gray fox
Red fox
Coyote
White-tailed deer
Eastern cottontail
Woodchuck
Thirteen-lined ground squirrel

Eastern chipmunk
Eastern fox squirrel
Eastern gray squirrel
Red squirrel
Southern flying squirrel
Harvest mouse
White-footed mouse
Beaver
Southern plains wood rat
Southern bog lemming
Meadow vole
Prairie vole
Pine vole
Muskrat
Jumping mouse

Oklahoma

Opossum
Nine-banded armadillo
Eastern mole
Least shrew
Short-tailed shrew
Little brown bat

Badger
River otter
Gray fox
Red fox
Kit fox
Coyote

Eastern gray squirrel
Black-tailed prairie dog
Southern flying squirrel
Plains pocket gopher
Silky pocket mouse
Plains pocket mouse

Eastern pipistrel
Red bat
Silver-haired bat
Hoary bat
Western big-eared bat
Big brown bat
Mexican free-tailed bat
Big free-tailed bat
Raccoon
Bobcat
Long-tailed weasel
Mink
Striped skunk
Spotted skunk
Black-footed ferret

Red wolf
White-tailed deer
Bison
Pronghorn
Black-tailed jackrabbit
Eastern cottontail
Desert cottontail
Porcupine
Woodchuck
Spotted ground squirrel
Thirteen-lined ground
    squirrel
Colorado chipmunk
Eastern chipmunk
Eastern fox squirrel

Kangaroo rat
Grasshopper mouse
Harvest mouse
White-footed mouse
Cotton mouse
Cotton rat
Rice rat
Beaver
Eastern wood rat
Southern bog lemming
Prairie vole
Pine vole
Muskrat
Jumping mouse

Oregon

Opossum
Shrew-mole
Pacific water shrew
Vagrant shrew
Northern water shrew
Little brown bat
Pallid bat
Western pipistrel
Silver-haired bat
Hoary bat
Western big-eared bat
Big brown bat
Mexican free-tailed bat
Big free-tailed bat
Black bear
Ring-tailed cat
Raccoon
Mountain lion
Bobcat
Lynx
Fisher
Marten
Short-tailed weasel
Long-tailed weasel
Mink
Striped skunk

Spotted skunk
Badger
River otter
Gray fox
Red fox
Kit fox
Coyote
Gray wolf
Elk
Mule deer
White-tailed deer
Pronghorn
Bighorn sheep
Pika
Pygmy rabbit
Snowshoe hare
White-tailed jackrabbit
Black-tailed jackrabbit
Mountain cottontail
Brush rabbit
Porcupine
White-tailed antelope
    squirrel
Yellow-bellied marmot
Ground squirrel
Yellow pine chipmunk

Least chipmunk
Western gray squirrel
Chickaree
Red squirrel
Northern flying squirrel
Northern pocket gopher
Giant pocket gopher
Pocket mouse
Little pocket mouse
Dark kangaroo rat
Grasshopper mouse
Harvest mouse
Beaver
Desert wood rat
Bushy-tailed wood rat
Pacific phenacomys
Mountain phenacomys
Tree phenacomys
Red-backed vole
Mountain vole
Prairie vole
Long-tailed vole
Muskrat
Aplodontia
Jumping mouse

Pennsylvania

Opossum
Hairy-tailed mole
Eastern mole
Star-nosed mole
Smoky shrew
Long-tailed shrew
Masked shrew
Pygmy shrew
Least shrew
Short-tailed shrew
Northern water shrew
Little brown bat
Eastern pipistrel
Red bat
Silver-haired bat
Hoary bat
Big brown bat

Black bear
Raccoon
Bobcat
Least weasel
Short-tailed weasel
Long-tailed weasel
Mink
Striped skunk
Spotted skunk
River otter
Gray fox
Red fox
White-tailed deer
Snowshoe hare
European hare
Eastern cottontail
New England cottontail

Porcupine
Woodchuck
Eastern chipmunk
Eastern fox squirrel
Eastern gray squirrel
Red squirrel
Northern flying squirrel
Southern flying squirrel
White-footed mouse
Rice rat
Beaver
Eastern wood rat
Southern bog lemming
Meadow vole
Red-backed vole
Muskrat
Jumping mouse

Rhode Island

Opossum
Hairy-tailed mole
Eastern mole
Star-nosed mole
Smoky shrew
Short-tailed shrew
Little brown bat
Eastern pipistrel
Red bat
Silver-haired bat
Hoary bat

Big brown bat
Raccoon
Short-tailed weasel
Long-tailed weasel
Mink
Striped skunk
River otter
Gray fox
Red fox
New England cottontail
Woodchuck

Eastern chipmunk
Eastern gray squirrel
Red squirrel
Southern flying squirrel
White-footed mouse
Beaver
Southern bog lemming
Meadow vole
Muskrat
Jumping mouse

South Carolina

Opossum
Eastern mole
Star-nosed mole
Masked shrew
Least shrew
Short-tailed shrew
Little brown bat
Eastern pipistrel
Red bat
Silver-haired bat

Raccoon
Bobcat
Long-tailed weasel
Mink
Striped skunk
Spotted skunk
River otter
Gray fox
Red fox
White-tailed deer

Eastern gray squirrel
Red squirrel
Southern flying squirrel
Pocket gopher
Harvest mouse
White-footed mouse
Cotton mouse
Cotton rat
Rice rat
Beaver

Hoary bat
Eastern big-eared bat
Big brown bat
Florida free-tailed bat
Black bear

Eastern cottontail
Marsh rabbit
Woodchuck
Eastern chipmunk
Eastern fox squirrel

Eastern wood rat
Meadow vole
Red-backed vole
Muskrat
Jumping mouse

South Dakota

Opossum
Eastern mole
Pygmy shrew
Short-tailed shrew
Northern water shrew
Little brown bat
Red bat
Silver-haired bat
Hoary bat
Western big-eared bat
Big brown bat
Big free-tailed bat
Raccoon
Bobcat
Least weasel
Short-tailed weasel
Long-tailed weasel
Mink
Striped skunk
Spotted skunk
Black-footed ferret
Badger
River otter

Red fox
Kit fox
Coyote
Elk
Mule deer
White-tailed deer
Bison
Pronghorn
Bighorn sheep
Snowshoe hare
White-tailed jackrabbit
Black-tailed jackrabbit
Eastern cottontail
Desert cottontail
Porcupine
Spotted ground squirrel
Thirteen-lined ground squir-
    rel
Woodchuck
Yellow-bellied marmot
Black-tailed prairie dog
Eastern chipmunk
Least chipmunk

Eastern fox squirrel
Eastern gray squirrel
Red squirrel
Southern flying squirrel
Northern flying squirrel
Plains pocket gopher
Northern pocket gopher
Silky pocket mouse
Plains pocket mouse
Kangaroo rat
Grasshopper mouse
Plains harvest mouse
White-footed mouse
Beaver
Wood rat
Bushy-tailed wood rat
Red-backed vole
Prairie vole
Long-tailed vole
Muskrat
Jumping mouse

Tennessee

Opossum
Hairy-tailed mole
Eastern mole
Star-nosed mole
Least shrew
Short-tailed shrew
Little brown bat
Eastern pipistrel
Red bat
Silver-haired bat
Hoary bat
Eastern big-eared bat

Least weasel
Long-tailed weasel
Mink
Striped skunk
Spotted skunk
River otter
Gray fox
Red fox
White-tailed deer
Eastern cottontail
New England cottontail
Woodchuck

Red squirrel
Southern flying squirrel
Northern flying squirrel
Harvest mouse
White-footed mouse
Cotton mouse
Cotton rat
Rice rat
Beaver
Wood rat
Southern bog lemming
Meadow vole

Big brown bat
Raccoon
Bobcat

Eastern chipmunk
Eastern fox squirrel
Eastern gray squirrel

Red-backed vole
Muskrat
Jumping mouse

Texas

Opossum
Eastern mole
Short-tailed shrew
Little short-tailed shrew
Little brown bat
Silver-haired bat
Big brown bat
Hoary bat
Red bat
Lump-nosed bat
Free-tailed bat
Mastiff bat
Black bear
Raccoon
Coatimundi
Ring-tailed cat
Long-tailed weasel
Mink
Black-footed ferret
River otter
Spotted skunk
Striped skunk
Hooded skunk
Hog-nosed skunk
Badger
Red fox
Desert fox
Swift fox

Gray fox
Coyote
Gray wolf
Red wolf
Jaguar
Ocelot
Cougar
Jaguarundi
Bobcat
Manatee
Thirteen-lined ground
    squirrel
Spotted ground squirrel
Black-tailed prairie dog
Antelope squirrel
Gray-collared chipmunk
Eastern gray squirrel
Fox squirrel
Eastern flying squirrel
Plains pocket gopher
Spiny mouse
Plains pocket mouse
Hispid pocket mouse
Desert pocket mouse
Kangaroo rat
Beaver
Long-tailed grasshopper
    mouse

Short-tailed grasshopper
    mouse
Harvest mouse
Desert harvest mouse
Pygmy mouse
White-footed mouse
Cotton mouse
Brush mouse
Rice rat
Cotton rat
Florida wood rat
White-throated wood rat
Prairie meadow mouse
Muskrat
Porcupine
Nutria
Jackrabbit
Eastern cottontail
Davis Mountains cottontail
Swamp rabbit
Peccary
Pronghorn
Elk
Mule deer
White-tailed deer
Bighorn sheep
Nine-banded armadillo

Utah

Dwarf shrew
Vagrant shrew
Northern water shrew
Little brown bat
Pallid bat
Spotted bat
Western pipistrel
Red bat
Silver-haired bat

Badger
River otter
Gray fox
Red fox
Kit fox
Coyote
Gray wolf
Elk
Mule deer

Beaver
Yellow pine chipmunk
Least chipmunk
Tassel-eared squirrel
Spruce squirrel
Red squirrel
White-tailed prairie dog
Northern flying squirrel
Townsend pocket gopher

Hoary bat
Western big-eared bat
Big brown bat
Mexican free-tailed bat
Big free-tailed bat
Black bear
Grizzly bear
Ring-tailed cat
Raccoon
Mountain lion
Bobcat
Lynx
Short-tailed weasel
Long-tailed weasel
Mink
Striped skunk
Spotted skunk

White-tailed deer
Pronghorn
Bighorn sheep
Pygmy rabbit
Pika
Snowshoe hare
White-tailed jackrabbit
Black-tailed jackrabbit
Mountain cottontail
Desert cottontail
Porcupine
White-tailed antelope
   squirrel
Yellow bellied marmot
Spotted ground squirrel
Grasshopper mouse
Harvest mouse

Pocket gopher
Desert pocket mouse
Silky pocket mouse
Kangaroo rat
Desert kangaroo rat
Desert wood rat
White-throated wood rat
Bushy-tailed wood rat
Meadow vole
Red-backed vole
Mountain vole
Prairie vole
Long-tailed vole
Muskrat
Jumping mouse

Vermont

Opossum
Hairy-tailed mole
Eastern mole
Star-nosed mole
Smoky shrew
Pygmy shrew
Short-tailed shrew
Northern water shrew
Little brown bat
Eastern pipistrel
Red bat
Silver-haired bat
Hoary bat
Big brown bat
Black bear
Raccoon

Bobcat
Lynx
Fisher
Marten
Short-tailed weasel
Long-tailed weasel
Mink
Striped skunk
River otter
Gray fox
Red fox
White-tailed deer
Snowshoe hare
European hare
New England cottontail
Porcupine

Woodchuck
Eastern chipmunk
Eastern gray squirrel
Red squirrel
Northern flying squirrel
Southern flying squirrel
White-footed mouse
Beaver
Southern bog lemming
Northern bog lemming
Meadow vole
Red-backed vole
Pine vole
Muskrat
Jumping mouse

Virginia

Opossum
Hairy-tailed mole
Eastern mole
Star-nosed mole
Pygmy shrew
Least shrew
Short-tailed shrew

Bobcat
Least weasel
Long-tailed weasel
Mink
Striped skunk
Spotted skunk
River otter

Eastern gray squirrel
Red squirrel
Southern flying squirrel
Northern flying squirrel
Harvest mouse
White-footed mouse
Cotton rat

Little brown bat
Eastern pipistrel
Red bat
Silver-haired bat
Hoary bat
Eastern big-eared bat
Western big-eared bat
Big brown bat
Black bear
Raccoon

Gray fox
Red fox
White-tailed deer
Snowshoe hare
Eastern cottontail
New England cottontail
Porcupine
Woodchuck
Eastern chipmunk
Eastern fox squirrel

Rice rat
Beaver
Wood rat
Southern bog lemming
Meadow vole
Red-backed vole
Muskrat
Jumping mouse

Washington

Opossum
Shrew mole
Pacific water shrew
Vagrant shrew
Pygmy shrew
Northern water shrew
Little brown bat
Pallid bat
Western pipistrel
Silver-haired bat
Hoary bat
Western big-eared bat
Big brown bat
Big free-tailed bat
Black bear
Grizzly bear
Raccoon
Bobcat
Mountain lion
Lynx
Fisher
Marten
Short-tailed weasel
Long-tailed weasel

Mink
Striped skunk
Spotted skunk
Wolverine
Badger
River otter
Gray fox
Red fox
Coyote
Moose
Elk
Mule deer
White-tailed deer
Mountain goat
Bighorn sheep
Pygmy rabbit
Pika
Snowshoe hare
White-tailed jackrabbit
Black-tailed jackrabbit
Mountain cottontail
Porcupine
Hoary marmot
Yellow-bellied marmot

Pocket gopher
Northern flying squirrel
Yellow pine chipmunk
Least chipmunk
Red-tailed chipmunk
Western gray squirrel
Chickaree
Red squirrel
Giant pocket gopher
Pocket mouse
Kangaroo rat
Grasshopper mouse
Harvest mouse
Beaver
Bushy-tailed wood rat
Bog lemming
Mountain phenacomys
Meadow vole
Red-backed vole
Mountain vole
Muskrat
Aplodontia
Jumping mouse

West Virginia

Opossum
Hairy-tailed mole
Eastern mole
Star-nosed mole
Smoky shrew
Long-tailed shrew

Big brown bat
Black bear
Raccoon
Bobcat
Least weasel
Long-tailed weasel

Eastern fox squirrel
Eastern gray squirrel
Red squirrel
Southern flying squirrel
Northern flying squirrel
Harvest mouse

Masked shrew
Pygmy shrew
Least shrew
Short-tailed shrew
Northern water shrew
Little brown bat
Eastern pipistrel
Red bat
Silver-haired bat
Hoary bat
Western big-eared bat

Mink
Striped skunk
Spotted skunk
River otter
Gray fox
Red fox
Snowshoe hare
Eastern cottontail
Porcupine
Woodchuck
Eastern chipmunk

White-footed mouse
Rice rat
Beaver
Wood rat
Southern bog lemming
Meadow vole
Red-backed vole
Pine vole
Muskrat
Jumping mouse
White-tailed deer

Wisconsin

Opossum
Eastern mole
Star-nosed mole
Smoky shrew
Pygmy shrew
Least shrew
Short-tailed shrew
Northern water shrew
Little brown bat
Eastern pipistrel
Red bat
Silver-haired bat
Hoary bat
Big brown bat
Black bear
Raccoon
Bobcat
Least weasel
Short tailed weasel

Long-tailed weasel
Mink
Striped skunk
Badger
River otter
Gray fox
Red fox
Coyote
Gray wolf
White-tailed deer
Snowshoe hare
European hare
White-tailed jackrabbit
Eastern cottontail
Porcupine
Woodchuck
Thirteen-lined ground
    squirrel
Eastern chipmunk

Least chipmunk
Eastern fox squirrel
Eastern gray squirrel
Red squirrel
Southern flying squirrel
Northern flying squirrel
Plains gopher
Harvest mouse
White-footed mouse
Beaver
Southern bog lemming
Meadow vole
Red-backed vole
Prairie vole
Pine vole
Jumping mouse

Wyoming

Eastern mole
Vagrant shrew
Northern water shrew
Little brown bat
Pallid bat
Spotted bat
Red bat
Silver-haired bat
Hoary bat
Western big-eared bat

Black-footed ferret
Badger
River otter
Red fox
Kit fox
Coyote
Moose
Elk
Mule deer
White-tailed deer

Cliff chipmunk
Least chipmunk
Red squirrel
Spruce squirrel
Eastern fox squirrel
Black-tailed prairie dog
White-tailed prairie dog
Northern flying squirrel
Plains pocket gopher
Northern pocket gopher

Big brown bat
Big free-tailed bat
Black bear
Grizzly bear
Raccoon
Mountain lion
Bobcat
Lynx
Fisher
Marten
Short-tailed weasel
Long-tailed weasel
Mink
Striped skunk
Spotted skunk

Mountain goat
Bison
Pronghorn
Bighorn sheep
Pika
Snowshoe hare
White-tailed jackrabbit
Black-tailed jackrabbit
Mountain cottontail
Desert cottontail
Porcupine
Yellow-bellied marmot
Spotted ground squirrel
Thirteen-lined ground
    squirrel

Silky pocket mouse
Plains pocket mouse
Kangaroo rat
Grasshopper mouse
Harvest mouse
White-footed mouse
Beaver
Bushy-tailed wood rat
Mountain phenacomys
Meadow vole
Red-backed vole
Mountain vole
Prairie vole
Muskrat
Jumping mouse

CANADA

Alberta

Masked shrew
Vagrant shrew
Pygmy shrew
Northern water shrew
Little brown bat
Red bat
Silver-haired bat
Hoary bat
Big brown bat
Black bear
Grizzly bear
Raccoon
Mountain lion
Bobcat
Lynx
Fisher
Marten
Least weasel
Short-tailed weasel
Long-tailed weasel
Mink
Striped skunk
Wolverine

Badger
River otter
Red fox
Kit fox
Coyote
Gray wolf
Moose
Elk
Mule deer
White-tailed deer
Barren Ground caribou
Woodland caribou
Mountain goat
Bison
Pronghorn
Bighorn sheep
Pika
Snowshoe hare
White-tailed jackrabbit
Mountain cottontail
Porcupine
Woodchuck
Hoary marmot

Thirteen-lined ground
    squirrel
Yellow pine chipmunk
Least chipmunk
Red-tailed chipmunk
Red squirrel
Northern flying squirrel
Pocket gopher
Kangaroo rat
Grasshopper mouse
White-footed mouse
Beaver
Bushy-tailed wood rat
Northern bog lemming
Brown lemming
Mountain phenacomys
Meadow vole
Red-backed vole
Yellow-cheeked vole
Prairie vole
Muskrat
Jumping mouse

British Columbia

Shrew mole
Pacific water shrew
Masked shrew
Pygmy shrew
Northern water shrew
Little brown bat
Pallid bat
Red bat
Silver-haired bat
Hoary bat
Western big-eared bat
Big brown bat
Big free-tailed bat
Black bear
Grizzly bear
Raccoon
Mountain lion
Bobcat
Lynx
Fisher
Marten
Least weasel
Short-tailed weasel
Long-tailed weasel
Mink

Striped skunk
Spotted skunk
Wolverine
Badger
River otter
Red fox
Coyote
Gray wolf
Moose
Elk
Mule deer
White-tailed deer
Barren Ground caribou
Woodland caribou
Mountain goat
White sheep
Bighorn sheep
Pika
Snowshoe hare
White-tailed jackrabbit
Mountain cottontail
Porcupine
Hoary marmot
Yellow-bellied marmot
Woodchuck

Arctic ground squirrel
Chipmunk
Yellow pine chipmunk
Least chipmunk
Red chipmunk
Chickaree
Red squirrel
Northern flying squirrel
Pocket gopher
Pocket mouse
Harvest mouse
Beaver
Bushy-tailed wood rat
Northern bog lemming
Brown lemming
Mountain phenacomys
Meadow vole
Tundra vole
Red-backed vole
Yellow-cheeked vole
Mountain vole
Muskrat
Aplodontia
Jumping mouse

Manitoba

Star-nosed mole
Masked shrew
Pygmy shrew
Short-tailed shrew
Northern water shrew
Little brown bat
Red bat
Silver-haired bat
Hoary bat
Big brown bat
Polar bear
Black bear
Raccoon
Bobcat
Lynx
Fisher

Spotted skunk
Wolverine
Badger
River otter
Gray fox
Red fox
Arctic fox
Coyote
Gray wolf
Moose
Elk
Mule deer
White-tailed deer
Barren Ground caribou
Woodland caribou
Snowshoe hare

Thirteen-lined ground
  squirrel
Eastern chipmunk
Least chipmunk
Eastern gray squirrel
Red squirrel
Northern flying squirrel
Pocket gopher
Northern pocket gopher
Pocket mouse
Grasshopper mouse
White-footed mouse
Beaver
Northern bog lemming
Brown lemming
Collared lemming

Marten
Least weasel
Short-tailed weasel
Long-tailed weasel
Mink
Striped skunk

White-tailed jackrabbit
Arctic hare
Eastern cottontail
Porcupine
Woodchuck

Meadow vole
Red-backed vole
Yellow-cheeked vole
Muskrat
Jumping mouse

New Brunswick

Hairy-tailed mole
Star-nosed mole
Masked shrew
Pygmy shrew
Short-tailed shrew
Northern water shrew
Little brown bat
Red bat
Silver-haired bat
Hoary bat
Big brown bat
Black bear
Raccoon
Mountain lion

Bobcat
Lynx
Fisher
Marten
Short-tailed weasel
Long-tailed weasel
Mink
Striped skunk
River otter
Red fox
Coyote
Moose
White-tailed deer
Woodland caribou

Snowshoe hare
Porcupine
Woodchuck
Eastern chipmunk
Red squirrel
Northern flying squirrel
Beaver
Southern bog lemming
Northern bog lemming
Meadow vole
Red-backed vole
Yellow-nosed vole
Muskrat
Jumping mouse

Newfoundland

Star-nosed mole
Masked shrew
Pygmy shrew
Northern water shrew
Little brown bat
Polar bear
Black bear
Lynx
Fisher
Marten
Short-tailed weasel
Mink
Striped skunk

Wolverine
River otter
Red fox
Arctic fox
Gray wolf
Barren Ground caribou
Woodland caribou
Snowshoe hare
Arctic hare
Porcupine
Woodchuck
Eastern chipmunk
Red squirrel

Northern flying squirrel
Beaver
Northern bog lemming
Brown lemming
Phenacomys
Collared lemming
Meadow vole
Red-backed vole
Yellow-nosed vole
Muskrat
Jumping mouse

Northwest Territories

Masked shrew
Pygmy shrew
Northern water shrew
Little brown bat
Hoary bat

River otter
Red fox
Arctic fox
Coyote
Gray wolf

Arctic ground squirrel
Least chipmunk
Red squirrel
Northern flying squirrel
Deer mouse

Big brown bat
Polar bear
Black bear
Grizzly bear
Lynx
Fisher
Marten
Least weasel
Short-tailed weasel
Mink
Striped skunk
Wolverine

Moose
Mule deer
Woodland caribou
Barren Ground caribou
Musk-ox
Bison
White sheep
Snowshoe hare
Arctic hare
Porcupine
Hoary marmot
Woodchuck

Beaver
Northern bog lemming
Brown lemming
Phenacomys
Collared lemming
Meadow vole
Red-backed vole
Yellow-cheeked vole
Tundra vole
Muskrat
Jumping mouse

Nova Scotia

Star-nosed mole
Masked shrew
Pygmy shrew
Short-tailed shrew
Northern water shrew
Little brown bat
Silver-haired bat
Hoary bat
Big brown bat
Black bear
Raccoon
Bobcat

Fisher
Marten
Short-tailed weasel
Mink
Striped skunk
River otter
Red fox
Moose
White-tailed deer
Snowshoe hare
Porcupine
Woodchuck

Eastern chipmunk
Red squirrel
Northern flying squirrel
White-footed mouse
Beaver
Southern bog lemming
Meadow vole
Red-backed vole
Muskrat
Jumping mouse

Ontario

Opossum
Hairy-tailed mole
Star-nosed mole
Masked shrew
Pygmy shrew
Least shrew
Short-tailed shrew
Northern water shrew
Little brown bat
Eastern pipistrel
Red bat
Silver-haired bat
Hoary bat
Big brown bat
Polar bear

Fisher
Marten
Least weasel
Short-tailed weasel
Long-tailed weasel
Mink
Striped skunk
Wolverine
Badger
River otter
Red fox
Coyote
Gray wolf
Moose
White-tailed deer

Eastern cottontail
New England cottontail
Porcupine
Woodchuck
Eastern chipmunk
Least chipmunk
Eastern gray squirrel
Red squirrel
Northern flying squirrel
White-footed mouse
Beaver
Bog lemming
Phenacomys
Meadow vole
Red-backed vole

Black bear
Raccoon
Bobcat
Lynx

Barren Ground caribou
Woodland caribou
Snowshoe hare
European hare

Yellow-nosed vole
Muskrat
Jumping mouse

Prince Edward Island

Masked shrew
Little brown bat
Raccoon

Mink
Striped skunk
River otter

White-tailed deer
Eastern chipmunk

Quebec

Hairy-tailed mole
Star-nosed mole
Masked shrew
Pygmy shrew
Short-tailed shrew
Northern water shrew
Little brown bat
Eastern pipistrel
Red bat
Silver-haired bat
Hoary bat
Big brown bat
Polar bear
Black bear
Raccoon
Bobcat
Lynx
Fisher
Marten

Least weasel
Short-tailed weasel
Long-tailed weasel
Mink
Striped skunk
Wolverine
River otter
Gray fox
Red fox
Arctic fox
Coyote
Gray wolf
Moose
White-tailed deer
Woodland caribou
Barren Ground caribou
Snowshoe hare
Arctic hare
European hare

New England cottontail
Porcupine
Woodchuck
Eastern chipmunk
Eastern gray squirrel
Red squirrel
Northern flying squirrel
Beaver
Bog lemming
Brown lemming
Collared lemming
Phenacomys
Meadow vole
Red-backed vole
Yellow-nosed vole
Muskrat
Jumping mouse

Saskatchewan

Masked shrew
Pygmy shrew
Short-tailed shrew
Northern water shrew
Little brown bat
Red bat
Silver-haired bat
Hoary bat
Big brown bat
Black bear
Raccoon
Bobcat

Black-footed ferret
Badger
River otter
Red fox
Kit fox
Coyote
Gray wolf
Moose
Elk
Mule deer
White-tailed deer
Barren Ground caribou

Least chipmunk
Red squirrel
Northern flying squirrel
Black-tailed prairie dog
Pocket gopher
Pocket mouse
Grasshopper mouse
Kangaroo rat
White-footed mouse
Beaver
Bushy-tailed wood rat
Bog lemming

Lynx
Fisher
Marten
Least weasel
Short-tailed weasel
Long-tailed weasel
Mink
Striped skunk
Wolverine

Woodland caribou
Pronghorn
Snowshoe hare
White-tailed jackrabbit
Mountain cottontail
Porcupine
Woodchuck
Thirteen-lined ground squir-
rel

Brown lemming
Phenacomys
Meadow vole
Red-backed vole
Yellow-cheeked vole
Muskrat
Jumping mouse

Yukon Territory

Masked shrew
Northern water shrew
Pygmy shrew
Little brown bat
Black bear
Grizzly bear
Big brown bear
Polar bear
Marten
Fisher
Least weasel
Short-tailed weasel
Mink
Wolverine
River otter
Red fox
Arctic fox

Coyote
Gray wolf
Lynx
Woodchuck
Hoary marmot
Ground squirrel
Least chipmunk
Red squirrel
Northern flying squirrel
Beaver
Wood mouse
Bushy-tailed wood rat
Meadow vole
Long-tailed vole
Phenacomys
Bog lemming
Brown lemming

Collared lemming
Red-backed vole
Muskrat
Jumping mouse
Porcupine
Collared pika
Snowshoe hare
Mule deer
Moose
Barren Ground caribou
Musk-ox
Mountain sheep
Dall sheep
Stone sheep
Mountain goat

8. THE NATIONAL PARKS OF CANADA

The National Parks Branch of the Department of Northern Affairs and National Resources supervises 29,276 square miles of superb natural settings in Canada's varied geological landscapes. Strictly controlled, beautifully kept, these great national parks, eighteen in all, are something in which the entire world can rejoice. It is devoutly to be wished that the people of Canada never lose interest in this priceless heritage. Surely these parks are the gifts each generation gives to the next. They are a sacred trust.

DATE FIRST VISITED	NAME OF PARK	LOCATION
_____	Mount Revelstoke	British Columbia
_____	Glacier	British Columbia
_____	Yoho	British Columbia
_____	Kootenay	British Columbia
_____	Jasper	Alberta
_____	Banff	Alberta
_____	Waterton Lakes	Alberta
_____	Elk Island	Alberta
_____	Wood Buffalo	Alberta– Northwest Territories
_____	Prince Albert	Saskatchewan
_____	Riding Mountain	Manitoba
_____	Point Pelee	Ontario
_____	Georgian Bay Islands	Ontario
_____	St. Lawrence Islands	Ontario
_____	Fundy	New Brunswick
_____	Prince Edward Island	Prince Edward Island
_____	Cape Breton Highlands	Nova Scotia
_____	Terra Nova	Newfoundland

9. NATIONAL PARKS OF THE UNITED STATES AND AREAS ADMINISTERED BY THE NATIONAL PARK SERVICE

As of January 1, 1966, The National Park Service controlled 26,548,693 acres of federally owned lands. These lands are divided into 192 units that come under sixteen category headings. These categories are:

TYPE OF AREA	NUMBER	FEDERAL LAND (ACRES)
National Parks	32	13,619,099+
National Historical Parks	10	33,358+
National Monuments	77	8,941,778+
National Military Parks	11	29,367+
National Memorial Parks	1	69,000+
National Battlefields	5	2,733+
National Battlefield Parks	4	7,162+
National Battlefield Sites	3	780+
National Historic Sites	23	3,088+
National Memorials	16	5,319+
National Cemeteries	10	220+
National Seashores	6	198,077+
National Parkways	3	106,411+
National Capital Parks	1	34,873+
National Recreation Areas	11	3,497,402
White House	1	18+
	192	26,548,685+

Of these sixteen categories, the National Parks, the National Monuments, and the National Recreation Areas will offer the most opportunities for the observation of wildlife. For the use of the reader the areas included under these headings are listed in the following tables. Anyone truly involved in the subject of North American wildlife will want to visit as many of these areas as possible. For that reason the lists are indicated as checklists. It will be no mere coincidence that your progress on the chart in Appendix 2 will be reflected in your progress on the charts that follow.

The National Parks of the United States

DATE FIRST VISITED	NAME OF PARK	LOCATION
————	Acadia	Maine
————	Big Bend	Texas
————	Bryce Canyon	Utah
————	Canyonlands	Utah
————	Carlsbad Caverns	New Mexico
————	Crater Lake	Oregon
————	Everglades	Florida
————	Glacier	Montana
————	Grand Canyon	Arizona
————	Grand Teton	Wyoming
————	Great Smoky Mountains	North Carolina–Tennessee
————	Haleakala	Hawaii
————	Hawaii Volcanoes	Hawaii
————	Hot Springs	Arkansas
————	Isle Royale	Michigan
————	Kings Canyon	California
————	Lassen Volcanic	California
————	Mammoth Cave	Kentucky
————	Mesa Verde	Colorado
————	Mount McKinley	Alaska
————	Mount Rainier	Washington
————	Olympic	Washington
————	Petrified Forest	Arizona
————	Platt	Oklahoma
————	Rocky Mountain	Colorado
————	Sequoia	California
————	Shenandoah	Virginia
————	Virgin Islands	Virgin Islands
————	Wind Cave	South Dakota
————	Yellowstone	Wyoming
————	Yosemite	California
————	Zion	Utah

The National Monuments of the United States

DATE FIRST VISITED	NAME OF MONUMENT	LOCATION
————	Arches	Utah
————	Aztec Ruins	New Mexico
————	Badlands	South Dakota
————	Bandelier	New Mexico
————	Black Canyon of the Gunnison	Colorado
————	Booker T. Washington	Virginia
————	Buck Island Reef	Virgin Islands
————	Cabrillo	California
————	Canyon de Chelly	Arizona
————	Capitol Reef	Utah
————	Capulin Mountain	New Mexico
————	Casa Grande Ruins	Arizona
————	Castillo de San Marcos	Florida
————	Castle Clinton	New York
————	Cedar Breaks	Utah
————	Chaco Canyon	New Mexico
————	Channel Islands	California
————	Chesapeake and Ohio Canal	Maryland–West Virginia
————	Chiricahua	Arizona
————	Colorado	Colorado
————	Craters of the Moon	Idaho
————	Custer Battlefield	Montana
————	Death Valley	California
————	Devils Postpile	California
————	Devils Tower	Wyoming
————	Dinosaur	Utah–Colorado
————	Effigy Mounds	Iowa
————	El Morro	New Mexico
————	Fort Frederica	Georgia
————	Fort Jefferson	Florida
————	Fort McHenry	Maryland
————	Fort Matanzas	Florida
————	Fort Pulaski	Georgia
————	Fort Sumter	South Carolina
————	Fort Union	New Mexico
————	George Washington Birthplace	Virginia
————	George Washington Carver	Missouri
————	Gila Cliff Dwellings	New Mexico
————	Glacier Bay	Alaska
————	Grand Canyon	Arizona

DATE FIRST VISITED	NAME OF MONUMENT	LOCATION
⸻	Grand Portage	Minnesota
⸻	Gran Quivira	New Mexico
⸻	Great Sand Dunes	Colorado
⸻	Homestead	Nebraska
⸻	Hovenweep	Utah–Colorado
⸻	Jewel Cave	South Dakota
⸻	Joshua Tree	California
⸻	Katmai	Alaska
⸻	Lava Beds	California
⸻	Lehman Caves	Nevada
⸻	Montezuma Castle	Arizona
⸻	Mound City Group	Ohio
⸻	Muir Woods	California
⸻	Natural Bridges	Utah
⸻	Navajo	Arizona
⸻	Ocmulgee	Georgia
⸻	Oregon Caves	Oregon
⸻	Organ Pipe Cactus	Arizona
⸻	Perry's Victory and International Peace Memorial	Ohio
⸻	Pinnacles	California
⸻	Pipe Spring	Arizona
⸻	Pipestone	Minnesota
⸻	Rainbow Bridge	Utah
⸻	Russell Cave	Alabama
⸻	Saguaro	Arizona
⸻	Scotts Bluff	Nebraska
⸻	Sitka	Alaska
⸻	Statue of Liberty	New York
⸻	Sunset Crater	Arizona
⸻	Timpanogos Cave	Utah
⸻	Tonto	Arizona
⸻	Tumacacori	Arizona
⸻	Tuzigoot	Arizona
⸻	Walnut Canyon	Arizona
⸻	White Sands	New Mexico
⸻	Wupatki	Arizona
⸻	Yucca House	Colorado

The National Recreation Areas of the United States

DATE FIRST VISITED	NAME OF RECREATION AREA	LOCATION
_____	Amistad	Texas
_____	Arbuckle	Oklahoma
_____	Bighorn Canyon	Wyoming–Montana
_____	Coulee Dam	Washington
_____	Curecanti	Colorado
_____	Flaming Gorge	Utah–Wyoming
_____	Glen Canyon	Arizona–Utah
_____	Lake Mead	Arizona–Nevada
_____	Sanford	Texas
_____	Shadow Mountain	Colorado
_____	Whiskeytown–Shasta–Trinity	California

10. DIRECTORY OF UNITED STATES NATIONAL WILDLIFE REFUGES

On June 30, 1964, there existed 297 National Wildlife Refuges in the United States and Territories administered by the Bureau of Sport Fisheries and Wildlife of the U.S. Fish and Wildlife Service in the Department of the Interior—28,301,288 acres thus dedicated to the preservation of our native species. The refuges are classified as follows:

CLASS	TYPE	NUMBER	ACREAGE
W or W-E	Migratory Bird Refuges, including 55 on private land (W-E)—Waterfowl	229	3,612,430
G	Migratory Bird Refuges—General	46	3,708,590
BG	Big Game Refuges	14	5,190,994
GR	Game Ranges	5	4,604,258
WR	National Wildlife Ranges	3	11,185,016
		297	28,301,288

REFUGE	COUNTY	ACREAGE	CLASS
	Alabama		
Choctaw*	Choctaw	4,218	W
Eufaula† (*see also* Ga.)	Barbour, Russel	†	W
Wheeler	Morgan, Limestone, Madison	34,988	W
	Alaska		
	(*Judicial Divisions*)		
Aleutian Islands	Third	2,720,235	G
Arctic National Wildlife Range	Fourth	8,900,000	WR
Bering Sea	Second	41,113	G
Bogoslof	Third	390	G
Chamisso	Second	641	G
Clarence Rhode National Wildlife Range	Fourth, Second	1,870,000	WR
Forrester Island	First	2,832	G
Hazen Bay	Fourth	6,800	W
Hazy Islands	First	41+	G
Izembeck National Wildlife Range	Third	415,015+	WR

* Unless otherwise designated, add "National Wildlife Refuge" to the name of each area.
† Refuge in process of establishment; not counted in totals.

REFUGE	COUNTY	ACREAGE	CLASS
Kenai National Moose Range	Third	1,730,000	BG
Kodiak	Third	1,815,000	BG
Nunivak	Second	1,109,384+	BG
Pribilof Reservation	Third	173	G
St. Lazaria	First	64+	G
Semidi	Third	8,422	G
Simeonof	Third	10,442	BG
Tuxedni	Third	6,439+	G

Arizona

Cabeza Prieta Game Range	Yuma, Pima	860,000	GR
Cibola† (see also Cal.)	Yuma	†	W
Havasu Lake (see also Cal.)	Mohave, Yuma	26,576+	W
Imperial (see also Cal.)	Yuma	28,711+	W
Kofa Game Range	Yuma	660,000	GR

Arkansas

Big Lake	Mississippi	9,900+	W
Holla Bend	Pope	4,082+	W
Wapanocca	Crittenden	3,789+	W
White River	Arkansas, Desha, Monroe, Phillips	112,312+	W

California

Cibola† (see also Ariz.)	Imperial	†	W
Clear Lake	Modoc	33,439+	W
Colusa	Colusa	4,039+	W
Delevan		5,633+	W
Farallon	Marin	91	G
Havasu Lake (see also Ariz.)	San Bernardino	17,753+	W
Imperial (see also Ariz.)	Imperial	14,670+	W
Kern	Kern	10,543+	W
Lower Klamath (see also Oreg.)	Siskiyou	21,458+	W
Merced	Merced	·2,561+	W
Modoc	Modoc	5,966	W
Pixley	Tulare	4,328	W
Sacramento	Glenn, Colusa	10,755+	W
Salton Sea	Imperial	36,366+	W
Sutter	Sutter	2,590+	W
Tule Lake	Modoc, Siskiyou	37,336+	W

REFUGE	COUNTY	ACREAGE	CLASS
	Colorado		
Alamosa	Alamosa	1,774+	W
Brown's Park†	Moffat	†	W
Monte Vista	Alamosa, Rio Grande	13,674+	W
	Delaware		
Bombay Hook	Kent	14,854+	W
Killcohook (*see also* N.J.)	New Castle	580	W
Prime Hook	Sussex	338+	W
	Florida		
Anclote	Pasco, Pinellas	208+	G
Brevard	Brevard	12+	G
Cedar Keys	Levy	378+	G
Chassahowitzka	Citrus, Hernando	28,617+	W
Great White Heron	Monroe	1,996+	G
Island Bay	Charlotte	20+	G
Key West	Monroe	2,019+	G
Lake Woodruff	Volusa	4,980	W
Loxahatchee	Palm Beach, Broward	145,524+	W
Merritt Island	Brevard	25,300	W
National Key Deer	Monroe	6,744+	BG
Passage Key	Manatee	36+	G
Pelican Island	Indian River	616	G
Pinellas	Pinellas	278	G
St. Marks	Jefferson, Taylor, Wakulla	65,135+	W
Sanibel	Lee	1,314	W
	Georgia		
Blackbeard Island	McIntosh	5,617+	W
Eufaula† (*see also* Ala.)		†	W
Harris Neck	McIntosh	2,686+	W
Oconee†	Wilkinson	†	W
Okefenokee	Charlton, Clinch, Ware	330,973+	G
Piedmont	Jones, Jasper	32,898+	W
Savannah (*see also* S.C.)	Chatham	5,413+	W
Tybee	Chatham	100	G
Wolf Island	McIntosh	538	W
	Hawaii		
Hawaiian Islands	Kauai	1,765	G

REFUGE	COUNTY	ACREAGE	CLASS
	Idaho		
Camas	Jefferson	10,535	W
Deer Flat	Canyon	11,403+	W
Kootenai†	Boundary	†	W
Minidoka	Cassia, Blaine, Power, Minidoka	25,629+	W
	Illinois		
Chautauqua	Mason	4,488+	W
Crab Orchard	Williamson, Union, Jackson	42,963+	W
Mark Twain (*see also* Iowa and Mo.)	Adams, Calhoun, Jersey, Mercer	12,459	W
Upper Mississippi River Wild Life and Fish Refuge (*see also* Iowa, Minn., and Wis.)	Carroll, Jo Daviess, Rock Island, Whiteside	23,260+	W
	Iowa		
De Soto (*see also* Nebr.)	Harrison, Pottawattami	3,463	W
Mark Twain (*see also* Ill. and Mo.)	Des Moines, Louisa, Muscatine	10,328	W
Union Slough	Kossuth	2,077+	W
Upper Mississippi River Wild Life and Fish Refuge (*see also* Ill., Minn., and Wis.)	All counties along the river from Scott County north	50,637+	W
	Kansas		
Flint Hills†	Coffey, Lyon	†	W
Kirwin	Phillips	10,777+	W
Quivira	Stafford, Rice	14,350+	W
	Kentucky		
Kentucky Woodlands	Trigg, Lyon	65,712+	W
Reelfoot (*see also* Tenn.)	Fulton	2,029+	W
	Louisiana		
Breton	Plaquemines	7,512	G
Catahoula	LaSalle	4,308+	W
Delta	Plaquemines	48,799+	W
East Timbalier Island	Terrebonne	337	G

REFUGE	COUNTY	ACREAGE	CLASS
Lacassine	Cameron	31,124+	W
Sabine	Cameron	142,716+	W
Shell Keys	Iberia	8	G

Maine

Moosehorn	Washington	22,565+	W

Maryland

Blackwater	Dorchester	11,216+	W
Chincoteague (*see also* Va.)	Somerset	417+	W
Eastern Neck	Kent	675+	W
Martin	Somerset	4,313+	W
Susquehanna	Hartford, Cecil	3+	W

Massachusetts

Great Meadows	Essex	216+	W
Monomoy	Barnstable	2,697+	W
Parker River	Essex	4,649+	W
Sudbury	Middlesex	151+	W

Michigan

Huron	Marquette	147	G
Michigan Islands	Alpena, Charlevoix	11+	G
Seney	Schoolcraft	95,455+	W
Shiawassee	Saginaw	6,323+	W
Wyandotte	Wayne	304+	W

Minnesota

Agassiz	Marshall	61,009+	W
Mille Lacs	Mille Lacs	1—	G
Rice Lake	Aitkin	16,476+	W
Tamarac	Becker	37,796+	W
Upper Mississippi River Wild Life and Fish Refuge (*see also* Ill., Iowa, and Wis.)	Houston, Winona, Wabasha, Goodhue	33,222+	W

Mississippi

Davis Island	Warren	69+	W
Horn Island	Jackson	2,418+	W
Noxubee	Winston, Noxubee, Oktibbeha	45,628+	W
Petit Bois	Jackson	748+	W
Yazoo	Washington	7,782+	W

REFUGE	COUNTY	ACREAGE	CLASS
	Missouri		
Mark Twain (*see also* Iowa and Ill.)	St. Charles	232	W
Mingo	Wayne, Stoddard	21,645+	W
Squaw Creek	Holt	6,809+	W
Swan Lake	Charlton	10,676+	W
	Montana		
Benton Lake	Cascade, Chouteau	12,382+	W
Black Coulee	Blaine	1,480	W–E
Bowdoin	Phillips	15,436+	W
Charles M. Russell National Wildlife Range (Fort Peck)	Valley, Garfield, Petroleum, Fergus, Phillips, McCone	375,677+ 575,624+	GR G
Creedman Coulee	Hill	2,728	W–E
Hailstone	Stillwater	2,240	W–E
Halfbreed Lake	Stillwater	3,096+	W–E
Hewitt Lake	Phillips	1,680+	W–E
Lake Mason	Musselshell	18,173	W
Lake Thibadeau	Hill	3,508+	W–E
Lamesteer	Wibaux	800	W–E
Medicine Lake	Roosevelt, Sheridan	31,457+	W
National Bison Range	Sanders, Lake	18,540+	BG
Ninepipe	Lake	2,022	W
Pablo	Lake	2,542	W
Pishkun	Teton	8,194+	W–E
Ravalli	Ravalli	1,006+	W
Red Rock Lakes	Beaverhead	39,946+	W
War Horse	Petroleum	3,192+	W
Willow Creek	Lewis and Clark	3,118+	W
	Nebraska		
Crescent Lake	Garden	45,996+	W
De Soto (*see also* Iowa)	Washington	4,324+	W
Fort Niobrara	Cherry	19,122+	BG
North Platte	Scottsbluff, Sioux	5,047+	W
Valentine	Cherry	71,515+	W
	Nevada		
Anaho Island	Washoe	247+	G
Charles Sheldon Antelope Range (*see also* Oreg.)	Washoe, Humboldt	520,524+ 23,372+	GR BG

REFUGE	COUNTY	ACREAGE	CLASS
Desert Game Range	Clark, Lincoln	2,188,455+	GR
		323+	BG
Fallon	Churchill	17,901+	W
Pahranagat	Lincoln	5,033	W
Ruby Lake	Elko, White Pine	35,697+	W
Sheldon National Antelope Refuge	Washoe	34,131+	BG
Stillwater	Churchill	24,203+	W

New Jersey

Brigantine	Atlantic	15,122	W
Great Swamp	Morris	1,870	W
Killcohook	Salem	906+	W
Troy Meadows	Morris	1,089	W

New Mexico

Bitter Lake	Chaves	24,083+	W
Bosque del Apache	Socorro	57,191+	W
Burford Lake	Rio Arriba	2,000	W
San Andres	Dona Ana	57,216+	BG

New York

Iroquois (formerly Oak Orchard)	Genesee, Orleans	6,328+	W
Montezuma	Seneca	6,803+	W
Morton	Suffolk	187+	W
Wertheim	Suffolk	11+	W

North Carolina

Mackay Island (*see also* Va.)	Currituck	5,981+	W
Mattamuskeet	Hyde	50,177+	W
Pea Island	Dare	5,880+	W
Pee Dee	Anson, Richmond	936+	W
Pungo	Washington, Hyde	11,895+	W
Swanquarter	Hyde	15,500+	W

North Dakota

Appert Lake	Emmons	1,160+	W–E
Ardoch	Walsh	2,676+	W–E
Arrowwood	Stutsman, Foster	15,934+	W
Bone Hill	LaMoure	640	W–E

REFUGE	COUNTY	ACREAGE	CLASS
Brumba	Towner	1,977+	W–E
Buffalo Lake	Pierce	2,096+	W–E
Camp Lake	McLean	1,224+	W–E
Canfield Lake	Burleigh	453+	W–E
Chase Lake	Stutsman	4,384+	W
Cottonwood Lake	McHenry	1,013+	W–E
Dakota Lake	Dickey	2,756	W–E
Des Lacs	Burke, Ward	18,881	W
Flickertail	Emmons	640	W–E
Florence Lake	Burleigh	1,888+	W
Half-Way Lake	Stutsman	160	W–E
Hiddenwood	McLean, Ward	568+	W–E
Hobart Lake	Barnes	2,073+	W–E
Hutchinson Lake	Kidder	478+	W–E
Johnson Lake	Nelson, Eddy	2,007+	W–E
Kellys Slough	Grand Forks	1,620	W–E
Lac aux Mortes	Ramsey	5,881+	W–E
Lake Elsie	Richland	634+	W–E
Lake George	Kidder	3,118+	W–E
Lake Ilo	Dunn	4,038+	W
Lake Nettie	McLean	2,400	W–E
Lake Zahl	Williams	3,823+	W
Lambs Lake	Nelson	1,286+	W–E
Little Goose	Grand Forks	359	W–E
Long Lake	Burleigh, Kidder	22,310+	W
Lords Lake	Bottineau, Rolette	1,915+	W–E
Lost Lake	McLean	960+	W–E
Lostwood	Burke, Mountrail	26,747+	W
Lower Souris	Bottineau, McHenry	58,693+	W
Maple River	Dickey	800	W–E
McLean	McLean	760	W
Pleasant Lake	Benson	897+	W–E
Pretty Rock	Grant	800	W–E
Rabb Lake	Rolette	260+	W–E
Rock Lake	Towner	5,506+	W–E
Rose Lake	Nelson	872+	W–E
School Section Lake	Rolette	680	W–E
Shell Lake	Mountrail	1,835+	C–E
Sheyenne Lake	Sheridan	797+	W–E
Sibley Lake	Griggs	1,077+	W–E
Silver Lake	Benson, Ramsey	3,347+	W–E
Slade	Kidder	3,000+	W
Snake Creek	McLean	13,498	W

REFUGE	COUNTY	ACREAGE	CLASS
Snyder Creek	Towner	1,550+	W–E
Springwater	Emmons	640	W–E
Stewart Lake	Slope	2,230+	W–E
Stoney Slough	Barnes	1,540	W–E
Storm Lake	Sargent	685+	W–E
Stump Lake	Nelson	27+	G
Sullys Hill National Game Preserve	Benson	1,673+	BG
Sunburst Lake	Emmons	327+	W–E
Tewaukon	Sargent	7,447+	W
Tomahawk	Barnes	440	W–E
Upper Souris	Renville, Ward	32,088+	W
White Lake	Slope	1,040	W
Wild Rice Lake	Sargent	778+	W–E
Willow Lake	Rolette	2,847+	W–E
Wintering River	McHenry	399+	W–E
Wood Lake	Benson	280	W–E

Ohio

REFUGE	COUNTY	ACREAGE	CLASS
Cedar Point†	Lucas	†	W
Ottawa	Lucas, Ottawa	2,322+	W
West Sister Island	Lucas	82	G

Oklahoma

REFUGE	COUNTY	ACREAGE	CLASS
Salt Plains	Alfalfa	32,431+	W
Tishomingo	Johnston, Marshall	16,619	W
Washita	Custer	8,200	W
Wichita Mountains Wildlife Refuge	Comanche	59,019+	BG

Oregon

REFUGE	COUNTY	ACREAGE	CLASS
Cape Meares	Tillamook	138+	G
Charles Sheldon Antelope Range (*see also* Nev.)	Lake	627+	BG
Cold Springs	Umatilla	3,116+	W
Hart Mountain National Antelope Refuge	Lake	239,933 731+	BG W
Klamath Forest	Klamath	15,225+	W
Lower Klamath (*see also* Cal.)	Klamath	1,336+	W
Malheur	Harney	180,850+	W
McKay Creek	Umatilla	1,836+	W
Oregon Islands	Curry	21	G

REFUGE	COUNTY	ACREAGE	CLASS
Three Arch Rocks	Tillamook	17	G
Upper Klamath	Klamath	12,532+	W
Willamette	Benton	3,842+	W

Pennsylvania

Erie	Crawford	3,994+	W

South Carolina

Cape Romain	Charleston	34,697+	W
Carolina Sandhills	Chesterfield	45,011+	W
Santee	Clarendon, Berkeley	73,308+	W
Savannah (*see also* Ga.)	Jasper	7,229+	W

South Dakota

Bear Butte	Meade	436	W–E
Belle Fourche	Butte	13,680	W
Lacreek	Bennett	9,442	W
Lake Andes	Charles Mix	861+	W
Sand Lake	Brown	21,430+	W
Waubay	Day	4,649+	W

Tennessee

Cross Creeks	Stewart	8,000	W
Hatchie†	Haywood	†	W
Lake Isom	Lake, Obion	1,849+	W
Reelfoot (*see also* Ky.)	Lake, Obion	9,141+	W
Tennessee	Henry, Benton, Humphreys, Decatur	50,819	W

Texas

Anahuac	Chambers	9,836+	W
Aransas	Aransas, Refugio, Calhoun	47,261+	W
Buffalo Lake	Randall	7,663+	W
Hagerman	Grayson	11,319+	W
Laguna Atascosa	Cameron	44,651+	W
Muleshoe	Bailey	5,809+	W
Santa Ana	Hidalgo	1,980+	G

Utah

Bear River Migratory Bird Refuge	Box Elder	64,895	W
Fish Springs	Juab	17,992+	W

REFUGE	COUNTY	ACREAGE	CLASS
Locomotive Springs	Box Elder	1,031	W
Ouray	Uintah	10,335	W

Vermont

Missisquoi	Franklin	4,226	W

Virginia

Back Bay	Princess Anne	4,588+	W
Chincoteague (*see also* Md.)	Accomack	9,029+	W
Mackay Island (*see also* N.C.)	Princess Anne	842+	W
Presquile	Chesterfield	1,328+	W

Washington

Columbia	Adams, Grant	28,406+	W
Copalis	Grays Harbor	5	G
Dungeness	Clallam	556+	W
Flattery Rocks	Clallam	125	G
Jones Island	San Juan	188+	G
Little Pend Oreille	Stevens	41,707+	BG
		2,251+	W
Matia Island	San Juan	145	G
McNary	Walla Walla	2,867+	W
Quillayute Needles	Clallam, Jefferson	117	G
San Juan	San Juan	52	G
Smith Island	Island	65	W
Toppenish	Yakima	260	W
Turnbull	Spokane	17,171+	W
Willapa	Pacific	8,174+	W

Wisconsin

Gravel Island	Door	27	G
Green Bay	Door	2	G
Horicon	Dodge, Fond du Lac	20,795+	W
Necedah	Juneau, Wood	39,607	W
Trempealeau	Trempealeau	706+	W
Upper Mississippi Wild Life and Fish Refuge (*see also* Ill., Iowa, Minn.)	Crawford, Buffalo, Vernon, Trempealeau, Grant, LaCrosse	87,974+	W

Wyoming

Bamforth	Albany	1,166	W
Hutton Lake	Albany	1.986+	W
National Elk Refuge	Teton	23,774+	BG

REFUGE	COUNTY	ACREAGE	CLASS
Pathfinder	Natrona, Carbon	46,341+	W
Seedskadee†	Sweetwater	†	W

Territories

Culebra	Humaceo District, Puerto Rico	3,000	G
Johnston Island	Pacific Ocean	100	G

11. CONSERVATION ORGANIZATIONS

One of the nice things about your interest in wildlife is that you are not alone. Thousands, millions of the nicest people in the world share your enthusiasm. Meeting with these people, learning from them, and contributing whatever share of your means you can to the work of the organizations they form, can be tremendously satisfying. Many of these groups publish excellent magazines on a regular basis and offer a subscription as one small reward of membership. Make your interest in the natural world around you an active one. Participate, contribute, make a gift of our natural world to the generations to follow.

Principal Conservation Groups

American Fisheries Society
1404 New York Avenue NW
Washington 5, D.C.

The American Forestry Association
919 17th Street NW
Washington 6, D.C.

American Ornithologists' Union, Inc.
Chicago Natural History Museum
Roosevelt Road and Lake Shore Drive
Chicago 5, Illinois

American Planning and Civic Association
901 Union Trust Building
Washington 5, D.C.

American Society of Mammalogists
Museum of Zoology
University of Michigan
Ann, Arbor, Michigan

Association of Midwest Fish and Game
    Commissioners
c/o C.H.D. Clarke, Chief Fish and Game
    Branch
Ontario Department of Lands and Forests
Parliament Buildings
Toronto, Ontario, Canada

Boy Scouts of America
National Council
New Brunswick, New Jersey

The Conservation Foundation
30 East 40th Street
New York 16, New York

Defenders of Wildlife
809 Dupont Circle Building
346 Connecticut Ave. NW
Washington 16, D.C.

Ducks Unlimited
165 Broadway
New York 6, New York

The Garden Club of America
598 Madison Avenue
New York 22, New York

The Izaak Walton League of America
1326 Waukegan Road
Glenview, Illinois

National Audubon Society
1130 Fifth Avenue
New York 28, New York

National Parks Association
1300 New Hampshire Avenue NW
Washington 6, D.C.

National Wildlife Federation
1412 Sixteenth Street NW
Washington, D.C. 20036

The Nature Conservancy
2039 K Street NW
Washington 6, D.C.

New York Zoological Society
30 East 40th Street
New York 16, New York

Sierra Club
1050 Mills Tower
San Francisco 4, California

The Wilderness Society
2144 Street, NW
Washington 7, D.C.

Wildlife Management Institute
709 Wire Building
Washington 5, D.C.

Wildlife Restoration, Inc.
17 West 60th Street
New York 23, New York

The Wildlife Society
2000 P Street NW
Washington 6, D.C.

World Wildlife Fund
American National Appeal
910 17th Street, NW
Washington, D.C. 20006

Canadian Audubon Society
46 St. Clair Avenue East
Toronto 7, Canada

Ottawa Field-Naturalist Club
Ottawa, Ontario, Canada

State Conservation Authorities

ALABAMA
Division of Game, Fish and Seafoods
Department of Conservation
Montgomery 4

ALASKA
Department of Fish and Game
229 Alaska Office Building
Juneau

ARIZONA
Game and Fish Commission
Arizona State Building
Phoenix

ARKANSAS
Game and Fish Commission
State Capitol
Little Rock

CALIFORNIA
Department of Fish and Game
722 Capitol Avenue
Sacramento 14

COLORADO
Game and Fish Commission
1530 Sherman Street
Denver 5

CONNECTICUT
Board of Fisheries and Game
State Office Building
Hartford 15

DELAWARE
Board of Game and Fish Commissioners
Dover

DISTRICT OF COLUMBIA
Superintendent, Metropolitan Police,
Washington

FLORIDA
Game and Fresh Water Fish Commission
646 West Tennessee
Tallahassee

GEORGIA
Game and Fish Commission
401 State Capitol
Atlanta 3

HAWAII
Division of Fish and Game
Box 5425
Honolulu

IDAHO
Department of Fish and Game
P.O. Box 25
Boise

ILLINOIS
State Conservation Commission
State Office Building
Springfield

INDIANA
Division of Fish and Game
Department of Conservation
311 West Washington Street
Indianapolis 9

IOWA
State Conservation Commission
East Seventh and Court Streets
Des Moines 9

KANSAS
Forestry, Fish and Game Commission
Box 581
Pratt

KENTUCKY
Department of Fish and Wildlife Resources
Frankfort

LOUISIANA
State Wildlife and Fisheries Commission
400 Royal Street
New Orleans 16

MAINE
Department of Inland Fisheries and Game
State House
Augusta

MARYLAND
Game and Inland Fish Commission
State Office Building
Annapolis

MASSACHUSETTS
Division of Fisheries and Game
73 Tremont Street
Boston 8

MICHIGAN
Department of Conservation
Lansing 26

MINNESOTA
Department of Conservation
State Office Building
St. Paul 1

MISSISSIPPI
Game and Fish Commission
Woolfolk State Office Building
Jackson

MISSOURI
Conservation Commission
Farm Bureau Building
Jefferson City

MONTANA
State Fish and Game Department
State Capitol
Helena

NEBRASKA
Game, Forestation and Parks Commission
Lincoln 29

NEVADA
Fish and Game Commission
Box 678
Reno

NEW HAMPSHIRE
Fish and Game Department
State House Annex
Concord

NEW JERSEY
Department of Conservation and
    Economic Development
Division of Fish and Game
230 West State Street
Trenton 7

NEW MEXICO
Department of Game and Fish
Santa Fe

NEW YORK
Conservation Department
1220 Washington Avenue
Albany

NORTH CAROLINA
Wildlife Resources Commission
Box 2919
Raleigh

NORTH DAKOTA
Game and Fish Department
State Capitol
Bismarck

OHIO
Division of Wildlife
Department of Natural Resources
1500 Dublin Road
Columbus 12

OKLAHOMA
Department of Wildlife Conservation
State Capitol Building
Oklahoma City 5

OREGON
State Game Commission
P.O. Box 4136
Portland 8

PENNSYLVANIA
Pennsylvania Game Commission
Harrisburg

PUERTO RICO
Department of Agriculture and Commerce
Division of Fisheries and Wildlife
Box 10163
Santurce Station, San Juan

RHODE ISLAND
Division of Fish and Game
Department of Agriculture and
    Conservation
State House
Providence 2

SOUTH CAROLINA
Wildlife Resources Commission
Box 360
Columbia

SOUTH DAKOTA
Department of Game, Fish and Parks
State Office Building
Pierre

TENNESSEE
Tennessee Game and Fish Commission
Cordell Hull Building
Sixth Avenue, North
Nashville 3

TEXAS
Game and Fish Commission
Austin

UTAH
Department of Fish and Game
    Commission
1596 West North Temple
Salt Lake City 16

VERMONT
Fish and Game Service
Montpelier

VIRGINIA
Commission of Game and Inland Fisheries
P.O. Box 1642
Richmond 13

WASHINGTON
Department of Game
600 N. Capitol Way
Olympia

WEST VIRGINIA
Conservation Commission of West Virginia
State Office Building No. 3
Charleston

WISCONSIN
Conservation Department
State Office Building
Box 450
Madison 1

WYOMING
Game and Fish Commission
Box 378
Cheyenne

Canadian Provincial Organizations

BRITISH COLUMBIA
Fish and Game Branch
Department of Recreation and Conservation
Victoria

ALBERTA
Fish and Wildlife Division
Department of Lands and Forests
8221 109th Street
Edmonton

SASKATCHEWAN
Wildlife Branch
Department of Natural Resources
Regina

MANITOBA
Game Branch
Department of Mines and Natural
  Resources
Winnipeg

ONTARIO
Division of Fish and Wildlife
Department of Lands and Forests
Toronto 2

QUEBEC
Wildlife Protection Service
Department of Game and Fisheries
Quebec

NEW BRUNSWICK
Fish and Wildlife Branch
Department of Lands and Mines
Fredericton

NOVA SCOTIA
Director of Conservation
Department of Lands and Forests
Halifax

PRINCE EDWARD ISLAND
Deputy Minister of Industry and Natural
  Resources
Charlottetown

NEWFOUNDLAND
Director of Wildlife
Department of Mines, Agriculture and
  Resources
St. John's

NORTHWEST TERRITORIES
Northern Administration Branch
Department of Northern Affairs and
  Natural Resources
Ottawa, Ontario

YUKON TERRITORY
Commissioner, Yukon Territory
P.O. Box 127
Whitehorse, Yukon Territory

12. BIBLIOGRAPHY AND READING LIST

Of necessity this list is abbreviated. In a book of this kind the number of reference sources actually drawn upon is vast. The list that follows is (1) a basic list of the most interesting or essential references and (2) a cross-section of the others. So that this list might serve as a selected reading list as well as a bibliography, a system of stars is employed. One star (*) indicates that the reference, in the author's opinion, is of special interest. Two stars (**) indicate that the reference is, again in the author's opinion, important to an understanding of the subject. Three stars (***) indicate that the author feels the particular work is essential for a complete understanding of the subject or that the work is a definitive arbiter in discussions of the animal or animals in question. The stars do not, however, indicate literary merit. No such value judgments are herein attempted. They refer only to value of information content and this, once more, only in the personal opinion of the author. The dozens of periodicals referred to in the preparation of this book are not included.

Allen, Glover Morrill, *Bats.* Cambridge, Massachusetts, Harvard University Press, 1939.

***Anderson, Rudolph Martin, *Catalogue of Canadian Recent Mammals.* Bulletin No. 102, Biol. Series No. 31. Ottawa, National Museum of Canada, 1946.

Animal Tracks: The Standard Guide for Identification and Characteristics, with an introduction by H. Marlin Perkins. Harrisburg, Stackpole Co., 1954.

**Anthony, H. E., *Field Book of North American Mammals.* New York, G. P. Putnam's Sons, 1928.

Baker, Ralph C., *Fur Seals of the Pribilof Islands.* Conservation in Action Series, No. 12, Fish & Wildlife Service, U.S. Department of the Interior, 1957.

Barker, Will, *Familiar Animals of America.* New York, Harper & Brothers, 1951.

Beebe, William, *Unseen Life of New York: As a Naturalist Sees It.* New York, Duell, Sloan & Pearce, 1953.

Booth, Ernest S., *How to Know the Mammals.* Dubuque, Iowa, Wm. C. Brown Co., 1950.

*Bourlière, François, *The Natural History of Mammals.* New York, Alfred A. Knopf, 1954.

**Burt, William Henry, and Grossenheider, Richard Philip, *A Field Guide to the Mammals* (Peterson Field Guide Series). Boston, Houghton Mifflin Co., 1952.

**Burt, William H., *Mammals of the Great Lakes Region.* Ann Arbor, University of Michigan Press, 1957.

**Butcher, Devereux, *Exploring Our National Wildlife Refuges.* 2nd ed. rev. Boston, Houghton Mifflin Co., 1963.

*Cameron, Austin W., *A Guide to Eastern Canadian Mammals*. Ottawa, Natural Museum of Canada, 1956.

***Clark, James L., *The Great Arc of the Wild Sheep*. Norman, University of Oklahoma Press, 1964.

*Colby, C. B., *Fur and Fury*. New York, Duell, Sloan and Pearce, 1963.

*———, *Wild Cats*. New York, Duell, Sloan and Pearce, 1964.

*———, *Wild Deer*. New York, Duell, Sloan and Pearce, 1966.

*———, *Wild Dogs*. New York, Duell, Sloan and Pearce, 1965.

*Crisler, Lois, *Arctic Wild*. New York, Harper & Brothers, 1956.

Dasmann, William P., *Big Game of California*. Sacramento, State of California Department of Fish & Game, 1962.

*Davis, William B., *The Mammals of Texas*. Austin, Texas Game & Fish Commission, Bulletin 27, 1960.

Dobie, J. Frank, *The Voice of the Coyote*. Boston, Little, Brown & Co., 1947.

Gard, Wayne, *The Great Buffalo Hunt*. New York, Alfred A. Knopf, Inc., 1960.

Garlough, F. E., *Capturing Foxes*. Circular No. 8, Fish & Wildlife Service, U.S. Department of the Interior, 1945.

Hamilton, W. J., Jr., *Mammals of Eastern United States*. Ithaca, New York, Comstock Publishing Co., Inc., 1943.

Hibben, Frank C., *Hunting American Lions*. New York, Thomas Y. Crowell Co., 1948.

Holzworth, John M., *The Wild Grizzlies of Alaska*. New York, G. P. Putnam's Sons, 1930.

***Jackson, Hartley H. T., *Mammals of Wisconsin*. Madison, Wis., University of Wisconsin Press, 1961.

Jones, J. Knox, Jr., *Checklist of Mammals of Nebraska*. Transactions of the Kansas Academy of Science, Vol. 60, No. 3, 1957.

Keith, Elmer, *Elmer Keith's Big Game Hunting*. Boston, Little, Brown & Company, 1948.

Kenyon, Karl W., and Scheffer, Victor B., *The Seals, Sea-Lions, & Sea-Otters of the Pacific Coast*. Circular No. 32, Fish & Wildlife Service, U.S. Department of the Interior, 1955.

*Kieran, John, *Natural History of New York City*. Boston, Houghton Mifflin Co., 1959.

**Laycock, George, *The Sign of the Flying Goose: A Guide to the National Wildlife Refuges*. Garden City, N.Y., The Natural History Press, 1965.

***Marsden, Walter, *The Lemming Year*. London, Chatto & Windus, 1964.

**Matthiessen, Peter, *Wildlife in America*. New York, The Viking Press, 1959.

***Miller, Gerrit S., Jr., and Kellogg, Remington, *List of North American Recent Mammals*. U.S. National Museum Bulletin 205, 1955.

Miller, Wilford L., *Wildlife in North Dakota*. Copyrighted pamphlet, 1959.

——, and Holmberg, Claire Anne, *Land of the Prairie Dog*. Bismarck, North Dakota, Miller-Holmberg Productions, 1963.

*Morris, Desmond, *The Mammals: A Guide to the Living Species*. New York, Harper & Row, 1965.

***Murie, Olaus J., *The Elk of North America*. Harrisburg, Stackpole Co., and Washington, D.C., Wildlife Management Institute, 1951.

***——, *A Field Guide to Animal Tracks*. Boston, Houghton Mifflin Co., 1954.

Murry, Robert, *Food for Wildlife*. Louisiana Wild Life & Fisheries Commission, Wildlife Education Bulletin No. 60, 1962.

National Geographic Book Service, *America's Wonderlands: The Scenic National Parks and Monuments of the United States*. Washington, D.C., National Geographic Society, 1959.

——, *Wild Animals of North America*. Washington, D.C., National Geographic Society, 1960.

***Norris, Kenneth S. (editor), *Whales, Dolphins and Porpoises*. Berkeley, University of California Press, 1966.

*O'Connor, Jack, and Goodwin, George G., *The Big Game Animals of North America*. New York, E. P. Dutton & Company, Inc., 1961.

*Palmer, Ralph S., *The Mammal Guide*. New York, Doubleday & Company, Inc., 1954.

***Peterson, Randolph L., *North American Moose*. Toronto, University of Toronto Press, 1955.

*Petrides, George A., *A Field Guide to Trees and Shrubs*. Boston, Houghton Mifflin Company, 1958.

*Rand, A. L., *The Southern Half of the Alaska Highway and Its Mammals*. Bulletin 98, Bio. Series No. 27. Ottawa, National Museum of Canada, 1944.

——, *Mammals of Yukon*. Bulletin 100, Bio. Series No. 29. Ottawa, National Museum of Canada, 1945.

Rhode, Clarence J., and Barker, Will, *Alaska's Fish and Wildlife*. Circular No. 17, Fish & Wildlife Service. U.S. Department of the Interior, 1953.

***Scheffer, Victor B., *Seals, Sea Lions and Walruses*. Stanford, California, Stanford University Press, 1958.

***Schwartz, Charles W., and Elizabeth R., *The Wild Mammals of Missouri*. University of Missouri Press and Missouri Conservation Commission, 1959.

Seton, Ernest Thompson, *Lives of Game Animals*. Charles T. Branford Co., 1909.

*——, *Animal Tracks and Hunter Signs*. New York, Doubleday & Co., Inc., 1958.

Seymour, George, *Furbearers of California*. Sacramento, State of California Fish and Game Commission, 1960.

**Shelford, Victor E., *The Ecology of North America*. Urbana, University of Illinois Press, 1963.

***Slijper, E. J., *Whales*. New York, Basic Books, Inc., 1962.

**Sumner, Lowell, and Dixon, Joseph S., *Birds and Mammals of the Sierra Nevada*. Berkeley, University of California Press, 1953.

***Taylor, Walter P., ed., *The Deer of North America*. Harrisburg, Stackpole Co., and Washington, D.C., The Wildlife Management Institute, 1956.

Teer, James G., *Texas Deer Herd Management*. Bulletin 44, Texas Game and Fish Commission, 1963.

Tener, J. S., *A Preliminary Study of the Musk-Oxen of Florsheim Peninsula, Ellesmere Island, N.W.T*. Wildlife Management Bulletin Series 1, No. 9. Ottawa, Canadian Wildlife Service, 1954.

***Trippensee, Reuben Edwin, *Wildlife Management*, Vols. 1 & 2. New York, McGraw-Hill Book Co., Inc., 1948.

U.S. Department of the Interior, National Park Service, *Areas Administered by the National Park Service*. Washington, D.C., U.S. Government Printing Office, 1962.

Waldo, Edward, *The Louisiana Nutria Story*. New Orleans, Louisiana Wild Life and Fisheries Commission, 1962.

***Walker, Ernest P., et al., *Mammals of the World*, Vols. 1 & 2. Baltimore, The Johns Hopkins Press, 1964.

**Wright, Bruce S., *The Ghost of North America: the Story of the Eastern Puma*. New York, Vantage Press, 1959.

*————, *Wildlife Sketches—Near and Far*. Fredericton, New Brunswick, Brunswick Press, 1962.

***Young, Stanley P., *The Bobcat of North America*. Harrisburg, Stackpole Co., and Washington, D.C., The Wildlife Management Institute, 1958.

***————, and Jackson, Hartley H. T., *The Clever Coyote*. Harrisburg, Stackpole Co., 1951.

***————, and Goldman, Edward A., *The Puma, Mysterious American Cat*. Washington, D.C., The American Wildlife Management Institute, 1946.

***————, *The Wolf in North American History*. Caldwell, Idaho, The Caxton Printers, Ltd., 1946.

***————, and Goldman, Edward A., *The Wolves of North America*. Washington, D.C., American Wildlife Management Institute, 1944.

13. WILDLIFE PHOTOGRAPHY

If spotting and observing a wild animal is an enriching experience, coming away with a good photographic record of the event is twice as exciting. The thrill of seeing the pictures for the first time, and later reliving your experience through your photographic record, can add immeasurably to your pleasures in our natural heritage.

To give advice on what equipment to use that will be meaningful for all budgets, and for all degrees of skill, is difficult. There are, however, certain ground rules that can help guide the beginner.

Generally, in choosing camera equipment for use in wildlife photography, these suggestions will be of help:

(1) Avoid the *photography-made-easy* trap. Don't be tricked into buying equipment that does everything for you. For, quite simply, no matter what the claim of the manufacturer, no camera does. The *fully-automatic-just-press-the-button-and-you-have-a-prize-winning-photograph*–type camera ad is very misleading. In certain limited ways, and seldom in the area of wildlife photography, all these gimmick-cameras can do is correct for exposure. No camera can select, compose, or adjust to the light-and-dark patterns of wooded areas. The things they can do automatically are the easiest things of all to do anyway. The tricky part of photography is judgment and choice, and we don't have machines for those functions yet!

(2) Avoid obtaining a mass of equipment all at one time. If you find yourself suddenly loaded with strange gear that you just have to get going with, you will not learn to use any of it well, but all of it in a mediocre fashion. And, unless you are very wealthy, you will settle for second best all down the line so that you can have "one of each." Remember, the camera is just a light-tight box to hold the film; it is the lens that takes the picture. Get one lens at a time, and get the very, very best you can possibly afford. It is far better to buy one lens a year and get a really good one, than to run out and buy a camera, a wide-angle lens, a normal lens, and a telephoto all at once.

(3) If you talk with half a dozen photographers, you are apt to hear half a dozen reasons why this type of camera or that is best. No one argument overrides all others, and no one man's opinion is sacred. However, as author of this book, I reserve the right to express my own opinion however contrary it may run to those of other people. Simply, I find 35-mm photography best for use with wildlife. There are many reasons; one is that superb equipment, fine enough for any professional, is available at a fraction of the cost needed to outfit a kit with a larger negative size. No negative size has more versatile equipment available to expose it. The 35-

mm system allows for 20 *or* 36 exposures for each camera loading, doing away with the frustration a smaller number of exposures is bound to cause sooner or later. No sooner will the two bull moose charge into each other, for a once-in-a-lifetime series of shots, than you will find your twelve-shot camera is on its twelfth shot!

(4) Avoid bargains on equipment whose name is not known to you. Categorically, buy the most expensive camera you can possibly afford and buy it with one lens only, the best lens you can afford. Learn to use it well, and then add other focal length lenses over the years.

(5) Give careful consideration to "camera systems." These are basic cameras of usually very high quality that have available for use in conjunction with them a vast range of equipment. This will allow you to expand in any direction you want later on without taking a terrible loss by selling your original equipment. Do NOT buy a middle-cost camera with the idea of replacing it later with a better one. It is no easier to learn on cheap equipment (the opposite is often the case), and you will lose virtually your entire original investment. You get next to nothing for second-hand camera gear. Buy the best at the beginning, learn with it, and grow into it.

(6) Personally, I favor the Nikon system, although it can hardly be claimed that there is no other that will serve your needs. The Nikon system does provide, however, for our purposes here, a case in point of how you can build your kit. The single-lens-reflex Nikon F allows you to see directly through the lens exactly what you are going to photograph. The automatic meter-reading facilities built into the system are as automatic as any camera should be if the man with the camera is to call himself a photographer.

A system like the Nikon has these added advantages:

a) A wide variety of fine lenses from extreme wide angle to very long telescopic.

b) Bellows and tube systems, as well as a special lens, to allow extreme close-up work in the field and in the laboratory.

c) Attachments so that the basic camera can be used with a microscope without any structural change.

d) Electric motors for remote use; radio-controlled tripping as well as excellent equipment for use in a camera trap to catch elusive species.

e) Time-lapse photography capabilities with intervolometer.

f) It is light in weight, small in size.

g) It uses 35-mm film so that thirty-six exposures can be made available with one loading. With the lens involved, some of the best ever manufactured anywhere, the 35-mm negative size is as good as will be needed in black and white or color.

h) Universal distribution so that equipment and repairs are available almost anywhere in the world where camera equipment is sold.

i) Extreme ease of use.

There are, as I have said above, other cameras of superb craftsmanship and great versatility. I could not claim that my Nikon kit is going to get me better pictures than somebody else's Leica, Canon, or what-have-you. However, all *I* can go on is experience, and in my experience the 35-mm system that can offer the kind of versatility outlined above is the kind of equipment to start with and grow with. It is a funny thing about photography; you very quickly get to be better than you ever thought you could be—if you have the right equipment to start with.

A word about your exposure. The most foolish economy in the world is film economy in wildlife photography. You may have traveled far (and at considerable expense) and waited long for a chance to photograph a hairy three-toed snit. Don't take one or two shots in order to save film. Film is the cheapest thing you are dealing with when you are also involved with time and travel. *Bracket your shots.* If your meter reading calls for 1/125 second at f5.6, shoot it that way, and also at f4 and f8. Don't take chances on losing the shot, and don't trust your meter that much.

In using your telephoto lens, take a careful look at the new spot meters that are appearing on the market. With their extremely narrow field (down, now, to one degree) they can be of inestimable use in nature photography.

Some more tips:

a) Before going on a trip where photography is important to you, put your camera in for minor repairs, cleaning, and adjustment. Avoid frustration.

b) Think seriously of owning two cameras that will both take the same lens. There are two basic advantages: if one camera sours, the other may remain sweet! And you can have two lens sizes or two film types instantly available at all times. Most manufacturers of really fine cameras have a second and often even a third body type in their line as back up equipment at far less cost. (Be certain your extra camera bodies take the same lenses.)

c) Buy a 1-A sky filter *immediately* for every lens you own. Put them on your lenses and leave them there *permanently*. A six- or seven-dollar filter is easier to replace than a lens. It doesn't affect color film at all, can only improve black and white, and has no filter factor to worry about. The one exception is if you intend to go to extremely large blowups, like murals. The filter is never as good optically as your fine lens. In any normal use, however, a good filter is good enough by a wide margin. And that 1-A on the front will save your lens from scratches many more times than you realize.

d) Use your sunshade.

e) Protect your camera from dust (particularly desert sand), moisture, and most particularly salt-water spray.

f) If your camera should fall into salt water, put the entire thing into a bucket of fresh water as quickly as possible and deliver it that way for repairs. It might be salvageable.

g) Insure your equipment.

h) Invest in a good book on nature-photography techniques.

No matter where you go, no matter what your budget, take a camera with you into the field. You will add great, new dimensions to your nature exploring that will be recallable years later. You will never describe what a raccoon looks like hunting for crayfish along the edge of a pond as well as a few color slides will illustrate. And, remember, the man who takes one really good wildlife shot is the most skilled hunter in the world. It is far, far easier to kill an animal than to capture his image in a way that will please the intellectually curious mind as well as the artistic soul.

Index